Exploring
Journalism
and the Media

SECOND EDITION

Lorrie Lynch

SOUTH-WESTERN
CENGAGE Learning

Australia • Brazil • Japan • Korea • Mexico • Singapore • Spain • United Kingdom • United States

SOUTH-WESTERN
CENGAGE Learning·

**Exploring Journalism and the Media
Second Edition**
Lorrie Lynch

Vice President of Editorial, Business:
Jack W. Calhoun

Vice President/Editor-in-Chief: Karen Schmohe

Acquisitions Editor: Michael Guendelsberger

Developmental Editor: Anne Merrill

Marketing Manager: Kara Bombelli

Marketing Coordinator: Julia Tucker

Marketing Communications Manager:
Libby Shipp

Content Project Manager: Jana Lewis

Manager of Technology, Editorial:
Matthew McKinney

Media Editor: Lysa Kosins

Manufacturing Planner: Kevin Kluck

Production Service: MPS Limited, a Macmillan
Company

Senior Art Director: Tippy McIntosh and
Michelle Kunkler

Internal Designer: Liz Harasymczuk

Cover Designer: Liz Harasymczuk

Cover Image:
   © Digital Vision/Getty Images;
   © blue jean images/Getty Images;
   © Jitalia17/iStockphoto;
   © Florian ISPAS/Shutterstock;
   © George Doyle/Getty Images

Rights Acquisition Specialist: Amber Hosea

Photo Researcher: Darren Wright

Text Researcher: Jennifer Wagner,
PreMedia Global

ExamView® is a registered trademark of eInstruction Corp. Windows is a registered trademark of the Microsoft Corporation used herein under license. Macintosh and Power Macintosh are registered trademarks of Apple Computer, Inc. used herein under license.
© 2008 Cengage Learning. All Rights Reserved.

ISBN-13: 978-0-8400-6899-6

ISBN-10: 0-8400-6899-9

South-Western
5191 Natorp Boulevard
Mason, OH 45040
USA

Cengage Learning products are represented in Canada by Nelson Education, Ltd.

For your course and learning solutions, visit **www.cengage.com/school**
Visit our company website at **www.cengage.com**

Printed in the United States of America
1 2 3 4 5 6 7 15 14 13 12

Contents

5 Collaborate on Content   112

6 Interviewing   140

7 Handling Quotations   170

Reviewers

Karen Bair
Business and Information Technology Instructor
Perkins-Tryon High School
Perkins, Okla.

Evynn Blaher
Journalism Teacher and Librarian
Prince William County Schools
Woodbridge, Va.

Beth Bloom
English and Journalism Teacher
Amelia High School
Batavia, Ohio

Andrea Brankel
English and Journalism Teacher
Claremore High School
Claremore, Okla.

Kimberly Stewart Brown
Science Department Teacher
Alexander Central High School
Taylorsville, N.C.

Jill M. Cook
English Department Instructor
Brookfield Central High School
Brookfield, Wis.

Kathi Couch
Journalism Teacher and Publications Advisor
Flower Mound High School
Flower Mound, Texas

Susan Duncan
Publications Adviser
Pine Tree High School
Longview, Texas

Ruby A. Dyer
Journalism and English Teacher
Wayne High School
Wayne, W.Va.

Christopher D. Fama
Assistant Professor of Business and Communications
Cayuga Community College
Auburn, N.Y.

Velisa Jewett
Journalism Adviser
Claudia Taylor Johnson High School
San Antonio, Texas

Renee Gearhart Levy
Freelance Writer and Editor
Fayetteville, N.Y.

Judy A. Moore
Mass Media Instructor
McKinley Technology High School
Washington, D.C.

Carolyn Harrington Richardson
Teacher
Carroll County Intermediate School
Hillsville, Va.

Cynthia Schneider
Principal
World Journalism Preparatory School
Flushing, N.Y.

Sara Waldron
Business Education Teacher
Birchwood Public School
Birchwood, Wis.

REAL WORLD
REAL PEOPLE
REAL JOURNALISM

2e

Exploring Journalism
and the Media

LORRIE LYNCH

About the Author

Lorrie Lynch is a news, feature and contemporary culture writer and editor with more than two decades of experience in the print and Web journalism worlds. Lynch is a channel editor at AARP.org, the website of the membership association for those 50-plus. Before her work at AARP, Lynch was at *USA TODAY* and its Sunday magazine *USA Weekend*, which is carried in 700 newspapers. She was on *USA TODAY*'s founding staff and worked as a reporter, San Francisco Bureau Chief and People editor. At *USA Weekend*, she was a senior editor, celebrity columnist and blogger.

Lynch also worked for newspapers in California and Michigan, where she won several writing awards. She teaches writing for communication in the School of Communication at American University and is a communications consultant in Washington, D.C., where she lives with her husband, a *USA TODAY* editor. Lynch earned her B.A. in Journalism at Central Michigan University. In November 2007 she was inducted into CMU's Journalism Hall of Fame.

FOR IMMEDIATE RELEASE

Dear Journalism Instructor:

The world of journalism today could not be more challenging. We are in the midst of profound change, experimenting with new forms of storytelling and news delivery. All of us who practice and teach are affected.

Yet, as we find new platforms on which to tell our stories, and as we learn to think WAY outside the box, we must not forego teaching the basic skills and values that make professional journalists different from unskilled, non-professionals.

That's why I'm excited to introduce *Exploring Journalism and the Media, 2e*. In it you will find: how multimedia story presentation is working, how convergence of print and digital platforms is playing out in the nation's news organizations and, most important, how all of it is relevant to your students. The text also stresses reporting, writing, editing and journalistic ethics and values.

My experience as a practicing professional gives me a different from perspective than those found in most other journalism texts. In addition, you will find in the book the experience and wisdom of many additional professionals and students. **Real People Real Careers** demonstrates various media occupations, including some new ones available in a multimedia world. *New* features include **Grammar Tips**, which showcase specific rules for essential grammar skills; **21st Century Skills**, which covers the skills, knowledge and expertise students must master to succeed in life and work; and **Scholastic Journalism**, which presents examples of authentic student writings for school publications.

In the pages that follow, you'll find more about the book's other strengths, which include cooperative learning features that emphasize editorial ethics, interesting journalism facts and statistics, the impact of the Internet on traditional journalism and much more. A Web site—www.cengage.com/school/langarts/journalism—keeps the book current with ongoing updates and important Internet links.

Find out for yourself why I believe *Exploring Journalism and the Media, 2e* will engage your students. I appreciate your partnership in the teaching process and look forward to working with you.

Sincerely,
Lorrie Lynch

THE REAL NEWS IN JOURNALISM

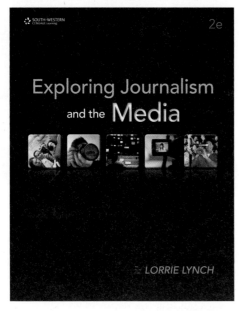

Exploring Journalism and the Media, 2e

Capture the dynamics of today's ever-changing world of journalism in your class with the real, hands-on, powerful approach found in **Exploring Journalism and the Media, 2e.** Written by award-winning journalist Lorrie Lynch, this engaging text offers a unique real-world perspective absent from most other journalism textbooks. Experiences from Lynch and other professionals, pulled straight from the field, help your students see for themselves how journalism is much more than what they see on television, read in newspapers or view on the Internet. Students will be able to learn, practice and immediately apply journalism concepts to their current scholastic journalist roles with the school yearbook, newspaper or Web site.

Using a wealth of captivating learning features and a practical writing style, this text and supporting technology connect with your students, no matter what their learning style. Lynch combines timeless journalism concepts and applications, such as strong writing techniques, with a meaningful discussion of current issues, including media convergence and the challenges of editorial ethics today.

With **Exploring Journalism and the Media, 2e**, your students will not only perform better in the classroom but also improve on standardized test scores because of the book's many academic connections. The text examines all media outlets and the interplay among them with coverage of all the fundamentals necessary for success.

> **FOR THE RECORD**

"I love writing tips from a current professional in the field."

—JUDITH COOPER, LEHMAN HIGH SCHOOL

> **FOR THE RECORD**

"The variety of activities, writing assignments and academic connections are valuable and pertinent. The material is current and necessary for today's journalist — and going into the future."

—ANDREA BRANKEL, CLAREMORE HIGH SCHOOL

PREPARE STUDENTS FOR THE EXCITING REAL WORLD OF JOURNALISM!

Exploring Journalism and the Media, 2e introduces students to the exciting world of journalism and the many different scholastic and career opportunities within the journalism field. To ensure ongoing student interest, author Lorrie Lynch keeps it as real in your classroom as out in the field!

NEW! Prepare students for scholastic journalism opportunities, such as a becoming a staff member of the school yearbook or newspaper. The new **Scholastic Journalism** feature presents authentic examples of student writings from scholastic publications.

Critical-thinking questions correlate to chapter content for application and reinforcement.

Scholastic Journalism

Elements of a News Story

By Victor Xu, Carmel High School, Carmel, Ind., "Spring (Oil) Cleaning"

Although her family traveled to Florida relatively frequently in past years, senior Andrea Czarnick said the oil spill is a major factor in her family choosing not to travel to the Gulf Coast states this spring break. Instead, she and her family will visit Hawaii for the upcoming spring break.

"Last year we were happy we went down to the Gulf shores in Florida, and my dad was happy that we were able to fit it in," Czarnick said. "They took us down to the ocean ri[ght] ... We might have gone this year, but we're [going] somewhere warmer and clean[er] ...

Jonathon Day, professor a[t] [the] [Re]search Center, said tourism t[o] [is] adversely affected by the oil s[pill] a large proportion of the eco[nomy ...] mated that tourism in 2010 a[lone] and employed more than 400[,000 ...]

The explosion of the Dee[pwater] last April 20 tore open a we[ll] crude oil, making it the larg[est ...] ing to a New York Times ar[ticle] well was sealed on July 15, [but] pated, the long-term effect[s ...]

"At this time we can b[...] have spent the last few m[onths ...] show they're in good shap[e ...] to beaches also tell that s[...] mouth' about the quality [...]

Although reports and [...] Gulf Coast states have en[...] will ultimately determin[e ...] tourism.

"The key issues will be whether people perceive that the beach destinations of the Gulf are clean and ready to welcome visitors," Day said. "We'll know for sure in a couple of weeks."

THINK *Critically*

1. Analyze this article in terms of the elements of a news story, discussed in Lesson 3.1 of this chapter.

2. Is this article reporting hard news or soft news? Explain your answer.

Source: Used by permission of Victor Xu.

21st CENTURY SKILLS

PARTNERSHIP FOR 21st CENTURY SKILLS

MEDIA LITERACY: A Media-Centered World

Journalists in the 21st century are part of a technology-driven world where news is available 24 hours a day, seven days a week through a variety of media platforms. To be competitive in a career in journalism, you must be savvy in all media platforms. The three major media platforms are

- **Print media,** which include newspapers and news magazines. Jobs in print media include reporters or correspondents, feature writers, columnists, editors and publishers.
- **Broadcast media,** which include radio and television. Jobs in broadcast news include reporters, analysts, anchors, broadcasters or newscasters, editors, camera people, videographers and producers.
- **Internet-based news sites,** where jobs include reporters or correspondents, bloggers, analysts, editors, videographers and Web designers.

USING MULTIPLE MEDIA

In addition to being confident writing for the various media platforms, today's journalists also must be comfortable working with multiple media, that is, combining audio, video and graphic elements to make the stories available for the Internet. For example:

A reporter who specializes in writing magazine articles on bands for Rolling Stone will need to write a story and provide photos of the band for the print magazine. For the Internet, the journalist will have to provide a shortened story and video clips of the band performing

the whole package — a story ready for print, along with photos, and a story ready for the Internet, along with video clips. Good reporters even in larger markets pay attention to the photographs or video clips and work in partnership with the camera person to be able to tell the best story and choose the photos or clips that do just that.

LEARNING ABOUT THE MEDIA

For most careers in journalism, a degree in journalism, mass communications or English is required. To be competitive in today's market, students planning to enter the field of journalism should also take courses in computer science, photojournalism, broadcast journalism and other technology-related courses.

Journalists who want to specialize in a particular area also should take courses in their field of interest. For example, if you have an interest in business and plan to write for a business magazine or news outlet, you will want to take business courses.

OPPORTUNITIES FOR JOURNALISTS

Entry-level jobs in journalism in print, broadcast and Internet news may not be high-paying. Competition is strong, especially in urban areas, but journalism can be a rewarding career, especially if you are working in a specialty you like.

All journalists entering the field today

NEW! 21st Century Skills features showcase the skills, knowledge and expertise students must master to succeed in work and life. These skills are established by the Partnership for 21st Century Skills, which is a national organization that advocates workplace readiness for every student to help them succeed in a global world.

REAL PEOPLE REAL CAREERS

Tony Dearing | Embracing Digital Media

Tony Dearing has been a journalist almost all his life. He was editor of his junior high school newspaper, his high school newspaper and his college newspaper. "I've always known what I wanted to do," he says, "and it never occurred to me to do anything else."

Dearing is now chief content officer (in the new-media world, that means editor) of AnnArbor.com, the news website serving the Michigan community outside Detroit. After three decades in the news business and 11 years at The Ann Arbor News before it folded in 2009, Dearing embraces the digital media.

"One big difference with online journalism is immediacy," Dearing says. "People want news in real time. If a mother is at work and gets a text from her son saying that his school has been locked down, she's not going to wait until the newspaper comes out tomorrow to find out what's going on. She expects to go to your website and find a report right then. And she'll expect to see updates throughout the day."

Another major difference between print and online journalism, Dearing says, is the interactivity website users expect. "People want to comment. They want to 'like' stories and share them. They want to upload their photos. This is the complete opposite of the passive, one-way experience newspapers offered." In hiring staff, Dearing says, he looks for journalists with "good, old-fashioned reporting skills. We want people who have a nose for news and know how to go out there and dig up stories and ask tough questions. But they also need to be comfortable with all the tools of new media so they can tell those stories in digital form, be it social media or video or a series of Web posts that rapidly update a breaking story. That's why we call our employees digital journalists rather than reporters."

ADVICE FOR ASPIRING JOURNALISTS

Dearing is upbeat about the future of journalism. He tells aspiring journalists: "First of all, don't listen to the gloom and doom you may hear about the news business. It is true, newspapers are facing real struggles right now, but journalism as a profession is as much in need as ever, and as we make the transition to the digital realm, I believe we are entering an exciting new era in which journalism will flourish again."

Young people who want to be part of the news revolution must learn solid reporting skills, Dearing says. "Today's journalists have to know how to be fast and accurate. Be an early adapter to emerging technology, and always look for new ways to report the news."

Source: Personal interview with Tony Dearing.

THINK *Critically*

Why do many people prefer to get their news via digital media rather than a printed newspaper?

Real People Real Careers features highlight the career paths of real journalism professionals and explore first-hand some of the rapidly evolving issues in media today. Additionally, they address up-to-date educational requirements and professional skills needed for various careers and occupations in the field of journalism and the media.

IMPROVE ACADEMIC PERFORMANCE IN THE CLASSROOM!

Exploring Journalism and the Media, 2e will not only introduce students to many career opportunities, but it will also help them perform better in the classroom. The text provides numerous tips, critical-thinking activities and opportunities for students to learn and apply their personal writing style, working individually or in teams.

Digging Deeper

First Amendment Rights of Student Journalists

In its 1988 decision in Hazelwood School District v. Kuhlmeier, the U.S. Supreme Court ruled that two high school newspaper reporters' First Amendment rights were not violated when the principal pulled articles th had written from the paper before publication. The principal deemed the topics of the articles — teen pregnancy and divorce — to be inappropriat for the high school audience. In its decision, the Court said, "First Amendment rights of students in the public schools are not automatically coexte sive with the rights of adults in other settings, and must be applied in ligh of the special characteristics of the school environment. A school need no tolerate student speech that is inconsistent with its basic educational mission, even though the government could not censor similar speech outsid the school."

To learn more about First Amendment rights for student journalists, access the Gale Journalism eCollection at www.cengage.com/school/langarts/journalism and click on the link to Chapter 1. Read the article entitled, "California eyes new free-speech protections in schools." The artic explains recent legislation in California that protects scholastic journalism advisors from being punished for not censoring articles later deemed objectionable by school administrators.

THINK Critically

School District

NEW! **Digging Deeper** boxed features elaborate on chapter concepts with our exclusive collection of online articles.

●grammar tip

Write in complete sentences, not in sentence fragments. A complete sentence has a subject and a verb. A sentence fragment is a word, phrase or clause that is treated like a separate sentence but should be added to surrounding words to form a complet sentence. Consider did not reveal h So she went phrase "So is a se gment. To turn ment into a did not reveal her so she went to jail"

under deadline pr posely write falseh

Truth is a defe Suppose you have the city council te and will retire at t write the story for publication in the who told you the plans to retire, an election, and now though it was a co you were assured story is false.

INVASION OF PI

Printing private i

NEW! **Grammar Tips** remind students to apply essential grammar skills in their writing with specific tips, rules and examples.

Think Critically

21. How has the Internet helped you become more informed about world news than your parents and grandparents were?
22. How did the Civil War change the way journalists wrote news stories?
23. How was competition among reporters during the Civil War similar to and different from competition among reporters today?
24. Why might a reporter have taken pride in being called a muckraker?
25. How might a government hurt journalism in a country that does not offer protection such as the First Amendment of the U.S. Constitution?
26. Do you think the administration of your school should be allowed to censor the school newspaper? Why or why not?
27. Why should news organizations provide information on multiple platforms?
28. What does it say about a community within the United States when the newspaper that most of the people who live there read is printed in a language other than English?
29. What benefits and drawbacks are associated with obtaining news from the Internet?
30. What should a reporter do when she has a hot story that will make her famous but hurt an innocent person?

Make Academic Connections

31. **HISTORY** Use the Internet to research the history of the First Amendment. Write a composition that includes information on the person who wrote the amendment and his reasons for wanting the amendment. Also, include your personal opinion on why you think the First Amendment is necessary and how it relates to your life in your school or community. Carefully examine your paper for clarity, engaging language, and the correct use of English.
32. **CAREERS AND PERSONAL FINANCE** Use the Internet or personal interviews to research pay for starting reporters for a local broadcast station and a local newspaper. Use a computer to create a spreadsheet for a budget that shows how you would live on the net income. Include major expenses such as rent, vehicle, food, clothing and entertainment.
33. **SCHOLASTIC JOURNALISM** Choose a topic that is relevant to your school and write a news story for your school newspaper. Include the history of the issue in your story. Be sure to use the inverted pyramid style.
34. **TECHNOLOGY** Telecommuting, working from home or another location outside the company's office, is rapidly becoming

Strong Assessments conclude each lesson and chapter to help offer a variety of hands-on activities.

- **Make Academic Connections** exercises at the end of the chapter link chapter content to core subject areas, such as social studies, language arts, music, writing, economics and others.

- Numerous writing activities and samples of good and poor writing will help students understand the importance of accuracy and attention to detail. Rubrics for the instructor will help evaluate student writing and provide feedback.

- **AP Stylebook Workshops** introduce students to the most widely accepted journalistic style standards and provide tips and rules with specific examples and applications.

nal, (d) the Los that shows the have in comm each paper th

37. **VISUAL ARTS** computer grap relevant to yo

38. **SOCIOLOGY** ments in newsgathering and reporting change with events in history. Using the information in this chapter and research, design a chart that illustrates how events in history changed journalism. For example, illustrate that the inverted pyramid style came out of the Civil War.

Writing Portfolio Activity

39. Keep a journal of news and news-related information you read for one week. Include newspapers and news magazines, radio and television news, and news from the Internet. At the end of the week, write an analysis of a story you read or listened to. In your analysis, answer these questions: What attracted you to the story? Did you read, or listen to, the entire story or only the beginning? What caught your interest about the story? What was the print headline or broadcast teaser? Was there a photo, chart or other visual with the story? Did you read or hear about the story from more than one source? What were the sources? How did the style of reporting differ? Which did you like the best? Why? Was the story written for someone in your age group or for an older audience? What elements in the story helped you determine the age group?

AP Stylebook Workshop

In your English class, you may have learned to use a comma before the conjunction, such as the word "and," in a simple series.
Example: Journalists research, plan, and write a draft before they turn in final copy.
AP style does not use a comma before a conjunction in a simple series.
Example: Journalists research, plan and write a draft before they turn in final copy.
Insert commas according to AP style in the following sentences:

40. The major television networks are ABC CBS Fox and NBC.

41. News delivery has gone from only newspapers to newspapers radio television and the Internet.

INSTRUCTIONAL RESOURCES

Annotated Instructor's Edition (ISBN: 978-1-111-42663-7)

Find all the teaching suggestions and answers you need to create a powerful journalism course within this valuable Annotated Instructor's Edition. Meaningful teaching notes and solutions are overprinted around student pages and include teaching method instructions for your convenience.

Instructor's Resource CD (ISBN: 978-1-133-43512-9)

Get quick access to all of the resources you need for dynamic classroom instruction with this CD. A variety of ancillaries include data and solution files, lesson plans and customizable PowerPoint® presentations. All of these tools help motivate students and enhance their knowledge and course appreciation.

ExamView® (ISBN: 978-1-111-42747-4)

This computerized testing tool allows you to create paper and online tests and is ideal for building tests, worksheets and study guides (practice tests). This assessment solution saves you time and improves student results by focusing on specific learning objectives.

Exploring Journalism and the Media Companion Web site
www.cengage.com/school/langarts/journalism

The companion Web site provides interactive quizzing and activities for students to apply their knowledge as well as corresponding updates with links to *USA TODAY* to keep examples current.

 Interested in a simple way to complement your text and course content with study and practice materials? Cengage Learning's *Exploring Journalism* CourseMate brings course concepts to life with interactive learning, study and exam preparation tools that support the printed textbook. Watch student comprehension soar as your class works with the printed textbook and the textbook-specific Web site.

Exploring Journalism CourseMate includes:

>> An interactive eBook

>> Engagement Tracker, a first-of-its-kind tool that monitors student engagement in the course.

>> Interactive teaching and learning tools, such as:
- Quizzes • Flashcards • News Scene*
- Digging Deeper eCollection • and more!

* **News Scene** is an award-winning, online program that features 11 interactive news assignments based on realistic news events. To help you assign writing projects and to help students sharpen their writing skills for print, broadcast and online media, News Scene uses extensive source material, including videotaped interviews, telephone messages, official documents and database information.

>> **FOR THE RECORD**

"Great writing style. Readable and full of great examples and tips."

—MELODY GRIGAR,
RICE HIGH SCHOOL

Introduce Your Students to the REAL *WORLD* and the REAL *PEOPLE* of REAL *JOURNALISM*!

SOUTH-WESTERN
CENGAGE Learning

2e

Exploring Journalism and the Media

LORRIE LYNCH

Student Edition ISBN: 978-0-8400-6899-6

TABLE OF CONTENTS

>> FOR THE RECORD

"Think of this important textbook as a map of a brand new journalism and media universe. You'll have as your explorer-in-chief Lorrie Lynch, one of America's most thoughtful and experienced journalists – supported by a team of 30 of the most innovative practitioners in the news business. It's a big media universe to explore these days. For high school students and teachers, this book, I predict, will become the essential guide."

—ROY PETER CLARK, SENIOR SCHOLAR, THE POYNTER INSTITUTE, & AUTHOR OF "WRITING TOOLS"

ISBN-13: 978-1-133-36437-5
ISBN-10: 1-133-36437-3

90000

9 781133 364375

Source Code: 11PJSC0001

Exploring
Journalism
and the Media

History, Law and Ethics

1.1 The History of Journalism

1.2 Matters of Law

1.3 Ethics in a Multimedia World

21st Century Journalism

Technology is changing American journalism in the 21st century more profoundly and more quickly than at any other time in its history. Computer technology is to journalism today what the printing press, the telegraph and television were in previous eras — an innovation that has had game-changing impact on how Americans keep up with current events.

Newspapers, once the predominant medium for news, are today struggling to stay alive even as editors have made their products more colorful, more readable and easier to navigate. In the 1990s, as computers became more and more a part of American households, the Internet became society's information superhighway. It became clear that information companies would need to look to the Web to reach their readers.

By 2010, the Internet was a dominant player in the news and information business. The newspaper that landed on your doorstep in the morning was delivering news at least eight hours old. News websites were delivering news as it happened.

Many newspapers — from big metropolitan dailies such as The Rocky Mountain News in Denver to community dailies such as The Ann Arbor News in Michigan — closed their doors. News-aggregating websites such as The Huffington Post and The Daily Beast were hiring top-notch writers away from traditional newspapers. Some journalism practitioners and scholars now predict that most paper-and-ink newspapers will not survive another 10 years.

> **THINK** *Critically*
> Do you think newspapers are relevant today? Will they survive another 10 years? Why or why not?

The History of Journalism

Goals

- Describe the history of newspapers in the United States.
- Discuss the history of mass media.
- Explain the influence of the Internet on journalism.

Key Terms

- newspaper 3
- penny press 4
- inverted pyramid 4
- yellow journalism 5
- muckraking 5
- mass media 5
- Golden Age of Radio 5
- network 6
- Skype 6
- multiple platforms 6
- multiple media 7
- convergence 7

FOCUS

In today's world, you have access to news 24/7 — 24 hours a day, seven days a week. This was not always so. Have you ever wondered how people in earlier times learned about their world? Think about how the early settlers of your community heard about news in nearby settlements. How did the founders of this country learn about events that were important to building a new nation?

History of Newspapers

In the United States, there were newspapers even before the American Revolution. **Newspapers** are publications printed on large sheets of folded paper that contain information about current events, features on different topics and advertisements. Newspapers provide information about your school, your community, your country and the world.

COLONIAL NEWSPAPERS AND THE PENNY PRESS

Most news in Colonial times was carried by merchants and other travelers and reported in letters exchanged among friends and families. The letters carried information about crops, marriages and babies, political opinions and news of a possible war with Great Britain.

These letters, along with essays, were the early newspapers and were mostly the opinions of the writer. By 1750, the Colonies had 14 weekly newspapers. By the time of the Revolution in the 1770s, 89 newspapers were being published.

////// *Why were penny press newspapers so popular with the public?*

Near the middle of the 19th century, the focus of newspapers shifted away from the publishers' personal letters and views to news about current events and people. In 1833 Benjamin Day began a new trend when he published the New York Sun and sold it on the street for a penny. Other newspapers followed this trend, and they soon became known as the **penny press**, so named because of the cost, one cent. The low price and easy street-corner access made the penny press newspapers popular with the public.

Soon, advances in printing technology revolutionized the newspaper business. New, massive presses meant thousands of copies of newspapers could be printed every hour. Newspapers' circulation increased, as did their influence. The first newspaper with a national circulation was the New York Tribune, established by Horace Greeley in 1841.

CIVIL WAR NEWS

Technology changed the news business, but the War Between the States changed journalism. During the Civil War of the 1860s, newspapers introduced special war correspondents. Competition among these war journalists was fierce. To get the news to newspapers in the North, journalists in the South used the telegraph to transmit stories. In case the telegraph broke down during transmission, journalists began writing in a more concise style, putting the most important facts first. This format — the **inverted pyramid** — is still used today.

YELLOW JOURNALISM

In the mid-1890s, newspapers competing for advertising dollars and readers began an era of sensationalism. Named after a comic strip character called the

Yellow Kid, **yellow journalism** came to represent screaming headlines and cheap melodrama. Stories were made up of half-truths, and newspaper publishers engaged in shameless self-promotion.

Two of the top newspaper publishers, William Randolph Hearst and Joseph Pulitzer, also were the most notable yellow journalists. Hearst published the San Francisco Examiner and later the New York Journal. Pulitzer published the New York World.

MUCKRAKING

As the era of yellow journalism came to a close, journalists moved into the role of promoting social responsibility. Journalists investigated corruption, especially in big business, social institutions and politics. It was the beginning of investigative journalism, which came to be called **muckraking**. The journalists investigating corruption were called muckrakers, a term in which they took pride.

checkpoint ✓

Briefly describe the history of newspapers in the United States.

History of Mass Media

Access to mass media through newspapers, magazines, radio, television and high-speed Internet connections can be found today in most American homes and workplaces. The term **mass media** refers to all the channels of communication that reach a large audience. Each new communications medium had an impact on our culture, and each has made information more accessible to the masses. You have already learned about the impact newspapers had on society. Now you will read about how radio at the turn of the 20th century, television in the middle of the century and the Internet at the end of the century also changed the way in which you receive news, information and entertainment.

RADIO

Italian inventor Guglielmo Marconi began experimenting with the wireless telegraph in 1894. It was 1926 before the first lasting U.S. radio network, the National Broadcasting Co. (NBC), was created by David Sarnoff. In 1927, the Columbia Broadcasting System (CBS) was formed. By 1930, in what is considered the **Golden Age of Radio**, Americans listened to their radios for music, drama, comedy, variety shows and news.

Radio played a big part in informing Americans during World War II, thanks to a CBS news correspondent named Edward R. Murrow. He brought the war home with his radio broadcasts from the European front.

TELEVISION

In the 1950s, television replaced radio as the most popular medium. Television's visual component gave it an edge over radio and soon made it the preferred source of information.

In the beginning, television adopted a lot from radio. Like radio stations, television stations were affiliated with **networks,** or groups of stations that broadcast regularly scheduled programs. Big radio names like Murrow transferred to television. In 1948, NBC started broadcasting the evening news with a 10-minute filmed newsreel. By the next year, a 15-minute broadcast anchored by John Cameron Swayze was live. CBS and ABC followed quickly into the nightly news arena. The growth of the audience for nightly network newscasts contributed to the decline, and eventual death, of the afternoon daily newspaper.

THE INTERNET

By 2000, the Internet had changed how journalists researched and reported the news, as well as the way news was delivered. With the Internet, people could access news, information and entertainment through websites.

Journalists use the Internet in many ways to get their jobs done. They use it for their preliminary research. They send completed articles to their editors via email. They may conduct interviews via email or real-time video chat using software programs such as **Skype**. Photographers use the Internet to send digital images to editors. Editors use email to send pictures of a completed page, or PDF files, to staff or freelance writers who worked on the story.

News organizations now realize that news consumers have **multiple platforms**. Some people may read a traditional newspaper. Others read that

AP Stylebook Concepts

Associated Press style differs from the style you read and write in school. Style refers to the way something is written. Most textbooks follow The Chicago Manual of Style. However this textbook follows the style journalists use, Associated Press style. Journalists use The Associated Press Stylebook as their reference. Throughout the textbook, look for this AP Stylebook Concepts feature to learn how to write in the style journalists use.

© domin_domin/iStockphoto.com

////// *Describe how the Internet has changed the way people can access the news.*

newspaper's website on a personal computer or smartphone. Some people choose to listen to an audio version of a journalist's interview on their MP3 players or iPods. These interviews are called podcasts, combining the words "iPod" and "broadcast."

The variety of platforms on which news consumers can receive information is forcing journalists to think in new ways about how they present stories. Journalists are thinking in terms of **multiple media**, that is, adding audio, video and graphic elements to print stories on the Web. Reporters and photographers are using digital audio and video recorders and digital still cameras to cover events, do investigative reporting or showcase human interest stories. Editors and Web designers are using various software programs to make the stories available and attractive online. Journalists write the same story in different forms for both a print publication and a website. This merging of the media with other platforms is called **convergence**.

check point ✓

Briefly describe the history of mass media.

1.1 | Assessment

Understand Concepts

Determine the best answer for each of the following questions.

1. To which newspaper practice did use of the telegraph during the Civil War contribute?
   a. the penny press
   b. inverted pyramid
   c. editorials
   d. news about local citizens

2. Networks are
   a. groups of radio and television stations.
   b. multiple media platforms.
   c. Civil War correspondents.
   d. Internet-based news sites.

3. **True or False**   Yellow journalism was honest and respected investigative reporting.

4. **True or False**   Mass media refers to all the channels of communication that reach a large audience, including newspapers, magazines, radio, television and the Internet.

Write Now!

Practice your writing skills with the following activities.

5. Interview two or more senior citizens to learn about the history of news delivery from their perspective. Include newspapers, radio, television and the Internet. Plan, draft and write a composition that describes the information from your interview. Carefully examine your paper for clarity, engaging language and the correct use of written English.

6. Choose a national news story that is being reported in a newspaper, on a televised newscast and on the Internet. Write an analysis that explains how the different media handle the same topic. Notice the words used, the length and depth of the reporting and photos or video used. Once you have written an analysis, rewrite the story for a national newspaper, a local newspaper, a national network broadcast, a local broadcast and news website.

7. Use a software program to create a multimedia representation of the history of journalism. Include in your presentation the information you learned from the text and outside information obtained through Internet research. Use a combination of the written word, music and visual representations as you create your presentation. Present your work to the class.

Matters of Law

Goals

- Understand the importance of the First Amendment.
- Identify the difference between public officials, public figures and private citizens.
- Explain legal issues and laws that pertain to journalists, including libel, invasion of privacy, shield laws and freedom of information laws.

Key Terms

- First Amendment 9
- censorship 10
- public official 10
- precedent 10
- public figure 11
- libel 11
- invasion of privacy 12
- shield laws 12
- freedom of information laws 12
- sunshine laws 12

FOCUS

It was a sad day for The New York Times when the newspaper published an editorial that began:

> This is a proud but awful moment for The New York Times and its employees. One of our reporters, Judith Miller, has decided to accept a jail sentence rather than testify before a grand jury about one of her confidential sources. Ms. Miller has taken a path that will be lonely and painful for her and her family and friends. We wish she did not have to choose it, but we are certain she did the right thing.*

Judith Miller went to jail for three months rather than obey a judge's order to tell a grand jury the name of a confidential source who had told her the name of an undercover CIA agent. The prosecutor, the main lawyer representing the U.S. government, used the court to try to get Miller to reveal her source. Even though it meant going to jail, Miller protected her source because she believed, as a journalist, that she was ethically bound to do so.

*"Judith Miller Goes to Jail," New York Times, July 7, 2005.

The First Amendment

All citizens have certain rights guaranteed by the **First Amendment** to the U.S. Constitution. The First Amendment leads off the Bill of Rights, the name given to the first 10 amendments to the Constitution. Among other rights, the First Amendment provides the rights to free speech and a free press, which helps journalists do their jobs.

The First Amendment states:

> Congress shall make no law respecting an establishment of religion, or prohibiting the free exercise thereof; or abridging the freedom of speech, or of the press; or the right of the people peaceably to assemble, and to petition the Government for a redress of grievances.

 **What First Amendment rights does this photo illustrate?**

This constitutional right to freedom of the press protects journalists and the media against censorship. **Censorship** is the prevention, or attempted prevention, of printing or broadcasting materials that some people consider objectionable. The First Amendment guarantees journalists the right to express themselves in publications, but no more so than other citizens. All U.S. citizens are protected under the First Amendment.

check *point* ✓

What constitutional rights are guaranteed to journalists by the First Amendment?

Public Officials and Public Figures

To understand the laws that concern journalists, you need to be able to distinguish public officials, public figures and private citizens. Private citizens include the vast majority of people who are not in the public spotlight.

PUBLIC OFFICIALS

Sometimes it's clear who is a **public official**. The mayor, your representative in the statehouse or the U.S. Congress, and the president of the United States are all public officials. Public officials are people whose salaries are paid with your tax dollars. They are elected by the people, have control of government and have access to the media. Sometimes it is not clear who is a public official. Is a police officer a public official? Is a teacher?

Court cases set precedents in determining who is a public official and who is not. In setting **precedents**, the courts use prior cases as a guide for deciding similar new cases. Journalists are legally allowed to write about public officials without their consent, so knowing who is considered by law to be a public official and who is considered a private citizen is important. For example, courts in most states have ruled that police officers may be considered public officials because they have the power to make arrests, which is a form of government control. Courts also have said teachers and other employees in public education are not public officials, because they carry out policies set by others. When trying to decide if someone is a public official, editors and reporters look at the outcomes of court cases and consult with lawyers who work in the field of communication law.

PUBLIC FIGURES

Journalists also are allowed to write about public figures without their consent. The definition of a **public figure** is broader than the definition of a public official. Public figures are people whose achievements or notoriety put them in the public spotlight. This includes actors and athletes in glossy magazines and newspaper sports pages. It includes people who attain some celebrity by being on a reality television show. People who seek attention by voluntarily putting themselves into public controversy also are considered public figures. This includes someone such as a community activist. People who end up in the spotlight involuntarily may not be public figures. If there is a question, it may need to be settled in court.

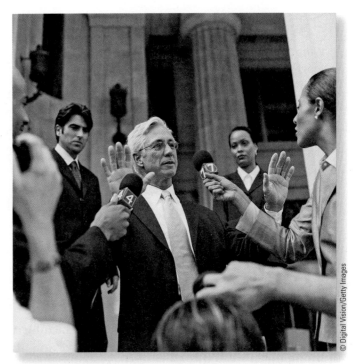

/////// *Why do journalists need to know whether the person they are reporting about is a public official, public figure or private citizen?*

What is the difference between a public official and a public figure?

Legal Issues

Legal issues that journalists need to understand include those involving libel and invasion of privacy. Journalists also need to understand shield laws and freedom of information laws.

LIBEL

The difference between public officials or public figures and private citizens is important because there are different standards for proving **libel**, or the making of a false and damaging statement about somebody. Journalists have less leeway in what they can say about private citizens than about public officials and public figures.

Journalists do not purposely set out to commit libel. Avoiding libel takes diligence in everyday reporting. Most libel cases happen because reporters under deadline pressure make careless mistakes, not because reporters purposely write falsehoods.

Truth is a defense against libel, but it doesn't always get you off the hook. Suppose you have been covering the city council meetings and a member of the city council tells you privately that the mayor of the city is in ill health and will retire at the next meeting. This is big news in your city, so you write the story for immediate posting on your newspaper's website and for publication in the morning's print edition. You quote the council member who told you the news. The story turns out to be false. The mayor has no plans to retire, and he's in excellent health. In fact, he plans to run for re-election, and now he'll have to contend with questions about his health. Even though it was a council member who said the mayor was in ill health, and you were assured it was true, you could be charged with libel because the story is false.

INVASION OF PRIVACY

Printing private information about a private citizen in a public forum is considered an **invasion of privacy**. Your school records, for example, are private and confidential. A reporter cannot print your grades in the school newspaper without your permission. Citizens also have the right to be left alone. A journalist coming onto your property without your consent is considered an invasion of privacy as well. You may have noticed that when covering a story, newspaper and television news crews often park across the street from someone's property.

News organizations that find themselves in court on privacy issues try to show that the published information was newsworthy. For public officials and public figures, almost anything can be considered newsworthy. For private individuals, it could be tougher to prove, but certain information could be considered newsworthy. For example, if a student is pictured in a photograph of a group of people at a political rally, the student might argue that media use of the picture is an invasion of privacy. The media argument could be that this student's — and other students' — attendance at the rally is newsworthy because it shows student interest in politics.

OTHER LAWS

Another set of laws that journalists need to understand are **shield laws** and **freedom of information laws**. Shield laws allow journalists to keep certain conversations confidential. Not all states have shield laws. There is no federal law to protect all journalists. News organizations have been trying to minimize the use of confidential sources in recent years. However, some stories, particularly those that reveal wrongdoing on the part of government or business, would never be told if reporters had to reveal their sources.

Freedom of information laws are sometimes called **sunshine laws** because they relate to the business of government being carried out in the open, or in the sunshine. Because our government belongs to the people, the notion behind freedom of information laws is that the people have the right to know what their government and government officials are doing.

 **check**point ✓

How do shield laws protect journalists?

Digging Deeper

First Amendment Rights of Student Journalists

In its 1988 decision in Hazelwood School District v. Kuhlmeier, the U.S. Supreme Court ruled that two high school newspaper reporters' First Amendment rights were not violated when the principal pulled articles they had written from the paper before publication. The principal deemed the topics of the articles — teen pregnancy and divorce — to be inappropriate for the high school audience. In its decision, the Court said, "First Amendment rights of students in the public schools are not automatically coextensive with the rights of adults in other settings, and must be applied in light of the special characteristics of the school environment. A school need not tolerate student speech that is inconsistent with its basic educational mission, even though the government could not censor similar speech outside the school."

To learn more about First Amendment rights for student journalists, access the Gale Journalism eCollection at www.cengage.com/school/langarts/journalism and click on the link to Chapter 1. Read the article entitled, "California eyes new free-speech protections in schools." The article explains recent legislation in California that protects scholastic journalism advisors from being punished for not censoring articles later deemed objectionable by school administrators.

THINK *Critically*

1. Search the Internet to find the text of the Hazelwood School District v. Kuhlmeier decision. Do you think the Supreme Court's decision was fair? Why or why not? Write a paragraph explaining the lessons you would take away from the Hazelwood decision.

2. What effect would passage of the Journalism Teacher Protection Act have on high school journalists in California?

Source: Daniel B. Wood. "California eyes new free-speech protections in schools." The Christian Science Monitor, Apr. 15, 2008.

1.2 | Assessment

Understand Concepts

Determine the best answer for each of the following questions.

1. What laws might have kept Judith Miller from going to jail?
   a. public figure laws
   b. invasion of privacy laws
   c. shield laws
   d. libel laws

2. **True or False**   A famous athlete is considered a public figure.

3. **True or False**   Courts in most states have ruled that police officers may be considered public officials because they have the power to make arrests, which is a form of government control.

4. **True or False**   Federal shield laws protect journalists in all states.

Write Now!

Practice your writing skills with the following activities.

5. Read a news story covered by an online U.S. newspaper. Read the same story covered by an online foreign newspaper. Write a report that compares and contrasts how the stories were handled. Cite specific lines of text that illustrate the similarities and the differences. After writing your report, reread it for clarity, engaging language and correct English.

6. Write a composition that discusses why censorship hurts journalism. Use the Internet to find an example of two current news stories. Include in your composition a discussion of how these stories might be different if they were censored. Plan and write a draft of the composition before writing the final paper. Carefully examine your paper for clarity, engaging language and correct English.

7. Write a news story about a public figure in your community for the school paper. Edit and proofread your story to ensure the story is well-written, states the facts in an interesting way and contains proper grammar.

Ethics in a Multimedia World

Goals

- Understand the ethical challenges journalists face.
- Explain the types of ethical violations that destroy a reporter's credibility.

Key Terms

- ethics 15
- accuracy 15
- credibility 15
- influence 16
- integrity 16
- anonymous source 17
- transparency 17
- on the record 17
- impartial 17
- conflict of interest 17
- plagiarism 20
- fabrication 21

FOCUS

One morning you read a newspaper story about the good deeds of a high-ranking political figure. That evening, on the television network news, you hear how that same politician used public funds to travel to exotic vacation spots. In the morning newspaper story, there was no mention of the politician using public funds for traveling, and in the evening television news story, there was no mention of the politician's good deeds.

The next day you see a photo of the newspaper reporter with the politician. The caption reads: "News reporter and politician longtime friends." What happens to your trust in the reporter and the politician when you learn about their friendship? What happens to your trust in the accuracy of the story about the politician's good deeds? Most likely your trust in the newspaper reporter and in the accuracy of the story will be lessened.

Everyday Ethics

Ethics are the moral principles that govern the conduct of individuals and organizations. Journalists must always conduct themselves ethically. What are the elements of ethical conduct in journalism?

When you read an article in a newspaper or on a website, or when you see a story reported on the television news, you most likely assume the story is true. There's nothing more important to a news organization than **accuracy**, which means getting all the facts right and always seeking the truth. Consistent accuracy gives the journalist and the news organization **credibility**, a reputation for being right. Credible news organizations and their employees strive to be fair and independent, that is, free from the influence of government, businesses or individuals.

Good journalists live in fear of making mistakes, and they work very hard to avoid them. Mistakes do happen, however, so news organizations make an effort to correct them as soon as possible. The willingness to correct mistakes is another mark of credibility.

There are many day-to-day situations in which journalists have to make ethical decisions. Some people try to **influence**, or persuade, reporters to write favorably about them or their businesses. Some ethical decisions for journalists are small, such as whether they should let a community leader pay for the lunch they have together. Some are larger, such as whether they should take a free trip offered by the resort about which they will write a travel story.

The Society of Professional Journalists has a broad code of ethics, but opinions may differ on how to handle some specific situations. For example, suppose you are a sports reporter for a high school yearbook. The bids for printing the yearbook are about to go out, and one of the printers offers you tickets to a professional football game. Would you accept the tickets? You might argue that you are not in a position to make a decision on who gets the printing bid (the editor and adviser decide that), so it is OK to accept the tickets. Or, you could argue that you are part of the yearbook staff and accepting the tickets obligates you and the others on staff to look favorably at the printer's bid. The best way to avoid ethical conflicts is to avoid even the appearance of impropriety. Taking tickets to a game from a potential yearbook printer at the least looks improper.

INTEGRITY

Journalists frequently face situations that test their **integrity**, that quality of possessing an inner sense of knowing right from wrong and adhering to high

////// *Why is accuracy important to a news organization?*

moral principles or professional standards. Often journalists have to decide the honorable way to handle a source, or the right way to deal with information they get from a source.

Suppose you agree to keep confidential the name of a source who supplies you with good information. Back at the news office, however, your editor says the information cannot run without attribution. Do you go back to the source and ask that person for permission to use his or her name? Do you publish the source and explain later that it was the boss's decision? Your natural instinct is probably to go back to the source and ask that person for permission because that's the right thing to do. Your integrity is guiding your decision making.

Journalists who act with integrity are honest in their reporting, and they are honest with readers and viewers about where they get their information. This principle of honesty is the reason many news organizations discourage or ban the use of **anonymous sources** except in extraordinary cases. Anonymous sources are sources who don't want to be named. News organizations now encourage **transparency**, which means writing into the story where the information came from and allowing readers to decide for themselves whether to believe the story.

Imagine you are a reporter for your high school newspaper and you find out from the principal's son, another student, that his mother will be moved to a different high school at the end of the semester. Because the son was not supposed to tell anyone this news, he wants to be anonymous, or unnamed, in the story. He says you should call him "a source close to the principal."

That would not be permitted by many news organizations. However, a good reporter may still go after the story by trying to get the information **on the record**, meaning that the information can be attributed to the source by name. If your source is still unwilling to go on the record, you might: (1) directly ask the principal if she is leaving at semester's end, or (2) ask the superintendent of schools if the principal will be moved. If the information comes from one of those credible, named, transparent sources, the truth of the story is verified and readers will know where it originated.

IMPARTIALITY

Journalists are expected to keep their distance from the people and organizations they cover so that they can be **impartial** in their stories. Impartiality means being objective and putting aside personal opinions when writing the news. It also means avoiding any **conflict of interest**. An example of a conflict of interest would be reporters writing about companies in which they own stock, or an organization to which they belong, or even the schools their children attend.

Journalists often are sent free books, CDs, movies and other material by sources who would like the journalists to write about the material in a story. Are these items given in an attempt to influence the reporters? Not usually. Most news organizations allow reporters to use and keep material that is clearly intended for mass press consumption, though some organizations strongly encourage employees to give such material to libraries or charitable organizations when their use for a story is complete. Critics and reporters on entertainment and sports beats often are offered tickets to games, concerts, theater productions or movies. Some organizations require that reporters buy tickets to any event they cover so there is no question about the impartiality of their reporting. Others allow reporters to attend screenings intended only for press or use seats set aside for press that would not be sold to the public. This is the case for sports reporters who sit in a press box to cover a game. If ever in doubt about accepting anything from a source or the source's representatives, a reporter should discuss it with his or her editors. If you encounter a situation involving possible conflict of interest while working on your school newspaper, talk to your faculty adviser.

ETHICAL GUIDELINES

Some journalists and ethics scholars say the new multiplatform, multimedia approaches to newsgathering and storytelling make for a news environment

///// *What are some ethical decisions a journalist might have to make?*

like the wild, wild West. When the rules aren't clear, it's easy to think there aren't any. Not true. The reality is that credible journalists working in multimedia are as concerned about getting everything right as are veteran print journalists. The principles of independence, fair play, responsibility, accuracy, truth, freedom of the press and impartiality apply to the work reporters do in any medium. See the American Society of News Editors' Statement of Principles in the Editorial Ethics feature on page 22.

New circumstances and forums raise ethical — and sometimes legal — questions. In 2006, the Poynter Institute, a journalism think tank in St. Petersburg, Fla., gathered together experienced reporters, editors, bloggers and online journalists. The group created guidelines for online news reporting. These guidelines, which are a work in progress, include information on blogs, truth and accuracy, and user-generated content.

1. **BLOGS**   On blogs, or Web logs, in Web discussions and even on radio and television shows, journalists can have trouble staying objective. Offering an opinion, particularly on a story the reporter covers, could compromise a reporter's impartiality. Journalists keeping personal blogs should recognize their responsibility to the news organization for which they work. If the blogger is a columnist rather than a news reporter, expressing an opinion in the blog is OK, but opinions should not be expressed on issues the blogger may cover in news columns either online or in print.

2. **TRUTH AND ACCURACY**   Multimedia journalists should be clear about the content they present, never manipulating it or presenting falsehoods. Photos and video should be shown in context and never doctored to make a point. The same goes for audio or video clips. In making publishing decisions on everything from how to report a story to what links to include in a story on the Internet, journalists take into consideration purpose, how much of the outside information is verified, the source and in what context the information was obtained.

3. **USER-GENERATED CONTENT**   News organizations generally have two types of user-generated content: self-published, which is often opinion or comment published on the organization's website, and specific solicited stories, photos and videos. In both cases, terms and conditions for publication should be spelled out and publicized consistently so the standards of the website are easy to find and can be effective. The publication also should make clear its policy on taste and judgment, anonymity, linking to outside sources and moderating.

check *point* ✓

What are ethics?

Ethics Violations

Ethics violations are serious because they break down the trust between a news organization and its audience. They have the power to destroy credibility. A reporter's credibility is destroyed when the reporter plagiarizes or fabricates a story or loses objectivity. Ethical issues are not always black and white, though most news organizations develop clear policies for their employees to follow.

News organizations have been faced with a number of cases where journalists have violated the ethical standards of truth, honesty and accuracy. These journalists caused great embarrassment for their employers and colleagues, and all were fired from their jobs.

PLAGIARISM

Copying others' work is not allowed in school, and it is not allowed in journalism. **Plagiarism** is copying the work of others and passing it off as your own. It is the same as stealing, and it is never allowed. Some journalists believe there have been more cases of plagiarism — whether stealing a sentence, a paragraph or a whole story — since the Internet became the first tool of research. The Internet and the computer programs journalists use to write and edit make it easy to cut and paste words from a research article into their own story, sometimes without realizing it. Still, there are no excuses for plagiarism.

///// **What precautions could a writer take to guard against plagiarism when conducting Internet research?**

It is acceptable, however, to use someone else's idea or concept for a story. News organizations routinely take ideas from each other. City newspapers like to localize a national story by getting their own sources and examples. The key is that they do their own reporting by finding new and different examples.

FABRICATION

There is no room for fiction writing in journalism, and fabrication is fiction writing. **Fabrication** covers everything from making up quotes and details, to making a story more exciting or interesting, to writing a whole story that never happened. In 2003, Jayson Blair, a young reporter for The New York Times, was forced to resign after it was discovered that in some stories he fabricated sources and descriptions, and, in some cases, the entire story.

Fabrication can be more difficult to detect than plagiarism. The editors at USA Today found this out the hard way. Also in 2003, an investigation of the work done by one of the paper's star reporters, Jack Kelley, revealed many instances where he had made things up. Kelley resigned, as did two top editors who worked with Kelley. Two other editors were reassigned because the investigation showed there were quotes, descriptions and whole stories fabricated over a number of years that should have been questioned by good editors.

LACK OF OBJECTIVITY

Should reporters and commentators be expected to keep their personal opinions to themselves at all times? Is objectivity compromised if a journalist speaks out on an issue? In 2010, Juan Williams, a commentator for National Public Radio (NPR), was fired from his job after he made statements about Muslims and terrorism on a Fox News Channel show. NPR agreed that Williams, a veteran journalist, had a right to say whatever he wanted to say on the Fox program. It contended, however, that he did not also have the "right" to continue to be paid by NPR. NPR said it fired Williams because his comments violated NPR's standards for commentary.

check point ✓

What is the difference between plagiarism and fabrication?

ASNE's Statement of Principles

The American Society of News Editors (ASNE) adopted a set of ethics for the profession in 1922. They were called the Canons of Journalism, and they acknowledged that the press had serious obligations and responsibilities. By agreeing to these canons, or principles, ASNE put newspaper editors around the country on the same page, at least on matters of ethics.

The canons have been revised over the years and are now called the Statement of Principles. The six basic ideas did not change. They are:

1. **Responsibility**   The primary job of editors and reporters is first to serve and inform the general public. Newspapers also should be a forum for debate, and they should bring independent scrutiny to the powers that be in society.

2. **Freedom of the Press**   Journalists must make sure the public's business is conducted in public. Freedom of the press must always be defended, and journalists must be watchful against anyone who exploits the press for selfish reasons.

3. **Independence**   Journalists must avoid conflicts of interest and impropriety. They shouldn't accept anything or pursue any activity that might compromise their integrity.

4. **Truth and Accuracy**   Every effort must be made to be sure that content is accurate and free from bias and that all sides are presented fairly. That goes for editorials and commentary, too. Significant errors of fact or omission should be corrected promptly and prominently.

5. **Impartiality**   Being impartial doesn't require being unquestioning. But there should be a clear distinction between news and opinion, and each should be clearly identified.

6. **Fair Play**   Journalists should respect the rights of people involved in their story, observe common standards of decency, and be accountable to the public for the fairness and accuracy of their reports. Pledges of confidentiality should be honored at all costs, and sources should be identified unless there is a clear and pressing need to maintain confidences.

THINK *Critically*

1. Why should all news organizations use the same ethical standards?
2. How might you balance freedom of the press with the rights of a school's administration to restrict private information about an action that affects the student body?

Source: From the American Society of News Editors. Used with permission.

1.3 | Assessment

Understand Concepts

Determine the best answer for each of the following questions.

1. Reporters need to keep a distance from the people and organizations they cover in order to
   a. get involved in conflicts of interest.
   b. avoid using anonymous sources.
   c. be impartial in their stories.
   d. be transparent.

2. Which is copying the work of someone and passing it off as your own?
   a. ethical dilemma
   b. plagiarism
   c. on-the-record copy
   d. fabrication

3. **True or False**   Plagiarism is acceptable as long as you do not get caught.

4. **True or False**   As a journalist, your integrity is important so people will believe the information in your stories.

Write Now!

Practice your writing skills with the following activities.

5. Do you believe news organizations should use anonymous sources? Write an opinion composition that describes your position and explains why you take this stand. Use the Internet to research cases where anonymous sources have been used successfully or unsuccessfully, and cite these cases in your composition. After you have planned your paper, write a draft, and then write the final composition. Before turning in your paper, examine it for clarity, engaging language, and the correct use of English.

6. Write a paper on the responsibilities of being a journalist that includes ethics, how you should treat sources and why you should serve truth. Be sure to edit and proofread your paper to ensure you have done your best job.

7. List the principles of your personal code of ethics, and then write a code of ethics for scholastic journalism.

CHAPTER 1 | Assessment

Review Journalism Concepts

1.1 The History of Journalism

The first American newspapers began in Colonial times as expressions of the editors' political opinions. By the mid-19th century, the focus of newspapers had shifted to current events and people. Popular penny press newspapers sold on street corners for one cent. Civil War journalists, using the telegraph to send stories, wrote in the inverted pyramid style, which is still used today. Competition among newspapers led to yellow journalism — sensationalism with screaming headlines and half-truths. Journalists with a social conscience began investigating corruption in big business, social institutions and politics. The investigations came to be known as muckraking, and the early reporters — or muckrakers — were the first investigative journalists.

Radio, television and the Internet have contributed to the way information is offered to, and received by, people. Radio began with the wireless telegraph in 1894. The Golden Age of Radio occurred during the 1920s and 1930s. In the 1950s, television replaced radio as the dominant broadcast medium. Like radio stations, television stations were affiliated with networks, or groups of stations that broadcast the same programs at the same time. By 2000, the Internet had changed how journalists researched and reported the news. Mass media — newspapers, magazines, radio, television and the Internet — have had an impact on our culture and made information more accessible.

1.2 Matters of Law

The First Amendment guarantees a free press. It is an important tool against censorship, which is the prevention, or attempted prevention, of printing or broadcasting materials. Journalists must understand the laws that govern their behavior. Public officials are politicians and others whose salary is paid by tax dollars. Public figures are famous people, such as rock stars, and private citizens are people who are not in the public spotlight.

Reporters can be taken to court for libel, the making of false or damaging statements about someone. Journalists must avoid invasion of privacy, which means not printing information about private individuals in a public forum. Shield laws allow reporters to keep certain conversations confidential, and freedom of information laws allow journalists to access government documents.

1.3 Ethics in a Multimedia World

Ethics are the moral principles that govern appropriate conduct for reporters and news organizations. Journalists must strive for accuracy and keep their integrity by remaining impartial and avoiding any conflict of interest.

Journalists must follow ethical guidelines. They must be objective and must avoid ethical violations, including plagiarism (copying the work of another and passing it off as your own) and fabrication (making up all or part of a story).

Develop Your Journalism Language

Write the letter of the term that matches each definition. Some terms will not be used.

_____ 1. Publications printed on large sheets of folded paper that contain information about current events, features on different topics and advertisements

_____ 2. Story format that puts the most important facts first

_____ 3. Beginning of investigative journalism

_____ 4. Guarantees a free press

_____ 5. Merging of print and other platforms

_____ 6. Printing a private citizen's private information in a public forum

_____ 7. The making of false or damaging statements about someone

_____ 8. Laws that allow some journalists to keep certain conversations confidential

_____ 9. Also called sunshine laws, these laws allow journalists to obtain information about government business

_____ 10. The moral principles that govern the conduct of individuals and organizations

_____ 11. Prevention, or attempted prevention, of printing or broadcasting materials

a. anonymous source
b. censorship
c. convergence
d. ethics
e. fabrication
f. First Amendment
g. freedom of information laws
h. impartial
i. invasion of privacy
j. inverted pyramid
k. libel
l. mass media
m. muckraking
n. network
o. newspaper
p. on the record
q. penny press
r. plagiarism
s. public figure
t. public officials
u. shield laws
v. Skype
w. transparency

_____ 12. A source who does not want to be named

_____ 13. Writing into the story where the information came from and allowing readers to decide for themselves whether to believe the story

_____ 14. The source's name can be used

_____ 15. Being objective and putting aside personal opinion when writing the news

_____ 16. Copying the work of others and passing it off as your own

_____ 17. Making up quotations or details or even the whole story

_____ 18. Refers to all channels of communication that reach a large audience

_____ 19. A group of radio or television stations that broadcast the same programs at the same time

_____ 20. People whose salaries are paid with tax dollars

Think Critically

21. How has the Internet helped you become more informed about world news than your parents and grandparents were?

22. How did the Civil War change the way journalists wrote news stories?

23. How was competition among reporters during the Civil War similar to and different from competition among reporters today?

24. Why might a reporter have taken pride in being called a muckraker?

25. How might a government hurt journalism in a country that does not offer protection such as the First Amendment of the U.S. Constitution?

26. Do you think the administration of your school should be allowed to censor the school newspaper? Why or why not?

27. Why should news organizations provide information on multiple platforms?

28. What does it say about a community within the United States when the newspaper that most of the people who live there read is printed in a language other than English?

29. What benefits and drawbacks are associated with obtaining news from the Internet?

30. What should a reporter do when she has a hot story that will make her famous but hurt an innocent person?

Make Academic Connections

31. **HISTORY** Use the Internet to research the history of the First Amendment. Write a composition that includes information on the person who wrote the amendment and his reasons for wanting the amendment. Also, include your personal opinion on why you think the First Amendment is necessary and how it relates to your life in your school or community. Carefully examine your paper for clarity, engaging language, and the correct use of English.

32. **CAREERS AND PERSONAL FINANCE** Use the Internet or personal interviews to research pay for starting reporters for a local broadcast station and a local newspaper. Use a computer to create a spreadsheet for a budget that shows how you would live on the net income. Include major expenses such as rent, vehicle, food, clothing and entertainment.

33. **SCHOLASTIC JOURNALISM** Choose a topic that is relevant to your school and write a news story for your school newspaper. Include the history of the issue in your story. Be sure to use the inverted pyramid style.

34. **TECHNOLOGY** Telecommuting, working from home or another location outside the company's office, is rapidly becoming popular among journalists. Think about how journalists might telecommute and then answer these questions: As a journalist, how could you benefit from telecommuting? What tools would you need to telecommute?

35. **WRITING** Why is integrity an important characteristic for a journalist to possess?

36. **BUSINESS**   Use the Internet to find the circulation of each of the following newspapers: (a) USA Today, (b) The New York Times, (c) The Wall Street Journal, (d) the Los Angeles Times, (e) The Washington Post. Create a spreadsheet that shows the circulation of each paper. Also show the elements the papers have in common, such as "is a national paper" and the elements unique to each paper that help make it a high-circulation paper.

37. **VISUAL ARTS**   Work with two or three other students to create a poster or computer graphic of the first page of an online newspaper with information relevant to your class.

38. **SOCIOLOGY**   Developments in newsgathering and reporting change with events in history. Using the information in this chapter and research, design a chart that illustrates how events in history changed journalism. For example, illustrate that the inverted pyramid style came out of the Civil War.

Writing Portfolio Activity

39. Keep a journal of news and news-related information you read for one week. Include newspapers and news magazines, radio and television news, and news from the Internet. At the end of the week, write an analysis of a story you read or listened to. In your analysis, answer these questions: What attracted you to the story? Did you read, or listen to, the entire story or only the beginning? What caught your interest about the story? What was the print headline or broadcast teaser? Was there a photo, chart or other visual with the story? Did you read or hear about the story from more than one source? What were the sources? How did the style of reporting differ? Which did you like the best? Why? Was the story written for someone in your age group or for an older audience? What elements in the story helped you determine the age group?

AP Stylebook Workshop

In your English class, you may have learned to use a comma before the conjunction, such as the word "and," in a simple series.

Example: Journalists research, plan, and write a draft before they turn in final copy.

AP style does not use a comma before a conjunction in a simple series.

Example: Journalists research, plan and write a draft before they turn in final copy.

Insert commas according to AP style in the following sentences:

40. The major television networks are ABC CBS Fox and NBC.

41. News delivery has gone from only newspapers to newspapers radio television and the Internet.

42. To understand the laws that concern journalists, you need to be able to identify public officials public figures and private citizens.

MEDIA LITERACY: A Media-Centered World

Journalists in the 21st century are part of a technology-driven world where news is available 24 hours a day, seven days a week through a variety of media platforms. To be competitive in a career in journalism, you must be savvy in all media platforms. The three major media platforms are

- **Print media,** which include newspapers and news magazines. Jobs in print media include reporters or correspondents, feature writers, columnists, editors and publishers.

- **Broadcast media,** which include radio and television. Jobs in broadcast news include reporters, analysts, anchors, broadcasters or newscasters, editors, camera people, videographers and producers.

- **Internet-based news sites,** where jobs include reporters or correspondents, bloggers, analysts, editors, videographers and Web designers.

USING MULTIPLE MEDIA

In addition to being confident writing for the various media platforms, today's journalists also must be comfortable working with multiple media, that is, combining audio, video and graphic elements to make the stories available for the Internet. For example:

A reporter who specializes in writing magazine articles on bands for Rolling Stone will need to write a story and provide photos of the band for the printed magazine. For the Internet, the journalist will have to provide a shortened story and video clips of the band performing as well as backstage clips of band members before or after the concert.

Some reporters work with a photographer or videographer, especially reporters in broadcast news. However, in smaller markets the journalist should be able to offer the media the whole package — a story ready for print, along with photos, and a story ready for the Internet, along with video clips. Good reporters even in larger markets pay attention to the photographs or video clips and work in partnership with the camera person to be able to tell the best story and choose the photos or clips that do just that.

LEARNING ABOUT THE MEDIA

For most careers in journalism, a degree in journalism, mass communications or English is required. To be competitive in today's market, students planning to enter the field of journalism should also take courses in computer science, photojournalism, broadcast journalism and other technology-related courses.

Journalists who want to specialize in a particular area also should take courses in their field of interest. For example, if you have an interest in business and plan to write for a business magazine or news outlet, you will want to take business courses.

OPPORTUNITIES FOR JOURNALISTS

Entry-level jobs in journalism in print, broadcast and Internet news may not be high-paying. Competition is strong, especially in urban areas, but journalism can be a rewarding career, especially if you are working in a specialty you like.

All journalists entering the field today must be media literate in all media platforms of journalism — print, broadcast and electronic news.

THINK *Critically*

Develop a plan for the college courses you would take in order to pursue journalism as a career. Be sure to include courses that will prepare you for jobs in print, broadcast and Internet-based news.

REAL PEOPLE REAL CAREERS

Tony Dearing | Embracing Digital Media

Tony Dearing has been a journalist almost all his life. He was editor of his junior high school newspaper, his high school newspaper and his college newspaper. "I've always known what I wanted to do," he says, "and it never occurred to me to do anything else."

© Photo courtesy of Tony Dearing

Dearing is now chief content officer (in the new-media world, that means editor) of AnnArbor.com, the news website serving the Michigan community outside Detroit. After three decades in the news business and 11 years at The Ann Arbor News before it folded in 2009, Dearing embraces the digital media.

"One big difference with online journalism is immediacy," Dearing says. "People want news in real time. If a mother is at work and gets a text from her son saying that his school has been locked down, she's not going to wait until the newspaper comes out tomorrow to find out what's going on. She expects to go to your website and find a report right then. And she'll expect to see updates throughout the day."

Another major difference between print and online journalism, Dearing says, is the interactivity website users expect. "People want to comment. They want to 'like' stories and share them. They want to upload their photos. This is the complete opposite of the passive, one-way experience newspapers offered." In hiring staff, Dearing says, he looks for journalists with "good, old-fashioned reporting skills. We want people who have a nose for news and know how to go out there and dig up stories and ask tough questions. But they also need to be comfortable with all the tools of new media so they can tell those stories in digital form, be it social media or video or a series of Web posts that rapidly update a breaking story. That's why we call our employees digital journalists rather than reporters."

ADVICE FOR ASPIRING JOURNALISTS

Dearing is upbeat about the future of journalism. He tells aspiring journalists: "First of all, don't listen to the gloom and doom you may hear about the news business. It is true, newspapers are facing real struggles right now, but journalism as a profession is as much in need as ever, and as we make the transition to the digital realm, I believe we are entering an exciting new era in which journalism will flourish again."

Young people who want to be part of the news revolution must learn solid reporting skills, Dearing says. "Today's journalists have to know how to be fast and accurate. Be an early adapter to emerging technology, and always look for new ways to report the news."

Source: Personal interview with Tony Dearing.

THINK *Critically*
Why do many people prefer to get their news via digital media rather than a printed newspaper?

The Journalist in the New Century

2.1	**Who Is a Journalist?**
2.2	**Multimedia Journalists**
2.3	**What Convergence Means**

Making a Name in Journalism

Many important names in the field of journalism have made their reputations in one particular medium. Edward R. Murrow made World War II come alive for the American audience listening to his legendary radio reports from Europe. "CBS Evening News" anchor Walter Cronkite was an authoritative presence on television in the 1960s, breaking the news of President John F. Kennedy's assassination and bringing the Vietnam War into America's living rooms. In the 1970s, the Watergate political scandal made print reporters Bob Woodward and Carl Bernstein journalism icons. Working for The Washington Post, they ushered in an era of investigative reporting as their work uncovering the details of Watergate led to congressional hearings and toppled Richard Nixon's presidency. Will a 21st century journalist make a reputation on the Internet? Chances are, yes.

> **THINK** *Critically*
> What do these journalists have in common that helped them make their reputations?

Who Is a Journalist?

Goals

- Describe modern-day journalists and their role.
- Explain the differences between reporters and editors.

Key Terms

- journalist 31
- journalism 31
- freelance journalist 32
- reporter 32
- correspondent 32
- editor 32
- photographer 32
- videographer 32
- copy editor 33
- designer 33
- artist 33

FOCUS

When your parents were growing up, they may have had a newspaper delivered to their doorstep every morning. At breakfast, they may have peeked at the sports page to get the score of last night's important game, or looked at the television schedule to check which of their favorite shows would air that night. They might even have read a few favorite comic strips before catching the bus for school.

In your world, the Internet has become as important a news source as the newspaper was to your parents. It's the modern way of keeping informed about what is going on in the world. The difference between newspapers and the Internet is that Internet users get video, audio and interactive graphics, as well as the printed word. Plus, the Internet is updated all day long. The Internet is more than a news source, though. It also is a place for regular folks to find information, build social communities and communicate — exactly the mission most news organizations see for themselves.

The Modern Journalist

Journalists in the 21st century are the reporters, editors, photographers, producers and camera crews who sift through the many events of a day to tell you what is important or interesting in your community and the world. They are modern-day storytellers who use all the technology available to them. Journalists work in the field of **journalism**, which is the business of news-gathering and reporting. Journalists like to know what is going on in their communities and why something happened. They like to get information, ask questions and tell good stories.

Journalists today may use a reporter's notebook and pen, but they also must know how to use the digital recorders on their smartphones and the latest video chat software on their laptop computers. New-century journalists keep up to date with new technology and use it as they develop their stories for print, broadcast and the Internet. In addition, today's journalists need traits and skills that good journalists always have needed: solid news judgment and sound ethics, the ability to write clearly and edit carefully, and the desire to investigate and verify.

Some people become journalists because they are naturally curious. Others enter the field because they are writers. They like the challenge of taking facts, interviews and observations and weaving them into interesting tales that help others understand the world, or at least one slice of it. Some are photographers who see stories through the lens of a camera, whether still or video. Whatever the reasons journalists have for getting into the field of journalism, they are in the business of storytelling. Whether the story is told in a magazine, in a newspaper, on a television or radio broadcast or on an Internet webcast, the traits and basic skills needed are the same.

THE ROLE OF JOURNALISTS

Journalists are people who collect information and report on current events, trends and issues in the community and around the world. In other words, they are people who help to keep their communities — and the world — up-to-date. Journalists work with government officials, businesses and community leaders, but they must remain independent of them and free from any association that would be — or might appear to be — a conflict of interest. Journalists often work for news organizations, such as newspaper publishers or broadcast networks. They are on staff and paid by those organizations to cover news, to find trends and to explain important issues.

Other journalists are **freelance journalists**. That means they do not work for a particular news outlet and they may cover stories for any news outlet that wants to hire them. Sometimes freelance journalists work for an employer on assignment, which means they work on, and are paid for, one story at a time. Freelance journalists also work on contract, which means they make an agreement to work for, and are paid for, a particular length of time. Whether journalists are on staff or freelance, they represent the organization employing them and adhere to their employer's standards as well as those of the profession.

The term "journalist" is broad. It often is used as a synonym for "reporter." However, many types of journalists are involved in putting out a news report.

- **Reporters**, also called **correspondents**, gather information for stories by researching, observing and interviewing. They then write most of the content. Most of their stories will be assigned to them by editors, but some will come from ideas of their own that were approved by an editor.

- **Editors** assign and approve the content — meaning stories, photos and videos — that will be produced for a print, broadcast or online news report. There are editors for news, sports, the arts, business and more.

- **Photographers** take still shots for a story.

- **Videographers** tell stories with moving images and capture the story in video.

- **Copy editors** edit the text of a story. They check the facts and correct errors in spelling and grammar before publication. Copy editors also write headlines and photo captions.

- **Designers** determine, with the top editors, where content will be placed on printed pages or how it will be arranged on websites.

- **Artists** work with editors and reporters to produce illustrations, charts, graphs, maps or other material that will help tell a story.

In the next section you will learn more about the role of reporters and editors, the backbone of the news media.

Name the types of journalists involved in putting out a news report.

Reporters and Editors

Reporters and editors are the journalists who work in print, broadcast and Internet operations to report and sort the news. They work for daily and weekly news operations, monthly magazines, and 24/7 broadcasts and websites.

As you have read, journalists on the front lines are usually called reporters or correspondents. They gather facts and prepare information to send out by mass media to the people who will read it, listen to it or watch it. When Japan was hit by a major earthquake and tsunami in 2011, journalists from national

////// *What would a journalist do in reporting the stories in a natural disaster?*

cable and broadcast networks and many major newspapers and websites scrambled to get reporters, photographers and videographers on the ground there quickly. They wrote and photographed thousands of stories about the devastation and the human impact of these disasters so that people in this country could understand what had happened. Some correspondents stayed for weeks or months after the quake to continue reporting on rebuilding and relief efforts.

Reporters don't have to go to the scene of an international disaster to be on the front line. A reporter who covers a school board or city council meeting in a small community also gathers and reports information that helps people in the community stay informed on important issues that affect their lives and personal budgets. How do you find out whether the city council voted to raise parking fees? How do you learn that the school board voted to cut the music and arts program? You learn from reporters.

Editors work with reporters to get the best stories to news consumers as quickly as possible. In addition to assigning reporters to breaking news stories or features, editors also may help reporters develop questions for interview subjects, decide where reporters should go to get the story and be a contact point in the office of the news organization.

While reporters were in Haiti covering the aftermath of the earthquake in 2010, editors were in the office reviewing photos, video and information coming in from all sources. They listened to reporters on the ground via cell or satellite phone, received text and email messages, and developed a list of stories the reporters would produce for the website and print editions. Editors also edited the material to be sure it could be understood easily by readers and website users.

checkpoint ✓

What is the job of a reporter, and what is the job of an editor?

AP Stylebook Concepts

In a scholarly text, the names of cities and states are spelled out, with a comma between the city and state.

Example   Los Angeles, California

AP style allows you to abbreviate most state names, but not all. Ohio, for example, is never abbreviated, but California is always abbreviated to Calif. when used with a city. Eight states are not abbreviated. They are Alaska, Hawaii, Idaho, Iowa, Maine, Ohio, Texas and Utah. To find the abbreviations of the other states, refer to the class copy of The Associated Press Stylebook. Note that the abbreviations are different from the two-letter abbreviations used by the U.S. Postal Service.

Get to Know Your First Amendment

The First Amendment to the U.S. Constitution is just 45 words, but they are important words. The First Amendment gives us the right to say what we want to say, write what we think and publish it. We may criticize our government, gather to do so, and worship where we like.

Citizens in some countries can't do all that. In the U.S., different opinions are valued, and the First Amendment allows for the exchange of thoughts and opinions. The media can create a marketplace of ideas. Whether the government likes the ideas doesn't matter. The ideas can't be repressed.

The First Amendment gives power to the people and the press. It recognizes that the people have a right to know what the government is up to. Most of us don't have time to keep tabs on all the movers and shakers in our government. We count on journalists to be the watchdogs, to tell us what's going on in our communities, from the local to the international level.

That doesn't mean everybody agrees on how much power the people and the press should have. Debate on the First Amendment has been robust since the ratification of the Constitution more than 200 years ago, and it keeps on going today. James Madison, who wrote the amendment, and the rest of the Founding Fathers agreed that the freedoms of speech, press, religion and assembly were necessary to have the open society they envisioned for America. However, like many Americans today, they did not agree on how the First Amendment should be applied.

Should reporters be allowed to give their sources anonymity for the sake of getting good information? Should the government be allowed to keep secret certain information it claims is sensitive? Those are just two of the questions still unsettled. More questions arise all the time as technology changes and expands our marketplace of ideas.

THINK *Critically*

1. Why are First Amendment freedoms important to our society?
2. Do you think freedom of the press should be unrestricted? Why or why not?

2.1 | Assessment

Understand Concepts

Determine the best answer for each of the following questions.

1. The journalist responsible for the final content of a story is the
   a. correspondent.
   b. copy editor.
   c. editor.
   d. designer.

2. **True or False** Freelance journalists are free to work for different news outlets.

3. **True or False** Reporters gather information and write most of the content for their stories.

4. **True or False** Videographers are the journalists responsible for producing illustrations, charts, graphs, maps and other graphics.

Write Now!

Practice your writing skills with the following activities.

5. Research, plan, draft and write a paper about your favorite journalist. The journalist can be from a local or national news source. The paper should include information on the journalist's background, education, body of work and awards won. Also explain why you chose this journalist. What do you admire about him or her? The composition should be carefully researched, planned, drafted and written, and edited for clarity, engaging language and the correct use of the conventions and mechanics of written English.

6. Write a few paragraphs that explain which you would rather be — a reporter or an editor. Explain your answer in a way that describes each job.

7. Choose a news website originating in a foreign country that is written in a language you can understand. If English is your second language, choose a news website in your native language. Study the website to find a reporter whose work you like. Read at least three of the reporter's stories, and then choose one of the stories to rewrite in English in a journalistic style for your high school paper.

8. Study three online news sources such as The Huffington Post, CNN and MSNBC. Compare and contrast the news organizations' websites. What is similar about the home screens? What is different? Do they all have bloggers? Breaking news stories? Features? Still photos? Videos? Audio? Create a chart that shows the similarities and differences, and then write a summary that describes your findings. Include information on which source you like best and why.

Multimedia Journalists

Goals

- Define "multimedia" and describe the multimedia tools journalists use.
- Explain how journalists use multimedia to tell stories.

Key Terms

- multimedia 37
- multimedia journalist 37
- print journalist 37
- backpack journalist 37
- digital video camera 38
- producer 39

FOCUS

When you watch an entertainment news show for the latest tidbit on your favorite movie star, or read your local newspaper to find out who won the race for mayor, you are looking at the work of journalists. The Internet and advancing technology have given rise to many more media outlets for gathering and delivering news in many more formats. Still, it takes educated, curious people to collect and tell the stories of the day.

Multimedia Journalists

Multimedia simply means that a Web story is some combination of the written word, photographs, video clips, audio clips, graphics and an interactive element, such as a quiz or a poll. Multimedia stories are presented in a nonlinear way, which means that Web users decide how to navigate through the elements. The elements are complementary, not redundant. **Multimedia journalists** are news and information gatherers who are comfortable working to produce all the elements mentioned above. A multimedia journalist is a combination of a **print journalist**, who writes the text for the story; a photographer; and a videographer. Multimedia journalists may conduct interviews, record videos or take photographs, write the story, write a script for the video, and post it all to a website. Multimedia journalists are multitaskers, too. They may use multiple tools — a video camera and a notebook, for example — during the same interview.

Multimedia journalists may be referred to as **backpack journalists** because they carry in a backpack all the technical tools needed to produce the multiple elements of the story. They understand how the video and other visual elements will work with text and how to integrate it, or make it work together. They go to the scene with a backpack containing a reporter's notebook, video camera, still camera and light laptop computer on which they can write and transmit all the elements to editors of the website.

Sam is a backpack journalist for a local newspaper assigned to cover a fire in the community. He arrives at the scene of the fire with his notebook and pen, light laptop computer, still camera and video camera. As he roams around the smoking debris, he observes and then makes written notes of what he sees in his slim reporter's notebook. As he conducts interviews with the people affected by the fire, he takes notes, writing quickly so the quotations are accurate. He asks interview subjects to spell their names, and he carefully writes the spelling into his notes. As he gets ready to go to the newsroom, he checks the notebook one last time to be sure he has made a record of everything he needs to write a compelling story about the event.

Sam knows the story also needs a visual element, so he takes his digital camera out of his backpack. He surveys the damage and begins to think about capturing one or two compelling images to help illustrate the print story. He also sees the possibility of a narrated slide show for the Internet and begins shooting images that he will later edit on the appropriate software program in his computer. He will use his reporter's notebook to get names and to put his images in context.

Next, he takes his **digital video camera** — one that captures images electronically — out of his backpack. After surveying the damage through the lens, he zooms in on vignettes that will bring out emotion in viewers — a teddy bear lying on a burned sofa, for example. He conducts a few interviews on camera with those affected by the fire. He also collects other bits of sound — the hiss of the water through the hoses still in use, the cries of children who can't get back into their homes. Before he leaves he may make a few additional notes in his reporter's notebook — phone numbers for the interview subjects, for example. When he arrives back at the office he has enough information to write a story as well as to write a script for the video, which he will edit on his computer to tell the story succinctly.

checkpoint ✓

What is multimedia, and what tools are used in multimedia?

Multimedia Stories

Most website stories produced by a news organization contain all the elements that Sam the backpack journalist used to tell the story of the fire. These elements include text, photographs, video and audio. Websites allow for multimedia storytelling. However, not all stories on websites are created from the beginning as multimedia stories. Sometimes the various parts of a story that are presented as multimedia are produced separately for their own platform, such as print, television or radio broadcast, or online. The text, for example, is prepared for a print product and may be used unchanged on the Web. The photograph used with the text is used in the print product, and the video is a version of what is shot and produced for a television report. The elements are there, but that is not always the best presentation for a website.

The best multimedia stories are organized and planned by a reporter, editor or producer who knows how to integrate all the content elements before the journalists set off to cover the story. The text written for a website is likely to be shorter than for print; photographs will not be produced at the same size for the Web as they would be in print; and video will be seen in smaller frames on a computer than on television, so the videographer will shoot with that in mind.

Sometimes an editor, who may be called a **producer** if part of a website team, takes charge of a multimedia story, particularly when it is a breaking news story. The editor will assign different journalists to each part of the story and assign people who use different tools to tell their stories. The editor may send a print reporter to gather important information from authorities and conduct some interviews; a photographer for photos for use in print and on the Web; a videographer to survey the scene and get interviews on camera with a short video story in mind; an artist to draw a map or an illustrative graphic from facts reported in the field. Once the editor knows everything is covered, the next step is to integrate the story as journalists at the scene send the pieces to the newsroom.

checkpoint ✓

How are multimedia stories produced?

////// *What is the producer's role when the news team is faced with a breaking news multimedia story?*

2.2 | Assessment

Understand Concepts

Determine the best answer for each of the following questions.

1. Journalists who work alone and use all the technical tools needed to produce the multiple elements of a story are called
   a. correspondents.
   b. freelance journalists.
   c. photojournalists.
   d. backpack journalists.

2. A multimedia journalist is a combination of a photographer, a videographer and a(n) _____, who writes the text for the story.
   a. editor
   b. producer
   c. print journalist
   d. backpack journalists

3. **True or False**   Most website stories include text, photographs, video and audio.

4. **True or False**   Stories on websites are always created from the beginning as multimedia stories.

Write Now!

Practice your writing skills with the following activities.

5. Find a news story in your high school that lends itself to both a print and a website audience. Think about how the story would work for a print publication and how it would work for a website. What photographs would work? Could you use audio and video for the website? Write the news story for both a high school print paper and a high school news website. Before you turn in your stories, add information on what elements you would add to the print and website stories. Be sure to edit your stories for clarity, engaging language and the use of correct English. Write in journalistic style and use the right format for each platform.

6. Write an outline that describes the multimedia elements to include in a news story about an upcoming sports rally at your school. Be creative!

7. Use a computer to write a story for a news website that explains why the Internet is a good place for consumers to read about new products. Upload your story and send it to your teacher over the Internet.

What Convergence Means

Goals

- Define "convergence" and explain how news organizations have merged operations and turned newsrooms into information centers.
- Understand how technology continues to change journalism.

Key Terms

- convergence 41
- posts 42
- desks 42
- information center 42
- content producers 42
- citizen journalism 43
- open-source or crowd-source reporting 43
- online journalism 44

FOCUS

A White House correspondent for a national, multimedia news organization has a busier job in the 21st century than White House correspondents have had historically. Today, when the president has a news conference, reporters may send out short reports by text messaging on their cellphones or by tweets on Twitter even as the news conference is still happening. When the news conference is over, reporters may quickly write a short news report and post it on the news site or, if the organization has one, on a blog devoted to breaking news. Once those pressing duties are done, reporters will settle into writing a story with more background, research and perspective for the print product. When the day is done, reporters will have written for three platforms: social media (Twitter), the Web and print.

Merging Operations

The variety of platforms on which news consumers can receive information is forcing journalists to think in new ways about how they will present a story. In addition to the print medium, journalists must think in terms of multiple media, the adding of audio and video elements to the story. Reporters and photographers use digital audio and video recorders and digital still cameras to cover events, conduct investigative reporting or showcase human interest stories. Editors and Web designers use various software programs to make the stories available and attractive online. Journalists are likely to write the same story in different forms for both a print publication and its website.

The merging of a news organization's operations — some combination of print, Web and broadcast — is called **convergence**, and it often requires a lot of collaboration. Convergence began at a time when the products an organization put out needed to be much different from traditional products. Instead of just offering print or broadcast news, organizations also had to keep up with the changing technology.

Just as 21st century journalists working in the field keep up with technology, so do 21st century information consumers. Today's news stories are told not only in black-and-white newspaper columns but also on the Web, where consumers expect something different. Web users prefer to interact with the story. Give these consumers a video on which to click, a podcast to download or a graphic that pops up little-known facts, and you may keep their attention. Internet users are likely to read a Web log, or blog, by a popular writer, but not the writer's newspaper column. In fact, Web users are likely to develop allegiance to certain blogs, returning to the blogs they like several times a day looking for additional **posts**, or updates.

News managers — who now oversee print publications, websites, and possibly television or radio broadcasts — are constantly rethinking how they organize their news operations. Some companies are training print reporters to operate digital cameras, video recorders and other equipment needed for multimedia presentation of news and features. Others have changed entirely the way their newsroom is set up to handle information and data. Although the changes these news managers make are not always comfortable for reporters and editors who have been accustomed to putting out only one type of product, the managers bring new thinking and new types of jobs to news information companies. Journalists are finding new ways to tell stories they think their communities should know.

THE NEW NEWSROOM

Journalists in traditional print and broadcast organizations usually call their base of operations a newsroom. The reporters and editors working there are assigned to **desks**, areas of designated specialties. Reporters might be assigned to a city desk, for example, because they cover topics related to city government, local schools and police activity in the community. Reporters who work on the foreign desk likely would be stationed in other countries, yet take assignments from the home office. As convergence continues, more news organizations are moving away from traditional labels.

The center of today's news operations may be called an **information center**, replacing the term "newsroom." The editors and reporters who continue to cover news of the day, as well as plan feature and other stories for all their platforms, may be called **content producers**.

Some content is produced simply by collecting data about community events, sporting events, local activities and even crime. That information may be entered into databases available to Web users to browse as they wish. Some information, such as news headlines, restaurant listings or movie times, may be available to customers immediately on platforms such as a mobile phone.

///// *Why is "information center" a better term than "newsroom" for a converged news world?*

Whatever the labels, 21st century journalists understand they must deliver the content their audiences want anytime, anywhere and to any device. This means meeting the 24/7 demands of customers. It requires asking editors and reporters to do new jobs or work different hours while expanding their skills beyond print into video, audio and other media. It means the news operation maintains the large databases their users might want to search or browse. Most important, the information center concept requires placing value on local news and on the community's interaction with the providers of news.

CITIZEN JOURNALISM

A buzz phrase often heard at news organizations experimenting with the new ways of informing people is **citizen journalism**, or journalism in which the audience participates. News sites started down this path by enabling Web users to comment on stories or blogs. Some news organizations embrace citizen journalism in a big way, asking the public to help them report stories. This is called **open-source** or **crowd-source reporting**. MSNBC.com, for example, asks its readers to send pictures and reports of their return to their homes after natural disasters such as hurricanes and brush fires.

Another way news organizations embrace citizen journalism involves allowing readers and users to file reports on events in which they have an interest, such as their children's soccer games or a PTA meeting. These reports are then posted on the website. Some news outlets ask readers to write blogs about their neighborhoods, or about specialties, such as gardening. Though there is some disagreement about citizen journalism and how far it can or should go, there is no doubt that in some form it's here to stay.

checkpoint ✓

What is convergence, and how has it changed the traditional newsroom?

Technology Continues to Change Journalism

Ride any public transportation system, such as the subway in New York or the "L" in Chicago, and you will see commuters catching up on the day's news on handheld devices such as a BlackBerry or iPhone. By 2010, the Internet was an important source of information for many Americans and was on its way to becoming America's main news source, according to the Pew Research Center for the People & the Press. One Pew report found that 61 percent of Americans get some of their news online on a typical day and 71 percent get news online at least occasionally. The Internet also facilitates sharing news stories as a social activity, and social media sites such as Facebook and Twitter are now important platforms on which to get news noticed.

ONLINE JOURNALISM

Journalism conducted on the Internet is called **online journalism**. The Internet makes it possible to deliver information anywhere to anyone who has access to a computer, a smartphone or other advanced technology. In your parents' generation, television helped make Earth a global village, but in the 1990s the Internet went beyond what television did. More and more people were using the Internet for email, research and information sharing. That's when it became clear to newsgathering companies that harnessing the Internet to deliver news could be a good idea.

Online journalism continues to change with new technological possibilities. Journalism scholars continue to look at how future citizens in a global world will obtain their news and information. Some industry leaders say news organizations should not worry about the media platform, focusing instead on the quality of the journalism produced. Some say that the content produced is gaining in value because Internet users choose where they will go on the basis of a website's content and presentation. The better the stories and the presentation, the more online readers the site will draw. Journalism also gains value when citizens have a stake in it, as do the many who post comments to stories, or write their own stories and blogs. Journalists of the future will deal with lots of questions about how best to perform their most important work, such as public service and investigative stories, in constantly changing environments.

WHY GO WEB?

Working on the Web is immediate. It allows reporters to get their work out even while they are in the middle of gathering facts. It means news can be reported in real time, not — as is typical in high school newspapers — days or weeks after the fact.

Whether you are on the newspaper staff or you are just an avid reader, you probably know more about events in the life of your high school than the newspaper offers. That's not a reflection on the newspaper. The staff must deal with a lag time before publication because of printing facility scheduling and expense.

If you are a reporter who writes for a school newspaper, you can cover Friday afternoon's baseball game but not publish your game report until the next week. With a website, a game story can be published as soon as the game begins, with updates throughout the afternoon. Writing for the Web, you learn to compose short pieces — or posts — on strict deadlines.

Websites, blogs, social media such as Facebook and Twitter, email, and text messaging are part of the way today's high school students communicate in the world. A student-run news website that offers daily reports also offers an experience more typical of the one student journalists will face in the real world. More important, the website may bring fellow students into the

////// **How does social networking contribute to the news?**

community of their high school by delivering news, information and feature stories that may make them active participants in the life of the school. Of course, online journalism demands more of your teachers and advisers and presents challenges because it is so immediate.

Those challenges exist in professional journalism as well. Reporters and editors are learning to write shorter, think in nonlinear ways and post stories straight to the website without the benefit of copy editing. Technological advances are expected to bring more change in the years ahead. Journalists who will thrive during periods of reorganization and transition will be those who are flexible as well as talented.

checkpoint

How has the Internet changed journalism?

Digging Deeper

Social Media: A Catalyst for Change?

Social media has received both praise and criticism as a tool for citizen journalists to convey information and tell stories. According to a story on the Canadian Broadcasting Corporation, social media has been hailed as a "tool of democracy" in the Arab world. However, in Britain it has been blamed for promoting anti-government sentiments, and in some cases, violence. To listen to and/or read this story access http://www.cengage.com/school/langarts/journalism and click on the link to Chapter 2. Then answer the questions and complete the activity below.

THINK *Critically*

1. Do you think social media is a good tool for citizen journalists? Explain your answer.

2. Search the Internet to learn more about social media and how citizen journalists use it to promote political awareness and change. Using the information from the article provided at the link above and your research, write an essay that takes a position for or against social media as a catalyst for change.

Source: "U.K. riots reveal social media double standard." The Canadian Broadcasting Corporation (CBC). Aug. 10, 2011.

2.3 | Assessment

Understand Concepts

Determine the best answer for each of the following questions.

1. Which is the name for newsrooms that have multiple platforms for delivering the news?
   a. desks
   b. information centers
   c. online journalism
   d. posts

2. Which is the term for an online news editor or reporter?
   a. citizen journalist
   b. blogger
   c. online journalist
   d. content producer

3. **True or False** Journalists are likely to write the same story in different forms for both a print publication and its website.

4. **True or False** High school students can be citizen journalists.

Write Now!

Practice your writing skills with the following activities.

5. Research the convergence process for your local newspaper or another newspaper in your state. Write a composition on your findings. Cite your sources. Before you begin writing the composition, research the subject, and then plan and draft the paper. Finally, edit your composition for clarity, engaging language, and the correct use of English.

6. Be a citizen journalist and write a breaking news story for the local newspaper or broadcast news program about an event at your school or in your community. Next, write two human interest stories that are related. Be sure to edit your stories for clarity and correct punctuation. Before beginning, study the newspaper or broadcast news program and gear your stories to its audience.

7. Take a survey of 50 people in different age groups to ask how they receive the news every day. Use spreadsheet software to record the information you receive. Include classmates and other high school students, middle school students and adults in a variety of walks of life. For example, you might ask your parents and neighbors or salespeople or customers in a retail store or supermarket. You also may use a social networking site, but make sure the responders represent different age groups. Once you have recorded your answers, write a paper that describes your findings and explain whether you were surprised by the findings and why.

CHAPTER 2 | Assessment

Review Journalism Concepts

2.1 Who Is a Journalist?

Modern journalists are storytellers who use all the technology available to them. Journalists include reporters and correspondents, editors, photographers and videographers, copy editors, designers and artists. They sift through the many events of a day to tell you what is important or interesting in your community and the world. Journalists work directly for a news organization or they freelance, which means they do not work for a particular news outlet but may cover stories for any outlet that wants to hire them.

Reporters are the journalists who gather facts and write stories. Editors assign stories to reporters and photographers and are responsible for the content.

2.2 Multimedia Journalists

Multimedia means that a Web story is some combination of the written word, photographs, video clips, audio clips, graphics and some interactive element, such as a quiz or poll. Multimedia journalists are news and information gatherers who work with all these elements. Print journalists work in printed newspapers. Videographers tell stories with moving images. Photographers use digital cameras to capture still photos electronically.

Most multimedia stories include all the elements of multimedia, including text, photographs, video and audio. Some journalists collaborate with others as part of a team, while others work alone in multimedia storytelling. Journalists who work alone are called backpack journalists because they carry in a backpack all the technical tools necessary to produce a multimedia story. Editors who work on websites may be called producers.

2.3 What Convergence Means

Convergence, the merging of news operations, is happening at a time when the products a news organization produces need to be different from what has been offered traditionally. Today's consumers can obtain news from print newspapers, broadcast news programs and the Internet. The newsroom has been replaced by an information center where reporters and editors who are assigned to desks — areas of designated specialties — turn out stories for the news organization's print newspaper and also for the website. Editors and reporters for websites may be called content producers. The Internet allows for stories and photos from citizen journalists, or journalism in which the audience participates. This open-source, or crowd-source, reporting is used by many news organizations.

Online journalism is conducted on the Internet. Web-based reporting is more immediate and allows reporters to get the story out as they gather facts.

Develop Your Journalism Language

Write the letter of the term that matches each definition. Some terms will not be used.

_____ 1. A blogger's update

_____ 2. The merging of a news organization's print, Internet and broadcast operations

_____ 3. A modern name for the converged newsroom

_____ 4. Journalism conducted on the Internet

_____ 5. A combination of the written word, photographs, video clips, audio clips, graphics and an interactive element

_____ 6. A journalist who writes text for a newspaper

_____ 7. A journalist who captures stories in video

_____ 8. Camera used by news videographers that captures images electronically

_____ 9. A journalist who works alone and carries all the tools needed to produce multiple elements for news stories

_____ 10. An editor who is part of a website staff

_____ 11. The business of newsgathering and reporting

_____ 12. A journalist on the scene gathering information and writing the story

_____ 13. A journalist responsible for all the content in a print newspaper

_____ 14. Journalism in which the audience is asked to help report stories

_____ 15. Areas of designated specialties where reporters and editors work

a. artist
b. backpack journalist
c. citizen journalism
d. content producers
e. convergence
f. copy editor
g. correspondent
h. designer
i. desks
j. digital video camera
k. editor
l. freelance journalist
m. information center
n. journalism
o. journalists
p. multimedia
q. multimedia journalist
r. online journalism
s. open-source or crowd-source reporting
t. photographer
u. post
v. print journalist
w. producer
x. videographer

16. Which journalist is responsible for the final content that appears on a news organization's website?
    a. copy editor   c. reporter
    b. producer   d. artist

17. Which refers to journalists who do not work for a particular news outlet and who may cover stories for any news outlet that wants to hire them?
    a. citizen journalists   c. copy editors
    b. freelancers   d. correspondents

18. News and information gatherers who are comfortable working in multimedia are called
    a. videographers.   c. print correspondents.
    b. freelancers.   d. multimedia journalists.

Think Critically

19. What do you think will be the future for many small news organizations that do not have the resources to converge?

20. Are news organizations in small communities as affected by convergence as news organizations in major cities or national news organizations? Explain your answer.

21. Why might it be difficult for reporters to have both an editor and a producer?

22. How is technology forcing news organizations to rethink how they deliver the news?

23. Should one business own all the news sources in your community? In the country? Why or why not? How might this affect news coverage?

24. How does reading or listening to more than one news source help you understand world events?

25. Is multimedia used to deliver the news in your high school? Which platforms are available? How do those platforms and elements work together?

Make Academic Connections

26. **SOCIAL STUDIES**   Reporters and news organizations must balance reporting the news from the world's hot spots with the personal safety of the reporters. Use the Internet to research information on foreign reporters in war zones or other volatile situations around the world, and then write a paper that answers these questions: Do you think reporters should or should not be embedded in war zones and in other areas that could put them in danger? What is the reporter's responsibility? For example, should a reporter intentionally enter a city that is involved in a civil war? What is the responsibility of a news organization for keeping its reporters safe? For example, should it keep reporters a distance from the city where there is civil unrest? How important is getting the story from the place of unrest? In your paper, cite at least three cases in which reporters have been physically harmed or killed while reporting from a hot spot. Distinguish between responsible and irresponsible action on the part of the journalist and the news organization in each case. Once you have completed your research, plan your paper, and then write a draft before writing the final paper. When you have completed the paper, carefully examine it for clarity, engaging language and the correct use of the conventions and mechanics of written English.

27. **CAREERS**   Research the careers of lawyers who specialize in media law. Create a fact sheet that includes information about what lawyers do who specialize in the converging news organizations.

28. **SOCIOLOGY**   Record the lead story of a broadcast news program for a local news channel. Look for the same story in the local newspaper. Look at the websites for both the broadcast news organization and the newspaper. Use a computer and word-processing program to write the news story for your high school newspaper. Rewrite the story, using the same information

and selecting the most appropriate format for a high school news website. Then write a summary that compares and contrasts the different versions of the story.

29. **TECHNOLOGY** List and describe three major pieces of equipment you will use as a reporter for your high school yearbook.

30. **COMPUTER TECHNOLOGY** Use a computer to create the main screen of a website that shows the main story and related elements of the story about a person or an event in your school. Include elements such as text, audio, video, photographs, graphics and illustrations. Decide whether you want the reader to interact with the website. Do you want open-source reporting? What are the related stories that complement the main story? Create and design the Web screen with a high school audience in mind.

31. **READING** Read an online newspaper, and then analyze the significance of online journalism in contemporary society. For example, are more people reading news on smartphones or laptops while they use public transporation to commute to work? If so, is this keeping people from talking to one another? Are people more aware of the state of the world because of the availability of news 24/7? Is more awareness of the state of the world helpful, or is it too much to take in?

32. **BUSINESS** Interview two businesspeople in your community about how they think business today influences journalism.

Writing Portfolio Activity

33. Create a list of websites that you regularly use for research and news information. Add the list to your portfolio. Use the following criteria to determine whether the news organization and its writers are credible. Beside each entry, make notes that help you distinguish between responsible and irresponsible media action and news reporting.
   - Is the website maintained by a reputable news organization?
   - Do the writers or organization show bias, or are they objective in their reporting?
   - Is the information current or out of date?
   - How can you determine whether this website is a responsible site for research?

AP Stylebook Workshop

Abbreviate, or do not abbreviate, and punctuate the following according to AP style.

34. | | | |
|---|---|---|
| Canton Ohio | Tacoma Washington | Buffalo New York |
| Springfield Missouri | Iowa City Iowa | Memphis Tennessee |
| Fresno California | Montgomery Alabama | Trenton New Jersey |
| Tampa Florida | Portland Maine | Fort Worth Texas |

TIME MANAGEMENT: Time Management for Journalists

Successful journalists know how to manage their time. As you learn and begin to use time-management skills, you will be able to

- Successfully manage your time
- Value other people's time
- Balance your work and personal life

SUCCESSFULLY MANAGE YOUR TIME

You need a way to plan how to use your time to accomplish all you want to get done in your life. A calendar will help you to do this. You can use a book or wall calendar where you add entries, or a calendar application on your computer or phone. At the beginning of each month, spend time with your calendar to record the things you must accomplish. For example:

A sports reporter would fill the monthly calendar with upcoming games, making sure each game is recorded on the correct date. Next the reporter would list other events taking place or assignments due.

Each week take time to look over your calendar. You will add events each week, such as an unexpected game, or subtract events, such as a canceled game. Spend a few minutes at the end of each day to ensure you will be ready for tomorrow. Do you have the phone numbers you need to call people for interviews? Do you know the websites you want to use for research? Also, look over your daily calendar in the morning to see what you have planned for the day and to see what changes you may want to make for the remainder of the week.

Your calendar should reflect the time you have committed to yourself and others.

It should include school assignments, club meetings, appointments, time with your family and friends, and other activities. You can use your calendar to plan the steps in an assignment such as time for research, interviewing and writing. Be sure to add time for editing and proofreading, too.

VALUE OTHER PEOPLE'S TIME

Part of time management is learning to value other people's time. You need to be on time for interviews, meetings, activities you're reporting on and deadlines. Making others wait for you is disrespectful and may cost you an interview. Deadlines in journalism are extremely important. News organizations rely on tight deadlines to get the stories into print or onto the Web before competing news organizations do. In journalism, missing deadlines on a routine basis will hurt your career.

BALANCE WORK AND PERSONAL LIFE

Successful journalists are able to balance their work and personal lives. In addition to listing classes, school assignments and other school or work-related events on your calendar, you also want to list recreational activities. For example, you might list time for exercise, time with your family, and time for fun and relaxation. Successful time managers know when to say "no" to friends and upcoming events.

THINK *Critically*
What can you do right now to improve the way you manage your time?

REAL PEOPLE REAL CAREERS

Laura Elizabeth Pohl did not begin her career as a digital storyteller, but that is who and what she has become. As Multimedia Manager at Bread for the World, a non-profit organization with a mission to end hunger, she has produced digital stories from Haiti, Liberia, Mexico and North Carolina on issues related to hunger, poverty and immigration. "I am lucky enough to have my dream job," she says. "I'm learning more every day and I hope to continue growing as a digital storyteller."

© Photo courtesy of Laura Pohl

There is little doubt that she will. Pohl has a fine education but she also teaches herself and takes advantage of opportunity. She was working as a business reporter in Seoul, Korea, when she bought her first camera and began sending photos home to the United States where her relatives and friends were delighted to receive them. "I realized my pictures were educating my friends and family about places a lot of them had never seen. I liked that feeling," Pohl says, "but I wasn't focused."

That changed in June 2002, when South Korea co-hosted the World Cup. "My neighborhood went nuts nearly every night with people celebrating the national team's victories over soccer powerhouses like Italy and Spain. Thousands of people swarmed the eight-lane boulevard in front of my apartment building . . . I even saw one guy climb on top of a bus — yes, on top! — and jump to the ground as the crowd cheered. He broke his legs. You could see it. I knew it would happen. But he was still cheering like crazy. Every night I was out there photographing the revelry and trying really hard to capture moments. By the end of the World Cup I knew I wanted to get paid to take pictures."

Pohl describes digital storytelling as "telling stories with video, audio, photography, text, graphics and sometimes music to tell a compelling, human-interest story. Sometimes all these elements are in a story, sometimes just two or three. Digital storytelling blends what I love most about print reporting and photography: getting attention-grabbing quotes and storytelling images."

And what about writing and editing, the skills that got her started in a journalism career? Pohl says, "writing and editing — and reporting, too — are the foundation of being a digital storyteller. I'm constantly writing: storyboards, text intros, captions, scripts, even e-mails about storyboards, text intros, captions and scripts. I storyboard before I go out in the field and sometimes again when I'm preparing to edit a story. Probably most crucial of all is being a thorough reporter. You must have all your facts and they must be correct, otherwise you'll be in a bind when you start editing."

Source: Personal interview with Laura Elizabeth Pohl.

ADVICE FOR ASPIRING JOURNALISTS

Her best advice to those who would like to become digital storytellers is to be unafraid of making mistakes. "Find someone to give you honest critiques about your work. Compliments feel nice but you don't learn from them; you learn from your mistakes."

THINK *Critically*

1. How did sending her photographs to family and friends help Pohl find her career?
2. How important to digital storytelling is writing and editing?

3 | Reporting

An Environmental Disaster

When BP's Deepwater Horizon oil well exploded in the Gulf of Mexico on April 20, 2010, killing 11 men working on the platform and sending oil gushing into the sea for months, there was little doubt that it was a big breaking news story. The day it occurred and for weeks after, the oil spill was played on front pages of newspapers and websites, as well as at the top of newscasts around the world.

The BP spill, as it became known, had all the elements of an important news story. The most compelling element was its impact — it was the worst environmental disaster the United States had ever faced, according to government officials — and the spill affected the U.S. coastline from Louisiana to Florida. Some of those whose livelihoods depended on the fishing and tourism industries that thrive along the coast lost jobs. Thousands of birds and hundreds of dolphins were found dead. Photographs of oil-covered pelicans brought home the impact of the catastrophe on wildlife.

After the explosion, a six-month moratorium on offshore drilling was enacted, but there was no doubt that the BP spill would affect offshore oil drilling policy in the United States for the foreseeable future.

THINK *Critically*
1. What made the BP spill front-page news?
2. Look at the front page of your local newspaper or news website today. What criteria do you think the editors used to decide whether it should be front-page news?

Report the News

Goals

- Identify the important elements of a news story and the difference between hard and soft news stories.
- Understand the difference between breaking news and enterprise stories.

Key Terms

- hard news 56
- soft news 56
- social media platform 57
- enterprise news 57
- breaking news 57

FOCUS

Listen to a local radio station as you get ready for school in the morning and you may notice that it touts the traffic and weather reports every 10 minutes. Why? Because traffic and weather have immediate impact on the listener. If you know there is a tie-up on a highway you take to school, you may choose another route. If you are aware that the morning's sunshine is expected to become rain by afternoon, you may take a coat and an umbrella with you. Journalists sometimes disagree on what is news or how they would play certain stories, but they generally agree that news stories have a number of important elements in common.

Elements and Types of News Stories

When thinking about what makes a good news story, journalists keep in mind the four functions of mass communication: to inform, to transmit culture, to persuade and to entertain. Reporters and editors make decisions about the news value of a story by determining the elements of the story. They also consider whether a story is a hard news story or a soft news story.

ELEMENTS OF A NEWS STORY

News is information that has **impact**. That could be anything from the outcome of your school's baseball game with a rival team to a power outage that affects whether your television and computer will work. News often is the unexpected. It has the element of **surprise** — a fire, for example, or a crime. Of course, expected events — a congressional vote on new taxes or the jury's decision in an important trial — are news, too.

Expected or not, news may involve **conflict**, and not just on a sporting field. Politicians have conflicting points of view every day. News stories are happening and have **relevance** at the time you are reporting them. Often, news involves someone who has **prominence**. That could be a national celebrity or a local one, your city's mayor, perhaps. In fact, **proximity** is another

Does this photo depict a hard news or soft news story in the making?

element of a news story. Generally, the more local a story, the more newsworthy it is.

Reporters and editors make decisions about news value by determining the elements of the story and whether it is a hard news or a soft news story.

HARD NEWS

A story is **hard news** if it is about a serious or important topic and has a sense of immediacy. Speeches, news conferences, actions taken by governing bodies, crimes, fires, and major weather stories such as hurricanes and blizzards are examples of hard news.

The president's annual State of the Union address is an example of a hard news story. Journalists know that the speech will occur and often have an idea of what the president will say, but they must hear it and report it on deadline to news consumers who want details quickly. Timeliness is an important element of hard news, so reporters might file their first reports to their organization's website, news blog or Twitter feed before they write a story for broadcast or print publication.

SOFT NEWS

Feature and human interest stories are **soft news**. Articles that are informational, educational, emotional or entertaining are also soft news. Heartwarming tales about ordinary people who overcome obstacles, do extraordinary deeds or accomplish something noteworthy are examples of soft news stories.

Journalists working on soft news stories often are not under a strict daily deadline. For example, a reporter for your high school paper might be assigned to do a story on arrangements for the senior prom. The reporter may conduct multiple interviews, spend time with various subjects working on the prom, and write the story in a more colorful way than a hard news story would be written. The soft news story may get a prominent place in a newspaper, but not as prominent as it would if it were a hard news story.

checkpoint ✓

What are the six elements of a news story?

Breaking and Enterprise News

The new world of multiplatform, multimedia journalism offers more options than ever before for bringing breaking news stories to information consumers. Journalists are getting more creative in how they report and tell their stories. Print journalists had all but given up the idea of breaking news, long ago surrendering that territory to radio and television media, which could have cameras and microphones at the scene and broadcast live. Now, however, print reporters see websites as a way to get their news reporting out immediately. They also use **social media platforms** to get their stories out. These are online tools that people use to connect with one another using websites such as Facebook and Twitter. Journalists recognize that they have the ability to make regular updates as they get more details. For non-breaking news, or **enterprise news**, journalists have even more options to offer, among them databases that can be searched to provide personalized information and interactive graphics that engage readers with their stories.

BREAKING NEWS

News that is happening now and that journalists must cover live and on deadline is **breaking news**. Journalists covering breaking news usually go to the scene and report what is going on as quickly as possible. They want to witness firsthand what the scene looks like so they can describe it to their readers, or collect video for Web and broadcast reports. Reporters also like to talk in person with people who are part of the story. Hundreds of reporters set out to witness the devastation of New Orleans after it was hit in 2005 by Hurricane Katrina. Many reporters had a difficult time getting into the city, however, because roads were impassable and the airport was closed. Journalists who did get into New Orleans despite the hurricane's raging winds found plenty of breaking news stories. Within hours of the storm, journalists were broadcasting on the air and writing on websites about the widespread flooding after a levee broke, the lack of help for the stranded and homeless, and the lawlessness and chaos that ensued without enough police to patrol the streets.

Breaking news such as devastating hurricanes or the earthquake that struck Haiti in 2010 usually requires constant reporting in the field and constant updating of the audience. Many journalists reporting on the New Orleans and Haiti disasters expected to stay only days to cover the breaking story. However, it soon became clear in both cases that the need for updated information would continue for months. Many of the journalists who had headed to the scene immediately remained on site long after the breaking news, talking to people who had lost businesses, homes, neighbors, friends and loved ones. Reporters looked for local officials and international or national authorities who could explain what the governments and volunteers were doing to help or rebuild, and what was happening with the money being sent to aid those who were suffering. They found no shortage of stories to tell.

ENTERPRISE REPORTING

In journalism, the term "enterprise" covers a lot of territory. An investigative reporter's exposing wrongdoing that results in government action to fix a problem is an enterprise effort. An in-depth report on crime in your city that uses computer databases full of statistics to pinpoint safe and unsafe areas also is an enterprise effort. Some journalists define enterprise as a story you find instead of a story that finds you. Some say it is a story that answers a question or defines or solves a problem. Often enterprise ideas take months to report, and when finished they become a series. The Washington Post developed a series on the mountains of red tape and deplorable conditions wounded Iraq War veterans encountered at Walter Reed Army Medical Center. The Post's stories resulted in the firings of top military personnel and hearings in the U.S. Congress.

*check*point ✓

What is the difference between a breaking news story and an enterprise story?

AP Stylebook Concepts

In scholarly writing, you usually spell out numbers from one to one hundred, round numbers, and numbers that begin a sentence. There are exceptions to this rule, which can become complicated. AP style is easier to follow.

1. Generally, spell out numbers one to nine; for 10 and larger, use the numeral.

Wrong	Each reporter wrote 3 stories.
Right	Each reporter wrote three stories.
Wrong	Each reporter wrote thirty-three stories.
Right	Each reporter wrote 33 stories.

2. Spell out all numbers at the beginning of a sentence, or rewrite the sentence to avoid starting with a number. The exception is a number that identifies a calendar year, for which numerals are always used.

Wrong	32 reporters were in the newsroom when we left.
Right	Thirty-two reporters were in the newsroom when we left.
Right	When we left, 32 reporters were in the newsroom.
Wrong	Nineteen ninety-six was the year the school published the first newspaper.
Right	1996 was the year the school published the first newspaper.

What We Don't Use

Reporters always are on the lookout for facts and details that make their stories come alive. However, that doesn't mean they will or should use every fact they record in their notebooks, or every bit of video or audio they have captured for a story.

Most news organizations are careful to observe common standards of decency when it comes to reporting on crime and crime victims. For example, many news organizations do not print the names of juveniles accused of crimes unless the accused are tried as adults. And authorities — police and the district attorney's office — often don't release the names of juveniles until they are charged with a crime.

Many news organizations continue to make it their practice not to name victims of rape, despite a legal right to do so. They believe that publishing victims' names discourages women from reporting the crime. In recent years, with the occurrence of cases where high-profile men accused of the crime were named in news reports but the women who accused them were not, some news organizations have been rethinking that practice.

The National Center for Victims of Crime developed voluntary guidelines for the media. One guideline advises that the media notify and ask permission from victims and their families before using photographs. The center also suggests that the media refrain from publishing unverified or ambiguous facts about the victim.

Journalists generally are careful to avoid sensationalism, or exaggerating stories just to hook their readers. They avoid using material their audience might find obscene or in poor taste, particularly photographs and video. Deciding the standards of good taste, however, may be tricky. Editors should ask themselves first if the story is newsworthy, and then how their readers will react to the story, to the language in the story and to other elements that help tell the story — photographs, video or audio.

THINK *Critically*

1. Do you think journalists should name juveniles accused of a crime? Why or why not?

2. How would you determine whether a story meets common standards of decency?

3.1 | Assessment

Understand Concepts

Determine the best answer for each of the following questions.

1. A story about a(n) _____?_____ would be considered a hard news story.
   a. upcoming art show
   b. earthquake
   c. rock star's new album
   d. new business

2. A story about a(n) _____?_____ would be considered a soft story.
   a. governing body passing a law
   b. ordinary person winning a prize
   c. fire
   d. crime

3. **True or False**   Hard news stories are often breaking news stories.

4. **True or False**   An example of an enterprise story is the president's annual State of the Union address.

Write Now!

Practice your writing skills with the following activities.

5. You are a reporter for a major daily newspaper. You want to persuade your editor to allow you to write an enterprise story. Write an outline for the story.

6. Find a breaking news story on a news website from a foreign country. If English is your second language, choose a news website in your native language. If you speak, or are studying, another language, choose a news website in that language. Rewrite the story for an audience of your peers for a high school newspaper, website, and radio or television station. Use appropriate journalistic style and the proper format for each medium.

7. Think about how your school should punish cheaters. Consider both those who plagiarize when writing papers and those who cheat on tests. Research, plan and write an enterprise story that describes the acts of cheating, how widespread cheating is in your school, the punishment that should be handed out and how cheating hurts the students who cheat and the entire student body. Also, indicate whether the students' names should be published. Carefully examine your enterprise news story for clarity, engaging language, and the correct use of English.

Generate Story Ideas

Goals

- Define beat and general assignment reporting.
- Describe how to generate ideas from beats.
- Explain how to generate ideas from personal experience and trend spotting.

Key Terms

- beats 62
- general assignment reporters 63
- pitching 63
- profile 64
- trend spotting 65
- tipping point 66

FOCUS

It's 6:30 p.m. on a Thursday and a high school sports reporter is working her beat by hanging around the gym. She's watching the varsity basketball team practice for Friday's important game. It determines whether the team goes to the state championships. As practice ends and the exhausted players head to the locker room, the reporter notices that one player hangs back. He picks up a ball and continues practice on his own, shooting free throws. Unaware a reporter is watching, the player sinks shot after shot after shot.

The reporter is impressed and curious. She uses her laptop computer to look up the player's stats in previous game stories and, sure enough, she quickly finds that when this player is in a game, he never misses a free throw. Because he's not a "star," the unblemished free-throw record has gone unnoticed. No more. The reporter sees a story in the unsung free-throw master. So, while others write about the coach's plan and the team's chances for victory on Friday, this reporter tells a different story — a soft news story about a player who with disciplined practice keeps his special talent sharp.

Beat and General Assignment Reporting

If journalists counted only on breaking stories to fill empty news columns and news broadcasts, there would be a lot of blank space in print news and dead air on radio and television news shows. Unfortunately, reporters and editors cannot count on breaking news every day. Fortunately, news organizations are full of curious, questioning people who have many ideas for stories. Editors and reporters work together to "find" news. They come up with stories from reporters' beats, the agendas of governing bodies and their own life experiences. Journalists are inspired by what they read and the people with whom they meet and talk. Reporters hear from readers and listeners, who often have good ideas. They also hear from sources who have insight on local or pertinent issues, such as information on city governments. Editors assign stories to either beat reporters or general assignment reporters.

BEAT REPORTING

Most newsgathering operations continue to organize staff with a system of beats. **Beats** are topics or areas of coverage such as sports or politics, but they are even further defined and specific. For example, a national news organization such as the Associated Press or NBC News has several political reporters. Some of those reporters may have the White House as their beat. The job of these reporters is to know everything about the president and the agenda the president pursues. At a local paper there is likely to be a reporter whose beat is to cover the mayor and city council or the school board that makes decisions affecting your school.

Beat reporters make it their business to get to know the people they write about and the issues that will be meaningful to readers. The idea is to have a professional and cordial relationship so the people on the beat will give reporters tips, information and insight. If you are covering the city council, for example, it would be best to know the council members, their staff (if any) and the heads of the city departments and programs the council oversees. At your school, student government might be a beat. To cover it well, you will need to know the officers, representatives from each class, what major events the organization oversees and where it spends the money it is allocated.

Movies, music, books, the arts and more are the beats of feature or entertainment sections. Sports is a broad topic area that includes many beats. Most large-city news organizations have several writers for baseball, several for football, and more. If your school has sports, your newspaper staff may decide that having beat reporters for each team makes sense.

Beat reporters often are journalists who like building expertise in their field and developing good long-term relationships with sources. Some like beat reporting because they are good at the organization, discipline and dedication required to keep up on everything that's happening on the beat, plus they like digging up stories on the beat that are not being told. Beat reporters usually come up with their own stories to work on rather than wait for an editor to assign stories. One of the best ways to find good human interest stories on a beat is to talk to the people who are touched by the policies or decisions made by the leaders on your beat. If you're covering city hall, you want to talk to city residents about whether they are getting city services. If you cover education, you want to get into classrooms.

The best beat reporters always have a list of stories they want to write, and they never have enough time to do all the stories on their list. The problem with a beat, many beat reporters say, is that there is always a daily story to do and little time to develop the news features, or enterprise stories, they would like to write. Nevertheless, they make time to write non-deadline enterprise stories as well as the daily ones because it keeps their job challenging and their audience informed.

GENERAL ASSIGNMENT REPORTING

Most news organizations have a number of **general assignment reporters**. Because these reporters do not have regular beats to cover, editors assign general news and feature stories to them. For the most part, these stories do not fall into another reporter's beat. Weather stories, such as hurricanes and blizzards, are often assigned to general assignment reporters who interview people affected by the weather as well as those who predict it. Sometimes, however, general

What kind of journalist might enjoy general assignment reporting?

assignment reporters help beat reporters with large, breaking news stories in order to complete the stories in a timely manner. A major air show that affects news, sports and traffic could be considered part of the news beat, but covering all the angles to write print and website stories will take more than one reporter.

General assignment reporters usually are journalists who like the freedom to jump from one story to another. They may cover an air show one day and a Fourth of July parade the next. When they go to work in the morning, they aren't sure what story will be theirs to tell, but that is what excites them about their profession. General assignment reporters thrive on tight deadlines, enjoy the challenge of learning about new issues and like meeting new people.

check *point* ✓

Describe the difference between a beat and general assignment reporter.

Beat Ideas

Many news organizations have daily and weekly meetings to generate potential stories for print, online and broadcast media. Reporters and editors arrive for these brainstorming meetings prepared to share with others their ideas and expertise, often called **pitching** a story. Whether the story is on a beat or not, the person pitching it will present some preliminary information. For example, a reporter suggesting a story on a new speed trap on a local highway would already have researched how many cars have been ticketed since it appeared. Questions and comments from colleagues may help define the story further. The whole purpose of these brainstorming sessions is to make everyone's ideas work well. No idea is too wacky, no one's opinion unwanted.

MAKE CONTACT

Beat reporters usually start their days with visits or phone calls to the people who can give them the information they need to know. Regular contact helps them get to know people and build trust.

Imagine you are a police reporter for your city's newspaper, a beat never at a loss for good stories. You start your day with a visit to police headquarters, where you can look over routine police reports drafted daily by the officers who work the cases. You won't write about every report. You look for anything unusual. In the pile of reports that have stacked up overnight, you find something interesting: A city council member was involved in a single-car accident at 2 a.m. This is the second accident in two weeks involving the same council member. In neither case did police give the council member a Breathalyzer test to determine whether alcohol was a factor in the accident. Usually a Breathalyzer test is a routine step in investigating such accidents. Back at the office you monitor other media to see if other journalists are reporting the accident. You discuss with your editor whether to do a straightforward news report about the accident or do further reporting to ask questions about the Breathalyzer and the council member's long-term driving record. Your visit to the police station has now provided two possible stories.

As you begin more reporting on the council member's driving violations, one of your police sources tells you that police give government officials special treatment when they are stopped for driving violations such as speeding. You and your editor decide to widen the scope of your reporting, looking at how police treat government officials who break driving laws. It won't be an easy story to report, but you have good contacts in the police department because you are there every day and treat your sources with respect.

PROFILE PEOPLE

Beat reporters meet all kinds of interesting people, some of whom become good subjects for stories called **profiles**. The obvious people to profile are those who are leaders or authorities, but journalists like to look for those who work behind the scenes and are offbeat or colorful. Business reporters may find entrepreneurs who have built a livelihood out of a passion. Political reporters look for the assistants and aides who do the work for politicians or shape their images. Speechwriters and campaign chiefs are helpful to political reporters. Education reporters who can get away from boards of education will find lots of stories in the teachers and students those boards oversee.

People profiles can be found on every beat and can serve two purposes. First, they inform the reader about someone in the news and reveal a person's character, not just a resume. In addition, profiles may help a beat reporter develop a rapport with the source, who can supply information, ideas and insight for future stories.

How does a beat reporter generate story ideas?

Ideas From Experience and Trend Spotting

Good journalists are curious and observant by nature and see stories all around them. They draw many stories from their experiences as well as from noticing social trends, or **trend spotting**. Reporters often share their story ideas in brainstorming sessions with colleagues who work in all media. Many news organizations hold such sessions daily and weekly. Whether they are reporters, videographers, editors or producers, all come prepared to share with others their experience and expertise and develop ideas into good stories. Whether the story is on a beat or not, the person pitching it will present some preliminary information. For example, a reporter suggesting a story about the increasing number of student absences due to the flu will have researched how many cases of the flu have recently been reported by the local health department and compared those numbers to the previous year.

STORIES FROM EXPERIENCE

Reporters often get story ideas from things they experience in their own lives. For example, you may live in an urban area where squirrels and raccoons are your usual wildlife. However, within a month you spot four deer in various city locations, including on a main thoroughfare. You do some preliminary research and find out that the number of deer sightings reported to your city animal control department has increased by 50 percent from the previous year. When you bring this up in a brainstorming meeting, some of your city-dwelling colleagues say they too have spotted deer in unusual city locations, including on a sidewalk in a busy neighborhood. Discussion centers on how to determine if the deer population has actually increased. You are assigned to develop a story on the urban deer population by talking with state and local animal-control specialists, state park specialists who track deer, and city residents who say the creatures are eating up their gardens and causing traffic accidents. You will want official numbers from those who track the population, but anecdotal evidence suggests that not only are there more deer, but the deer are not deterred by traffic and human contact.

Reporters often get stories from things they experience in their lives, such as noticing deer in urban settings. Think of three story ideas for your school newspaper based on your current life experiences.

More serious social problems that we all experience often make important stories. If you share in a brainstorming session that you've noticed more homeless men on the street, you may find that others have noticed the same thing. Another colleague may know that a local men's shelter has closed. There may be a story in what will happen to those men if another shelter doesn't open. Many good stories and collaborations come from ideas and experiences shared with colleagues.

STORIES FROM TREND SPOTTING

Because they are keen observers of social and popular culture and usually have access to information before the general public, journalists often spot trends before other people do. They like to write about what they see just before it hits the **tipping point** — the point at which something unique becomes mainstream. Did you ever feel like a certain phrase you'd heard a couple of times suddenly had become common usage? Or a gadget you'd recently heard about was suddenly in everyone's hands? The phrase or gadget probably has hit the tipping point.

Arts and entertainment writers often spot trends in the popular movies and television shows being produced. For example, the immediate success of the CBS series "Survivor" started a reality show craze that has lasted more than a decade, which television reporters could spot before the general public. Why? TV beat writers talk with people who make series for all the networks as well as the network executives who buy their series. Observant TV reporters could gauge the number of such shows being made and talk to executives about how many they would buy.

Fashion reporters look for trends among designers that they can interpret for consumers each season. They talk to the designers long before the designers ever show their collections at a fashion show so the writers have a good idea of what common elements will be shown. Keenly observant reporters have noted trends in everything from food — one year it was pomegranates — to favored dogs — one year it was the Labradoodle.

*check**point***

How do reporters develop ideas from trend spotting?

Elements of a News Story

By Victor Xu, Carmel High School, Carmel, Ind., "Spring (Oil) Cleaning"

Although her family traveled to Florida relatively frequently in past years, senior Andrea Czarnick said the oil spill is a major factor in her family choosing not to travel to the Gulf Coast states this spring break. Instead, she and her family will visit Hawaii for the upcoming spring break.

"Last year we were happy we went down to the Gulf shores in Florida, and my dad was happy that we were able to fit it in," Czarnick said. "They took us down to the ocean right before the spill happened. We might have gone this year, but we're going somewhere else for spring break, somewhere warmer and cleaner."

Jonathon Day, professor at the Purdue Tourism and Hospitality Research Center, said tourism to the Gulf Coast states will most likely be adversely affected by the oil spill. The tourism industry there commands a large proportion of the economy. A report by Oxford Economics estimated that tourism in 2010 along the Gulf was worth $34 billion per year and employed more than 400,000 people.

The explosion of the Deepwater Horizon oil rig in the Gulf of Mexico last April 20 tore open a well that released up to 185 million gallons of crude oil, making it the largest unintentional oil spill in history, according to a New York Times article published in February. Although the oil well was sealed on July 15, and the majority of the surface oil has dissipated, the long-term effects are still in question.

"At this time we can be optimistic," Day said. "Many destinations have spent the last few months with webcams and other promotion to show they're in good shape. Locals and frequent visitors who have been to beaches also tell that story to potential visitors, and so the 'word of mouth' about the quality of the beaches has been very positive."

Although reports and projected statistics about the turnout in the Gulf Coast states have emerged, Day said he believes travelers' thoughts will ultimately determine the effect of the oil spill on spring break tourism.

"The key issues will be whether people perceive that the beach destinations of the Gulf are clean and ready to welcome visitors," Day said. "We'll know for sure in a couple of weeks."

THINK *Critically*

1. Analyze this article in terms of the elements of a news story, discussed in Lesson 3.1 of this chapter.

2. Is this article reporting hard news or soft news? Explain your answer.

Source: Used by permission of Victor Xu.

3.2 | Assessment

Understand Concepts

Determine the best answer for each of the following questions.

1. Many reporters say the biggest problem with a beat is that
   a. breaking news takes the top headlines.
   b. writing about the same beat gets boring.
   c. their contacts are seldom around.
   d. there is little time to develop enterprise stories.

2. Which could be the subject of a profile?
   a. the causes of earthquakes
   b. a local electronics store that's having a big sale
   c. a local woman who became a presidential speechwriter
   d. the Internet

3. Which is an example of a television trend?
   a. the evening news
   b. Saturday morning cartoons
   c. reality shows
   d. car commercials

4. **True or False**   Social problems often make important stories.

5. **True or False**   If you notice that a phrase you have heard a few times is beginning to be used a lot, you know the phrase has reached its tipping point.

Write Now!

Practice your writing skills with the following activities.

6. You are a beat reporter in an subject area that interests you. Generate ideas for a news story and two related stories. List the sources you would contact to write the stories, and then contact your sources. Research, plan, draft and write the three stories for the local newspaper, for a news website and for a local broadcast news program. Be sure to edit your stories for clarity, engaging language, and the correct use of the conventions and mechanics of English. Stories should be in journalistic style and in the correct format for each medium. Send your stories electronically to your teacher.

7. Think of a person you would like to profile for your high school newspaper. This can be a famous person, someone from your community or someone in your school. Use a word-processing program on a computer to write a paper that describes why this person would be a good person to profile. What makes the person interesting? What has he or she accomplished? Be sure to edit your paper for clarity, engaging language and the correct use of English. Send your papers to your teacher electronically.

Get Started With Research

Goals

- Explain how to use the Internet to begin reporting.
- Recognize how foot and phone work contribute to research.

Key Terms

- pre-reporting 69
- jargon 70
- interview 71

FOCUS

Every morning across the country, news editors and reporters, photographers and Web producers, and entire news teams meet to plan their day's work. In the meeting, they brainstorm and discuss topics for possible stories to cover. Before pitching their story ideas, reporters spend some time and energy researching the topics. One reporter might pitch a story on how food prices are affecting the economy. To pitch this story, the reporter must have facts and figures and have some idea where the story is going. Reporters can find much of that information through research on the Internet.

The Internet

At some news organizations, the process of determining whether a story is newsworthy is called **pre-reporting**. Pre-reporting a story takes time and the same research skills needed to do the full reporting. Sometimes pre-reporting results in scrapping a story idea, but most often it does not. Either way, good research is the basis for a solid story, and good research skills are crucial to talented reporters.

Using the Internet for pre-reporting — or for staying on top of a beat — saves hours of time reporters used to spend on the phone and on foot. Most businesses, educational facilities, government offices, recreational organizations and more — from the national to the most local — have websites that supply basic information about their mission as well as the people who can be contacted for comment. There is no reason to call people for information you can find easily on an official website, unless there is information you don't understand.

Keep in mind, however, that official websites for some agencies and organizations highlight only what the organization thinks is important, not necessarily what reporters want to know. The U.S. Department of Education site, for example, lists the priorities of the secretary of education and defines what the secretary sees as "top stories" of the day. It is the secretary's way of saying

////// **Why is the Internet a valuable tool in pre-reporting?**

to journalists, "These are the stories you should cover." Good journalists will take those ideas into consideration but pursue their own story ideas always.

With access to the Internet, journalists, like their readers, can travel the world to get information on a range of topics. But for curious reporters, Internet information is a guide, one that suggests people and other places to go to for more in-depth information. Interesting stories need lively quotes and anecdotes that can come only from interviews. Reporters often ask their sources to avoid **jargon**, or language specific to their business, and explain information in "lay terms," language that can be understood by a non-expert reader.

If you were assigned a story on the rising cost of college in your metropolitan area, you could use the Internet to take the first steps. Among them:

1. Use your favorite search engine to look for information on your topic. For example, go to the websites for colleges and universities in your area and compare tuition costs from the last several years. You will want to find charts or graphs that tell you how much tuition has increased in real dollars and the percentage of increase. Look for numbers that go back at least five years.

2. Now search for national and local news stories on tuition increases. You want to see what your competition has reported and compare your findings to any national trends. Search for stories reported by reputable news organizations. Some of the stories you find probably will discuss reasons for increases. The stories also will contain the names of people who may be good sources for your own further reporting.

3. Return to your local colleges' websites for any explanation by the presidents or boards of trustees for the tuition increase in this or past years. Do their explanations mirror those of college presidents elsewhere?

4. Investigate student reaction to tuition increases by searching student organization sites, including college newspaper websites. Make note of student leaders — the student body president, perhaps — who could become sources for your own story.

With that research done, you are ready to move on.

checkpoint ✓

Why is the Internet a good preliminary resource for reporters?

Foot and Phone Work

In the fast-paced age of technology, journalists are not always encouraged to leave their offices to do some old-fashioned reporting. However, seeing people face to face or talking to them on the phone is important to making a story come alive. It also makes the job infinitely more interesting and gives reporters more multimedia possibilities. Researching a story for a journalist is like investigating a crime for a detective. The more people relevant to the case the detective talks to, the more likely she is to solve the case. In researching a story, you may not use all the information you collect from people, but the effort you make will give you confidence that your facts are correct and you are ready to pursue it.

Sometimes it takes effort to find a particular person, or subject. If you have done preliminary research on the Internet, you may already have the phone numbers and addresses you need to get started. If not, telephone directories may be of some help, or a city directory that provides addresses with names. If there is time to make an appointment by phone, you may be more politely received than if you arrive unexpectedly. However, if you are on deadline and cannot reach the subject by phone, you may have to go to the subject's office or home. If you can't find your subject's phone number or address in directories or on the Internet, you may have to work through the last known contact with a job, friends or family.

Why go to the effort of tracking people down? Because talking to real people — conducting **interviews** — always makes a story better. Writing about the expense of a college education becomes a more compelling story if the reporter talks to real students who are working two jobs and pinching pennies to make escalating tuition payments. Writing about urban deer becomes more poignant if the journalist can document their trail into the city and show that the deer's natural habitat is being destroyed. Getting out of the office to talk to students, park rangers, business owners or police officers on

////// **Why should a journalist go to the effort of conducting interviews?**

the street is as important as poring over a computer screen full of carefully chosen official words.

To get started with foot and phone work:

1. Identify broadly whom you want to talk to for your story. For your story on cost increases at local colleges you probably would list the following: students affected by the increase, college budget officials, college presidents or members of their boards of trustees.

2. Call the offices of the presidents and budget officials. Ask to speak to them immediately if you have a deadline. If you can wait, make an appointment to speak by phone.

3. Drive to one or more of the college campuses in your area to interview students. Find the student union or other gathering place where you can find a large number of students. Identify yourself as a reporter (show your ID if you have one) and explain the story. Ask for their opinion on the increase and how it specifically affects them. Will they cut back on social outings? Eat fewer meals out? Eliminate expenses such as gas for a car? When you interview people face to face you will get more personal information.

checkpoint ✓

Why is foot and phone work important to reporters?

3.3 | Assessment

Understand Concepts

Determine the best answer for each of the following questions.

1. Some news organizations call the process of determining whether a story is newsworthy
   a. editing.
   b. interviewing.
   c. pre-reporting.
   d. foot and phone work.

2. Which is an example of journalism jargon?
   a. Web 2.0
   b. goal and defensive line
   c. beats, desks and assignments
   d. mens rea and habeas corpus

3. The ultimate goal of foot and phone work is to
   a. gather information for pre-reporting.
   b. find the phone numbers of people to interview.
   c. find the addresses of people to interview.
   d. interview people close to a story.

4. **True or False**   Reporters should rely on the Internet for all their research.

5. **True or False**   Interviews help to make a story better.

Write Now!

Practice your writing skills with the following activities.

6. Choose a favorite reporter from a local or national newspaper. Clip out the reporter's stories over several days until you have collected at least six or seven stories by this reporter. Analyze the stories by marking the quotations from interviews in one color, the information learned from interviews in another color, information learned through research in a third color. Use a computer and word-processing program to write a paper that analyzes the reporter's work. Cite the articles you analyzed.

7. Choose a news story from your school or community. Use the Internet for background information. Identify two or three people you want to interview for the story. Make a short list of questions you want to ask these people who are connected with the story. Conduct the interviews, and then write a news story for (1) your high school newspaper; (2) your local newspaper or a national print newspaper; (3) a news magazine, such as Newsweek or Time.

Review Journalism Concepts

3.1 Report the News

All news contains certain elements, including impact, surprise, conflict, relevance, involvement of someone prominent, and a local tie or angle. News is divided into hard news and soft news. Hard news is about a serious or important topic and has a sense of immediacy. Soft news includes feature articles and human interest stories. These stories are informational, educational, emotional or entertaining.

Breaking news is news that is immediate. These stories are covered by journalists who get to the scene as quickly as possible. Print journalists had all but given up the idea of breaking news, ceding that territory to radio and television media that could have cameras and microphones at the scene and broadcast live. Now, however, print reporters see websites and social media platforms such as Facebook and Twitter as a way to get their news reporting out immediately. Non-breaking news is called enterprise news. These stories are investigative or include in-depth reporting.

3.2 Generate Story Ideas

Journalists generate story ideas through their beats, the agendas of governing bodies and their own life experiences. Editors assign stories to either beat reporters or general assignment reporters. Beats are topics or areas of coverage such as sports or politics. Beat reporters generate story ideas by regular contact by phone and in person with the people on their beat. They hear about stories from these sources. Some of these contacts may become profile subjects. They also find stories through written material such as police reports. Journalists meet daily or weekly to discuss story ideas. Reporters and editors arrive for these brainstorming meetings prepared to share with others their ideas and expertise. This is often called pitching a story. Curious by nature, journalists watch trends and like to report on them just before they hit the tipping point — the point at which something unique becomes mainstream.

3.3 Get Started With Research

Journalists use the Internet as a valuable research tool. The Internet is only the beginning, however, because good reporters also use foot and phone work when researching. Reporters use the Internet to help them find sources and background information. Interesting stories need lively quotations and anecdotes that can come only from interviews. When interviewing, or talking to people about a story, reporters often ask their sources to avoid jargon, or language specific to their businesses, and explain information in lay terms, language that can be understood by a non-expert reader

Develop Your Journalism Language

Write the letter of the term that matches each definition. Some terms will not be used.

_____ 1. News about serious or important topics that has a sense of immediacy

_____ 2. In-depth or investigative reporting that is non-breaking news

_____ 3. Online tools that people use to connect with one another

_____ 4. Topics or areas of coverage such as sports or politics

_____ 5. The point at which something unique becomes mainstream

_____ 6. News that is happening now and that journalists must cover live and on deadline

_____ 7. Language specific to a particular business

_____ 8. A story about an interesting person

_____ 9. Talking to real people to gain information about a story

_____ 10. Features and human interest stories

a. beats
b. breaking news
c. enterprise news
d. hard news
e. interviewing
f. jargon
g. pitching
h. pre-reporting
i. profile
j. social media platforms
k. soft news
l. tipping point
m. trend spotting

11. An example of a profile is a story about
    a. a dog that was rescued.
    b. the person who rescued the dog.
    c. the house where the dog lives.
    d. medals the dog won.

12. A profile is considered
    a. hard news.
    b. breaking news.
    c. Internet news.
    d. soft news.

13. Which refers to a reporter telling other reporters and editors about a possible story idea?
    a. pitching the story
    b. speaking in jargon
    c. reaching the tipping point
    d. conducting an interview

14. Which is an example of an interview?
    a. talking to someone in jargon
    b. asking someone questions for a story
    c. researching someone on the Internet
    d. reading about someone in the newspaper

15. An example of a breaking news story is a story about
    a. a horse show.
    b. an upcoming test.
    c. a fire.
    d. changes on the school board.

Think Critically

16. Before the Internet, why did broadcast journalists have an advantage over print journalists with breaking news?

17. Why is impact necessary in a news story?

18. If something happened a long time ago, is it news? Explain your answer.

19. Would a reporter ever write a profile about someone who is not prominent? If so, give an example.

20. Why is a local news tie important to a news story?

21. Why should you name the people you interview for a story and properly attribute quotations?

22. Why do reporters need to be flexible with their schedules when on breaking news assignments?

23. Why do journalists need to go to the scene of breaking news?

24. Can enterprise reporting lead to hard news stories? Give an example.

25. Should reporters use sensationalism to hook their readers for an enterprise story? Why or why not?

26. Why might reporters be interested in hearing from their readers and other sources?

27. Why do reporters need to have a natural curiosity?

28. Why are profiles popular with readers?

29. How do brainstorming sessions in news organizations help reporters pitch their story ideas?

30. Why do journalists write about trends before the tipping point occurs?

31. How does enterprise reporting satisfy the four functions of mass communication, which are to educate, inform, persuade and entertain?

Make Academic Connections

32. **CAREERS** Write a few paragraphs that explain whether you would prefer writing hard news or soft news.

33. **TECHNOLOGY** Use the Internet and interviews with people involved in technology to learn about electronic tools for reporters on the go. Interview someone who works in an electronics store or other type of technology firm, or someone who teaches technology. Make a list of the tools that you would find helpful as a hard news reporter. Describe each tool and explain how each tool would help you be a better reporter.

34. **LANGUAGE ARTS**   Choose an enterprise story of interest to you from one news source, print or online. Conduct research using various sources to try to confirm the validity of the information. Write an analysis of your findings.

35. **ENGLISH**   Read your school or community newspaper or newsletter and check the stories for proper grammar, spelling, punctuation and sentence structure. Make a list of the errors and then explain how you would correct each one.

36. **RESEARCH**   You are a political beat reporter. Identify sources and the way to locate sources appropriate for gathering information about activities within your school, your community and your state for a political beat. Make a list of sources for in-person interviews and for Internet research. Beside each source, provide an explanation about who or what the contact is and the type of information you would receive from each. For example, one list might be the names of members of the school board who would provide information on issues about education and your school such as funding needed or cuts to be made in programs. To locate the people, you would need their names and phone numbers or email addresses. For the state, you might have the governor's website.

37. **BUSINESS**   Interview a parent or other adult about the jargon he or she uses on the job. Write a soft news story about the jargon. Locate additional information sources about the use of this jargon. Then write a soft news story using your interview and research. Include a list of words and phrases and a translation of each word or phrase. Use quotations in your story.

Writing Portfolio Activity

38. Clip several hard news and soft news stories from your local newspaper. Analyze what elements the hard news stories and the soft news stories share. Use quotations from the stories when possible in your analysis. Keep your news stories and analysis in your portfolio.

AP Stylebook Workshop

If necessary, rewrite the following sentences using AP style.

39. At the last head count, thirty-three students were in the journalism class.

40. The newspaper has one hundred five reporters, twenty-two editors and fifty-five photographers.

41. When he arrived, three reporters were ahead of him.

42. Twenty eleven was the year the school launched its website.

COMMUNICATION AND COLLABORATION: Work as a Team

Journalists in the 21st century are part of an increasingly complex world which calls for complex and diverse news organizations. Most journalists work with a team. Working together effectively during a team meeting requires journalists to have both good communication skills and good collaboration skills. Team members may include

- **Reporters** One or more beat or general assignment reporters may work on a big story to write the story from different angles.

- **Photographers and/or videographers** Photographs are needed for the print story, and video is needed for the Web story.

- **Designers and artists** Newspapers and Web pages must be designed for the best effect of news coverage.

- **Copy editors** Before the stories are published, copy editors edit the text for clarity, style and accuracy.

- **Editors** The final word and approval of all story copy, photographs, art and video come from the editors.

MEETING TOGETHER

Journalists have meetings to brainstorm story ideas and to plan stories. For example:

During a meeting, one reporter mentions there is a motocross competition over the weekend. The sports beat reporter has the competition on the calendar, but she suggests it might also work as a human interest story because some of the competitiors are local high school students. The editor assigns a general assignment reporter to cover that story while the beat reporter is assigned the

sports angle. A photographer is assigned to take photos of the local students and a videographer is assigned to record footage of the competitors in action.

Broadcast news meetings would go much the same way except the stories would be geared for radio or television and the Web. Photos might be used on the Web and video of the students might be shown on the nightly newscast.

GOOD COMMUNICATION SKILLS

Regardless of the job the journalist is performing, good communication skills are necessary. These include being able to listen to other people and respect their ideas and opinions; being able to think clearly and express your thoughts clearly and succinctly; being knowledgeable about the topic; and being confident in yourself and your abilities as a journalist.

GOOD COLLABORATION SKILLS

Journalists also need good collaboration skills to work with the entire team. These skills begin with good interpersonal relationship skills, which means being able to get along well with others. When journalists work as a team, they share information and credit while recognizing the skills and talents each member brings to the story. All members of the team may not always agree on how a story should be handled, but journalists with good collaboration skills work with the team to produce the best story.

THINK *Critically*
What can you do today to improve your communication and collaboration skills?

REAL PEOPLE REAL CAREERS

Elizabeth Chuck | Forging a Career in the Social Media

When Elizabeth Chuck's grandfather died, a copy of the The New York Times was put into his casket. "Every morning he would have his banana and read his New York Times," says Chuck, who clearly comes by honestly what she calls her "news junkie" personality. Like her grandfather, she reads the Times every day, too. The difference between Chuck and her grandfather, however, is that she gets The Times and all her other news on a computer or other digital device.

© Photo courtesy of Elizabeth Chuck

As Social Media and Breaking News Editor for MSNBC.com, Chuck monitors all types of news sources. "I spend a good part of my day tweeting from the @breakingnews account on Twitter. I'm constantly searching the wires and other news sites for breaking news."

MSNBC.com, which relies on its broadcast partners MSNBC and NBC for some reporting, sees social media as a crucial platform for delivering news, Chuck says. "The hardest demographic to reach has always been students. Putting our content on Facebook and Twitter gives us a direct line to that demographic. In addition, it offers an area where news organizations can show some personality. We rarely get the chance to respond directly to our readers on our site, but in a Facebook discussion, we can."

Chuck, who graduated from Wesleyan University in Middletown, Ct., in 2005, never took a journalism class. "I graduated with a liberal arts degree," says Chuck. "But I was editor of my high school newspaper and editor of my college newspaper and I interned at The Hartford Courant, where I had a great editor who taught me a lot." In fact, Chuck says she had such a positive experience at The Courant that it was there she settled on a career choice. "I thought, 'Print journalism. That's what I want to do.'"

It took just one day on a second internship at MSNBC.com to change her thinking. "My co-workers were going over some numbers and talking about the millions of users and I thought, 'Wait a minute: This isn't journalism of the future. This is journalism now.'" When after her college graduation she was offered a full-time position at MSNBC.com, Chuck accepted.

ADVICE FOR ASPIRING JOURNALISTS

"Having a wider reach through online media is still satisfying," she says, "but the goal has shifted from 'How many people can we share this information with?' to 'What is the most innovative way to share it?' Because everyone from individual bloggers to other mainstream media organizations have the ability to reach the masses, the focus is now on how we disseminate the news. Even Twitter and Facebook are starting to feel like stale ways of getting the word out. My most satisfying work experiments these days are ones that use a new platform or give our readers a unique way to interact with our reporters or each other."

Source: Personal interview with Elizabeth Chuck.

THINK *Critically*

1. Which news platform offers more opportunity to young journalists — a print publication or a website?

2. How might you prepare for a career at a news website?

4

Write to Communicate

4.1	Identify the Central Point
4.2	**Write Inverted Pyramid Stories**
4.3	**Write the Body of Stories**

"Portraits of Grief"

In the days after Sept. 11, 2001 — the day the Twin Towers of the World Trade Center fell — reporters and editors at The New York Times struggled with the enormity of human loss that was both a local and global story. They knew that neither they nor their readers could comprehend the loss of 2,937 dead in the aftermath of a terrible terrorist attack. Then one reporter had the answer. Tell one story at a time.

Out of that idea came the Pulitzer Prize-winning "Portraits of Grief." Times reporters wrote 1,800 portraits of those who died, each about 150 words. The stories were reported so well that the essence of each lost life came through in the memories and anecdotes collected from friends and family.

The portraits ran daily for more than three months — sometimes three or four pages of them at a time. Perhaps not until the last full page ran did the Times team realize the impact of their project. They had given their city, their nation and their readers a gift of perspective.

THINK *Critically*

1. Why did Times reporters want memories and anecdotes about each person who died in the Twin Towers?

2. Why was it important for reporters to talk to the widows, widowers, children, parents, friends and colleagues of the people who died?

Identify the Central Point

Goals

- Identify the central point of a news story.
- Explain how to write leads.

Key Terms

- central point 81
- five W's and H 82
- lead 83
- summary lead 83
- descriptive lead 86
- question lead 86
- quotation lead 86
- direct address lead 86
- surprise lead 87
- free writing 87

FOCUS

Today's information consumers are busy people with lots of options. Over breakfast, they may scan the morning news headlines on a computer tablet such as the iPad. If they don't have time to read thoroughly, they may save for later any article they want to read in depth. In the car on the way to work, they may listen to an all-news radio broadcast. During working hours, information consumers can get news headlines sent to them on their smartphones or work computers. In the evening at home, they can choose from local or national television news broadcasts as well as a number of satirical news shows. Professional journalists writing and editing in this multi-option world must work harder than ever to deliver stories that get their point across clearly and quickly. They must be able to write an opening that makes the reader or listener want to move into the story and stay until the end.

Identify the Central Point

News stories are written in a journalistic style that allows readers and listeners to absorb quickly the most important information. The **central point** is the most important piece of information the writer wants to get across to the reader. It's the information that will have the most impact, or emotional punch, on the reader. In an English composition you would call the central point the "thesis statement."

When reporting a story, journalists collect all kinds of information. As they gather information, good reporters ask themselves: "What is this story really about? What is the point I want to make?" For example, if you are reporting a story about inconsistent temperatures in classrooms around your school, you need to ask yourself: "What is the main focus — the central point — of the story?" Maybe it is the effect of classroom temperature on student learning, or maybe it's the age of the infrastructure of the building. Once you establish a central point, it becomes easier to write a clear and succinct story.

FIVE W'S AND AN H

How do you figure out the central point on which to hang your story? Ask yourself the **five W's and H** questions: Who? What? When? Where? Why? and How? All are questions you want to answer somewhere in the story. Ask these questions before you start writing and you should find: (1) whether you have the information to answer all the questions, and (2) which one of the six questions seems most important to you.

In the story about inconsistent temperatures in classrooms, your central point might be how learning is affected by the change in temperatures from classroom to classroom. A different approach might be to make your central point about fundraising for a new heating and air conditioning system, or you might choose to focus on how a different energy source might save taxpayers money and help the environment.

There is no absolute right way to determine the central point of your stories. You must make the best judgment given the facts you have at the time. As more facts come in, you may even decide to change your central point and revise what you have written.

Whatever you choose as your central point, you want to establish it in the first sentence. In a news story your central point should be clear in the first few words.

checkpoint ✓

How do you identify the central point of a story?

The Five W's and H Questions	
Who	Who is the story about?
What	What happened or will happen? What event is the story about?
When	When did the event take place, or when will it take place?
Where	Where did the event take place, or where will it take place?
Why	Why did the event take place? What circumstances led up to it?
How	How did it happen? What makes this story newsworthy?

Leads

The **lead** is the beginning of the story. Every story has a lead. Leads are the door to the story. They invite readers in. Whether the reader stays for the whole tale depends on the lead. Summary leads are a standard and traditional way to bring readers into a story. Alternatives to the summary lead include the descriptive lead, quotation lead, direct address lead and surprise lead.

SUMMARY LEADS

The **summary lead** is the first paragraph of a news story. It summarizes the story in a clear, factual beginning paragraph. A summary lead answers who, what, when, where, why and how and establishes what the story is about.

The summary lead is the most recognized element of journalistic writing. It helps writers organize the story by establishing the angle or central point. It gives readers the most important information immediately, and it is written so that the information can be easily understood. Some journalists argue that the summary lead takes away from a story because it gives readers the conclusion at the top. It's a little like writing at the beginning of a murder mystery, "The butler did it." Other journalists argue that the summary lead has survived for more than a century in the news industry because it works.

Writing summary leads is an acquired skill. It takes practice. Many writers new to journalistic style find that if they make an outline, they can more easily construct the summary lead. For example, imagine that your school district board of education votes to cut athletic programs next year from your high school's budget. You attend the meeting and hear dozens of parents and students tell the board that they are against the athletic program cuts. You have quotations from some of these people, statements from some of the board members, and background information on the high school budget.

Back at your desk, you struggle with a summary lead. You begin an outline, a document to help clarify your thinking, and determine the newsworthy point. It won't be as formal as an outline you do for an English paper. It may look more like a list. But it will help you pull from your notes all the points you want to make.

Your outline might read like the following:

1. No athletic programs at the high school next year. That means no football, baseball, swimming, wrestling — any sports of any sort.

You want to tell readers why the above statement is true, which brings you to the second point of the outline:

2. Athletic programs will be cut because there is no money to pay for them. They cost about $100,000 a year.

Readers should know that many people opposed the cuts, so you make that note:

3. Dozens of student athletes and parents told the board of education they should not cut athletics. Some people got angry or emotional about it.

Readers should also know that the board voted unanimously to cut athletics even after hearing from parents and students, but the board had a reason:

4. If athletics were not cut, they would have to cut educational programs. In fact, one board member said, "We have no choice. It's sports or math."

With those four points outlined, you can begin constructing your lead. You might start your story with this paragraph:

There will be no football, baseball, swimming or other athletic programs at Kennedy High School next year. The board of education voted unanimously Tuesday to cut all athletics to save $100,000 and keep the school from cutting academics. Dozens of parents and students opposed the plan, but board member John Smith said, "We have no choice. It's sports or math."

What tool can you use to help yourself construct a summary lead?

Writing your summary lead should help you think critically and simplify the story. You would not want to write:

> After listening to lots of angry students and parents who were upset about the possibility of no athletic programs at the high school next year, the board of education voted 11 to 0 on Tuesday night to cut athletic programs from Kennedy High School next year.

What's wrong with the last lead? It does make some of the same points, but it's not clear what will be cut and why. The single sentence is long and redundant, and it doesn't clearly — in the first breath — give readers the main point, which is <u>there will be no sports</u>.

Here are other examples of good and not-so-good summary leads:

Rumors of a strike at ABC Co. in Rockville, Texas, became a reality Monday when a majority of union workers citing unfair labor practices voted to strike.	Good summary lead
Union workers said they were being treated unfairly by the ABC Co.	Poor summary lead
Tory High School's Yoseff Yelton won the first-place $1,500 prize Saturday at the Iron Teens Triathlon Series in Grissom Park.	Good summary lead
Yoseff Yelton was in the Iron Teens Triathlon Series and did very well. In fact, he won the first place prize of $1,500.	Poor summary lead

AP Stylebook Concepts

To express time in AP style, use figures except for "noon" and "midnight." To separate hours from minutes, use a colon: 10 a.m., 2 p.m., 5:30 p.m.

Do not write 9 a.m. this morning, 2 p.m. this afternoon or 11 p.m. Monday night. Instead, write 9 a.m., 2 p.m. or 11 p.m. Monday.

AP style allows the construction "o'clock," but writing times with a.m. or p.m. is preferred.

ALTERNATIVE LEADS

You may use alternative leads to the summary lead to invite readers into a story. These include the descriptive lead, quotation lead, direct address lead and surprise lead.

The **descriptive lead** allows the writer to become a storyteller and hint at interesting things to come. For example, suppose you want to write a story about singer Justin Bieber, who quickly rose to stardom. You might write a lead that gives the reader some description of the young man.

> Justin Bieber is not yet 16 but he moves with the style and confidence of an older performer. His slouchy jeans and rumpled T-shirts, his adorable baby-faced good looks and his hair — all brushed forward and shaggy — that was part of his signature before he cut it in 2011, made him a magnet for tweens and teens, who buy his CDs and tickets to his performances. In a short two years, Bieber went from a 12-year-old competitor in a local singing competition in his Canadian hometown of Stratford to an international superstar with a lucrative record deal.

Descriptive leads such as the one on Bieber are alternatives to the summary lead. This story could have had a summary lead, but it would have been much less inviting to readers. Consider:

> Justin Bieber, who won a local singing contest two years ago, is now an international star with a record deal.

Other leads journalists use include:

- The **question lead**, in which readers are asked a direct question.

  What would you do if you won an internship at The New York Times? College student Robert Davis is asking himself that question this morning.

- The **quotation lead**, which starts the story with something one of the subjects has said:

  "I'm lucky to be alive," said Marie Johnson as she surveyed the rubble of the home in which she survived a tornado.

- The **direct address lead**, in which readers are told to do something. In this case, they are asked to imagine:

  Imagine tile floors so shiny they glow, bright-colored hallways and sunny classrooms.

- The **surprise lead**, in which the writer supplies a twist:

  Residents of Reston, Va., were used to cats prowling their suburban neighborhood in the night, until a 60-pound bobcat appeared.

USE FREE WRITING TO GET STARTED

Many young writers have trouble writing leads for their stories and find themselves staring at blank computer screens in frustration. **Free writing** is an exercise many professional writers employ to move the ideas in their heads onto the screen or paper. It is the act of doing just what the term implies, writing with freedom. Free writing doesn't require sentences structured with proper nouns and verbs. Punctuation is helpful but not required. Whether you free write with paper and pen or on a laptop computer, the goal is to see where the words lead you.

Reporters use free writing to find the central point of an article. When they come back from the scene of a story or event, they begin by writing without referring to their notes.

In addition to using the five W's and H to find the central point of a story, ask yourself some of the questions below. You can use free writing, as well as your notes, to write the answers.

Name the technique you can use to move the ideas in your head to the paper and to help you find the central point of an article.

Questions to ask yourself to find the central point include:

- What is my story really about? (Example: An unexpected winner of a student election.)

- Who is the story about? Who are the major characters, the minor ones? (Example: The winner, of course, but also his or her supporters and the loser, too.)

- Where and when are the best places to find the story? Go to the location of the story. (Example: See the winner at a student government meeting, or just holding court at the local after-school hangout.)

- When should the story begin and end? What about the middle? (Example: the day after the election, describing the winner's day.)

- How did the story happen, unfold, come to be? What's the plot? (Example: The winner got a surge of support because he or she made incredible promises.)

- Why am I telling this story? Why does it matter? (Example: Because students need to know the person who is leading them and the winner influences how student fees are spent.)

Another trick is to ask yourself, "What's my story really about in one word?" Maybe the word is redemption or destruction or hope. In the story described above it might just be about victory. Whatever the word, it is the essence, or central point, on which the rest of the story will build.

/////// **How might asking the questions on this page help you find the central point of the story?**

Legal Issues

Citizen Journalists: Be Careful What You Say

Citizen journalists — those who write blogs, contribute to message boards, or maintain profiles on networking sites such as Facebook and Twitter — are not immune from libel or other laws governing speech and the free press.

In its 2007 report on the state of the news media, the Project for Journalism Excellence said, "Blogging is on the brink of a new phase that will probably include scandal, profitability for some and a splintering into elites and non-elites over standards and ethics." The report was correct. Indeed, in the ensuing years there has been much discussion about standards bloggers should follow. Lawsuits against bloggers and others who publish online are increasing; suits jumped from 17 to 106 in just four years, according to a Wall Street Journal report.

"It was probably inevitable, but we have seen a steady growth in litigation over content on the Internet," Sandra Baron, executive director of the Media Law Resource Center in New York, told the Los Angeles Times.

The Electronic Frontier Foundations (EFF), a civil liberties organization defending journalists' rights in the digital world, says that "freedom of the press applies to every sort of publication that affords a vehicle of information or opinion, whether online or offline."

However, EFF also notes that not all bloggers are journalists. Blogging software may be used for purposes other than journalism. Only those engaged in the practice of journalism are afforded some protections under the law.

Independent bloggers should know that they may say what they want to say online, but courts have allowed them to be sued for their comments. Truth remains the best defense against libel, in print or on the Internet.

THINK *Critically*

1. Do you think citizen journalists should be free to write anything they please online?

2. Do you always believe what you read in blogs? Why or why not?

4.1 | Assessment

Understand Concepts

Determine the best answer for each of the following questions.

1. The most important piece of information the journalist wants to get across to the reader is the
   a. summary lead.
   b. hourglass style.
   c. central point.
   d. how of the story.

2. Which will help you the most when trying to find the central point?
   a. summary lead
   b. focus style
   c. wire service
   d. five W's and H

3. Where do leads occur in a story?
   a. in a quotation
   b. first paragraph
   c. third paragraph
   d. last paragraph

4. **True or False** The summary lead is the only method journalists use to write a lead.

5. **True or False** Free writing is a way to help you get started writing.

Write Now!

Practice your writing skills with the following activities.

6. Choose a feature story from an online newspaper. If English is not your first language, choose an online paper in your native tongue. Using a computer and word-processing software, rewrite the lead as a summary lead, a descriptive lead, a quotation lead, a direct address lead and a surprise lead. Identify the type of lead. If English is not your native language, first translate the information into English before rewriting the lead.

7. Choose a news story from a national print newspaper or online news source. Rewrite the story with a local angle for your community newspaper. For example, if the news story is about severe weather crossing the country, your local angle could be about the weather in your area — the problems facing your community because of the weather, weather conditions in your region, or even about past weather problems and how the community came together as a result. Highlight your lead and indicate the type of lead you have used. Be sure to use proper journalistic style.

Write Inverted Pyramid Stories

Goals

- Understand inverted pyramid construction.
- Apply Associated Press style to stories.

Key Terms

- inverted pyramid 91
- wire services 91
- Linotype 91
- copy 91
- Associated Press style 93

FOCUS

In Chapter 1, you read about how the Civil War changed journalism and the way reporters wrote. Special war correspondents often worked for newspapers in the North, but they were stationed in the South. They had to use the telegraph to transmit their stories to their newspapers. Competition was fierce, and telegraph lines were unreliable. Reporters started putting the most important information in the leading paragraph in case transmission was interrupted. This format — the inverted pyramid — is still the most widely used format in newspapers and news magazines.

The Inverted Pyramid

Picture a pyramid turned upside down, an inverted pyramid. Most news stories are written using the **inverted pyramid** format. The most important information is at the top, in the lead paragraph. Subsequent paragraphs provide additional information in order of importance. When news was sent by telegraph in the Civil War era, it made sense to put the conclusion at the beginning, because transmission could be dicey. It still makes sense today.

With the development of wire services and Linotype for newspapers, the inverted pyramid style was still important. **Wire services** are news agencies that send out syndicated news items to media by means of telephone wires or satellites. **Linotype**, or hot type, was a traditional way of setting newspaper type for printing. An operator sat at the keyboard at the Linotype machine and operated the machine to produce the **copy**, or text. If the Linotype operators ran out of space at the bottom of a column, they just cut the copy to fit the news columns. Journalists wrote in the inverted pyramid style, so the most important information was never cut.

Technology changed the need to use the inverted pyramid style as a production tool, because journalists typically send their stories by computer.

Yet, the inverted pyramid maintains its popularity because it is the best way to give readers the most information quickly.

THE UPSIDE-DOWN APPROACH

Inverted pyramid construction requires writing upside down. Your conclusion becomes the beginning paragraph and you use your research — notes, quotes and information gathered — to support the central point, or theme, you established at the top.

In inverted pyramid construction, the second, third and subsequent paragraphs give the reader more details of the story and support your lead. The second paragraph is almost as important as the first and also should emphasize the news.

In the story example used earlier about athletic program cuts at a high school, the second paragraph would emphasize the news and its effect on students. The second paragraph might read:

> More than 200 male and female students who play on two dozen teams, including intramurals, will be without after-school activities. Prominent Kennedy athletes on interscholastic competitive teams may lose scholarship opportunities for college.

Your next paragraphs would continue with the news. You would include quotations from athletes and parents who opposed the cuts, background on

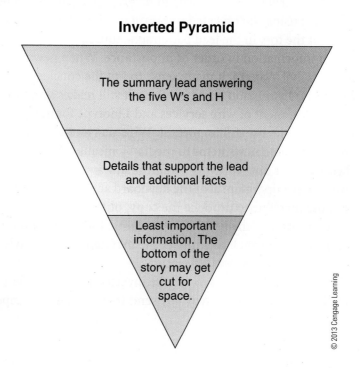

Inverted Pyramid

The summary lead answering the five W's and H

Details that support the lead and additional facts

Least important information. The bottom of the story may get cut for space.

© 2013 Cengage Learning

why the high school needed to reduce its budget by $100,000, and whether alternatives were considered.

Inverted pyramid stories don't require an ending. Students used to writing conclusions to English papers sometimes feel the need to finish the story with a summary or wrap-up paragraph. Remember that news stories are written in the inverted pyramid style and may be ended anywhere.

THE PYRAMID AND THE WEB

The inverted pyramid structure remains the most useful way to write news stories, whether writing for print or electronic publication. Readers of news pages on the Web spend even less time reading the news than do readers of newspapers or news magazines. Web readers want quick takes on the news. They "scan and land," meaning they look all over a Web page before landing on something that interests them. Web writers and editors use the inverted pyramid construction for news because it allows them to use short paragraphs and leave white space after each paragraph. They also use bold headlines and bold subheads to attract the readers' eyes and keep them focused on the story.

A summary lead in an inverted pyramid construction also can be updated easily as information changes. The Web allows for 24/7 news updating, so it is similar to the wire services, which continue to use the inverted pyramid in breaking news stories.

check *point* ✓

Explain how to write an inverted pyramid story.

Apply Journalistic Style

When we think of the word "style," it often brings to mind fashion, music or home decorating. For writers, style is what makes them unique. You may read news or sports columnists in print or on the Web every day because you like the topics the columnists pick, the opinions they hold and the way they say things. You like their style.

Journalists use a common style to make their stories easy to read. Newspapers such as USA Today or The New York Times employ hundreds of writers. If all those writers all used their own style, the newspaper would have no consistency and readers would find it difficult to go from one story to another. Journalistic style also helps the flow from one story to another.

JOURNALISTIC STYLE FOR PRINT AND ELECTRONIC NEWS

Most news organizations use **Associated Press style**, or AP style, in all stories, whether the stories are for print or the Internet. AP style is

grammar tip

A noun is a word or group of words that names a person, place, thing or idea. A noun can be either common or proper. A common noun names non-specific people, places or things. A proper noun names a specific person, place or thing.

Common nouns are capitalized only when they begin a sentence.

Example: Journalists are part of a club.

In this case, the noun "journalists" is capitalized because it begins the sentence. The noun "club" is not capitalized because it is not a specific name.

Proper nouns are always capitalized.

Example: Journalists may belong to the National Press Club.

the first layer of consistency, one most journalists learned in high school or college. Journalists learn AP style from The Associated Press Stylebook. You have been learning about AP style in the AP Stylebook Concepts feature.

Journalists must be familiar with The Associated Press Stylebook, but that doesn't mean they must memorize every passage. Many accomplished journalists keep the book handy and look up style points as they come up in their writing.

Print journalists strive to keep sentences clutter-free. William Zinsser, author of "On Writing Well," calls clutter "the disease of American writing." He writes, "We are a society strangling in unnecessary words, circular construction, pompous frills and meaningless jargon." Good writers simplify. They avoid unnecessary words, frills and jargon. They write short sentences with one idea. Their sentences have clear subjects and active verbs. Paragraphs are short. Each one provides more details of the story.

Journalistic writing for the Web is equally spare and clutter-free. It follows the print model, with short sentences and paragraphs. Web writers have the added challenge of making their stories as easy as possible for readers to scan and navigate, because reading a computer screen is harder than reading a newspaper or magazine. Short, straightforward headlines and many subheads in the copy propel Web readers forward through the story. Bulleted lists also help Web readers see points you want them to understand. Web writing should appeal to the eye.

Some news organizations have a few style rules of their own. For example, in contrast to AP style, The New York Times uses courtesy titles on second reference, so John Smith becomes Mr. Smith, not just Smith. One newspaper in San Francisco always referred to that city as "the City," as if there were

////// *Why can writing for the Web be more challenging than writing for print?*

© Lilyana Vynogradova/Shutterstock.com

no other city. When USA Today began publishing in 1982, it referred to the United States only as the USA, never the U.S.

JOURNALISTIC STYLE FOR BROADCAST NEWS

Broadcast journalists also use AP style when writing news copy, but these journalists must write for the ear, or the listener, not the reader. Broadcast journalists use short sentences with familiar words that can be understood easily by television or video viewers and radio listeners. Television writers have the challenge of writing to make visual images understood without saying in words what the pictures already make clear.

The newest challenge for all journalists is the hybrid of Web and broadcast. Video and slide-show presentations on the websites of many news organizations enhance or add to stories in the print publication. These website presentations require a script of their own, written in broadcast style.

GRAMMAR, PUNCTUATION, SPELLING AND WORD USAGE

Consistency in using correct grammar, punctuation, spelling and word choice keeps sloppiness from creeping into news stories. Think of the rules of grammar as similar to the rules of the road. Just as good drivers adhere to traffic signals, travel at the legal speed and obey signs that tell them to yield to pedestrians, good writers observe correct grammar, punctuation, spelling and word usage.

Adhering to rules for writing keeps you on safe ground. Readers know what to expect. You rely on news writers and editors to be good at what they do so you can read a newspaper or magazine confidently, knowing the story will provide you with the correct information in an organized and comprehensible way.

Correct grammar, punctuation, spelling and word usage are keystones to good writing. You must know the rules and use them well to become an accomplished writer.

Here are a few basic rules journalists try to live by:

1. **Begin sentences with a subject and a verb**. Sound simple? Many writers forget this simple point.

Print journalists (subject) cut (verb) clutter to simplify sentences.	Good example

To simplify sentences, print journalists cut clutter.	Poor example

2. **Use active verbs.** Strong verbs help readers visualize.

> David Gregory, host of NBC's "Meet the Press," *strides* across the White House lawn to *shout* a question at a departing president.
>
> Good example

> David Gregory, host of NBC's "Meet the Press," *walks* across the White House lawn to *ask* a question of the departing president.
>
> Poor example

3. **Use adverbs sparingly.** In the example below, the adverb "totally" adds nothing to the sentence. The home is destroyed, so the reader knows the home was totally destroyed.

> The tornado destroyed their home.
>
> Good example

> The tornado totally destroyed their home.
>
> Poor example

4. **Use adjectives, but use them sparingly.** Adjectives can help describe the noun. In the following sentence, the adjectives "dark" and "vast" do help readers visualize the funnel cloud. Without them the sentence is less effective.

> The dark funnel cloud was a vast presence in the Kansas sky.
>
> Good example

> The funnel cloud was a presence in the Kansas sky.
>
> Poor example

5. **Use punctuation to control the flow.** Periods and commas are your most effective punctuation marks. Periods stop your readers for a moment. Commas help you group ideas, words and phrases.

> Soccer practice is on different days each week. Check the schedule each week to see if practice is on Monday, Tuesday or Wednesday.
>
> Good example

> Soccer practice is on Monday one week and Tuesday the next and Wednesday after that.
>
> Poor example

"Word usage" refers to using words in a way that conveys the correct meaning. Journalists need to make decisions about using trendy words and phrases. You often hear words misused in everyday speech, which can cause you to misuse them in your writing. For example, "can" and "may" mean different things, but they are used interchangeably in everyday speech. "Can" refers to ability, as in: You can drive now that you've had lessons. "May" refers to permission, as in: You may take my car to school today. Reporters need to know the difference and use words correctly.

Fashionable phrases may be used to make your writing sound more conversational. Calling a subject "sweet" may be fitting in the story you are writing or it may not. Be careful that you don't sound dated or unnatural. Use a trendy word or phrase because it is fitting, not because your friends will like it. You might have written that something was cool a decade ago, but today? No way.

check *point* ✓

Why do all journalists follow the same style?

© Stockbyte/Getty Images

///// *How is writing news copy for broadcast different from writing copy for print and electronic news?*

4.2 | Assessment

Understand Concepts

Determine the best answer for each of the following questions.

1. In which style are most news stories written?
   a. narrative
   b. inverted pyramid
   c. focus
   d. hourglass

2. Which is the stylebook that most journalists use?
   a. AP
   b. APA
   c. MLA
   d. Chicago Press

3. **True or False** Most major newspapers today are set with Linotype machines.

4. **True or False** Only print journalists need to be concerned about using AP style.

Write Now!

Practice your writing skills with the following activities.

5. Using the information below, and any information you want to add, write a news story in three formats — a print story, a Web-based story and a broadcast story. Use correct journalistic style and write for a high school audience. Before you begin, plan your story, conduct research and then write a draft. Examine your stories for clarity, engaging language, and the correct use of English. Give your teacher a print copy of the print news story, send the Web story electronically, and provide an audio or video version of the broadcast story.

   Who: Omar Davidson

   What: A new social studies teacher

   When: Beginning this year

   Where: In your school

   Why: Replacing a retiring teacher

   How: Honors graduate of Western University

Write the Body of Stories

Goals

- Identify narrative, hourglass and focus styles.
- Understand how to achieve tightly written stories by writing short.

Key Terms

- narrative style 99
- hourglass style 101
- focus style 101
- nut graph 101
- kicker 101

FOCUS

Fast-forward a few years. You have just graduated from college and have your degree in journalism. You are looking for a job in a fast-paced news organization that operates multiple platforms and uses multimedia. In turn, the reporters and editors who work in the profession, and job seekers like you, must be able to work with words, photos and video and write well for each medium. Editors are looking for workers who are equally comfortable writing scripts for the video presentation or a story for a print platform. Reporters who can write in the inverted pyramid style plus a variety of other journalistic styles are the ones most likely to get jobs.

Narrative, Hourglass and Focus Styles

Three ways of organizing news and feature stories other than the inverted pyramid are the narrative, hourglass and focus styles.

NARRATIVE STYLE

The **narrative style** is a storytelling style. Journalists use it to draw readers in through the drama of an event, the personalities and characters of the subjects, and the overall scene. Stories written in narrative style often are written as a novelist might write. These stories are written in chronological order, use dialogue, and have a beginning, middle and end.

Newspapers are filled with reports on people and events. Some of those reports can become good stories when the journalist becomes a storyteller and narrates a compelling tale.

How do you make a story compelling? You write scenes that have detail and description. You turn your subjects into characters, and make your subjects active and quotable. You move the story forward and end it with a splash.

© Karl Schumacher/Time & Life Pictures/Getty Images

///// **In the USA Weekend narrative about reporter Sam Donaldson, what makes the story compelling?**

Here's the opening of a magazine article in narrative style about retired ABC News reporter Sam Donaldson. A 42-year veteran of ABC News, Donaldson served twice as the chief White House correspondent. His first term was from 1977 to 1989, and his second was from 1998 to 1999. He reported on Presidents Jimmy Carter, Ronald Reagan and Bill Clinton. This narrative is about his return to the White House beat in 1998.

Notice the active verbs — "striding," "sharpening," "injecting" — and a quick, pointed explanation of why he is important — he covered three presidents, Vietnam, Watergate and more.

The reporter who defined confrontational journalism is in his element — striding around the White House working a big story. Sam Donaldson, who made his reputation covering three presidents, Vietnam, Watergate and more, is sharpening pointed questions, cackling with colleagues and generally injecting new life into a White House press corps that was, until Monica Lewinsky appeared, settling in for a lame-duck term. With double the energy of reporters half his age, Donaldson, 64, works the phones, revels in a scoop and stands in freezing rain for a soap-opera-stopping "special report." That way, competitors like CNN's Wolf Blitzer, toasty indoors, won't know Donaldson got the story first. Forty-five minutes later, Blitzer broadcasts the story, too, and Donaldson chuckles.

Reporters from various outlets say Donaldson's January return to the White House beat has "raised the bar." Everyone is working harder and smarter. Clearly pleased to hear it, he arches one of his famous eyebrows and booms: "Let the games begin!"

Source: From USA WEEKEND Magazine. Used with permission.

HOURGLASS STYLE

The **hourglass style** is a combination of the inverted pyramid and narrative styles. The term was coined in 1983 by the Poynter Institute's senior scholar Roy Peter Clark when he noticed a story written in that style in his morning newspaper. Think of a misshapen hourglass — the bottom bigger than the top. That's the shape of the hourglass story, the frame on which you'll hang a story. Clark divides the hourglass into three parts:

1. **The top** This is the beginning of the story. This includes the summary lead and three or four paragraphs giving the most important news. If readers stop at the top, they'll understand the story and be informed.

2. **The turn** This is the transition paragraph. It tells the reader that the narrative will begin. It often has a phrase attributed to a source in the story. For example: According to police, it all began when …

3. **The narrative** This is the bottom part of the story. It is told chronologically with a beginning, middle and end. Details, quotations and background information all go here.

FOCUS STYLE

The **focus style**, a favorite of The Wall Street Journal, has four parts:

1. The story starts with a lead that focuses on a person, place or situation. The lead may be more than one paragraph.

2. The story moves on to a **nut graph**. This is a paragraph that states the central point of the story. The central point may be bigger than the focused lead suggests.

3. The body of the story develops the central point in as many paragraphs as needed.

4. The **kicker** is the conclusion. It finishes the story. Kickers often are good quotations, saved for last, or a short concluding sentence.

checkpoint ✓

What are the three parts of an hourglass structure?

Writing Short

Writing tight, detailed stories is a challenge for journalists. It requires "writing short" and is harder than writing long. Writing short often takes more time. Regardless of the length of the story, the same amount of research and good reporting is necessary.

ORGANIZE AND FOCUS

Writing short requires focus and detail. Once you have completed the research and you know what you want to say, write one short sentence, six or seven words, that explains the story. Answer this question for yourself: Why am I writing this? Why will the reader care? Keep that six- or seven-word sentence in front of you as you write. Be realistic. You can't write a full profile of Microsoft's Bill Gates in 800 words, but you can write about why he likes to give away money.

Go through your research notebook and circle the best quotations, the most important information and the key people. You will use these items in your story. The fact that you made a note doesn't mean you must include it. Edit yourself ruthlessly before you even begin writing.

TIPS FOR WRITING SHORT

Writing short is about rewrite and revision. Use short words, short sentences and short paragraphs. Every word must earn its spot. Your verbs should be active. In the example on page 100, Sam Donaldson is "cackling" with colleagues, not just laughing or joking. He is "injecting" new life, not just putting new life, into the press corps. Following are more tips to help you write short and achieve strongly written, detailed stories.

- Your writer's voice should be active, not passive.

The student government asks all seniors to use assigned parking.	Good example

All seniors are requested by the student government to use their assigned parking places.	Poor example

- Go after details and use them. Your sentences will be more powerful. As Clark from the Poynter Institute says, "Get the name of the dog." Read the examples below. Which is more powerful?

A cream-colored Labrador named Murphy pulled a 3-year-old boy out of the murky lake Tuesday.	Good example

A toddler was pulled from the lake by a dog Tuesday.	Poor example

- Short writing calls for simple sentences: a subject (noun) and a strong verb. Sentences don't need a sprinkling of adjectives and adverbs to make them lively; they need precision and the right words. Ice cream, for example, need not be really good, when it can be delicious.

- Prune all the clutter out of your sentences. Do it word by word. Take out words like "at present" when you mean "now." Don't use the word "experiencing" — as in, Are you experiencing shortness of breath? — when you can say more clearly, Can you breathe?

- Use quotations sparingly to move your story along, not to emphasize a point you have already made.

- Vary the length of sentences in your short story so that you set the pace. If every one of them is short, your story will sound choppy.

CHECKLIST FOR WRITING SHORT

- Do the research and reporting. You need as much information for a short story as for a long one.

- Organize or outline. Don't just empty your notebook.

- Simplify every sentence. Use clear nouns and strong, active verbs.

- Cut clutter. Remove all extra words and phrases.

- Use the best quotes. They are the ones that move the story forward.

- Be precise with words and details. Say "now," not "currently"; say "202," not "about 200."

check *point* ✓

Name three things you can do to write short.

© Creative/Getty Images

///// **Why is writing short harder than writing long?**

Write Short for Maximum Impact

By Monica Cheng, Carmel High School, Carmel, Ind., "CHS Carbon Footprint"

When sophomore Cleo Hernandez looked up in the main cafeteria one day during lunch, it occurred to her that the ceiling lights, particularly in the center of the room where she was sitting, used a large amount of energy.

"The school should try to conserve electricity and be more environmentally friendly," Hernandez said.

The Carmel Green Initiative is a program whose goal is to create awareness of the connection between Carmel citizens and their impact on the environment as well as to reduce energy waste and pollution. According to this program, as of February 2009 Carmel High School, among other schools in the district, took part in the replacement and conversion of light bulbs with new GE "Green" energy-saver bulbs, significantly lowering the quantity of pollutants in the atmosphere.

According to the U.S. Department of Energy, 40 percent of all electricity used to power electronics is consumed while the products are on standby mode, making it even more important to conserve energy by turning off computers and lights when not in use.

Even though turning off computers and lights are trivial things, Irene Gibson, a member of Carmel Green Team and junior, said every step counts toward helping the environment on a larger scale and contributing to one goal: protecting the Earth. The Carmel Green Team is a club at CHS that encourages "green" projects within the city of Carmel by giving grants of money to other teams that want to help the environment, according to Gibson.

"It's important to protect our environment for future generations," George Ohmer, an AP Environmental Science teacher, said. One thing that would be beneficial to the environment is recycling. "It takes an awful lot more energy to make materials, such as aluminum, cans and glass, from raw materials than it does to make those materials from recycled material."

Gibson said some students and teachers are active in these "green" procedures, but not everyone is doing it.

"It's really important [to help the environment] because it is our duty as humans to protect the environment in which we live," Gibson said. "We are the problem. We can also be the solution."

THINK *Critically*

1. This story appears to be written in the focus style, as explained on page 101 of this chapter. Identify the parts of the focus style in the story.

2. Did the writer succeed in writing short in this piece? Explain your answer using specific examples from the story.

Source: Used by permission of Monica Cheng.

4.3 | Assessment

Understand Concepts

Determine the best answer for each of the following questions.

1. The conclusion of a story written in the focus style is the
   a. nut graph.
   b. kicker.
   c. hourglass.
   d. narrative.

2. A journalistic style that is similar to a novelist's style is the
   a. narrative style.
   b. focus style.
   c. inverted pyramid style.
   d. hourglass style.

3. **True or False** Journalists are more valuable to news organizations if they can write in a variety of styles.

4. **True or False** Journalists rewrite and revise to help them write short.

Write Now!

Practice your writing skills with the following activities.

5. Choose a news article from a national newspaper. Use the Internet to gather background information to research the story in depth. Use at least three sources so that you can evaluate and confirm the validity of the background information. Rewrite the article for your high school paper in the narrative, hourglass or focus style. Include information from your research, and be sure to include a local angle in your story. Provide your teacher with a list of sources.

6. Record a national broadcast news show. As you listen to the news, notice how the stories are organized. Find three stories in the broadcast that are organized differently. Write a summary of each. For each story, identify the organization (inverted pyramid, narrative, hourglass or focus style) and explain why you think this organization was used. Next, rewrite one of the stories for broadcast in a journalistic style that is different from the one used originally. Use language that would be suitable for broadcast in your high school. Deliver your story to the class.

7. Research a topic of your choice to write a news story for your high school newspaper. Use the tips you learned in this section on how to write short when planning and writing your story. Using a computer, write one short sentence that explains the story. Keep this sentence in front of you as you go over your research. Circle the best quotations, the most important information and the key people. Write a draft, and then edit, deleting all unnecessary words. Be a ruthless editor of your work. Edit for clarity, engaging language and correct grammar. Identify the type of lead used in the margin beside the lead. Turn in your notes and drafts along with your final story.

CHAPTER 4 | Assessment

Review Journalism Concepts

4.1 Identify the Central Point

The central point is the most important piece of information the writer wants to get across to the reader. It's the information that will have the most emotional punch or impact on the reader. In English composition, you would call it the thesis statement. To help you find the central point, ask the five W's and H questions — who, what, when, where, why and how. All of the five W's and H questions should be answered in the summary lead in news stories. Alternative leads include the descriptive lead, question lead, quotation lead, direct address lead and surprise lead.

Free writing is an exercise that many writers employ to move the ideas in their heads onto a computer screen or paper. Reporters use free writing to find the central point of an article. Writers need to know what the story is about before they begin writing.

4.2 Write Inverted Pyramid Stories

Most news stories are written in the inverted pyramid style. This form of story construction places the most important information at the beginning. The inverted pyramid style came out of the American Civil War when correspondents sent stories over unreliable telegraph wires. Transmission often was interrupted before the entire story could be sent. The style continued to be used when newspapers were set for printing on Linotype machines, or hot type. Linotype operators often cut off the bottom of stories to make the copy fit into the newspaper columns. Today, although stories usually are sent from computer to computer, the inverted pyramid is the best style for busy readers.

Most journalists follow Associated Press style to assure consistency in stories written by different reporters. Journalists must also pay attention to grammar, punctuation, spelling and word usage.

4.3 Write the Body of Stories

In addition to the inverted pyramid, other journalistic ways of organizing stories include the narrative, hourglass and focus styles. The narrative is a storytelling style. The hourglass is a combination of the narrative and inverted pyramid styles, and the focus has four parts — a lead that focuses on a person, place or situation; a nut graph; a body that develops the central point; and a kicker.

Journalists need to write short. To do so, they need to be organized and to revise and rewrite copy. They also need to use active voice, include details, use simple sentences, prune clutter, use quotations sparingly and vary the length of sentences.

Develop Your Journalism Language

Write the letter of the term that matches each definition. Some terms will not be used.

_____ 1. Most important piece of information in a story

_____ 2. Hot type

_____ 3. Agencies that send out syndicated news items to media by means of telephone wires or satellite

_____ 4. Text

_____ 5. A storytelling style

_____ 6. Style used by news organizations

_____ 7. The format used for most news stories

_____ 8. Way to identify central point of a story

_____ 9. The most recognized element of journalistic writing, it answers who, what, when, where, why and how in the first paragraph

_____ 10. This lead allows the writer to become a storyteller and hint at interesting things to come

_____ 11. An exercise many professional writers employ to get ideas out of their heads and onto the screen or paper

_____ 12. The conclusion of a story in the focus style

_____ 13. The beginning of the story

_____ 14. A lead that tells readers to do something

a. Associated Press style
b. central point
c. copy
d. descriptive lead
e. direct address lead
f. five W's and H
g. focus style
h. free writing
i. hourglass style
j. inverted pyramid
k. kicker
l. lead
m. Linotype
n. narrative style
o. nut graph
p. question lead
q. quotation lead
r. summary lead
s. surprise lead
t. wire services

15. Which style contains the top, the turn and the narrative?
   a. focus
   b. inverted pyramid
   c. hourglass
   d. narrative

16. Which style contains the nut graph and kicker?
   a. focus
   b. inverted pyramid
   c. hourglass
   d. narrative

Think Critically

17. How do the five W's and H help you find the central point?

18. What questions do you need to ask with the five W's and H?

19. How is the central point in a news article like the thesis statement in a scholarly paper?

20. Can the central point of a story change as you begin writing? Explain your answer.

21. Why is the summary lead so named?

22. How can an outline help you write a summary lead?

23. What type of story might you be writing when using a descriptive lead?

24. How might free writing help you write a story's lead?

25. Why are most news stories written in the inverted pyramid style?

26. How did the telegraph and Linotype operators contribute to the inverted pyramid style?

27. What purpose do the second, third and subsequent paragraphs serve in the inverted pyramid?

28. Why might professional journalists keep the AP Stylebook handy?

29. Why must broadcast journalists write for the ear rather than the eye?

30. Why is word usage important to journalists?

31. What do narrative stories have in common with novels?

32. Why would it help your career as a journalist to learn to write in more than one journalistic style (inverted pyramid, narrative, hourglass and focus)?

33. Explain why the following statement is or is not true: "You should use all of the research in your story to assure good coverage."

Make Academic Connections

34. **CAREERS** Choose something that interests you, such as fashion, science, politics or sports. Use the Internet to research the career of a journalist who specializes in that subject. Request an interview with the journalist. The interview can be conducted via the phone or email. Use quotes from your interview if your request was granted and/or your research. Write a story that includes information about the publication the journalist writes for and any needed education, or knowledge in addition to journalism. Use at least three sources to evaluate the validity of the information and cite them in your story. The story should be suitable for a print or Web publication that has an audience of high school students. Before turning in your story, be sure to examine it for clarity, use of engaging language, and the correct use of English.

35. **SOCIAL STUDIES** Use the Internet to read the leads of five stories in a foreign-language newspaper. Choose both news stories and feature stories. If you do not read a foreign language, choose a British or Irish newspaper, or a foreign newspaper written in English. Identify the type of lead for each story. If English is your second language, read a newspaper in your native language.

36. **ECONOMICS** Use your research skills to obtain the starting salaries of journalists in major news organizations and in the news organizations in your community. Make a chart of starting salaries.

37. **READING** Read two leads in newspaper stories, and then read leads of stories on a similar topic written by a blogger. Identify the style of the leads, and then write a paragraph that compares and contrasts the newspaper leads with the bloggers' leads.

38. **ART** Using computer graphics and other art supplies, create a bulletin board that identifies and describes the five W's and H.

39. **WRITING** Use free writing to write about how you feel about journalism in this section of your course. Do you still want to pursue journalism as a possible career? Why or why not? Have you decided it's not for you? Why or why not? What type of journalism might you like to investigate further? Why are you drawn to that type of journalism? Is journalism harder or easier than you thought it would be?

40. **HISTORY** Use your research skills to research the history of the Associated Press. Write a paper that details the organization's history and how AP style became the accepted style for journalists. Before writing your first draft, plan the paper. After writing, edit your paper for clarity, engaging language, and the use of correct English.

41. **LANGUAGE ARTS** Ottmar Mergenthaler was the inventor of the Linotype machine. Use the Internet and other resources including past interviews, articles and reports to gather background information to write a biography of Mergenthaler. Give citations for sources you used in your research as well as for quotations. Be sure to plan your paper and write a draft before completing your final paper. When done, carefully edit your paper for clarity, engaging language, and correct word usage, grammar and punctuation.

Writing Portfolio Activity

42. Choose a profile story about your favorite movie star from a magazine or website. Analyze the story to determine the type of lead used — summary lead, descriptive lead, question lead, quotation lead, direct address lead and surprise lead. Rewrite the lead in each of the other types of lead so that you have one example of each type. Identify each lead. Add this to your portfolio.

AP Stylebook Workshop

Write the following times in AP style:

43. half past four in the afternoon

44. six thirty in the morning

45. twelve o'clock at night

46. eight in the morning on Thursday

INITIATIVE AND SELF-DIRECTION: Find Your First Job

Just as you research and plan your news stories, you must also spend time researching and planning to find that first job. This takes initiative and self-direction. To begin you will need to

- Decide which journalism job is right for you
- Research the job opportunities
- Prepare a resume

WHICH JOURNALISM JOB IS RIGHT FOR YOU?

You may already know that you want to be a foreign correspondent for a major broadcaster or a sports reporter for an online paper. Or, you may just know you want to work in journalism but aren't sure of the specific area. To narrow this down, the first step is to list your interests, values and abilities. Next, list the types of stories you are drawn to. In making your list, you will learn more about the type of journalism to gear your education and job search toward.

The next step is to look at what education will serve you best in your future career. Certainly you want to take journalism courses, but if you plan on becoming an art reporter, you will also need classes in art history and related subjects. If you want a career reporting the news, courses in social studies will be helpful.

If you have many interests, you might want to be a general assignment reporter, which is where most reporters begin. In addition to journalism courses, courses in technology and English will help you.

RESEARCH THE JOB OPPORTUNITIES

The next step is to look at the job offerings in the categories that interest you, including general reporting. To find out more about jobs in journalism, go to the "Occupational Outlook Handbook" published by the U.S. Bureau of Labor Statistics. Also look through news magazines, newspapers and online sources for available jobs for journalists. Make a list of available sources.

PREPARE A RESUME

To begin preparing your resume, make a list of your skills, abilities and work experiences. Add your education and your personal information — your name, address and phone number. Add a portfolio of news articles published.

Use the Internet to find sample resumes. Put your list into your preferred resume format. At the top of the resume, add an "Objective." The objective is what you want in a job. It's also useful to include what you bring to a job. Your objective might read: "To be a reporter for a news magazine where I can use my background and education in theater arts to help the magazine reach its goal of entertainment news stories 24/7."

Next, compose a cover letter. Use the Internet to research cover letters. Read several before writing yours. Plan what you want to write, write a draft, and then edit it. Have someone else read your letter for typos, grammar, engaging language and correct syntax and punctuation. If your cover letter if full of mistakes, the potential employer will not think much of your ability as a journalist.

THINK *Critically*

Take the first step in deciding which area of journalism is right for you. Make a list of your interests, values and abilities. Then list the types of stories you like to read and the topics you like to read about. What area or areas of journalism do these lists suggest?

REAL PEOPLE REAL CAREERS

Tina Johnson-Marcel | Hybrid Journalist in a Fast Medium

Tina Johnson-Marcel describes herself as a hybrid. The senior manager for digital communications for the nonprofit website Global Impact, Johnson-Marcel had training in both traditional and new media during her college years at Howard University in Washington, D.C., and in her early professional jobs.

"Howard's journalism department started offering Web writing and Web building classes and I took as many as I could," Johnson-Marcel says. "In addition to my summer internships, I was a new media intern for Congressional Quarterly during the school year for two years."

Those internships gave her all kinds of solid print experience so when she got out of college, at first she worked in print. After a couple of early professional newspaper jobs, however, she moved to the Web and never looked back.

Being on the Web, Johnson-Marcel says, means being fast. "And I mean fast in every way — not just filing a story quickly. The technology is constantly changing. You have to stay abreast of what's new. Even if you're not a 'producer' you still have to know what's going on or you will be left behind."

ADVICE FOR ASPIRING JOURNALISTS

She says up-and-coming journalists must learn the foundation of journalism — the writing and editing skills. "Don't let anyone convince you there is a shortcut just because you're on the Web. The basic knowledge is still required," she says.

She advises aspiring journalists to "start a blog on something you're passionate about. Participate in social media (but be aware — your future boss will be watching everything you post). Build your own brand. That's how the Web is changing the game." Now potential employers expect to see your resume and examples of your writing and editing on a website or professional-looking blog.

As part of her job, Johnson-Marcel peruses several news websites every morning. "I also have a few go-to blogs, as well. But I'm very old-fashioned. I still subscribe to The Washington Post. I like to hold the paper and browse. Even when I'm on vacation or visiting a city, I'll buy the local newspaper. There's still a lot you can get from the print version that you can't see on the Web — photo placement, the prominence of a story (was it on A1? above the fold?) — and I miss that. I also love, love, love the classified ads. One of my journalism professors told me you can learn a lot about a city by what folks are selling."

Source: Personal interview with Tina Johnson-Marcel.

THINK *Critically*

1. In what ways do you think that journalists who write for the Web need to be "fast"?
2. Judging from Johnson-Marcel's example, what are effective ways to build experience in journalism?

5

Collaborate on Content

A News Team Gets Ready for the Super Bowl

There is no bigger day on the advertising beat at major newspapers than Super Bowl Sunday. Businesses devote millions of dollars to producing special commercials and debut them on the most-watched live event on television. Most of the companies creating ads want to win USA Today's Ad Meter. The Ad Meter is a real-time system for measuring an ad's popularity with viewers.

It takes teamwork to make Ad Meter the respected measure of Super Bowl commercials that it is. It begins with viewing the 40 or so screening copies of commercials that will be seen during the Super Bowl game. Reporters look for trends, groundbreaking ideas or creative production techniques that might make interesting preview stories. While the reporters work on the ads, their editor gets preparations under way for having the ads rated by focus groups of randomly selected television viewers. The editor also prepares a list of stories that the reporting team will cover.

Like the coaches of the teams in the Super Bowl, the editor keeps a close watch on the players. The editor helps reporters sharpen ideas for the stories they will write before and after the game. The editor edits the finished stories for the newspaper's website and print editions; collaborates with designers, providing guidance, photos and video; and answers copy editors' questions.

Because everyone is prepared and working together, the editor is confident that the game day plan for Ad Meter will succeed.

THINK *Critically*
If you were editor of your school newspaper, how might you prepare for a big event?

112

Edit Content and Copy

Goals

- Identify the types of editors and explain their roles.
- Explain the role of copy editors and their responsibility in copy editing and proofreading.

Key Terms

- content editor 113
- copy editor 113
- managing editor 113
- executive editor 113
- storyboard 114
- news meetings 114

FOCUS

Does the newspaper in your community or online news site you read regularly publish corrections? Even the most reputable news organizations must correct mistakes, sometimes multiple mistakes. The mistakes may be as minimal as getting wrong the setting for a popular novel or as grave as misspelling someone's name. In any case, the errors must be corrected to keep the readers' trust. Corrections send a message to readers that the newspaper cares about accuracy. The people responsible for making sure news stories are accurate are the editors. Editors work hard to prevent mistakes in stories. If mistakes are made, editors make sure they are corrected.

Editors and Their Roles

Reporters and correspondents are the public faces of most news organizations. Behind them are editors whose job it is to make their reporters' work accurate and easy to understand. Editors decide what stories their news consumers see or hear and how prominently the stories are displayed in newspapers or on websites or told on air. There are different types of editors inside newsrooms or information centers.

Content editors work with reporters to produce content of all kinds — text, video and graphic. They coach, cajole, teach, advise and assist their reporters as stories begin to take shape. **Copy editors** check for errors in the copy, and keep reporters from making embarrassing mistakes in grammar, spelling and word usage. **Managing editors** are responsible for the day-to-day operation of the news organization. The **executive editor** is the top editor, responsible for the entire news organization. The executive editor often is the conscience of the organization. Together the editors protect the integrity and credibility of their news organization's work.

CONTENT EDITING

"Content editor" is the broad term for editors who work with reporters — or producers for Web-based news — to provide content, which includes the stories, photographs, graphics, headlines and photo captions for a print publication, a website or both. Content editors usually have a more specific title that identifies the section of the newspaper for which they work. Most daily newspapers, for example, have a city or metropolitan editor. That content editor has responsibility for stories about the local governments, as well as events and news in the city or metro area.

Sports editors are content editors who oversee reporters covering all types of sports. Some news organizations are big enough to have more than one sports content editor. Large organizations may have a baseball editor, a football editor and a hockey editor. Each is a content editor because each editor produces baseball, football or hockey content for the sports section. Your local newspaper also might have a lifestyle or an arts editor, whose reporters cover leisure pursuits, theater, movies, books and other performing and fine arts.

Your high school newspaper or yearbook can be organized with content editors responsible for different areas of interest to high school students. You may decide you want an editor for academics, one for student life, one for sports, another for arts and so on. If your staff is large enough, you might organize with more specific concentrations. In sports, for example, you could have a crew editor or women's sports editor. Under arts, you might have a music editor and a movies editor. Your staff will need a news editor to handle breaking stories, particularly if you also have a website. The way you organize should reflect the types of stories that are important to your publication or website's coverage.

DEVELOPING CONTENT

Content editors are involved in stories before any words are written. They help reporters determine what the story is, whom they need to talk to, what questions they need to answer and what obstacles they may encounter. In newsrooms where reporters are producing for a website, too, content editors work with reporters to create a **storyboard** — a visual outline of the story. This assures that everyone is clear on all the elements a Web story will have and helps journalists know what equipment is needed for video or audio components.

After content editors talk to their reporters about the story, deadlines, how long the story should be and whether photographers or videographers may be assigned, the content editor informs other editors about the story. Together they consult on which section the story should be published in. Content editors usually attend several daily **news meetings**, gatherings of editors from each department where placement and deadlines of stories are discussed. One

 *What do you think is the value of having frequent news meetings in a newsroom or information center?*

comprehensive news meeting also is attended by the top editors, including the managing editor and the executive editor. At this news meeting all editors share details of the stories their reporters are working on and how each is coming along.

check *point* ✓

> What do content editors do?

Edit Copy

Content editors are the first editors responsible for editing the reporters' stories. They look closely at the writers' words, checking for the five W's and H. They check for clarity, fairness, accuracy and the central point of the story. They also look for errors in grammar, style, spelling and facts. After content editors complete editing a story, they send it to the copy editors, who double-check the grammar, style, spelling and facts. One cliche in the world of journalism is that copy editors are the last line of defense, the final gatekeepers. For the best copy editors, that statement is true and remains uppermost in their minds.

COPY EDITORS

Copy editors are the last gate between the news organization and its readers, viewers or users. They are the quality controllers. They have no vested interest in your story except to make it clear and accurate for readers.

Copy editors usually sit together at desks in the middle of a newsroom, because they need access to reporters and content editors, of whom they ask questions. Copy editors are the editors that other people in the newsroom seek when they need an answer to a grammar or AP style question, because copy editors have a firm grasp of both. Their job involves more than putting commas in the right place or deleting repetitive phrases, however. Copy editors also protect the news outlet's reputation by checking facts in the story, pointing out potentially offensive language, or finding questions a story raises but doesn't answer. Copy editors cut stories to fit the available space. Most also write the headlines and subheads in the body of stories. At many large news organizations, copy editors work with the copy for both the print and online editions. They write separate headlines for print and online sites. For online sites, copy editors use keywords in the headlines that will be picked up by search engines attached to Internet browsers. Copy editors also pull out quotations and photo captions from the copy to go with the visuals in the stories. In some organizations, copy editors lay out pages, too. Copy editors make your story look inviting to readers.

Today, most copy editors make editing changes directly in the copy in the electronic file. Some copy editors may still make editing changes on a printed copy of the story. These copy editors use symbols such as those shown on page 117.

TRAITS OF GOOD COPY EDITORS

You cannot know enough about language if you want to be a copy editor. Studying English grammar, spelling and style is vital. Knowing newspaper style in general, AP style and your own publication's style also is crucial. Many copy editors know a foreign language. They say it helps them understand English even better.

Like doctors, good copy editors say, "First, do no harm." They want to improve copy. They don't want to make changes that would hurt the flow of the story or, worse, edit in a mistake.

The best copy editors know a little about a lot. As one top-notch copy editor puts it, they tend to be "broad but shallow." Copy editors are precise. They have a reverence for rules, and there are plenty of rules in journalism. However, good copy editors try not to fixate on the rules at the expense of the story. Copy editors know grammar and also have an "ear" for language. They can "hear" if a sentence or paragraph isn't doing its job. Common mistakes that copy editors catch are shown on page 118.

Copy Editing Symbols

¶ Is a paragraph mark.	paragraph mark
⌊Start a new paragraph.⌐	new paragraph
⌒This means run in—no new paragraph.	run in
Transpose, words these.	transpose
A circle around (ninety) or other spelled out numbers means use numerals.	use numerals
A circle around a numeral, such as ②, means spell it out.	spell out
Circling a full name, such as (Pennsylvania), means abbreviate.	abbreviate
Circling an abbreviation, such as (PA), means spell out as a full name.	don't abbreviate
Three lines under letters or words, such as u.s., means use uppercase.	uppercase
A slash through a /etter means use lowercase.	lowercase
A wavy line under text means use boldface.	boldface
A straight line under text means use italics.	italics
These marks mean close up the space.	close up space
This mark means insert space.	insert space
The word "stet" means retain the text as originally written.	retain original
A caret means insert word.	insert word
This symbol means to delete.	delete
]These marks mean center.⌊	center
A right bracket means flush right.]	flush right
⌊A left bracket means flush left.	flush left
For example this means insert comma.	insert comma
Its easy to insert an apostrophe.	insert apostrophe
I said, Please insert quotation marks.	insert quotation marks
Insert a period after this sentence⊙ or ⊗	insert period
These are ready made correction symbols.	insert hyphen
To insert a dash do this.	insert dash

© Cengage Learning 2013

COMMON MISTAKES COPY EDITORS CATCH

Subject–verb agreement

Everyone said they wanted to go. ("Everyone" is singular, so the pronoun should be "he or she." But that would make for an awkward sentence. Better to rewrite it.)	Poor subject–verb agreement
They all said they wanted to go.	Good subject–verb agreement

Dangling modifiers

Swimming in the local pool, I saw an alligator. (Who was swimming in the pool? You or the alligator?)	Poor sentence structure
I saw an alligator swimming in the local pool.	Good sentence structure

Personification

The accident happened when a car slammed on its brakes. (This reads as if the car is a person. A car can't do anything without a driver.)	Poor sentence structure
The accident happened when the driver of a car in front slammed on the brakes.	Good sentence structure

When copy editing, it is useful to have a checklist to remind you to look for various items. Some copy editors read through a story several times, each time watching for a different type of error. Following is a sample checklist.

COPY EDITORS' CHECKLIST

- Check copy for correct spelling, grammar, word usage and style.
- Eliminate cliches, redundancies and jargon.
- Tighten sentences by eliminating wordiness.
- Spot "holes" or unanswered questions or inconsistencies.
- Ask questions of reporters and content editors.
- Check facts in the story as time allows.

COPY EDITING FOR THE WEB

Copy editing stories for the websites of news organizations has become increasingly important. In the early stages of website development, copy editors were not part of the process because staffing budgets were not big enough to hire more copy editors, or because no one could figure out where in the process they should work.

When reporters can post a story while at the site of an event directly to a website from a laptop computer, or a blogger can post by using a smartphone directly from an event, copy editing becomes an afterthought. Still, as convergence continues and multimedia reporting becomes more common, copy desks are playing a more active role. Some journalism scholars say copy editors will be at the center of the

Photodisc/Getty Images

 How does copy editing a print story differ from copy editing a story to appear on the Web?

information center in the future, preparing copy for every platform. They will use different standards for preparing Web-based copy because readers read differently on the Web. They move around quickly, and they use a keyboard. They bounce from place to place. Just as you would not try to transfer a print story to a television newscast without change, you cannot transfer print to the Web without change.

check point ✓

What is the role of copy editors?

AP Stylebook Workshop

In April 2010, The Associated Press (or the AP) announced an important change in style rules. No longer would it be correct to write "Web site" (two words), as had been the case since the World Wide Web became part of mainstream language. AP said it was changing the style to "website" (one word, no capitalization). The AP said the change was based on increasingly common usage both in print and online. "Web," however, as shorthand for "World Wide Web," is capitalized, as is "Internet."

Avoid Sexist or Other Offensive Language

There is no room for sexism, racism or other "isms" in news writing. Editors and reporters make every effort to avoid stereotypes in language, as well as in design and photography.

Journalists watch carefully the words they use, because words are powerful. They try to eliminate bias in terms of race, ethnicity, gender, sexual orientation, lifestyle or philosophy, because it is the right thing to do. Writing without gender bias means using the right word and/or sentence structure. Don't say "fireman." It's "firefighter." Don't say "policeman." It's "police officer." A "chairman" can become, simply, "the chair."

Getting rid of "he" and "she" when they unfairly or illogically exclude the opposite sex takes a little more work. Most often the best solution is to change the pronoun to plural.

Don't write   A student who gets into Harvard will find himself surrounded by accomplished peers.

Do write   Students who get into Harvard will find themselves surrounded by accomplished peers.

Journalists should not use race and ethnicity as identifiers when more precise words are more descriptive.

Don't write   Police are looking for a Hispanic man about 5 feet 8 inches tall, 180 pounds, in his 20s.

Do write   Police are looking for a man in his 20s, 5 feet 8 inches tall, about 180 pounds, with light brown skin and dark, wavy hair.

Avoid using words that offend or diminish any group. For example, people who care about the environment should not be referred to as "tree-huggers." A racial or sexual slur should never be repeated unless the act of speaking it, by a prominent person perhaps, results in a news story.

Editors take care to avoid stereotypes in photographs. They show people of different races and ethnic backgrounds in the pages of their publications and on their broadcasts. Photos should not suggest that certain jobs or stations in life are limited. Teachers are not only women; presidential candidates are not only men.

THINK *Critically*

1. Why should news organizations avoid offensive language?
2. What are some ways writers can avoid sexist language?

5.1 | Assessment

Understand Concepts

Determine the best answer for each of the following questions.

1. Which editor is responsible for helping reporters through the process of selecting, researching and writing the stories?
   a. copy editor
   b. managing editor
   c. content editor
   d. executive editor

2. Which is the purpose of news meetings?
   a. To decide on reporters' salaries
   b. To discuss placement and deadlines of stories
   c. To plan the news organization's budget
   d. To copy edit the newspaper and website

3. **True or False**   In order to do their job, copy editors must know English grammar rules, newspaper style and their publication's style.

4. **True or False**   Executive editors are the final editors to check copy for errors.

Write Now!

Practice your writing skills with the following activities.

5. Write a paper that describes the job of high school yearbook editor and its qualifications. Interview one of the editors from your high school yearbook staff to learn more about the specifics of that job and the qualifications needed. Before the interview, write a list of questions to ask. During the interview listen for quotations from the interview to use in your paper. Plan your paper, write a draft and then, after completing your paper, examine it for clarity, engaging language and the correct use of English. Use the copy editing symbols shown on page 117 when editing and proofreading your paper. Along with your final paper, turn in your first draft with the copy editing symbols that show changes.

6. Write a broadcast news story about an event that is suitable for a local television station. Make a storyboard and edit the story using the copy editing symbols shown on page 117. Have someone videotape you while you deliver the story.

5.2 | Coach Reporters

Goals

- Understand what coaching is and what makes a good coach.
- Know how coaching editors work with reporters.

Key Terms

- coaching 122
- coaching editors 122
- culture 124
- Wikipedia 125

Did you ever wonder why the players on a winning pro football or baseball team sometimes douse their coaches with Gatorade or hold the coach aloft for all the fans to see? The players are paying tribute to the person who helped them do their personal best and work as a team. There may be no Gatorade dumping in the offices of news gatherers, but there are plenty of coaches who make the print and digital stories you read, or the newscasts you see or listen to, the very best.

What Is Coaching?

Coaching means guiding and training journalists to do their best work. **Coaching editors** help reporters define the stories even before they begin writing. The coaching editors, or coaches, help writers draft good questions for interviews and discuss what sources are credible. They anticipate and point out any obstacles the writer may encounter while working on the story. Coaching editors typically are assigned to coach specific reporters.

Some news organizations have editors whose only job is to coach. Most, however, leave coaching to the content editors who work with reporters. Coaches focus on the person, not the copy, though coaching is a way to improve the news writing in any organization. Coaches know their individual reporters and they see the big picture, too. Coaches want everyone on their team to feel like a winner while producing the best news product possible.

WHAT MAKES A GOOD COACH?

Content editors who are good coaches get to know their reporters. They make deadlines clear and leave time to edit the story with the reporter. Good coaches do not just fix mistakes without pointing them out to the reporter, but they work with the reporter to make the story better. Going over the changes with reporters helps them understand why the changes were made.

///// **What would be the value of having coaching editors in a school news organization?**

Good coaching helps reporters learn and grow, so their future stories will be stronger.

Coaches read their reporters' stories for accuracy, clarity, structure, information and flow. They respect the writers' words and ideas and make changes only for clarity and accuracy.

UNDERSTAND THE BEAT

Content editors who are good coaches get to know their reporters' beats. They know all the issues and the key players. For example, a city editor at a midsized newspaper might oversee a city hall reporter, a local schools reporter and a police reporter. To coach them well, the city editor needs to understand what issues are important on each beat. For example, the city editor may talk to the city hall reporter about how the paper should cover the city council's proposal to tear down a historic building. Together they will figure out the best sources of information, what audio or visual elements might help tell the story, how long the story will be and what time it is due. The editor will then go through the same process with the schools reporter, who has an early copy of the plan to build a new state-of-the-art high school, and the police reporter, who has new statistics showing the crime rate is down.

Editors on a school newspaper staff can work with reporters in a similar way. If you are the sports editor, for example, you want to know about all your high school teams and their key players so you can talk intelligently with the reporters who cover the teams. If you are the arts editor and your school is producing a musical, you want to know who is cast for the parts and who is directing the play, so you can develop stories with your theater writer.

check point ✓

What is coaching?

How Editors Coach Writers

Editors coach by working with reporters to make stories better. However, sometimes on deadline, editors fix things in stories without talking to the writers. That can lead to resentment or dependence, so good editing coaches prefer to help people fix things themselves. They help their reporters get better by pointing out strengths as well as weaknesses. Good coaching editors have a variety of techniques for helping their reporters and writers become better journalists. Some of these techniques are discussed next.

OFF-DEADLINE TIME

Coaches build trust through genuine, honest and regular contact with the people they coach. The more an editor and reporter work together, the more comfortable they can become.

On a high school newspaper, senior content editors may be responsible for getting younger staff members to produce good stories. Those younger staff members may need direction for reporting and help in focusing their writing. Think of coaching the less experienced staff as peer editing in an English class. Critiques can be honest, but gentle.

Coaches understand the **culture** of the news organization. This refers to the set of attitudes that characterizes the group of journalists. The culture may be supercompetitive, with reporters vying for the best stories and front-page play. The culture also could be laid back, with much banter and compatibility, until it is time to focus on writing. Coaches help reporters fit into the culture. In off-deadline editing sessions, editors and reporters look over the reporters' work carefully. Coaches use the opportunity to build the writers' confidence by praising stories for their strengths and pointing out ways to make the stories better.

Coaches give their least experienced writers the short, focused assignments. They set deadlines to leave time for revision. They help the writers but leave ownership of the story with the writers. They change only what must be changed to make the story better.

////// *Why is it necessary for coaching editors to use off-deadline time to give new reporters feedback on their work?*

COACHING FOR ELECTRONIC MEDIA

Researching on the Internet presents challenges for reporters. Coaches help reporters figure out which Internet sources are reliable and which are not. Some news organizations have developed lists of what they consider reliable Web sources. You may want to make a list of what your school newspaper considers credible. For example, most publications won't accept **Wikipedia** as a source. Wikipedia is an online open-sourced encyclopedia. This means that anyone can change the information, so there is no way to gauge its reliability.

Editors and reporters need to agree on acceptable research sources at the beginning of the story. Coaches ask where the information comes from and whether it is Internet-related. Coaching editors praise reporters for using credible sources and for uncovering new reliable sources.

Coaches also help writers adapt to new platforms. Journalists who have been writing only for print now must write for websites in a shorter, just-the-facts style. Journalists may be asked to write a script to go with video coverage, which requires matching words to the pictures. Coaches point out the differences and take time with their writers to go over stories, scripts or anything else they must do for the Web.

How can coaching editors work with reporters to make them better writers?

5.2 | Assessment

Understand Concepts

Determine the best answer for each of the following questions.

1. Which is not true of good coaching editors?
   a. They get to know their reporters.
   b. They get to know their reporters' beats.
   c. They make changes only for clarity and accuracy.
   d. They limit their comments to fixing reporters' mistakes.

2. Of the following, which would not be considered a reliable source?
   a. redcross.org
   b. usa.gov
   c. Wikipedia
   d. princeton.edu

3. **True or False**   Good coaches edit reporters' stories without explaining the edits to the reporters.

4. **True or False**   Coaching is a way to help reporters do a better job.

Write Now!

Practice your writing skills with the following activities.

5. You are a content editor and a coaching editor for your school newspaper's website. Your assignment is to coach a print news reporter on how to revise stories for the website. Research by studying your local print newspaper and its corresponding website. Notice whether the same photos are used with the stories. Is video added? Are the leads the same or different? Are the remaining paragraphs the same or different? Write a plan for coaching the print reporter. Include information on how to coach, what information will be discussed and when the coaching will take place — a few days before deadline? As soon as you learn about the assignment? On deadline? Write a draft of your plan, and then use copy editing and proofreading symbols to make corrections.

6. Many radio and television talk shows bill themselves as news shows, but the reporting often lacks objectivity. Choose two news shows. Listen to or watch the two shows and then, using a computer and word processing software, write a paper that (1) describes the shows, the topic and the hosts' political opinions; (2) compares and contrasts the content and delivery of the shows; (3) distinguishes between responsible and irresponsible media reporting; and (4) explains your opinion of each host, and then examines your opinion.

Manage a Team

Goals

- Define "team" and explain how to build a team.
- Understand how good team leaders use their skills to direct team members.

Key Terms

- team 127
- bios 128
- team leader 129
- story budget 129
- touchstone 131

FOCUS

Homecoming weekend is full of events and festivities. There is a big game, of course, often with a school rival. A week of spirit-raising events before the game gets everyone interested and invested in homecoming. A parade, which takes place at the game, features floats built by each class. A dance on the night after the game features a hot local band. The homecoming king, queen and court, chosen by students in balloting the previous week, reign at the dance. Homecoming may be just another event to most students, but to student journalists homecoming means multiple stories with many journalists needed to cover everything.

What Is a Team?

When a story has multiple elements that will take more than one reporter to cover, you need a team. A **team** is the group of journalists needed to cover a large event. Team members may include reporters, producers, editors, photographers, videographers and everyone else who plays a part in putting together stories about the event. News teams cover breaking news and non-breaking news, hard news and soft news. They cover stories about political elections and natural disasters and stories about events such as sports events and homecoming at a local university or high school.

Coverage can be planned, roles assigned and an editor or team leader decided without deadline pressure. Teams also can be pulled together quickly when the scope of a news story justifies doing so.

BUILDING A TEAM

Teams need people who have different talents and strengths. The team also needs a goal or purpose. For example, the news team that covers homecoming at your school will need photographers, reporters, videographers, editors and print and Web page designers. The team's purpose is to cover all the events of homecoming, both on the Web in real time and in the print product, which will come out the week after homecoming.

The team leader is the newspaper's news editor, who assigns roles and responsibilities to each person on the team. The news team might look like this:

- The **football reporter** is the game reporter. This person is responsible for two pregame stories to run on the website the week before the big weekend, a Web story on the night of the game and an analysis of the game for the print product.

- The **photographer** takes pictures of football practices to go with the pregame stories and also covers the game. The photographer may put several pictures of the best plays on the website on game night, for which the football reporter writes captions.

- A **researcher**, using your newspaper's archives, puts together a sidebar story and a timeline of the rivalry between the two teams with the scores of all games they've played in the past 10 years.

- A **student life reporter** reports a story on building the floats. The reporter must be good with a video camera to take videos for use on the website. This reporter also covers the parade on the night of the game.

- A **general assignment reporter** covers several stories. First is the voting for homecoming king, queen and court and the announcement of the winners. This reporter also is responsible for short **bios**, or biographical sketches, on each person and collecting photos to be posted on the website and possibly in the newspaper. This reporter also covers school-spirit events such as the day everyone dresses in school colors and the bonfire before the game. The general assignment reporter also writes a preview story about the band that will play at the dance and information about the dance. This story will run in the paper and on the website before the dance, with follow-up stories to run the day after the dance on the website and in the next edition of the paper.

The size of a team varies with the size of the publication and the scope of the story. At smaller publications, one person might be responsible for reporting the stories, taking pictures and video and producing versions for both a print and online publication. One editor might edit the material for the website and print stories, and design both. Whether the team is as small as two people or as large as a major newspaper's Super Bowl team, the key to making it work is good leadership and communication.

check *point* ✓

When is a team needed?

///// *What do you think are the keys to making the team approach work for a high school newspaper?*

Direct the Teams

Team reporting is a terrific way to bring the best journalism to readers and Web users. However, if no one takes charge, the team can fall apart. Teams require a **team leader**, someone who oversees the entire project. The team leader decides what stories need to be written, assigns stories to reporters and decides who is needed on the team for full coverage of the event. The best team leaders are people who are good at juggling a lot of information. They usually are content editors who can think critically and make decisions on deadline. They need leadership and relationship skills in addition to their excellent journalism skills.

THE STORY BUDGET

The key to making a team approach work is good leadership and good communication between all of those with roles to play. Team leaders create a **story budget**, or a list of what stories need to be covered.

The story budget for your homecoming team might look like this:

- **Game strategy** Sports reporter covers practice and looks at coach's strategy for winning the big game. For Web with photos.

- **Pregame lineup** Covers who will start and who will play in the big game. For Web with photos.

- **Sidebar** Timeline on teams' rivalry. For Web and print.

- **Homecoming game** Sports reporter covers game as it happens. For Web immediately and print with photos.

- **Game analysis** Sports reporter talks to coach and players and analyzes the win or loss. For print with photo.

- **Homecoming floats**   Student life reporter looks at each class's float as it comes together, with quotes from students who designed and constructed them. For Web with video, and print with photo.

- **King, queen, court**   Student life reporter writes about the possible king and queen candidates and court members, how many are expected to vote and when and where to vote. For Web only.

- **Court follow up**   Update on who wins king, queen and court. Short bios on each with photos. Bios include the student's name and grade and details such as the student's interests and future plans. For Web and print with photos.

- **Spirit day and bonfire**   Student life reporter and photographer do photo essay. For Web and print (if space allows).

- **Band**   Student life reporter previews the local band playing for homecoming dance. For Web, with photo.

- **Sidebar**   Where to get tickets for the dance, how much they cost and security measures.

- **Dance**   Student life reporter covers dance. For website immediately, with video. For print publication with photos.

As this story budget shows, video and still photography are important to the stories being produced for both the Internet and print publication, so team leaders are quick to bring people with those skills onto the team. Print and website designers, graphic artists and photo editors should be part of the team, too. Designers who are part of the story development process have a better idea of how to effectively use the elements together. Graphic artists may

What skills are needed to be a good team leader?

add charts, graphs or other visuals to present information. Photo editors may be able to help both photographers and videographers prepare for taking the best pictures and video.

PLAY TO STRENGTHS

Editors who head teams know the strengths of each member of their publication's staff. They first assess the mix of skills needed to produce the stories. Then they match people to each story. In the homecoming example, the team needs a sports reporter with experience covering the school's football team. Also needed is a reporter who is good at talking to students about school events. The stories need video and photos, so the team leader looks at who is best at covering these tasks. If one of the reporters is the best videographer, the editor and reporter may decide the reporter can both write the story and take the video.

All team members should understand their own role and the role of others. Clear communication about who is in charge and who makes decisions is important. Your team leader will help resolve conflicts and adjust the plan as more information is learned. The team leader is the **touchstone** for all team members. He or she sets the standard by which the project is judged.

SORT THE MATERIAL

Whether it is event coverage requiring more than a dozen stories reported and written over days or weeks, such as the homecoming story, or a breaking news story where the entire news staff is gathering information for stories to be written on deadline, the editor in charge of the team makes the first decisions on where information goes. With a story budget such as the one for homecoming, the editor has predicted what information will come in and where each story will be placed. A few surprises are likely, however. For example, the star quarterback could get hurt in practice. This would require stories on the injury, the change in lineup for the team, and a profile on the replacement. Still, good planning will pay off in an organized approach to getting all the information onto the newspaper's website and into the print publication by set deadlines.

Breaking news is a different situation. Reporters may call in information, send copy by email over laptops and upload video footage from the scene. Team-leading editors have to see the big picture, and then funnel the smallest pieces of the story to the right writers. The editor in charge will listen critically to what reporters have to say, decide who will write which stories and assign deadlines so that the copy comes in at staggered times. A copy desk can't read every story at once, so story deadlines vary.

check point ✓

How do team leaders use their skills to direct team members?

Reporting World News in a Student News Organization

By Victor Xu, Carmel High School, Carmel, Ind., "Egypt Turmoil Hits Home"

After the outbreak of the demonstrations in Egypt agitating for a new government, senior Crestin Andrews said she was concerned for her relatives in Cairo and other Egyptian cities. Although her relatives did not participate, they still needed to protect themselves during the protests.

"I do know that a lot of them had to stand outside with weapons in an attempt to protect their buildings and families when the police told the citizens to protect themselves early on in the protests," Andrews said.

The protests in Egypt started on Jan. 25 and lasted for less than three weeks, culminating in the resignation of Egyptian President Hosni Mubarak, according to CNN's website. The protests erupted in major cities across the nation, including Cairo and Alexandria, and most famously in Tahrir Square in Cairo. According to Hicham Bou Nassif, a senior graduate student in the Indiana University Department of Islamic Studies, Egyptians are fighting for the end of the political repression, corruption and economic issues under Mubarak's regime.

"It was humiliating to have to listen for years and years that Egypt is not yet ready for democracy," Nassif said. "It is certainly humiliating to… know that you can find yourself in jail just for venting out opinions that happen to be 'politically incorrect.' The accumulation of all these frustrations, over decades, led to the eruption we are witnessing."

Andrews' relatives told her that the country was in chaos, and all the stores, schools and banks had shut down. "I have been told that the sight in Tahrir Square is close to unbelievable," Andrews said. "Millions of people from all different backgrounds are gathered together to stand up for the same cause, and it looks like they are not going to leave until they get what they want."

Despite some instances of violence, Nassif said the Egyptian protests and the government's response to them have been peaceful, and family members in Egypt remain safe. With the resignation of Mubarak and the dismantling of his government, Nassif said he looked forward to a future Egypt in the hands of the people.

"People want freedom and dignity everywhere," he said. "The Tunisians seem to be well on their way toward democracy. I hope the same will be true in Egypt."

THINK *Critically*

1. What makes this story on a world event work for a student newspaper?
2. Assume that this writer was part of a team assigned to write the story for his high school news organization that has a printed newspaper, website and radio station. Rewrite the story as if you were assigned to provide copy for both the website and the radio station based on this print article.

5.3 | Assessment

Understand Concepts

Determine the best answer for each of the following questions.

1. A team is required when
   a. reporters are inexperienced.
   b. the news organization is understaffed.
   c. journalists must travel to another state.
   d. a project has multiple elements.

2. The journalist who oversees the entire project for the team is called a
   a. coaching editor.
   b. editorial coach.
   c. team leader.
   d. content producer.

3. **True or False**   A story budget can help the team see the whole picture.

4. **True or False**   Breaking news stories happen so fast that there usually is no time to pull a team together to cover them.

Write Now!

Practice your writing skills with the following activities.

5. Use the Internet to research Elton Mayo and the Hawthorne Experiments to learn more about the origins of team building. Use at least two reliable sources. After you have finished your research, plan and write a draft of a paper on the history of team building. Use a computer and word processing program to write your paper. Use correct copy editing and proofreading symbols on your draft to edit and correct your paper for clarity, engaging language and the correct use of English.

6. Journalists need to be objective, but often emotions get in the way. Being part of a team can help. For example, as a reporter you are asked to cover a story on animal abuse. As an animal lover you are appalled by the terrible conditions of the animals and have trouble writing an objective story. A member of your team who is in charge of background research learns the owner of the abused animals was taken to the hospital in an ambulance and then moved to a nursing home. Because there were no relatives, no one knew about the animals until neighbors began to complain to authorities about the smell. Think about a story that would be hard for you to write objectively. Now imagine you are a member of a team of journalists working on this story. How might you see the story differently from the other team members? Who on the team might help you? The coaching editor? Researcher? Photographer? How might they help? Write an analysis about how being part of a team helps you see the bigger picture of a story and become a better reporter.

CHAPTER 5 | Assessment

Review Journalism Concepts

5.1 Edit Content and Copy

Reporters and correspondents are the public face of most news organizations. Behind them are editors whose job it is to make their reporters' work accurate and readable. Editors decide what stories to run and how prominently they will be displayed. Editors include content editors, copy editors, managing editors and executive editors. Content editors work with reporters to produce copy for a newspaper or news magazine. Content editors coach, cajole, teach, advise and assist their reporters in producing stories. Copy editors check for errors in the copy. They are the last gate between the news organization and its readers, viewers or users. Managing editors are responsible for the day-to-day operation of the news organization, and executive editors are the top editors over the entire news organization.

5.2 Coach Reporters

Coaching is a way to help journalists do their best work. Coaches, or coaching editors, help reporters define the stories before they begin writing. Coaching editors help reporters draft good questions for interviews and discuss what sources are reliable. They anticipate and point out any obstacles reporters may encounter while working on the story. Coaches get to know their reporters and their reporters' beats. They understand the culture of the news organization and help reporters fit into that culture. They also guide reporters to reliable Internet sites for research. Coaching editors may help reporters write for unfamiliar platforms, such as teaching a print reporter to write for broadcast news or a website.

5.3 Manage a Team

When a story has multiple elements, a team of journalists is required to cover it for print, broadcast and electronic news outlets. Teams are made up of journalists with diverse talents and strengths. Teams may be planned ahead of time for non-breaking news or quickly for breaking news. Teams are led by a team leader, usually a content editor. The team leader oversees the entire project, which includes creating a story budget, or list of stories to cover. He or she then decides what stories to pursue, making assignments to reporters and photographers, and directing the entire effort. Team leaders play to each team member's strengths and set the standards for the project.

Develop Your Journalism Language

Write the letter of the term that matches each definition. Some terms will not be used.

_____ 1. Checks for errors in the copy and keeps reporters from making mistakes in grammar, spelling or word usage

_____ 2. Responsible for day-to-day operation of the news organization

_____ 3. Editor who helps and encourages reporters

_____ 4. Background on a person

_____ 5. Top editor of the news organization

_____ 6. A set of attitudes that characterizes a group of journalists

_____ 7. The person who oversees a project completed by a team

_____ 8. Gathering of editors from each department where placement and deadlines of stories are discussed

_____ 9. Group of journalists needed to cover a large event

_____ 10. Way to help journalists do their best work

_____ 11. Not a reliable Internet source

_____ 12. Standard by which a project is judged

_____ 13. Editors who work with reporters to produce content of all kinds

_____ 14. A list of stories that need to be covered

a. bio
b. coaching
c. coaching editor
d. content editor
e. copy editor
f. culture
g. executive editor
h. managing editor
i. news meeting
j. storyboard
k. story budget
l. team
m. team leader
n. touchstone
o. Wikipedia

15. Which is the public face of a news organization?
   a. managing editor   c. team leader
   b. reporters   d. content editor

16. Which editors would you go to when you have a question about AP style?
   a. content editors   c. copy editors
   b. team leaders   d. managing editors

Think Critically

17. When do news organizations use teams of journalists?

18. Why do news organizations have coaching editors for different beats?

19. How does a news editor decide who is needed on the team?

20. Why do copy editors need to have an "ear" for the English language?

21. How do you think Web reporters would benefit from having copy editors review their stories?

22. As a reporter, why might you prefer working with a coaching editor to working with an editor who does not coach?

23. What type of organization might have a hockey editor, a football editor, a soccer editor, a baseball editor and a basketball editor rather than just a sports editor?

24. How does a story budget help the team leader?

25. Why are news meetings valuable?

26. Why are copy editors needed if content editors also look for errors?

27. Why do copy editors sit at desks in the middle of the newsroom?

28. Why do copy editors use different standards for preparing website copy than for print publications?

29. How do reporters benefit from having coaching editors work with them to define the stories before starting the research or writing?

30. Why do news organizations put senior editors in charge of younger staff reporters?

31. Why do news organizations avoid using Wikipedia, the online encyclopedia, as a research source?

Make Academic Connections

32. **COMMUNICATION** Editing can enhance a story or change its meaning. To demonstrate this, photocopy or download two copies of a news story. Using copy editing symbols, edit one copy of the story to change the story's meaning. Use your computer to create an edited version of the story. Do the same with the second version, but be careful to avoid changing the meaning of the story. Next, using examples from the stories you just edited, write a paper that addresses the following: (1) how editing can change the meaning of a story; (2) why it is important for editors to be careful not to change the meaning of a story; and (3) why it is important for editors and reporters to work together closely to retain the integrity of the story.

33. **COMPUTER SCIENCE** You are the team leader for a large national news organization. Choose a major national or international news story. Use a computer to create a spreadsheet that shows (1) the story budget; (2) a list of team members; and (3) the type of stories each team member will cover for both print and the Web.

34. **LANGUAGE ARTS** Choose an international news organization. If English is your second language, choose a news organization that publishes stories in your native language. Write a critique of the organization's website. Explain what you do and do not like. Ask yourself the following questions: How well do the elements on the home page work together? Do the leads pull you into the stories? What type of lead is used for each story, and how do the leads pull you in? Which news elements are used? Are the stories well written? Is there a video? If so, is it well done? What changes, if any, would you make? Why would you make these changes? Include in your critique what type of team members were used for the main stories (for example, reporters, researchers, photographers, videographers, Web designers, copy editors, content editors). Would you have used the same team members? Why or why not? Who might you add or subtract? Download a copy of the home page and attach it to your critique.

35. **WRITING**   Write a paper that addresses the following questions: Why is the team approach popular with large news organizations? Does the team approach work with smaller news organizations? Does the team approach work with student publications? What are the advantages and disadvantages of the team approach? Before beginning your paper, plan it, write a draft and then, after completing the writing, carefully edit and proofread your paper using copy editing and proofreading symbols. Before turning in your paper, make sure you have checked it for clarity, engaging language, and the correct use of the conventions and mechanics of written English. Attach your draft, with the edits shown in copy editing and proofreading symbols.

36. **SPEECH**   Choose a news story from your high school. This may be about an event or about someone's accomplishment. Use a computer to write a broadcast news story appropriate for your high school. Deliver the newscast to your class using electronic broadcast equipment, if possible.

37. **RESEARCH**   Choose a major story from a news magazine. Analyze how many people you think are part of the team. Use the knowledge you gained about teams in this chapter and study the magazine's masthead, the bylines of stories and the credit line on the photos and other visuals. Also remember to include all the editors who are most likely involved. Make a list of the team members and describe what each member may have been responsible for.

38. **TEAM BUILDING**   Practice your coaching skills by working with another student. Exchange a news story you have written for this class. First edit the story using copy editing and proofreading symbols, and then take turns coaching each other about ways the story could be improved.

Writing Portfolio Activity

39. From a national newspaper, choose a major news story. Plan the team members and the story budget to cover the story for your high school newspaper, website and broadcast radio and television stations. Be sure to add a local angle and use language that is appropriate for your audience.

AP Stylebook Workshop

Using copy editing symbols, edit the following sentence to make it conform to AP style.

40. The school's web site is up and running on the web.

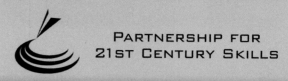
FLEXIBILITY AND ADAPTABILITY: Ace the Job Interview

Your cover letter and resume landed you a job interview. The interview is your time to shine, to let the interviewer know you are qualified for the job and want to work with the organization. It is a time to show you can be flexible and adaptable, needed abilities in today's fast-paced world. It also is a time for you to ask questions.

The job interview is a face-to-face meeting between you and your prospective employer. If you are interviewing for a job in journalism at a large organization, you may be interviewed first by someone from the human resources department. Eventually, you will be interviewed by the editor of the paper or magazine or the producer of the website.

During an interview you will want to show that you

- Have prepared for the interview
- Are self-assured
- Communicate effectively

PREPARE FOR THE INTERVIEW

To prepare, research the news organization. Read its print and electronic news and listen to its broadcast news. Know its style. Read about its corporate culture and ask yourself how well you would fit in. Be prepared to tell the interviewer how you would add value to the organization. Use words that fit the organization's corporate culture. Make a list of questions you have about the organization. These should not be questions that are easily answered by research.

Pack the materials you will need: copies of your resume and references; samples of your writing, photography, videography or design; your Social Security number; and copies of correspondence between you and the prospective employer. Also pack a pen and paper to take notes. Double-check the address, where you are to meet, the name of the person you are to contact, the phone number and the time of the meeting.

Your grooming and dress also influence the interviewer, so dress neatly and professionally. Make sure everything is clean and in good condition.

SHOW SELF-ASSURANCE

Be self-assured and confident without being boastful. You want the interviewer to know you are able to think quickly, adapt to situations readily and navigate complex situations. Let the interviewer know that you are able to cover stories alone but that you also work well on a team.

COMMUNICATE EFFECTIVELY

Journalists must have good communication skills. Demonstrate your ability to listen well by paying attention to what the interviewer is saying. Make eye contact with the interviewer and stay focused. Express your thoughts clearly and succinctly when you answer the interviewer's questions. Demonstrate you care about this interview by turning off your cellphone before you enter the interview room.

THINK *Critically*

Use the Internet to research a news organization you might like to work for. Make a list of questions you could ask in an interview.

REAL PEOPLE REAL CAREERS

Carol Stevens | A Top Editor with Responsibility to Readers

Carol Stevens, a veteran reporter and editor who now is director of media relations at the American Bar Association, asks a lot of questions. The difference is, she asks questions of her reporters instead of news sources. As the managing editor of the News section at USA Today, she was responsible for the accuracy of every story published every day. Nothing was more important to her than knowing that everything was correct, that the staff was talking to qualified experts and that the reporters followed the newspaper's policies on sourcing.

USA Today tries not to use unnamed sources in reporting news stories. If a reporter cannot tell the story without using an unnamed source, the story must be approved by top editors. Before she would sign off on use of a confidential source, Stevens would have a conversation with the reporter. She needed to know the name of the source and be convinced of why they were in a position to know what they were telling the paper.

Photo courtesy of Carol Stevens

IMPORTANCE OF SOURCE ATTRIBUTION

In Washington, D.C., press briefings by government agency officials are given only with the agreement that reporters will not name the spokesperson. USA Today reporters routinely protest this policy and ask that the briefings be on-the-record. Stevens says the goal is to be transparent about whom reporters are talking to. "It's too easy for reporters to write, 'Experts say….' [USA Today is] insisting they back it up. Facts must be attributed unless they are widely known." Also, Stevens says she would not let an unnamed source, no matter how high level, "be disparaging or speculative or self-serving. Why should you have to defend yourself from accusations by someone who won't put his name to the remark?"

Of course, USA Today editors keep other ethical concerns such as fairness and objectivity in mind, too. But the newspaper's practices on use of sources set it apart. Stevens says it's what news consumers want. "The audience is demanding," she says. "They see the work as a product and they want to know where information comes from."

Source: Personal interview with Carol Stevens.

THINK *Critically*

1. Why does USA Today want to name the sources of its stories?
2. In what circumstances would USA Today use unnamed sources?

6

Interviewing

6.1	**Choose Sources**
6.2	**Develop Questions**
6.3	**Conduct the Interview**

Celebrity Interviews

Interviewing a celebrity like John Travolta may seem easy, but before the interview, as the reporter, you must put in hours and hours of research. First, there are movies to watch. In Travolta's case that would be hits like "Hairspray," "Saturday Night Fever," "Pulp Fiction" and "Grease." There are articles to read, too. Travolta has been profiled in publications such as People, Entertainment Weekly, Vanity Fair and GQ. The good news is, those stories make it clear that Travolta is a good interview subject. He doesn't shy away from questions.

Neither do the friends and family of Travolta you talk to about him. Siblings say he's always been generous; friends say he's always enjoyed life. Soon an outline begins to take shape. You want to ask questions about Travolta's career, of course, and his latest movie. But you also want to touch on his family — both the one he grew up in, as the sixth and youngest child of Italian- and Irish-American parents, and the one he and wife Kelly Preston share.

On the interview day, you are prepared with file folders of relevant clips, notebooks and voice recorder. Travolta is delighted that you have prepared so well and, asked where he'd like to start, he decides to begin with family, and the interview begins.

> **THINK** *Critically*
> 1. How do you begin research on a personality you will interview?
> 2. Why do you talk to people who know the subject of your interview?

Choose Sources

Goals

- Understand the importance of interviewing and how to choose the right sources.
- Define the three types of unnamed sources and explain how to treat information from unnamed sources.

Key Terms

- interviewing 141
- deadline 142
- primary source 143
- quotation 143
- secondary source 145
- unnamed source 145
- off the record 145
- on background 146
- confidential source 146

FOCUS

When you read a news story online or in print, you may not pay close attention to the names of the people who are quoted. That's not surprising. It is the information you are most interested in, not the sources — the people who supply the information. However, to journalists the names of the sources are very important, because the quality and credibility of the information are determined by the source. Journalists want sources who know what they are talking about and who can be trusted to have the information needed for the stories they are writing. They want sources willing to be named because that shows credibility. Journalists want to have a conversation with their sources that ultimately will make the topic understandable to the reader.

Interview Sources

Even in today's fast-paced world of email, Twitter and texting, picking up the phone or going out and talking to people face to face is important. When you meet your source eye to eye and have the give-and-take of a conversation, you find yourself asking follow-up questions that provide more specifics, or a detailed account of an event witnessed by the source.

Interviewing — asking questions of knowledgeable people — is important because it leads reporters to a complete and true story. Interviewing remains the most useful technique for gathering accurate information for both news and feature stories. Think of it this way: Anytime you ask someone a question, you are interviewing.

No matter where they work, journalists around the world head to their computer every day not knowing whom they are going to interview and what questions they will ask the people they interview. Some reporters will talk to prime ministers and presidents. Reporters want to ask the world leaders questions on topics that make news. They particularly want to ask questions that get the leaders' answer on an important point or policy.

Other journalists talk to families who have lost a loved one in a natural disaster such as a tornado, or in a preventable disaster like a fire or a car accident. These journalists want to ask questions that are sensitive but evocative. They want to give the families a chance to say some final, meaningful words about their loss. At the same time the reporters want to tell a dramatic story about how life can change in a minute.

Still other reporters talk to business leaders about the health of their companies. The companies' well-being may be tied tightly to the state of the local economy. These journalists ask precise, specific questions about the companies' stability. An unhealthy company may mean a loss of area jobs.

In all these situations, journalists must do their homework. They must research the world leaders' politics and policies, the impact a disaster has on homes and families or a company's financial status. In their research, reporters seek the input of experts, editors, colleagues and readers to develop a list of thoughtful questions. They also interview as many people as possible in the time they have before **deadline**, the time their story is due. Interviews add information, detail and insight to stories. Interviewing is the core of most stories.

There are two types of sources reporters turn to for interviews — primary sources and secondary sources. Primary sources are the most important and the first people interviewed. Secondary sources also are helpful but have less direct involvement in the situation.

////// *What kinds of questions do reporters want to ask of government and world leaders?*

PRIMARY SOURCES

Primary sources are the people who can give you, the reporter, the most thorough or best information because they are the investigators, the witnesses or the people who are affected by the event. If circumstances and deadlines allow it, journalists try to get face-to-face interviews with primary sources because the reporters are likely to get more information in person than if they conduct the interview by telephone.

You ask good and relevant questions so you can use **quotations**, or quotes, in your story. Quotations are words a source says during an interview. When you quote a source, you repeat or copy the exact words spoken or written by the source, and you give the person credit. Quotations allow reporters to stand back and let the subject talk directly to the reader. Great quotations can turn what may seem like a boring story into colorful, interesting reading. Quotations give stories character. It is compelling to read the words of someone affected by an event. Using the words of the people you interview helps you explain things clearly and adds color — description, humor, insight or fun — to your story. Good quotations bring stories to life. Notice in the examples below how the good example is much more colorful than the poor example.

> Jesse Arbitron, a tornado survivor, said, "The funnel cloud looked like a dark, swirling triangle and sounded like a loud train approaching. We ran for the basement and huddled in a corner, afraid we would die."

Good example

> The dark funnel cloud sounded like a train, and frightened families took shelter in basements.

Poor example

Before you rush out the newsroom door or pick up the phone to interview someone, figure out what you need to know and then who has the information. If you are assigned to write a story about cutbacks in the extracurricular programs at your school, where would you begin?

- **Make a list of people involved.** The school principal, advisers to the programs that will be cut and students who participate in those programs.

- **Make contact with each of those sources.** Call the offices of the principal or advisers, or talk to students personally to set up times to discuss the story.

- **Research the reason for the cutbacks.** Use the Internet to find any stories that may have been published in the local newspaper about reduced funding for extracurricular programs at your school. Search for stories that discuss any history of cutbacks in these programs.

- **Get copies of pertinent documents.** Did the decision to cut back extracurricular programs come as the result of a study? Get a copy of the study. Get a copy of the school district's budget so you can compare spending on extracurricular programs with spending in other areas.

- **Prepare your questions.** Did the principal decide which extracurricular programs would be cut back at your school? Who else was involved in the decision? Why were the particular programs chosen? How many students are affected? What will students do with the time they spent in extracurricular programs? Were students consulted on the cutbacks? Will the loss of any of the programs affect whether students will be able to get into colleges?

Always interview people who are directly involved with the topic of the story. Here are some examples of stories and the types of people you might consider interviewing for them:

- **Stories about academic achievements**   Students who have special achievements or have won scholarships; teachers involved in any outstanding achievements; administrators; people who awarded scholarships

- **Stories about sports events**   Coaches, referees, players, cheerleaders, spectators

- **Stories about the arts**   Art teachers; students who excel in the arts; students who act in the plays or write or edit for the newspaper or yearbook; students who have artwork displayed in your school

- **Stories about the financial state of your school**   Administrators; members of the board of education; people who work in local government;

///// *If you were writing a story about the financial state of your school, whom could you interview?*

people in the community who pay property taxes; and administrators in neighborhood schools (to learn about their budgets)

SECONDARY SOURCES

Secondary sources are people who have information relevant to your story but are not officials, eyewitnesses or directly affected by the event. Even after they've completed interviews with primary sources, good journalists continue to think about other details they need and who can provide those details. In the case of the story about cutbacks in extracurricular programs, there are several further possibilities for the story and further interviews you may choose to do. An Internet search may turn up studies linking participation in extracurricular activities with good grades, so you may choose to interview college admissions directors at local or state universities about the importance of extracurricular activities when they evaluate applicants.

Here are some examples of stories you might do where secondary sources would contribute:

- **Stories about scholastic achievements** College or other guidance counselors; previous scholarship winners

- **Stories about athletic events** Local businesses or organizations that support school teams; police who manage traffic and crowds

- **Stories about the financial state of your school** Parents who pay "extra" fees; students who are affected by reductions in programs

*check*point ✓

Why is interviewing so important to stories?

Unnamed Sources

Unnamed sources are people who ask that their names not be used and, sometimes, that the information they give reporters not be used. Three types of unnamed sources that reporters turn to are those who want to speak off the record, those who want to speak on background, and those who want to speak confidentially. In every case, reporters want to know that the source asking for secrecy is credible. Reporters must know whether their sources are government officials, eyewitnesses to an event, or people who other-wise have access to reliable information — and how they have access to that information.

OFF THE RECORD

Off the record means that the information you are given by the source is not written down in your notebook or recorded. In fact, the source probably will ask that the recorder be turned off. It is as if the information were not shared at all. You may use the information to help you develop better questions for other sources who will be named. However, journalists are expected not to use off-the-record information in a story in any way unless they get it from another credible source on the record.

ON BACKGROUND

On background means you may use the information but must not attribute it to the source. White House and other high-level government officials often do business this way, even conducting official "background briefings" with multiple reporters and giving them the information they need, but insisting that the information be attributed in any story to a generic "administration" or "high-level" source.

CONFIDENTIAL

Confidential sources are those who want to remain anonymous, often because they fear reprisals from authorities who may not want the information out. Confidential sources provide information that reporters may use, but without being obvious about where it came from. Usually the journalist and the source agree that the source's name will not be revealed. Reporters usually discuss confidentiality agreements with their editors before agreeing to keep sources secret.

News organizations have become increasingly wary of using unnamed sources, and many have set up guidelines about their use. Journalists argue that some leeway in using anonymous sources is needed to get important stories. They say certain government officials would not give reporters any information at all if the information had to be attributed to them. Most publications now have specific guidelines for using confidential sources. The Associated Press Statement of News Values and Principles says AP journalists will strive to name all sources, "shielding them only when they insist upon it and they provide vital information."

///// **Why should news organizations be cautious about using unnamed sources?**

© Mlenny/iStockphoto.com

Your high school publication and other newsgathering operations such as your school website or television or radio station should develop a policy on anonymous sourcing. Be sure everyone who works for the organization understands the policy.

Policies notwithstanding, all reporters should ask themselves a number of questions before they consider granting anonymity, among them:

- Can I get this information elsewhere on the record?

- Why is this source unwilling to put a name on this information? Does the source have an interest or bias?

- Can I verify this information?

- If the truth is called into question, can the source be revealed?

*check*point

Define unnamed sources, and list and explain the three types of unnamed sources.

AP Stylebook Concepts

In written works, you will often see long quotations set off by wider margins. In this case, quotation marks are not used.

This is not done in AP style. Newspapers and news magazines usually do not have room for lengthy quotations. In AP style, quotations are run in with the text, and quotation marks are put around the source's exact words. Quotations may be one or more sentences or part of a sentence. Rarely put quotation marks around just one word even if that is the exact word used by the source.

Correct
"School will be dismissed early," Principal John Jones said.
Because of the hot weather, "school will be dismissed early," Principal John Jones said.

Incorrect
Because of the "hot" weather, school will be dismissed early, Principal John Jones said.

Recording Telephone Conversations

Recording your interviews with sources may seem like a good idea. After all, it is a useful way to be sure that you quote your sources accurately and that you understand the information they are sharing. Be careful, though. The recording could be illegal.

Different states have different laws about recording telephone and in-person conversations, so you need to know the law in the state in which you are recording. If you are recording a telephone call to someone in another state, you should know that state's law, too. If it came down to a court case, the person bringing suit could file in whichever jurisdiction better suited the case. That means the person you interviewed could file suit against you in the state in which you conducted the interview or in the state in which the source was at the time of the interview.

In 38 states and the District of Columbia, it is legal for anyone — not just journalists — to record conversations in which they are involved without informing the person or people with whom they are talking. Those are "one-party consent" states.

In the other 12 states, everyone involved in the conversation must be aware of the recording and agree to it. These are often referred to as "two-party consent" states, but note that they apply when more than two people are involved as well.

In all states, it is illegal to record conversations that you aren't involved in, don't have permission to record and could not naturally overhear. To avoid trouble, tell your interview subjects that you would like to record them and ask them to agree. Get that agreement on the recording.

To check the law in your state, go to the Reporters Committee for Freedom of the Press website at www.rcfp.org.

THINK *Critically*

1. What is the best way to avoid trouble if you want to record an interview?

2. Do you think all states should have the same laws when it comes to recording two-party conversations? Why or why not?

6.1 | Assessment

Understand Concepts

Determine the best answer for each of the following questions.

1. Which sources do reporters try to interview first?
   a. off-the-record sources
   b. secondary sources
   c. unnamed sources
   d. primary sources

2. Which term means that journalists may use the information the source provides but may not attribute it to the source?
   a. primary source
   b. on background
   c. off the record
   d. secondary source

3. **True or False** Primary sources are the people who can give the reporter the most thorough or best information because they are the investigators, witnesses or the people who are affected by the event.

4. **True or False** Interviewing secondary sources often can lead to new stories.

Write Now!

Practice your writing skills with the following activities.

5. Use a computer and computer software to write a paper that addresses the following questions: Is it unethical to use the name of a source who asked to stay off the record? Why or why not? Are there any circumstances where you could reveal the source's name and still be ethical? What are these circumstances? Would you reveal your source if a court declared you would go to jail if you did not reveal your source? Revise and edit your paper using copy editing symbols. Make sure you have carefully examined your paper for clarity, engaging language, and the correct use of English. Turn in your draft with copy editing symbols and your final paper.

6. Choose three articles from your school newspaper or magazine that use primary, secondary or unnamed sources. Highlight or underline the places in the article where the sources are used, and then in the column identify the type of source. Write a report on what types of sources were used, and how you identified each source. Explain what you might have done differently.

7. On the Internet, go to the website of the Reporters Committee for Freedom of the Press. Search the site for the laws in your state on recording interviews and hidden-camera laws. Write a fact sheet that explains the laws in your state.

6.2

Develop Questions

Goals

- Prepare effective interview questions.
- Know how to ask the right questions.

Key Terms

- anecdote 151
- open-ended question 152

FOCUS

In the cramped quarters of the West Wing, dozens of White House reporters are bent over laptops while talking on cellphones to their sources or their editors. They are hurriedly preparing for an upcoming press briefing with the White House press secretary. They know the press secretary will want to stay on the announced topic (the visit of a foreign dignitary), but the reporters have other topics in mind. They are trying to craft questions that are specific and interesting, that will get the press secretary "off topic," and get answers for stories on health care, immigration or other policies.

Prepare Interview Questions

An interview is all about the questions. Good ones are specific and get the subject to open up. To ask good questions, you have to be prepared. Whether you are getting ready to interview a local police chief or a United States president, you will get the best responses when you do your homework. No journalist would go into the Oval Office of the White House without being capable of discussing all major issues of the day.

Many journalists, even the most experienced, consider practicing their questions to be part of their preparation. After they write their questions, they say them aloud. They want to be sure they are clear and get to the point quickly. Preparing for every interview as thoroughly as possible is the hallmark of a good reporter.

PREPARATION

Before you can prepare your questions for an interview, you need to determine the goals you want to reach in your interview. What kind of information do you need from your subject? Is the information you need strictly factual or do you want reaction and emotion too?

You also need to learn about the background of the topic and the sources. Check the Internet for previous articles on your subject and topic. Gather any information you can from other sources, such as court documents and police or fire department reports. Read the information thoroughly so you can have an informed discussion.

PRACTICE

If you have time, practice your questions on other people. Saying them aloud will help you decide whether some questions are too long and should be shortened, whether the questions are clear, and whether they offer the subject a chance to open up. You want sources to answer with more than "yes" or "no." You could practice the questions on your editor or another reporter, who may help you make the questions more concise or sharper. If a colleague isn't available, try practicing the questions on a friend or family member. If all else fails, practice alone. You will be more at ease as you conduct your interview if you have said aloud the questions you want to ask at least once. You also will sound more polished and professional.

CHECKLIST FOR PREPARING FOR AN INTERVIEW

√	Determine the goals you want to reach in your interview.
√	Research the background of the topic.
√	Research the background of the subject.
√	After you write your questions, practice them by saying them aloud.
√	Make sure questions require more than a "yes" or "no" answer.
√	Practice questions on your editor, another reporter, or a friend or family member.

How do you prepare questions for an interview?

Ask the Right Questions

What's the right question? That's a good question. The answer is different for every story you write or subject you interview. The specifics vary, and your goal should be to get the kind of information that will make your story accurate and memorable. To do that, you want to ask questions that get your subject to give you quotations that provide depth, insight and sometimes even humor to the story.

You also will want to collect **anecdotes** that might help you make your interview more revealing. Anecdotes are short personal stories about an event or occurrence. Sometimes an anecdote is about a childhood memory.

Pronouns are words used in place of a noun. The singular subject pronouns are I, you, he, she and it. Pronouns also can be plural. The plural subject pronouns are we, you and they. Like nouns, pronouns must agree with the verb. If the pronoun is singular, the verb must be singular. For example, in the sentence, "She is an outstanding reporter," the singular pronoun she uses the singular verb is.

If the subject is plural, the verb must be plural. For example, in the sentence "They are outstanding reporters," the plural pronoun they uses the plural verb are.

Baseball players, for example, might tell an anecdote about the first time they picked up a bat and ball. Anecdotes help the subject's story become more real. Journalists strive to ask questions that allow their interview subjects to tell good anecdotal stories about themselves. The more you know about the people you interview, the easier it will be to get them to tell you anecdotes.

BE READY

Reporters have different ideas about how to ask the questions they develop to get the best possible quotations and anecdotes. All reporters and interview subjects are different, so there are different ways of asking questions. The following general guidelines will help you when preparing a list of questions for your story:

- Do save your toughest questions for last. You will get more honest answers after you have established a good relationship with your subject.

- Don't ask questions that can be answered in one word such as "Yes," "No," "Great" or "Awesome."

- Do ask **open-ended questions**, ones that allow the subject to talk, such as "What do you mean?" or "Can you give me an example?"

- Do be prepared with a long list of questions, but don't think those are the only ones to ask. Go with the flow. If you think of a question during the interview, it is probably a good question to ask even if it is not on your list.

- Do look around. Ask questions about what you see. If you are in an office where there are family photos, ask about them. If you in a home where there is a collection of modern art, ask about it.

What is a reporter's goal when asking questions in an interview?

- Do ask the subject to slow down if need be so you can take better notes.

- Do ask, "Did I miss anything?" or "Is there something you might like to add?"

- Do listen carefully.

TAKE GOOD NOTES

Print and Web reporters need to take notes during interviews. Taking notes during an in-person interview is one of the hardest tasks for a journalist to master. You want to maintain eye contact and show interest in your subject and the topic, but at the same time you are trying to write what is being said in your notebook and keeping track of the questions you want to ask. Many journalists use a voice recorder for in-person interviews because it allows reporters more freedom to interact with the subject and concentrate on questioning. However, some reporters find a recorder makes a source nervous and limits open conversation. Still, reporters usually use a recorder to be safe.

Even with a recorder, reporters still take careful notes because almost every reporter has a disaster story to tell about recorders that have been lost or malfunctioned. In addition to taking notes on what the subject says, reporters make notes on what they observe — details of the office or home they are in and the subject's dress or mannerisms, for example.

Technology, such as audio and video recorders, is increasingly important for multimedia reporting because journalists may be supplying podcasts or audio for slide and video presentations to their news organization's website.

CHECKLIST FOR TAKING NOTES IN AN INTERVIEW

√	Have the recorder ready to start taping; don't fuss with it during the interview.
√	Have your notebook and pen in hand.
√	Sit across from your subject.
√	Maintain eye contact by looking up from your notebook often.
√	Ask your subject to slow down if need be so you can get accurate quotes.
√	Make notes on the environment and your observations.

check point ✓

Why do you need to ask the right questions in an interview?

6.2 | Assessment

Understand Concepts

Determine the best answer for each of the following questions.

1. Good _____ bring stories alive.
   - **a.** unnamed sources
   - **b.** convergence
   - **c.** anecdotes
   - **d.** gatekeepers

2. Which does the smart reporter use when interviewing sources?
   - **a.** open-ended questions
   - **b.** anecdotes
   - **c.** quotations
   - **d.** off-the-record information

3. You want to maintain eye contact and show interest in your interview subject and at the same time _____.
   - **a.** tell good stories
   - **b.** explain you're a new reporter
   - **c.** take good notes
   - **d.** take photos

4. **True or False** Anecdotes help make a story about a personality more interesting.

5. **True or False** Saying your questions aloud before the interview will be helpful.

6. **True or False** In an interview, always ask the toughest questions first.

Write Now!

Practice your writing skills with the following activities.

7. You have been assigned to interview a student who was awarded a full college scholarship for your high school magazine. Prepare, and then practice, your list of questions for an in-depth interview.

8. Choose a news story from a newspaper, news magazine or Internet news site about a celebrity or other well-known personality. Use online sources to obtain background information on the subject. Read past interviews and current stories about the subject's work. From your research, choose an angle you would use to write a story about this person. For example, you might write about the person's involvement in a charity, the person's body of work, about an award recently won or an honor recently granted, or about something the person recently did that helps the world. Write a list of questions you would want to ask this subject in an interview. Find the answers to your questions in your research material, and then write a draft of a news story for a news magazine that would be appropriate for an adult audience. Use copy editing symbols to edit your draft. Rewrite the copy, editing your story to make sure you have written it in the proper journalistic style.

Conduct the Interview

Goals

- Describe three types of interviews and how to conduct them.
- Prepare to write the story using information from the interview.

Key Terms

- phoner 157
- feature 159
- Q-and-A (question and answer) 159
- read-back 160

FOCUS

TV personalities like Katie Couric and Oprah Winfrey have built reputations and multimillion-dollar incomes on their interviewing skills. Couric, a longtime news correspondent and anchor, often is seen with her interview subjects in a sit-down exchange during which she refers to notes in her lap. She appears prepared, her research all done. Winfrey doesn't use notes, but talks to her subjects in a conversational way, sometimes missing the obvious question. Viewers don't mind. They tuned in to see Winfrey as much as or more than the personality she will interview. Couric and Winfrey have different styles because they are different personalities. No two journalists conduct interviews in exactly the same way because no two journalists have the same style and personality. All journalists eventually develop an interview style that works for them.

Types of Interviews

Are you nervous about interviewing someone you don't know? That's natural. All journalists have been nervous before an interview at some time in their careers. Some journalists with years of experience still get nervous, particularly if they have to ask tough questions.

Remember that most people want to talk with you. They are eager to share their thinking, their knowledge and their skills. They would rather have the opportunity to answer tough questions than not be asked. If you are writing a personality profile, all the better. People love to talk about themselves.

Interviews can be conducted in person or with a video Internet application such as Skype, over the telephone or by email. Although many of the same rules for interviewing apply, each method is a little different.

IN-PERSON INTERVIEWS

In-person interviews are those where you go to the source's home or place of business, meet the source somewhere, or use a video Internet application. These are face-to-face interviews. Here are some interviewing tips used by experienced journalists. They may ease your nerves before the interview:

- Dress appropriately. If you are going to interview the mayor, you need to wear business clothes. If you are interviewing prize winners at the county fair, jeans are fine. You will feel more comfortable if you feel like you fit in with the environment.

- Start with a smile, a handshake and a thank-you for the appointment. People appreciate it when you acknowledge that they are giving you their time. Is it ever appropriate not to smile when meeting a source? Yes, if talking to the source about a serious or tragic subject, a smile may not be appropriate.

- Treat your time together as a business meeting. Arrive with the tools you need. Have your notebook, a pen, a tape recorder and your list of questions ready to go. Even if your meeting takes place outside an office, your tools and a polite, professional manner will signal that you are serious.

- Take notes, but make eye contact and show that you are listening carefully. Follow up on any new information you hear, even if it isn't on your question list. Your conversation will flow.

- Don't make a long speech when you ask a question. Put it simply. Be inquisitive, but neutral. Sometimes people are passionate about their cause or position. It's not your job to agree or disagree.

- Remember the basics. Ask your subject to confirm name spelling, age, college degrees and anything else that is relevant. Some reporters like to use those basic questions to start an interview. Others like to close with them.

- When you are finished, thank your interview subject again. Let him or her know that you will call back if you need more information, you need to check a fact, or an editor has further questions.

- After the interview, call to thank everyone involved in setting up your meeting. It's good manners, and you may need help again.

The best thing about an in-person interview is that you can observe the subject's home or office, appearance and

///// *What is an advantage in conducting an in-person interview?*

reaction to your questions. Ask questions and take notes on the things you observe. Family photos, collections, travel memorabilia or interesting books all can be topics of conversation and could lead to a telling anecdote. Notice your subject's demeanor. Is she nervously tapping her fingers? Does he become animated when talking about his children? These may be ideas you use in your story. They help describe the person you are interviewing.

Interviewing over the Internet, which allows you to see the subject on your computer screen, may give you the feel of an in-person interview and more insight into the subject's environment and personal traits, but it limits your observation opportunities.

TELEPHONE INTERVIEWS

Unfortunately, not every interview is done in person. In fact, most news-related interviews are done by telephone. These interviews are commonly called **phoners**. Journalists often are on a tight deadline and cannot take the time to travel to meet every source. The telephone saves time. Also, telephone interviewing allows reporters to use sources all over the world.

Conducting a telephone interview can be a little more difficult than the in-person interview. You need to keep your subject focused on your conversation, but you don't have the advantage of eye contact and body language. You can't see if he is distracted by email on a computer screen or an assistant signaling that he has another call.

Here are a few tips for conducting a phone interview:

- Use a friendly, upbeat voice. For example, "Hello, Coach Johnson. This is Stephen Noble from The Eagle. I'm calling to talk to you about the new physical education policy you have recommended to the principal."

© Photodisc/Jupiter Images

////// *Why is conducting a telephone interview more difficult than an in-person interview?*

- Ask your subjects where they are and whether it's a good place and time to talk. Cellphones have made it possible for business to be conducted in the aisles of grocery stores, on the corners of busy city streets, even at airport gates. These are not the best environments for good interviews. You don't want your interview subjects discussing important topics such as school policy while their thoughts are elsewhere. If your subjects are not in an office, home or other quiet environment, and your deadline allows for it, suggest that you call back when they will not be distracted.

- Once you are ready to begin, thank your subjects for their time. It signals that you are ready to ask questions. Listen carefully and respond appropriately. A well-placed "I see" or "Really?" or "Tell me more" will keep a connection between you and your subjects.

- When you have finished asking questions, ask if there is anything your sources would like to add. It signals the end of the interview and shows sources you remain interested in their opinion.

EMAIL INTERVIEWS

Using email to conduct interviews is becoming an increasingly useful option in a world where tracking down sources in person or by telephone is not feasible for 24/7 news organizations. While some journalists depend on email contact and use it regularly to conduct interviews, others have resisted using email to ask their questions of sources and will use it only when no other way will do.

Reporters who don't like to conduct interviews by email say that people interviewed by email have time to consider their response, to craft it carefully or vaguely, or to seek the help of others in answering questions. Reporters argue that they lose the tone of the interview or the openness of responses. Many newspapers now have policies requiring reporters to specify whether an interview was conducted by email. For example, "Our students need to get more exercise," gym teacher Philip Johnson said in an email.

Reporters who advocate conducting interviews by email (among them are people who have been sources themselves) say that the sources can be quoted with greater accuracy, that full transcripts of the interview are automatically and immediately available, and that giving sources time to think about the questions journalists ask is only fair to the source and provides better information to the readers. Email often is the quickest way to reach a source, which makes it efficient on deadline, too. Sources, some of whom are concerned about their quotes, ideas and explanations being used in context, favor email interviews because they believe the record of the interview means journalists will be more careful as they construct their stories.

checkpoint ✓

What are the three types of interviews?

Write From the Interview

You have completed your research and finished the interview. Now it's time to prepare to write your story. Begin by reviewing your notes and highlighting the quotations and anecdotes you think you want to use. Making an outline also will help (see page 162 for a sample outline). Next you need to talk with your editor to determine the type of story you are writing — news or **feature**. A feature story has all the journalistic elements of a news story but is written with a beginning, middle and end like a short story. You will also decide the format you will use — Q-and-A (question and answer) or straight write-through. Finally, you need to make sure all the facts you want to use in your story are correct.

NEWS AND FEATURE STORIES

Highlight in your notebook the quotations that illustrate the points you want to make in your story. Note the best anecdotes and short explanations. These will be the essence of your story. Now outline the story. If it is a news story, you probably will put the most important points at the top of the story. If it is a feature, you may start with an anecdote that has impact. Whichever style you choose, let your own words link the ideas and provide context for your subjects' quotations, anecdotes and explanations.

Do not use quotation marks unnecessarily. If Coach Johnson said students are becoming obese, it isn't necessary to put the word obese in quotation marks. Single-word quotations rarely add impact. If the coach said, "I see that students are becoming more obese every year, and I'm worried about their health," you would want to put the statement in quotation marks. The statement, coming from him, has impact.

Use specifics and details from your observation in your article. Don't write: George Clooney is good-looking. Instead, tell readers: George Clooney has dark eyes, salt-and-pepper hair, and a smile that was made for a movie screen. Former USA Weekend editor Jack Curry tells his writers to get "facts, not feelings." What does he mean? Do not write that the coaches "feel bad" about losing the big game. Go for the details. Find out what the coaches did after losing the game. Find out if they closed themselves in their offices for hours, or if they huddled with the team, or left the stadium without saying anything to anyone. Give the readers the facts.

THE QUESTION-AND-ANSWER FORMAT

One way to solve the problem of how to turn an interview into a story is to write in a **Q-and-A (question-and-answer)** format. A Q-and-A is written in the format of the reporter asking a question, and then the source answering that question.

Reporter Will jobs be cut if the school levy does not pass?
Principal We will have to look at that very carefully. For now, let's be positive that the levy will pass.

Reporter   What are you doing to assure passage?

Principal   We're talking to the parents and homeowners in the community to explain the importance of the levy.

When you have colorful quotes and thoughtful answers from a single subject, the Q-and-A can be a good way to go. Most reporters like to know going into the interview that they will write a Q-and-A, because they want to carefully prepare the questions they will ask and the order in which they will ask them. Recording the interview or using email is essential to get full and accurate quotations for a Q-and-A.

Unfortunately, no matter how carefully prepared you are, the interview subject may not speak or write clearly. Sometimes people interviewed have a particular quirk of speech. For example, saying the word "like" frequently ruins the flow of sentences and makes them particularly difficult to read in print. Is it ever OK to change or clean up quotes? Most journalists agree that it is acceptable to modify a quotation for clarity or to take out unnecessary words so the subject can be better understood and the prose isn't cluttered with repetitive words. Journalists who specialize in lengthy interviews argue that when presenting the interview as a Q-and-A, they must be permitted to edit freely or some Q-and-A's would be too literal to be readable.

FACT-CHECKING INTERVIEWS

Accuracy is the most important part of your job. That includes using all of the quotations and information you get from your interview correctly. Journalists resist giving copies of their work in advance of publication to any source. It is acceptable practice, however, to let your source know which quotes you are using by reading a summary or the gist of your story and paraphrasing the quotations you plan to use. Why do this kind of fact checking? To avoid mistakes, of course. It also shows your source that you care about accuracy. You want to maintain a good relationship with a source you may want to use again.

Sometimes reporters read portions of the story they are working on to their source to ensure accuracy. This is called a **read-back.** A problem can arise with read-backs if the source asks for changes that have nothing to do with the accuracy of the facts. The reporter must explain that the purpose of the read-back is to check for accuracy, not to edit content or style. You are not obliged to change anything unless the information is inaccurate. If you have taped your interview, you can check

© Photodisc/Getty Images

////// *When is a read-back important?*

the tape to be sure that you have used the exact words and that they are used in the correct context.

checkpoint

After you have reviewed your notes and made an outline, what other steps do you need to take as you prepare to write your story?

Digging Deeper

Online Activism with Change.org

In May of 2011, Eman al-Nafjan, a Saudi Arabian blogger, contacted a group of activists in San Francisco that hosts online petitions to encourage social change. Eman wanted the group to help him support Saudi Arabian women who were protesting a ban on female drivers in their country. The group, Change.org, agreed and created an online petition for the cause. The group also went a few steps further by organizing demonstrations, sending press releases and emails, and asking Secretary of State Hillary Clinton to speak out against the driving ban. Saudi protesters were happy to hear Mrs. Clinton's affirmation of their work in a news conference on the subject. She said, "What they are doing is right."

In 2011 Change.org's visibility increased rapidly. The group has hosted many ground-breaking petitions for change. Read this article by accessing the Gale Journalism eCollection at www.cengage.com/school/langarts/journalism, and clicking on the link to Chapter 6. Then answer the questions below.

THINK *Critically*

1. List the social media tools mentioned in the article. Write a brief paragraph about each one explaining how it could be used to raise awareness and gain supporters for social change.

2. Identify the disadvantages of online activism as listed in the article. Write a paragraph arguing in support of one of the disadvantages.

3. Visit the Change.org website. Look at several of the petitions the group hosts. Using the free petition maker, make your own petition for a social change you feel is important. Share your petition with the class and convince your classmates to sign it.

Source: Shih, Gerry. "Online Activism Finds a Home in San Francisco." New York Times 1 July 2011: A17A(L). Global Issues In Context. Web. 11 July 2011.

SAMPLE OUTLINE FOR A NEWS STORY

Main goal of the story To inform readers about summer jobs in the community for high school students

Interview sources Mr. Reid, the high school guidance counselor; 2 students

Research City government records for the city's employment status

Topic statement Students may have a hard time finding jobs in the area this summer.

Quotes

(Mr. Reid) "The local unemployment rate is at an all-time high, and students are forced to compete for jobs with adults."

"Most restaurants hire only people who are 18 years old or older."

"Only so many people can work at the Coffee House. There have to be more customers than servers."

(Students)

(Rachelle Mendenhall) "I need a summer job in order to help pay for college that's coming up in a couple years. I don't want to take a job in another town, because I'll use up all my earnings on gas."

(Tory Ashid) "Last summer I helped out at a landscaping company, but this year they said they don't need any help. I'm still looking. Can't give up."

Anecdote Bartlett's Ice Cream Parlor advertised for counter help, and 112 students showed up.

Introduction Open with anecdote

Main points

1. Explain that jobs are scarce for students and why.
   a. Research from the city's employment status
   b. Mr. Reid's quotes

2. Explain why students want or need to work.
   a. Rachelle's quote

Conclusion Tory's quote

6.3 | Assessment

Understand Concepts

Determine the best answer for each of the following questions.

1. _____ interviews are those where you go to the source's home or place of business, or meet the source face to face somewhere.
   a. In-person
   b. Off-the-record
   c. On-background
   d. Email

2. Which refers to an article written in the format of the reporter asking a question and then the source answering the question?
   a. read-back
   b. phoner
   c. fact-checking
   d. Q-and-A

3. **True or False** It's natural to be nervous about interviewing someone you do not know.

4. **True or False** In a read-back, sources are asked to edit the reporter's story.

Write Now!

Practice your writing skills with the following activities.

5. You have been assigned to interview several students in your school about their thoughts on an upcoming school levy. It is important to have diversity in the students you choose to interview for the story. Write a paper that explains why diversity is important in school publications, and explain how you can show diversity by the people you choose to interview. Plan your paper before writing a draft, and then use copy editing symbols to edit your story. Carefully check your paper for clarity, engaging language and the correct use of English.

6. Read an online foreign newspaper or news magazine. If English is your second language, choose a news source in your native language. If English is your first language and you have studied a foreign language, choose a news source in that language, or else choose a news source in English. Study three stories where sources have been interviewed. Choose at least one feature and one news story. Write an analysis of the three stories and how quotations and information from sources were used.

7. Choose a school-related topic for a news or feature story for a publication in your school — the newspaper, yearbook or magazine. As part of your research, conduct an interview with at least one student in your school. Prepare and practice your questions in advance. Following journalistic style, write your story in regular format that incorporates direct and indirect quotations, and then rewrite the story in a Q-and-A format.

CHAPTER 6 | Assessment

Review Journalism Concepts

6.1 Choose Sources

Interviewing — asking questions of knowledgeable people — remains the most useful technique to gather good information for both news and feature stories. Anytime you ask a question as a reporter, you are conducting an interview. There are three types of interview sources — primary sources, secondary sources and unnamed sources. Primary sources give the reporter the most thorough or best information because they are the investigators, the witnesses or the people who are affected by the event. Secondary sources have information relevant to your story but are not main investigators, eyewitnesses or directly affected by the event. Unnamed sources include off-the-record sources, on-background sources and confidential sources. Off-the-record information is not written in your notebook or recorded and must not be used in your story unless you get it from another source on the record. On-background information may be used but must not be attributed to the source. Confidential sources also want to remain anonymous. They provide information that may be used but ask reporters to avoid being obvious about the source of the information.

6.2 Develop Questions

Before the interview, you need to prepare the questions you want to ask, and you need to know how to ask the questions. Begin by determining the kind of information you need from your source. Then research the topic and the source. Once you write a list of questions, practice them on other people. Repeating the questions aloud will help you sound more polished and professional in the interview. Listen carefully during the interview for good quotations and anecdotes that will add color and bring stories alive. You also want to ask open-ended questions and take good notes. Some print and Web-based journalists use a recorder during interviews.

6.3 Conduct the Interview

Interviews can be conducted in person, over the phone or by email. In-person interviews are those where you go to the source's home or place of business, or meet the source for a face-to-face interview. Most news-related interviews are phoners, or those conducted over the phone. Using email to conduct interviews is becoming an increasingly useful option in a world where tracking down sources is not always feasible for 24/7 news organizations. Once the interview is complete, use your research, observation notes, anecdotes and the quotations from your interviews to prepare to write the story. One format that can be used is a Q-and-A format. With the Q-and-A, the reporter asks a question, and then the source answers that question. Fact checking is an important part of the process of preparing to write your story.

Develop Your Journalism Language

Write the letter of the term that matches each definition.

_____ 1. Question that allows the source to talk

_____ 2. Neither source nor information can be used

_____ 3. Reporters can use the information in a story, but not the source's name

_____ 4. Time the story is due

_____ 5. Includes off-the-record, on-background and confidential sources

_____ 6. Short personal story that helps make a story interesting

_____ 7. A source who has information relevant to your story but is not directly involved

_____ 8. A format where the reporter asks a question, and then the source answers that question

_____ 9. Best-informed source

_____ 10. Reading parts of the story to the source to check for accuracy

_____ 11. Words a source says or writes during an interview

_____ 12. You can use the information but not attribute the information to the source; often used by White House sources

_____ 13. Interview conducted over the telephone

_____ 14. A news story written like a short story with a beginning, middle and end

_____ 15. Asking questions of knowledgeable people for a story

a. anecdote
b. confidential source
c. deadline
d. feature
e. interviewing
f. off-the-record
g. on-background
h. open-ended question
i. phoner
j. primary source
k. Q-and-A (question and answer)
l. quotation
m. read-back
n. secondary source
o. unnamed source

16. Which is a primary source?
   a. a county official
   b. an eyewitness
   c. a meteorologist
   d. a fire inspector

17. Which helps you avoid mistakes and may show your sources that you care about accuracy?
   a. using quotes
   b. using anecdotes
   c. read-back
   d. phoner

Think Critically

18. Why is interviewing so important to a story?

19. Why does a reporter want to ask world leaders questions on important points or policy?

20. Why might sources give information more readily to a reporter in person than on the phone?

21. Why might you interview spectators for a sports story?

22. Why is it important to respect off-the-record sources and not use the source's name?

23. Why is preparation so important before an interview?

24. Why should you save the toughest question for last in an interview?

25. Why is it so hard to take good notes in an in-person interview?

26. Which is the best type of interview to use when interviewing the following people: a disabled student in your school; a pen pal in another country; a hard-to-reach business leader; a friend who moved away; a soccer player at a rival school?

27. With what type of interviews does the Q-and-A format work best?

28. Can unnamed sources be primary sources? Explain your answer.

29. Should you prepare more questions for a feature than for a news story? Why or why not?

30. What would you do if a source insisted on changing a quotation during a read-back, but changing the quotation changes your entire story?

31. How does outlining your notes help you?

Make Academic Connections

32. **SOCIAL STUDIES**   Use Internet news sites, newspapers, news magazines or blogs to find a reporter in a foreign country. Choose a reporter who writes in English. Use the Internet to research the reporter and the reporter's work, and then write five questions for an email interview of the reporter. Your questions should all be about the reporter's work or about a specific story on which the reporter worked. Do not ask personal questions, other than to verify the spelling of the reporter's name. Do explain this is for a school assignment. Be sure to thank the reporter for responding.

33. **ART**   From newspapers, news and popular magazines, and Internet sites, collect articles written in a Q-and-A format. Create a poster to present the interviews. Highlight direct quotations in each interview. Display your posters in the classroom.

34. **CAREERS**   Use newspaper classified sections and the Internet to research jobs for journalists. Choose three jobs. Describe the job specifics and write a short paragraph for each, explaining why this job interests you.

35. **MUSIC**   Research one of your favorite recording artists. Use at least five sources from popular magazines and the Internet. Evaluate and confirm the validity of background information from a variety of sources such as qualified persons, books, or news stories about your chosen artist. Compile a list of 12 questions you want to ask this recording artist. Then compile a list of at least three people connected to the artist you could interview to add interest to the story. Develop an outline and a draft of your story before writing the final story.

36. **LANGUAGE ARTS**   Use your Internet research skills to research the trial of John Peter Zenger, who was found not guilty of seditious libel, and thus began freedom of the press. Locate information sources such as persons,

databases, reports and stories to gather background information. Use several sources to evaluate and confirm the validity of the background information. Then imagine you are able to interview Zenger. Prepare a list of questions. Imagine how he might answer the questions. Then write a draft of a feature story about him. Use quotations and anecdotes in your story. Using copy editing symbols, edit your draft into finished copy for a feature that is appropriate for a high school Internet publication. Be sure to check for clarity, engaging language, and the correct use of English. Use your computer skills to design an online feature. Place your finished story and all drafts and notes in your writing portfolio.

Writing Portfolio Activity

37. Choose an adult in your school or community you think would be an interesting interview subject. You might choose a teacher who has been helpful to you or has a unique and successful teaching method, or you might choose someone in the community who is known for helping others. Ask the subject's permission for an interview, set up a meeting time, and then prepare for the interview by writing and practicing your list of questions. Review the Checklist for Preparing for an Interview on page 151, the Be Ready section on page 152, and the Checklist for Taking Notes in an Interview on page 153. After the interview, be sure to thank the person.

Use your notes from the interview to make an outline for a story. Turn the outline into a story that is suitable for one of the publications in your high school. Use quotations in your story along with additional research. Put your list of questions, your reporter's notes from the interview, the outline and the story to your instructor.

AP Stylebook Workshop

Add quotation marks where needed in the following sentences according to AP style.

38. Prepare and practice before an interview, the teacher said to the class.

39. The editor asked the new reporter, Are you prepared for this interview?

40. Good interviews make for good stories, the editor said.

41. The reporter told us that the interview with the rock star was juicy.

42. The reporter was happy with the interview, and good interviews make for good stories, the news editor said.

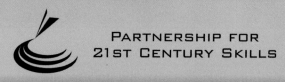
LEADERSHIP AND RESPONSIBILITY: The New Job

You've landed your new job. You are to report to the Human Resources Department of the news organization on Monday for new-employee orientation. What's next?

- What can you expect on your first day?
- How do you make a good impression?
- How can you prepare?

WHAT CAN YOU EXPECT ON YOUR FIRST DAY?

Most news organizations have a new-employee orientation where you learn about the company's policies and procedures. With large news organizations, this might be an all-day meeting with several other new employees. With smaller news organizations, you most likely will work with your editor or supervisor for a few days. Before you are sent out on your own to cover a news story, you might work with another reporter.

HOW DO YOU MAKE A GOOD IMPRESSION?

You want to set the right tone and get off on the right foot. You want to show that you are responsible, that you are willing to learn and that you have leadership qualities that will benefit the news organization. How do you do all this?

- Pay close attention to details about your new job. Notice where you are to sit so you can go directly to that space when you come into the office tomorrow. Make sure you know what hours you are expected to work. Plan to arrive about 10 minutes early and stay a little later than asked. Make sure you know your supervisor's and editor's names and the names of your immediate co-workers.
- Ask appropriate questions at the appropriate time. In large orientations,

you may need to write down your questions and ask them later. When working with one person, ask if you may ask questions while instructions are being given. Always ask for clarity on anything you do not understand.

- Take notes. You are not expected to remember everything. Plus, taking notes in a newsroom makes you look professional.
- Show self-assurance and confidence. Make eye contact with other people and offer a strong handshake when appropriate. Show that you think quickly and that you have leadership potential by demonstrating good interpersonal skills, acting respectfully toward others, and showing your interest in the greater good of the entire organization, not just your personal goals.
- If you become anxious during the day, take a deep breath and remind yourself that excitement and anxiety feel similar, and that you are excited, not anxious.

HOW CAN YOU PREPARE?

You want to be at your best on the first day of your new job. Begin by preparing earlier in the week. Choose the clothes you plan to wear and make sure they are clean. Choose clothes that fit into the organization of which you are now a part. Make sure you get a good night's sleep and are well-rested.

Pack a backpack or briefcase with any information you will need such as your Social Security number and contact information. Put at least one reporter's notebook and at least two pens or pencils into your pack.

THINK *Critically*
What can you do today to show leadership and responsibility in your life that will prepare you for your future career?

REAL PEOPLE REAL CAREERS

Daryn Kagan | Creator, DarynKagan.com

Daryn Kagan, a television reporter and former CNN news anchor who now has her own media company, says that, for her, the art of interviewing boils down to one word: wonder. "What do I wonder about the person?" she asks herself as she prepares for an interview. "What do I wonder about the situation?"

Kagan has done a lot of wondering in more than two decades of reporting and interviewing people in situations both good and bad. That much experience brings with it self confidence and a lot of lessons about interviewing. She shares a few:

- There's no such thing as a stupid question. "You are going to feel a lot more stupid if later you have to call back because you didn't get the explanation the first time."

- "Really listen. Don't get so locked into your questions that you don't follow up on what's been said."

- "Be prepared. Read up on the person. Know something about them."

- "Put your best questions first. For TV and radio interviews you may have only a few minutes. People may stay or leave, based on what they hear first."

Kagan was a local television reporter in both news and sports, earning her stripes in Santa Barbara, California, and Phoenix, Arizona, before she moved to CNN in Atlanta, Georgia, for twelve years. There she worked in sports before anchoring a three-hour morning newscast daily. When she and CNN mutually parted ways, she decided to become her own media company and set up her website, DarynKagan.com.

WRITING INSPIRATIONAL STORIES

Having her own website allows Kagan to report and produce the kind of stories she always liked best — inspirational stories. She wants stories on the website to be entertaining, but stimulating and surprising. Most of all, she wants the stories "to show what's possible." Visitors to DarynKagan.com find an inspirational video story each day, along with Kagan's blog entries and other features. She does the initial reporting to be certain the story has the elements she requires, and then she interviews her subjects by phone while they speak into a video camera. She anchors the video and narrates the stories. Her production costs are minimal, and she makes money with advertising on the site.

The Internet has allowed Kagan to practice her profession on her own terms. Soon after departing CNN, she thought she would produce and report inspirational stories for another news organization. She was soon convinced she could be successful doing it on her own. Soon after DarynKagan.com was available on the Web, Kagan got a book deal to share in print more stories of what's possible.

Source: Personal interview with Daryn Kagan.

THINK *Critically*

1. How has the Internet and technology allowed people like Kagan to practice journalism the way they would like?

2. Daryn Kagan specializes in inspirational stories on her website. What types of stories would you specialize in if you decided to start a similar site?

Handling Quotations

Clinton and the Teleprompter

President Bill Clinton, 42nd president of the United States, had been in office just nine months when he was to give an important speech to a joint session of Congress. The topic was his new health care policy. The president's staff distributed print copies of the speech to reporters who would be covering it.

When the president arrived at the Capitol, an aide took a computer disk with the speech on it to be loaded into the teleprompter. A teleprompter is equipment with a screen similar to a television monitor. The president, or any speaker, can then read a speech from the screen.

Before the president's speech began, the teleprompter operators needed to get the words at the right height for the president, so they loaded an old speech into the machine to practice. Unfortunately, they didn't take it out. As Clinton stood at the podium to begin his important address, he looked down at the teleprompter and knew immediately an old speech was scrolling on the machine.

It took aides and operators nine long minutes to locate and load the correct speech. For those nine minutes, Clinton outlined his policy without looking at notes. Though reporters had a printed copy of the speech in hand, the president's words were different for the first nine minutes of the speech. During these nine minutes, the press reporters had to scramble to take notes. It was a night where reporters again were reminded of the value of staying alert.

> **THINK** *Critically*
> What would you do if the speaker you were covering was not speaking the words you had on an advance hard copy of the speech?

Define Quotations

Goals

- Define three types of quotations.
- Explain where to get quotations.

Key Terms

- quotation marks 171
- direct quotation 171
- indirect quotation 173
- jargon 173
- partial quotation 175
- sound bite 175

FOCUS

When you watch the news on your local television station or on your computer, you will see stories in which people are interviewed on camera. You can see the people being interviewed. They face the camera and talk into a microphone, so you have no trouble understanding who is speaking or what is being said. In written stories, for print or the Web, things are not always so clear. Readers do not have visual images or sound. You cannot see or hear the speaker, so writers need to give readers clues to recognize when a source is speaking. That is when writers use quotation marks.

Types of Quotations

Quotations, or quotes, are the words a person speaks. In print and digital journalism, quotes are set between **quotation marks**, the punctuation marks that go at the beginning and end of the quoted words. Quotation marks tell your readers that these are the words of your source. You may see quotation marks at the beginning and end of one or several sentences. Sometimes you will see quotation marks around a few words or a phrase. You also may see statements attributed to sources with no quotation marks at all. As you read through this chapter, you'll learn when and when not to use quotation marks when quoting a source.

The ways in which journalists handle their source's quotations are direct quotations, indirect quotations and partial quotations. Let's take a closer look at each of these as well as learning about sound bites.

DIRECT QUOTATIONS

In journalism, **direct quotation** means you are using the exact words spoken by the source. The sentence or sentences placed inside quotation marks are written as they were spoken by the source, without change. Direct quotations work best when reporters want to do the following:

- Let the source talk directly to the reader

- Show the source's sense of humor or other emotion

- Reveal a controversial opinion

- Show the source's character or intellect

The best direct quotations in journalistic writing are short and memorable. Presidential inaugural addresses contain good examples of fine direct quotes. In his inaugural speech, President John F. Kennedy said, "My fellow Americans, ask not what your country can do for you; ask what you can do for your country."

The nation was deep into the Great Recession when President Barack Obama said in his inaugural speech: "Starting today, we must pick ourselves up, dust ourselves off and begin again the work of remaking America." Both quotations are short and memorable, set the tone for the new presidential administration, and reveal something of the character of the man.

The quotes you use usually will not be as dramatic as those in a presidential address. That doesn't mean they won't have impact. Suppose you interview the injured star quarterback on your school football team, who cannot play for the rest of the year. He tells you, "I feel terrible about letting down my team and my school." You have a quote with impact.

You want to give credit to the source of the quotations you use so your readers know who is speaking. You can insert the speaker's identification in the middle of the quotation. If you do so, be sure to put quotation marks around only what the speaker says. Do not enclose the speaker's identification within the quotation marks.

"That report on downtown parking is incomplete, the mayor said. I don't care if it takes six more months to get more information. I won't accept it until it's complete."

Incorrect use of quotation marks

"That report on downtown parking is incomplete," the mayor said. "I don't care if it takes six more months to get more information. I won't accept it until it's complete."

Correct use of quotation marks

Sometimes journalists break long quotations into more than one paragraph. In that case you would not put the closing quotation mark at the end of the first paragraph. You would begin a new paragraph with an opening quotation mark. In the following example, notice there is no closing quotation mark at the end of the first paragraph, because the writer wants to indicate the mayor is still speaking.

/////// *When should reporters use direct quotations in their stories?*

© jpbcpa/iStockphoto.com

"That report on downtown parking is incomplete," the mayor said. "I don't care if it takes six more months to get more information. I won't accept it until it's complete.

"In fact, I will appoint a task force to work with the city council on the parking issue. I want statistics from the parking enforcement division and evidence of a need to increase fines."

INDIRECT QUOTATIONS

With **indirect quotation**, or paraphrasing, a journalist rephrases the source's words for clarity. Indirect quoting is a useful tool when sources do not express themselves well. Indirect quoting lets the writer shorten and summarize what was said. Indirect quoting is a good way to get rid of bureaucratic words such as implement, utilize or prioritize, and to eliminate **jargon**. Jargon is the vocabulary that relates to a particular field.

"We intend to fully implement a new reading program when school begins in September," the superintendent said.

Direct quotation

A new reading program will begin in September, the superintendent said.

Indirect quotation

////// *When can indirect quotations be a useful tool for journalists?*

Journalists find that using indirect quotations is a helpful option when their sources say something obvious or their quotes are weakened by the speaker rambling.

Chamber of Commerce President Jennifer Jones introduced the luncheon speaker, saying, "We are so lucky to have with us today — and I should know because I've had the chance to meet him many times — a man who wants only the best for our downtown — which of course we all do — city planner Brian Smith."

Direct quotation

Chamber of Commerce President Jennifer Jones introduced luncheon speaker Brian Smith, a city planner who she said wants the best for downtown.

Indirect quotation

PARTIAL QUOTATIONS

Partial quotations are exactly what they sound like — part of the source's actual spoken words. The quotation marks go around only the words that the source said, not the whole sentence. Be wary of partial quotations because they are fragmented and choppy. They are often unnecessary because the sentence containing a partial quote can be paraphrased.

The local university will "turn down plenty" of good students because the number of applications "is higher than ever," says one admissions official.	Acceptable use of partial quotation
The local university will turn down many good students because it has more applications than ever, an admissions official says.	Better to paraphrase
He said the family had a "really fabulous" time at Water World because "the park is huge" and "everyone could go on the ride they liked best."	Acceptable use of partial quotation
He said the family had a fabulous time at Water World because the park is large and "everyone could go on the ride they liked best."	Better use of partial quotation

THE SOUND BITE

Broadcast news and reporters who use video on websites are always listening for sound bites. A **sound bite** is a cut of an audio- or videotape that has the sources' best quotes or quotes that end on a point the broadcaster wants to make. Sometimes broadcast writers use a full quotation in the story. Sometimes they use only part of a quotation. Either way, reporters set up the quotation with an introduction. The reporter or the news anchor gives the introduction and then switches to the tape.

In an interview for the Poynter Institute, CBS News radio correspondent Peter King says writing for broadcast leaves no time for details. He often uses sound bites with his reporting. He looks for sentences or partial sentences that underscore the points he wants to make or that finish the thoughts he started. In a story on a drought in Florida his broadcast went like this:

> King's partial sentence: Some parts of Lake Okeechobee are so dry . . .
>
> Sound bite: . . . there is not a drop of water anywhere.
>
> King's full sentence: Kim Day was looking at what used to be a boaters' canal that surrounded the J&S Fish Camp.
>
> Sound bite: There's just nothing there but grass now.

Like print reporters, broadcast journalists often use indirect quotes. Paraphrasing, or indirect quoting, is a good way to introduce a piece of tape or a sound bite that completes the story. For example:

> Anchor: City Council Chair Carolyn Mitchell announced today that she is running for mayor.
>
> Mitchell's taped words: "I want to make a bigger difference in this city."

The anchor states the news of Mitchell's announcement and lets the tape explain why she is running.

checkpoint ✓

What are three types of quotations?

Where to Get Quotations

Journalists find quotations in all their research and reporting. The most common places include interviews that are conducted in person, on video, on the telephone or by email; meetings that range from local planning commissions to the U.S. Congress; and speeches wherever a speaker is present, from the local Rotary Club to the White House.

INTERVIEWS

Sources speak, and reporters listen and write down what they hear. It seems easy enough, but it's not. Every time you interview someone for a story you are listening for great quotations. When you hear a great quotation, you need to put it in your notes. How do you know when you hear a great quote? That comes with listening carefully, knowing the background of the source and story, and practice.

When Hillary Rodham Clinton was speaking to reporters during her husband Bill Clinton's first presidential campaign in 1992, she faced questions from the press about her career in law and its possible conflicts with her husband's political career. She said, "You know, I suppose I could have stayed home and baked cookies and had teas, but what I decided to do was fulfill my profession, which I entered before my husband was in public life." Experienced journalists knew the impact that quote would have the moment they heard it, because it had the elements reporters look for. It was character-revealing and opinionated, and had emotional punch. However, Hillary Clinton, who went on to become a U.S. senator and the country's secretary of state, and to run for president herself, was unprepared for the outrage from people who thought she was expressing disdain for women who had chosen to be homemakers. She did all she could to undo the damage to her husband's political ambitions, even sharing some of her cookie recipes.

Interviews like those with Clinton usually are conducted in person or on the telephone. Reporters anticipate the need for good quotations in their stories and prepare their interview questions so they will get them. Using a recorder (and properly advising the source you are recording) helps reporters get lengthy quotations down accurately. Good note taking can be just as efficient. As you hear a quote you think is important, you can stop and repeat it for the source, or ask them to say it again for accuracy. For example, "I'm sorry, Mr. Mayor, I just want to be certain I heard you correctly. You said, 'I'll never run for office again.' Is that correct?"

The use of email as an interview tool gives reporters yet another option for quoting from an interview. Your source may answer questions directly and succinctly enough that you want to use his or her responses as they are written. Written responses can be treated as direct quotations, but it should be noted that they came by email. For example, "We will begin summer vacation one week early," the principal said in an email. An email exchange with a source also is fair game for paraphrasing. For example: The principal said in an email that summer vacation will begin a week early.

MEETINGS

Beginning reporters often are assigned to cover government meetings such as those of city councils, school boards and county boards. As news organizations continue to emphasize local news in print and on the Web, meeting coverage is even more likely to be part of a new reporter's assignments. When there is a lively issue involving public comment, a meeting can become a source of a good story and good quotes.

/////// *What are the advantages of collecting quotations through email interviews? What are the disadvantages?*

Suppose there is a city council meeting about a developer's plan to tear down a historic building in your city to build a shopping mall. You arrive to find the usually empty city council chambers filled with residents who oppose the idea. The developer is there, too, as are all council members, including some who believe the mall will be good for the local economy. As resident after resident comes to the microphone to speak, you dutifully take down quotations, knowing you will paraphrase most of them. You are listening for the one great quote that will help the story become more than just another pro-and-con report on a development issue. Finally, an elderly resident who was born in the community steps before the microphone and tells the council, "I don't want to live in a city that values a dollar more than its history." Does that sound like a good quote? Yes!

Most meetings you cover won't be so lively, but the people participating will talk nonetheless. Your job is to stay alert for the things that are said that bring your story to life. Another way to get quotations for a routine meeting story is to talk to participants after the meeting. Approach them with your notebook or handheld recorder and introduce yourself. In the city council example, you would ask council members why they voted the way they did, or how they think the action will affect the community. Ask residents why they made the time to attend the meeting, and if the vote didn't go their way, will they do something more? Ask open-ended questions so you will get good quotes, not a simple yes or no.

SPEECHES

Speeches are all about quotations. Quotations, both direct and indirect, will be the frame on which you build your speech story. That's why you must listen closely for specific lines as well as overall themes when you are covering a speech.

Good speeches are written to appeal to the ear with the cadence and rhythm of poetry. Peggy Noonan, a well-known journalist and speechwriter for Presidents Ronald Reagan and George H. W. Bush, was expert at putting together the words she knew would resonate with journalists and most Americans. Among the lines she wrote was a quote by then presidential candidate Bush: "Read my lips: no new taxes." That quote came to haunt the president, however, because once in office he found it impossible to keep his promise.

Speeches, whether given at a school assembly, at the local Rotary Club, or in front of both houses of Congress, usually are written well in advance. The best way to ensure accurate reporting of the quotations from the speech is to ask for a copy of the speech before you get to the event. Most speakers are happy to supply copies to the press because they understand it helps the press write accurate stories. Public officials routinely supply copies of their

 *If reporters receive a copy of a public official's speech in advance, why is it also important for them to pay close attention to what the person is saying?*

speeches to reporters. These officials may have a press secretary whose job it is to supply the press with speeches because they want their words reported correctly.

Having a copy of the speech in hand doesn't mean you can sleep through the event, however. You must follow along during the speech to be sure the speaker does not break from the script. Reporters who cover presidential campaigns may hear the candidate give the same speech so many times they can say it themselves without looking at a copy. Even so, they follow candidates on every stop, listening carefully, because they never know if the candidates will make a change.

check *point* ✓

Name three situations in which reporters may get quotations.

AP Stylebook Concepts

The purpose of punctuation is to make the story clear for the reader. Punctuation with quotations clarifies who is speaking and the thought being expressed. Follow these guidelines to help you when using quotations:

Use beginning and ending quotation marks (" ") to enclose the exact words of the speaker.

"I aced the test," Katicia said.

"I aced the test," Katicia said. "That makes me really happy."

When you are quoting more than one person and want to show a dialogue, each person's words should be in a separate paragraph. Quotation marks enclose each person's words.

"I aced the test," Katicia said.

"Does that make you happy?" Jeremy asked.

"That makes me really happy," she replied.

Editorial Ethics

Defining Prior Review and Prior Restraint

Are you familiar with the terms "prior restraint" and "prior review"? High school journalists often encounter them. The Journalism Education Association clearly defined the terms in spring 2010:

- "Prior review" occurs when anyone not on the publication or media staff requires that he or she be allowed to read, view or approve student material before distribution, airing or publication.

- "Prior restraint" occurs when someone not on the publication/ media staff requires pre-distribution changes to or removal of student media content.

- Prior review itself is a form of prior restraint. It inevitably leads the reviewer to censor and student journalists to self-censor in an effort to assure approval.

- An officially designated adviser, when working with students and offering suggestions for improvement as part of the coaching and learning process, who reads or views student media before publication is not engaged in prior review.

- However, when an adviser requires pre-distribution changes over the objections of student editors, his/her actions then become prior restraint.

THINK *Critically*

1. How might prior review cause prior restraint to occur in a story on which you are working?

2. Do you agree that editors of student publications should provide articles or other material to school officials before publication? Why or why not?

7.1 | Assessment

Understand Concepts

Determine the best answer for each of the following questions.

1. Which is an example of a direct quotation?
   a. Constance said the material would be here tomorrow.
   b. "Everyone would have an equal chance," Mr. Wong said.
   c. Brittany said she plans to "ace" the test.
   d. Henderson said she is going to plan the "surprise party."

2. Which punctuation marks do you use to enclose a quote?
   a. commas
   b. quotation marks
   c. colons
   d. periods

3. Asking for a copy of a speech before it is given
   a. ensures that you know what will be said.
   b. means you do not have to attend the speech.
   c. irritates the speaker.
   d. helps you accurately report the quotations in the speech.

4. If your quote is a written response from an interview conducted through email, you must
   a. paraphrase the quote.
   b. mention that the quote is taken from an email.
   c. not quote the writer.
   d. always use quotation marks.

5. **True or False** Interviews are a good source of quotations.

6. **True or False** Sound bites are used by electronic and broadcast reporters.

Write Now!

Practice your writing skills with the following activities.

7. Broadcast news often uses sound bites to promote an upcoming news show. On three occasions, listen to sound bites. Write down the sound bites, and then write a draft of a story that you think will be developed from each sound bite. Later, listen to the news to see if the sound bites correctly summarized each story or if any sound bite was misleading. Write a paper that explains why the sound bites were accurate or misleading, and distinguish between responsible and irresponsible media action in the use of sound bites. In your paper, use both direct and indirect quotes from the original sound bite and from the stories. Write a draft before writing the final paper. Carefully revise and edit your paper for clarity, engaging language and the correct use of written English. Use appropriate copy editing symbols. Turn in the original sound bites, your draft and your paper.

7.2

Modify Quotations

Goals

- Describe the journalistic issues around changing quotations.
- Explain the importance of accuracy in quotations.

Key Terms

- ellipses 182
- offensive language 183

ellipses 182

offensive language 183

FOCUS

Have you ever talked to a correspondent for a television station or a reporter for a newspaper? Did you eagerly await the evening broadcast or the next morning's newspaper to see if the reporter quoted you? When you saw yourself quoted, was it exactly as you put it to the reporter? If so, was it put in context correctly? Handling the quotations of their sources is a challenge for reporters, because people don't speak in perfect sound bites.

Journalistic Issues With Quotations

Changing quotations is not OK, except when . . . It's that "except when" that divides journalists. Even the best of journalism practitioners and scholars do not agree on whether it's proper to modify a source's quotations. The issue puts journalists in two camps — the do-not-change-a-word camp and the make-minimal-changes-for-good-reason camp.

DO NOT CHANGE QUOTATIONS

There is no law against changing quotes. The American Society of Newspaper Editors' Statement of Principles does not admonish against changing quotes. In fact, court cases have found that it doesn't matter if the words are changed if the spirit of the quote is accurate.

Yet, the Associated Press Stylebook clearly states: "Never alter quotations even to correct minor grammatical errors or word usage. Casual minor tongue slips may be removed by using **ellipses** but even that should be done with extreme caution. If there is a question about a quote, either don't use it or ask the speaker to clarify." Ellipses, also called an ellipsis, are three dots that indicate something has been omitted from the copy. For example, Jeremy said, "This classroom needs reorganizing . . . the disaster left everything in a mess." In this example, you know that Jeremy said more than what is printed. Some of what he said is omitted because it was unnecessary to the story, or because he used offensive or inappropriate language.

Many respected journalists and scholars agree with the AP guideline. The problem is that other respected journalists and scholars disagree with the AP guideline. Those who refuse to alter quotations under any circumstances argue that if you change a quote to correct the speaker's grammar or word usage, you are being condescending and giving readers a false picture of the speaker. The Los Angeles Times says in its statement of principles, "We do not manufacture, embroider or distort quotes, either in print or in the video and audio clips posted on our website."

Los Angeles Times Statement of Principles

CHANGE QUOTATIONS SOMETIMES

The policy of the national newspaper USA Today allows for some alteration of quotations under specific circumstances. The policy on quotations begins, "Do not tamper with quotations." The policy then goes on to state, "The only exception to this rule: Errors of grammar that are inadvertent, reflect a lack of education or are common in everyday speech may be corrected to avoid embarrassing an individual. If a source says, for example, 'I seen the crash from my front porch' it is proper to write it, 'I saw the crash from my front porch.'"

USA Today, Policy on Quotations

The Poynter Institute's writing scholar, Roy Peter Clark, believes some alteration of quotes helps the reader. Clark has little patience for those who believe in untouched, pristine quotes. Clark says that because words on paper are different from recorded words, journalists show respect for the reader by cleaning up quotes so they can be more easily read. "When someone speaks a word it flies by. So if someone makes a grammatical mistake it is not what you focus on," says Clark. "But in print it's there forever. A little tidying up without adding words, without altering or heightening the meaning is OK."

One area in which journalists tend to agree is changing or editing quotes for **offensive language**. Offensive language includes any words or remarks that offend, insult or threaten a person or group. Most news organizations try to avoid offensive language by not using the quote at all. If there is a compelling reason to use the quote, most news organizations call for using a long dash in place of the offending word.

////// *In what area do journalists tend to agree on the changing or editing of quotes? What does this include?*

check point ✓

What are the two circumstances in which some journalists think it's acceptable to change quotations?

Accuracy in Quotations

Regardless of the camp they are in — changing quotes or not changing quotes — journalists agree that the accuracy of the quotation is most important. Ensuring accuracy requires using quotations in context and with accurate reporting of tone and gesture. The AP Stylebook reminds journalists that they can misquote people by reporting their words without qualifiers, or words that explain the context. Writers who change quotes are warned to be extremely careful because deleting sentences or fragments of sentences can change a speaker's meaning. The speaker's manner of delivery also may be necessary to reporting a quotation accurately. As the AP Stylebook points out, a facial expression or a hand gesture may be as important as the words.

Suppose there is a debate at student council over whether to cancel the homecoming parade. A record crowd of students attends the meeting. You are reporting the remarks of the council president. Notice how the meaning changes in the two examples.

In this example, it sounds like no one showed up at the meeting.

> "I see no one wants a homecoming parade," said Student Council President Emma Lewis.

In the next example, it is clear that a lot of people came to voice their opinion. Lewis's remark is said lightly. You can see her smiling while standing in front of a large crowd.

> "I see no one wants a homecoming parade," Student Council President Emma Lewis said, acknowledging the large crowd at the debate.

checkpoint ✓

What do journalists agree is the most important aspect of quotations?

7.2 | Assessment

Understand Concepts

Determine the best answer for each of the following questions.

1. Which do you use if you want to show you have omitted a few words in a quotation?
   a. quotation marks
   b. ellipses
   c. commas
   d. [sic]

2. Which organization states: "Never alter quotations even to correct minor grammatical errors or word usage"?
   a. USA Today
   b. The New York Times
   c. Poynter Institute
   d. Associated Press

3. **True or False**   All journalists agree there is never any reason to change a quotation.

4. **True or False**   Most journalists agree that quotes should be edited, changed or not used at all if they contain offensive language.

Write Now!

Practice your writing skills with the following activities:

5. Go to the website of the Poynter Institute. Use the search tool to find articles about changing quotes. Read several articles for and against changing quotes. Use a computer to write a paper that states your position on whether quotations should ever be changed, and if so, under what circumstances. Use information from the text and from your research to support your position and to show the other side of the issue. Incorporate both direct and indirect quotations in your paper. Cite your sources. Before writing your final paper, write a draft, and then use correct copy editing symbols to edit and rewrite your draft for greater clarity, engaging language, and the correct use of English. Turn in your draft with your final paper.

6. Use the Internet to research the News Literacy Project, a partner of the Poynter Institute. Use a computer to design a front page and write the opening of three or four stories suitable for an online high school website about the program. Quote information from the source in your stories. Be prepared to explain whether you changed any wording in the quotes and why or why not.

7.3

Use Quotations

Goals

- Describe how to use quotations effectively.
- Explain how to attribute quotations.

Key Terms

- redundant 186
- dialogue 188
- attribution 189

FOCUS

"Let quotations in your stories do some of the work in your writing," the college professor said to the Writing for Communication class. "Quotations are helpful to readers, who like to hear directly from the source. You can help your story along with quotations."

"Mostly we've written papers for English class. We didn't hear a lot of quotes," Jose said. "How can we learn to use quotes effectively?"

The professor replied, "Using quotations effectively is a skill that serves both the writer and the reader. It's a skill we're about to learn."

Effective Use of Quotes

Writers need words. Journalists need information and quotations. Often the information comes from the mouth of good sources, though not all of what you hear is quotable. Quotations should be the spice of your news story. They should add something, surprise the reader, maybe even entertain. Journalists use quotes to move their stories forward, make a point or create dialogue. Remember, as the writer, you are the one who decides what gets used as a direct quote and what may be paraphrased.

MOVE STORIES FORWARD

Moving action forward is simply good storytelling. There is nothing more distracting than to read a news story in which quoted material repeats points the writer already has made. Use quotes to move your action or explanation forward, not backward.

Look at the following examples. In the first boxes the same information is written in both sentences. The quotation is **redundant**, which means information is repeated. Paraphrase some of the information and let the quote move the story to the next point.

Police believe the burglar had been casing the house for days.
    "We think the burglar had been casing the house for days," the police chief said. "Neighbors saw a white van driving by at odd hours."

Poor use of quote

Police believe the burglar had been casing the house for days. "Neighbors saw a white van driving by at odd hours," the police chief said.

Good use of quote

The National Zoo's baby panda turned two Sunday, and his birthday was celebrated with a party and treats for all children. "We had a party for the baby panda and celebrated with treats for all visitors under 13," the zoo director said.

Poor use of quote

One of the National Zoo's most famous residents turned two Sunday. "We had a party for the baby panda and celebrated with treats for all visitors under 13," the zoo director said.

Good use of quote

The Jefferson High School Mock Trial team won the state competition this year and will represent the state this year in the national championship. "We are very excited about representing our state in the national competition in June," said Alicia Marion, faculty adviser.

Poor use of quote

The Jefferson High School Mock Trial team won the state competition this year. "We are very excited about representing our state in the national competition in June," said Alicia Marion, faculty adviser.

Good use of quote

MAKE A POINT

The quotes in your reporter's notebook should make or support the main points you want to make in the story. As you pick and choose which of the many quotations to put into your story, look through your notebook with an eye for those that define the story.

In a story on weight loss surgery in The Herald-Dispatch in Huntington, W.Va., the reporter sprinkled several quotations throughout the story, which made important points, including those below.

> "We're seeing about 64 percent of adults over age 20 overweight or obese," says a specialist from the CDC.
>
> "Everyone wants a quick fix," says a registered dietitian in Cincinnati.
>
> "If you have the genetics to become obese, this is a bad time to be living," says a weight-loss surgeon at a local hospital.

CREATE DIALOGUE

Dialogue is not just for screenwriters and playwrights. Journalists use it too, if sparingly. You might find **dialogue** — the back-and-forth of conversation — at a public meeting when people on opposite sides of an issue speak. For example:

> School board member 1: "If we don't close Bancroft High School, we will have to cut sports at all high schools, and that would be a tragedy."
>
> School board member 2: "You don't think it's tragic to close Bancroft High School? Bancroft is the oldest high school in the city."
>
> School board member 1: "Precisely why it should be closed. The repairs it needs are too costly. We can't fund that and sports."
>
> School board member 2: "Our mission is academics, not athletics."

Dialogue works well in narrative stories, too. You need only snippets of dialogue to move the action forward or underscore your theme. In a story about two elderly women who walk their neighborhood streets together every morning, you might use this snippet:

"We've been walking this same route for 25 years," says Bessie Smith.

"I thought it was 26," says May Jones.

"Whatever it is, we sure have seen the neighborhood change," says Smith.

"And not for the better," says Jones.

The dialogue helps you see that the women are close. They finish each other's sentences and have walked together more than two decades. You also learn that the neighborhood changes have not been good.

What are three ways to use quotations effectively?

Attribute Quotations

Attribution — giving the reader the name of your source — is important in all news stories. Attribution lends credibility to your reporting because it shows that you found the right people to interview or the right documents from which you might learn more. Equally important is attributing sources for charts, graphs, graphics, photographs and other material your news organization may use in print, on camera or on the Web.

HOW TO ATTRIBUTE

Many words can show attribution, but generally none is better than the word "said." Other words, such as "declared," "noted" or "stated," may be used under the right circumstances. It's OK to write, "The principal pointed out that the student has a good academic record," if the principal really pointed this out in some way. If not, then it is more accurate to write, "The principal said the student has a good academic record."

Using other words to show attribution is attractive to new writers who think "said" is boring or repetitive. The reality is "said" blends in. It is the beige wallpaper of a story. It's not noticeable. Readers glide right over the word. Notice how easily "said" blends into the following sentences.

> The mayor said he won't raise taxes.
>
> She said, "I'm not going to the party."

It is possible the mayor declared that he will not raise taxes, or stated so, in a formal way. However, if said in a conversational way, then "said" is the best choice. Similarly, the woman may have declared, "I'm not going to the party!" If so, both "declared" and the exclamation point are appropriate. However, if she simply is informing the family that she's staying home, then "said" is the best choice.

Other verbs you may be tempted to write as an attribution word are "smiled," "frowned," "grimaced," "shrugged," "laughed" and so on. None are appropriate or accurate. You cannot talk and smile at the same time. No words come out of a shrug. So leave those words and others like them out of your arsenal of attribution words.

WHERE TO PLACE ATTRIBUTION

Beginning writers often find placement of attribution tricky. Generally, attribution goes in the middle or at the end of a sentence. For shorter quotes, attribution works best at the end.

> "We are cracking down on red light runners," the police chief said.

Longer quotes can take attribution in the middle of a sentence.

> "We are cracking down on red light runners," the police chief said, "because of the number of accidents at intersections."

AVOID PLAGIARISM

You may be used to attributing information in your academic work, using footnotes and end notes, or placing attribution in the text itself. You know it is important to give credit where credit is due. Using proper attribution helps you avoid plagiarism, which is copying someone else's work or taking credit for what someone else has written. Giving proper credit is important in both your journalistic and academic work.

Be sure to give credit to all sources, not just the people with whom you speak. The difference between giving credit in a news story and a scholarly work is that in the news story you do not use footnotes. All attribution goes in the copy. If you use government reports, case studies, legal documents or other official information, you name the document near the information you use.

> America is getting fatter, according to a new report by the Centers for Disease Control and Prevention in Atlanta.

If you use information or quote material you find in another publication, credit that publication.

> They said they were sorry for their inappropriate statement.

Incorrect

> They told The New York Times they were sorry for their inappropriate statement.

Correct

check *point*

How do you attribute quotations in a story?

////// *What is the difference between giving credit in a news story versus giving credit in a scholarly work?*

Effective Use of Quotations

By Monica Cheng, Carmel High School, Carmel, Ind., "General Fund Referendum"

On May 4, the Carmel Clay community will vote on a $12 million general fund referendum that would increase local sales and income taxes in order to keep up with the deficit and continue to provide students with a quality public school system. That referendum, if it were to pass, would provide Carmel schools with an additional $12 million per year for a total of seven years.

According to Tricia Hackett, vice president of the school board, with the $1.5 million budget cut from 2009 and a $3 million reduction proposal this year due to recession, the Carmel Clay school district has already lost 60 teaching positions and is struggling to hire enough teachers to keep class sizes down, a struggle that is becoming evident at CHS.

"Every school budget in Indiana is made up of seven different funds to pay for the public school system. Six of them are supported by property and excise taxes," Hackett said. "The state used to supply dollars to the general fund, the largest and most crucial fund, through local property tax, state sales tax and income tax. But now, the general fund can draw revenue from only state sales and income taxes, both of which may fluctuate depending on the economy."

According to Hackett, 93 percent of the general fund goes to salary and benefits. The remaining 7 percent goes to supplies and other services.

"If this general operating referendum is passed May 4, 2010, the Carmel Clay School District will receive the funding in calendar year 2011. However, changes can be enacted well before this," Hackett said in an interview via email.

Pete O'Hara, member of the Carmel Clay Education Association (CCEA) and social studies teacher, said he is in favor of the referendum.

"We want to be able to continue our high academic standards and make sure the kids get everything they deserve," O'Hara said. "This referendum is a great way for the people of Carmel to support the kids."

"(The referendum) is a worthwhile thing," O'Hara said. "This is for kids. I don't think it's digging so deep in our pockets that it's going to hurt us as much as it's going to help us."

THINK *Critically*

1. Analyze the writer's use of quotations using the topics in this chapter as your guide.

2. In your opinion, is the writer's use of quotations effective? Why or why not?

Used by permission of Monica Cheng.

7.3 | Assessment

Understand Concepts

Determine the best answer for each of the following questions.

1. Which is NOT a good use of quotations?
   a. To move stories forward
   b. To make a point
   c. To create dialogue
   d. To show the source speaks poor English

2. The quotations in your story should
   a. be redundant.
   b. make or support the main points.
   c. be from only the main person in the story.
   d. be followed by the word that describes the action, such as "declared."

3. **True or False**   You must always attribute quotations to the source.

4. **True or False**   Dialogue should be used only in feature stories and not in news stories because it slows down the action.

Write Now!

Practice your writing skills with the following activities.

5. Select a current feature story from a newspaper, news magazine or electronic news site. Highlight the quotations, noticing how they are attributed. Reorganize and rewrite the story, using the same quotations but a different lead. Send your final story to your teacher electronically.

6. Interview a student about how he or she plans to use the skills learned in this journalism class in the future. Listen for good quotations. Write a feature story about the student that is suitable for a high school newspaper or news magazine. Effectively use both direct and indirect quotes in your story. Write a draft, and then, using correct copy editing symbols, edit and rewrite your story, checking for clarity, engaging language, and the correct use of English. Send your story to your teacher electronically.

7. Use the Internet to read a foreign newspaper. If English is your second language, read a newspaper in your native language. Print out three or four stories and highlight the quotations using three colors: (1) Moves the story forward, (2) Makes a point, and (3) Creates dialogue. Rewrite one of the stories, reworking the quotations. If English is your second language, you may want to first rewrite the story in your native language, and then translate it into English. Be sure to attribute each quotation.

CHAPTER 7 | Assessment

Review Journalism Concepts

7.1 Define Quotations

There are three types of quotations — direct quotations, indirect quotations and partial quotations. Direct quotations are the exact words spoken by the source. With indirect quoting, you paraphrase the source's words for clarity or brevity. With partial quotations, you quote part of a source's actual words. Quotations are enclosed within quotation marks to show the exact words of the speaker. Broadcast and electronic news reporters listen for sound bites the way print reporters listen for quotations. Sound bites are cuts of an audio or video recording that contain the source's best quotes or that make a point. Journalists obtain quotations from sources during interviews, in meetings and from speeches.

7.2 Modify Quotations

Journalists disagree over whether quotations should be modified. One camp believes quotes should not be modified even to correct minor grammatical errors or word usage. The other camp believes quotes can be modified to correct grammar. Most journalists agree that quotes should be changed to remove offensive language. All journalists agree that all quotations must be accurate, even if modified.

7.3 Use Quotations

Reporters know how to use quotations effectively to add to the story or surprise or entertain the reader. Quotes move a story forward, make a point and create dialogue. Quotations move a story forward by avoiding redundancy. You do this by paraphrasing some of the information and let the quote move the story to the next point. Quotations should support the main points of your story. Dialogue should be used sparingly by journalists. It is useful in narrative feature or news stories and when showing the back-and-forth interchange of opposing sides.

All quotations must be attributed to the source. Equally important is attributing sources for charts, graphs, graphics, photographs and other materials. The word "said" is preferred for attributing quotations. Attribution usually is placed in the middle or at the end of a quote.

Plagiarism, using another person's words or works and passing them off as your own, is never acceptable. In journalism, all attribution goes into the copy.

Develop Your Journalism Language

Write the letter of the term that matches each definition. One term will not be used.

_____ 1. Describes words or sentences that provide the same information

_____ 2. Punctuation that shows words have been omitted from the copy

_____ 3. Punctuation marks that enclose a source's exact words

_____ 4. Paraphrase

_____ 5. Cut of an audio- or videotape used in broadcast and electronic news

_____ 6. The back and forth of conversation

_____ 7. Part of a source's spoken words

_____ 8. Words or remarks that offend, insult or threaten a person or group

_____ 9. A source's exact words

_____ 10. Naming your source

a. attribution
b. dialogue
c. direct quotation
d. ellipses
e. indirect quotation
f. jargon
g. offensive language
h. partial quotation
i. quotation marks
j. redundant
k. sound bite

11. A remark that insults a group of people would be considered
    a. an indirect quotation.
    b. offensive language.
    c. a sound bite.
    d. conflict of interest.

12. Which goes at the beginning and end of the source's spoken words?
    a. quotation marks
    b. commas
    c. ellipses
    d. semicolons

13. Which needs quotation marks to indicate a source's words?
    a. indirect quotation
    b. direct quotation
    c. paraphrase
    d. sound bite

14. Which refers to the vocabulary that pertains to a particular field?
    a. sound bite
    b. ellipses
    c. jargon
    d. attribution

15. Which is the same as an indirect quotation?
    a. ellipses
    b. sound bite
    c. partial quotation
    d. paraphrase

16. Which is a conversation between sources?
    a. direct quotation
    b. dialogue
    c. partial quotation
    d. sound bite

Think Critically

17. Why might you want to use quotations to reveal a source's controversial opinion?

18. Why might you paraphrase a source's words when the source uses jargon?

19. In paraphrasing, why is it important to stay close to the source's words rather than change them significantly?

20. Which is better to use — indirect quoting or partial quoting? Explain your answer.

21. Why do television stations use sound bites as commercials for the upcoming news?

22. Why is a recording device helpful when listening for quotations?

23. As a reporter, what meetings might you cover in your school?

24. Why should you use ellipses with extreme caution?

25. What could you do in an interview when your subject uses offensive language in answer to a question?

26. Why is accuracy so important with quotations?

27. Why omit redundancy in your writing?

28. Why should reporters make sure they credit their sources?

Make Academic Connections

29. **LAW**   A famous Supreme Court case — the 1991 case of Jeffrey Masson vs. The New Yorker magazine — added to the confusion among journalists over whether to change quotations even though the court wrote a definite answer. The court had the opportunity to decide if a "deliberate alteration" of an interviewee's words is protected by the First Amendment. Use the Internet to research this case. Incorporate at least three sources in your paper to evaluate and confirm the validity of the information. Write a paper that answers the following questions: As a journalist, do you think the courts should decide about news outlets changing quotes? Do you agree with the court's decision? Does the court's decision add to your confusion or help clarify your position on changing quotes? Explain your answer. Write a draft of your paper, incorporating both direct and indirect quotations, and then, using copy editing symbols, edit and rewrite your paper, paying attention to clarity, engaging language, and the correct use of English. Turn in your draft with your final paper.

30. **LANGUAGE ARTS**   Research plagiarism in journalism, and then write a news story suitable for a high school news publication that answers: What is plagiarism? What happens to journalists who are caught plagiarizing? How can you avoid plagiarizing? How does plagiarism undermine the foundation of journalistic ethics?

31. **CAREERS**   Research the careers of journalists who specialize in financial reporting. Create a fact sheet that includes information about the type of news financial reporters write and for which publications they write.

32. **SOCIAL STUDIES**   Read a current news story in your local newspaper and read about the same event in a foreign newspaper. Notice how quotations are used. Write a feature story suitable for a news magazine for a high school audience that compares and contrasts the way the two papers use quotations in stories.

33. **MULTIMEDIA**   List five famous quotations, and then edit the quotations into sound bites. Create a colorful bulletin board of the quotations. Then record the sound bites using a recorder. Use multimedia to add audio to the bulletin board.

34. **WRITING**   Develop a stylebook for your own reference. Use a notebook with tabs and notepaper. Select titles for the tabs. You might want to use the following titles: punctuation, abbreviations, sports words, ethics and attribution. Add more titles as needed. Add the AP Stylebook Concepts feature and any notes you have taken on style from the text. Also add any notes and examples that will help you easily find answers to your style questions. Continue to add to your stylebook as you progress through this course and in your future journalistic efforts.

Writing Portfolio Activity

35. This is a three-step activity. (1) Interview an adult about that person's job. Listen carefully for quotations. Write a feature story using at least one direct quote and one paraphrase. (2) Attend a meeting in your school or community. Listen carefully for quotations. Write a news story using at least one direct quotation and one partial quotation. (3) Listen to a speaker in your school or community. Listen carefully for quotations. Write a news story using at least two direct quotations. Revise and edit your three stories to ensure effective, grammatically correct writing. Add the stories to your portfolio.

AP Stylebook Workshop

Add quotation marks where needed in the following sentences according to AP style.

36. Journalists need to make sure the speaker's words are accurately reported, Amerato said at last night's meeting.

37. Journalists need to make sure the speaker's words are accurately reported, Amerato said. Too often I see what I've said misquoted.

ICT LITERACY: Multimedia Skills for Journalists

Today's world of technology-driven journalism requires journalists to offer employers a range of multimedia technological skills. In addition to knowing how to write tight, clear copy, journalists are expected to

- Be skilled in technology, including taking sharp digital photos that have impact and being proficient in the use of computers, smartphones, and audio and video recorders.
- Keep up with technological changes.

BE SKILLED IN TECHNOLOGY

While in high school, you want to prepare for your future career as well as use the information you gain in your current life. Take advantage of offerings in your school course schedule to put yourself one step ahead.

In addition to taking English and journalism courses to help you become a better writer, you also want to take classes in computer science, photography and Web page design.

If your schedule allows, consider courses in the drama department as well to learn about the technology of audio and video recording. These courses — along with classes in communications — will help you if you plan to enter the field of broadcasting.

When you plan your college classes, keep these same courses in mind, expanding them as the college offers. When choosing a college in which to study for a career in journalism, keep in mind the availability of technology-related courses.

KEEP UP WITH CHANGES IN TECHNOLOGY

Once you have graduated from college and are a working journalist, you need to stay abreast of the newest technology. Technology changes almost daily, and to make your contribution as a journalist, you must be up on the latest trends and equipment.

Many large news organizations offer ongoing training in the technology they use. Smaller news organizations expect employees to learn on their own or from peers. Backpack and freelance journalists do not have an organization with information-technology people backing them up, so they must keep up to date by talking with other journalists in the field or by taking continuing education courses offered through colleges and by reading journalism and technology-related magazines.

THINK *Critically*

Make a list of the technology-related courses in your high school and in the colleges you are considering attending. Review your list of current courses. Is it possible to add a technology-related course to your schedule? With your parents or guardians and school counselor, plan next year's schedule to allow for a technology-related class, such as computer science.

REAL PEOPLE REAL CAREERS

Susan Page has interviewed eight presidents. She interviewed Presidents Ronald Reagan, George H. W. Bush, Bill Clinton, George W. Bush and Barack Obama while they were in office. Page interviewed Presidents Richard Nixon, Gerald Ford and Jimmy Carter after they left office. As Washington bureau chief for USA Today, as well as in previous reporting roles, Page has interviewed untold numbers of high-level government officials. Still, she does her homework before her interviews, so she gets the best information and the best quotes.

Photo courtesy of Susan Page

"The hardest thing when you go in for an interview with a president or presidential candidate," she says, "is they've been interviewed so often it is hard to break through the boilerplate," meaning the same topics they always talk about. The challenge, she says, is to break new ground. Reporters get a set amount of time with the president or candidate and they have to make the most of it.

"The first president I interviewed was President Reagan," Page says. "I had a hard time. I was nervous. I hadn't gone in with a strategy." Experience is the best teacher and now, Page says, she thinks through her strategy before she goes in for an interview. She consults with other editors at the paper to get a different perspective and share her ideas. She talks to colleagues and she thinks about what readers will want to know. Of course, "I try to think through what would be newsworthy."

ADVICE FOR ASPIRING JOURNALISTS

When it comes to quoting presidents, Page says, it's important to be exact. "Remember, when a president is in office ... there is a whole division of the White House that records every word. You've got to quote them exactly." If you don't have the full quote or it's too rambling to use, "you paraphrase or use ellipses." Presidential candidates are a little more difficult. "Often you're catching them more on the fly," Page says. Yet, with cellphones and video recorders and other electronic equipment available, candidates too can be recorded, even on the fly. "I think in general you shouldn't change anything," Page says. "If it's between quotation marks it should be the person's words." It's also important to put quotes in context, she says. If a source tells you, "I disagree with the president on this issue, but I agree with him on everything else," you should use both parts of the quote to be fair.

Source: Personal interview with Susan Page.

THINK *Critically*

1. Why does Page, an experienced reporter, consult with others at the paper before an interview with a president or presidential candidate?

2. Should you ever change a president's quotes?

8

Writing Features

- **8.1** Types of Features
- **8.2** Narrative Stories
- **8.3** Personality Profiles

Planning a Feature Project

Leonardo DiCaprio, like many other Hollywood stars, calls the press when he has a movie about to be released. With his 2007 release, "The 11th Hour," it was especially critical to receive wide press coverage, because its subject is something everyone should care about. "The 11th Hour," a movie DiCaprio produced and narrated, is a documentary on the dire state of our natural environment.

At the same time, USA Weekend magazine editors were planning an issue devoted entirely to the environment. Newspapers know that using a celebrity on the cover draws readers, so they planned the issue to coincide with the opening of "The 11th Hour."

The editors negotiated with DiCaprio's press agent for permission to interview DiCaprio for a story and put him on the magazine cover. The editors also wanted an exclusive online piece that included movie footage with an introduction by DiCaprio. This was a sticking point with the press agent.

Negotiations between the magazine and the celebrity's press agent went back and forth, taking weeks. In the meantime, the editors planned alternative cover stories. Finally, while still negotiating the Internet part of the story, the editors had permission to go ahead with the cover and print interview story.

Negotiations between media outlets and celebrities are routine, with both sides giving a little. Although it's not unusual for negotiations to continue until the 11th hour, in this case, it was slightly ironic.

THINK *Critically*

1. Plan your strategy for getting an interview with an important figure in your high school. What will you propose and how will you make it attractive to your subject?

2. What should editors do while negotiating for an important story?

Types of Features

Goals

- Define types of feature stories.
- Describe the characteristics of feature stories.

Key Terms

- feature story 201
- human interest story 201
- informational feature story 202
- trend 203
- sidebar 204

FOCUS

Where do you begin when you pick up a newspaper? Is it the front page, where you will find the news of the day? Or do you go straight to a second or third section, where you expect to find features, profiles, entertainment and sports? When you go to a media outlet's Internet site, do you skip the front screen and the short news digests and instead click on your favorite sports or entertainment blog?

Features, profiles, sports and entertainment stories may be more appealing to you because they are written on topics you care about and in a different style than most news.

Types of Features

A **feature story** has all the journalistic elements of a news story but is written like a non-fiction short story. There is no formula for writing a feature, such as the inverted pyramid used for news. Features may be less timely than a news story. They may be longer; have a beginning, middle and end; and describe a person or place rather than an event. They are stories that can be found everywhere. Reporters on every beat in every part of a news organization come up with feature ideas from their interaction with people on their beats or in their everyday lives. Some of the best reporters covering news, sports, lifestyle, business or politics say they find features by observing the world around them. And some of the best feature writers say they find good stories by getting out of the newsroom, by going somewhere they have not gone before. Most of the feature stories you write for any section of the school newspaper probably will fall into the categories of human interest, informational or trends.

HUMAN INTEREST STORY

Human interest story is a catchall category for stories that are unusual, off-beat or just the result of keen observation. Stories about survivors of disasters are human interest, but so are stories about long-lost loves who reunite, or people who pursue their passions.

Photodisc/GettyImages

///// *If snowboarding is popular among students at your school, find out who is really good at it, go to the slopes and conduct an interview for a human interest story.*

Human interest stories have an emotional aspect — they make you smile or bring a tear to your eye. They detail something out of the ordinary, coyotes in New York's Central Park, for example. Or, they put an interesting spin on the ordinary, for example, people who stand in a ticket line days before tickets to a popular concert go on sale.

Your school is full of human interest stories. Listen to students talk at lunch or in the hallways about the places they go and the things they do after school or on weekends. Some of them may be very involved in activities that will make good human interest stories. Go where they go. You may find people who volunteer at local charities, show horses and win equestrian awards, compete in teen beauty pageants, perform in local theater or have unusual jobs. Report what they do, learn why they do it and get the details.

INFORMATIONAL FEATURE STORY

Informational feature stories provide information. They are stories in which experts help writers explain the story for readers. Media outlets are full of informational features on nutrition, diet, exercise, home improvement, travel and more. Informational features often answer the question "why?" Former Wall Street Journal reporter Jeff Bailey once wrote a feature story about why shoelaces don't stay tied.

Your newspaper staff may think about informational features as "how-to" stories. For example, how to prep for the SAT or ACT without taking an expensive course, how to lighten the nightly homework load, or how to dress for the prom for $100 or less are all good topics for an informational feature story. Just about any topic on which you would like to know more can become an informational feature story if you find the proper experts.

Your school is full of experts because that's what teachers are. Your calculus teacher may know a thing or two about budgeting. When you find out she also has dressed three daughters for proms, you have an expert on prom dressing on a budget. The math and English department heads probably have good ideas on how to prep for the SAT and will be more than willing to share them. Students who have special skills also can be experts for informational stories. Suppose you want to do a story on why skateboarding is popular with teen boys. Find a student who frequents the local skateboarding park to help you explain why it's popular and how to do it well.

Don't feel limited to sources at your school. Local colleges have a wide variety of experts, and their public relations offices usually keep a list of those who will speak to reporters. You also can go outside of the academic community to other experts in your city or state. Most people like to share their expertise and are willing to help reporters explain the topics in which they are interested.

TREND STORY

Trend stories often are the result of observation. A **trend** is a current style, what's in vogue, particularly when it comes to popular culture. It can be a tendency to use certain words or phrases, or go to certain places or events. Reporters sometimes jokingly say they think they have a trend when they have spotted or observed something three times or more. Yet it's not enough to tell readers you have observed something they should know about. In reporting on trends, you try to explain how the trend developed.

Some trends are very easy to spot. Fashion reporting is all about trends, which are strutted before fashion writers on the runways of New York and Milan. If miniskirts are shown by several designers, it's fair to say that the miniskirt is back in style. Fashion writers will declare it so, and they will talk to the designers about what inspired them to bring it back.

Entertainment writers are good trend spotters, scouring the daily trade newspapers, such as Variety and The Hollywood Reporter, to assess whether there are trends in the movies being made (action pics over romantic comedy flicks?), television shows being scripted (are we edging away from reality television?) or the top-selling music on iTunes.

Student journalists work in a world of trendsetters, so looking for trends can lead to good features. Keep your eyes open and ears tuned in everywhere you go. You might find a new local hangout or hear the latest catchphrase. Take notes, ask questions. It all could be part of the story.

*check*point ✓

What are three types of feature stories?

Characteristics of Features

Just as news stories have certain identifying characteristics — the five W's and inverted pyramid style, for example — so do the "other" stories you may read in the newspaper or on the Web: feature stories. Features can be written on any topic and found in every part of the newspaper or a media website. Features all have certain characteristics in common.

- **Facts**   Like news stories, feature stories are factual and reported. They are not the writer's opinion.

- **Relevance**   A feature story may not be as timely as a news story (though some are) but it will have relevance to your readers. It might grow out of a news event, such as a story about a family that survives a natural disaster. It might be a topic of importance to your readership because of location, such as whale watching in a Pacific Coast community. Or it might concern a timely topic, such as back-to-school trends in September.

- **Structure**   Feature stories have a beginning, middle and end. They have anecdotes that help bring the story to life quotes or dialogue that reveal and explain character; and pacing so it's easy for the reader to get through. Feature stories have a central point but it is not unveiled in the same manner as in a news story.

Feature stories can have impact. The story on a family that survives disaster might show through their loss the actual effect of the disaster. Features also can be entertaining. A back-to-school article on what students are wearing, carrying and talking about can be written with a humorous touch.

Features sometimes are written as a **sidebar** — or secondary story — to the news of the day. Suppose there's a power outage at your school and classes are unexpectedly dismissed. The news is the power outage, but your feature sidebar could be what students do with an unexpected day off.

checkpoint ✓

What are the characteristics of feature stories?

AP Stylebook Concepts

AP style includes guidelines for writing about business. Money is a big topic in business. AP style always uses lowercase for the words "dollar" and "cents." It uses figures and the dollar sign for most amounts. The word "cents" is spelled out. Numerals and the word "cents" are used for amounts less than a dollar. A dollar sign and decimals are used for amounts greater than a dollar.

Correct   Most items cost less than $10. For example, a salad is $2.25 and a pear is 45 cents.

Incorrect   Most items cost less than ten dollars. For example, a salad is 2 dollars and 25 cents and a pear is 45¢.

Use the following as a guide for numbers less than $1 million: $6, $56, $456, $3,456, $23,456 and $123,456. For amounts greater than $1 million, use up to two decimal places: $9.12 million. Do not use a hyphen to connect numerals to the word "million."

Correct   Granger is worth $98.12 million. He has a $30 million estate in Grant County and his annual salary is $5 million.

Incorrect   Granger is worth $98.123 million. He has a $30-million estate in Grant County and his annual salary is $5,000,000.

Human Interest Story

By Victor Xu, Carmel High School, Carmel, Ind., Excerpted from "Japan Disasters Leave Lasting Impact on Students Here"

Earthquake, tsunami and nuclear disaster create personal repercussions for students with loved ones in Japan.

Following the earthquake and subsequent catastrophes of tsunami and nuclear meltdown in Japan, junior Youkow Homma said he was concerned for the status of his family and friends who live in Tokyo and in the badly damaged city of Sendai. When the U.S. government advised travelers to cancel their visits, his family had to change its spring break travel plans.

"Going back to the normal way of life is going to take a long time, especially with the radiation," Homma said. "Tokyo is going back to normal, but the affected areas like Sendai are going to be hard to adjust. I saw some video footage of the high school where my friend goes; it's changed."

The 9.0 magnitude earthquake, the largest ever in Japan and the fourth largest in recorded history, struck Japan's Miyagi prefecture on its east coast in the afternoon of March 11, according to cnn.com. The temblor was exacerbated by a towering 30-foot tsunami on its heels and a nuclear meltdown. Its effects were felt across the Pacific Ocean with tsunami alerts on faraway coasts in the United States, Chile and Canada.

Masako Kamano, chaperone of the Carmel-Seikyo exchange program and English teacher at Seikyo Gakuen, said the devastating earthquake is a defining moment of Japan.

"We know this was the biggest earthquake after the war, during this century, even in the world—not only in Japan, but all over the world," Kamano said. "We just experienced the Kobe earthquake about 10 years ago, but this was much bigger than that one. This will remain in our people's minds longer, I think."

Homma said he has been able to speak with his family in Tokyo and his friend in Sendai several times since the catastrophes occurred. Sendai, which was the nearest major city to the epicenter, was one of the most severely damaged cities in Japan, due to its proximity.

"They can't really make food right now, and the emergency relief efforts are good, but sometimes they're not enough," he said. "I have a friend who lives in Sendai, where the earthquake was worse, and they had to split an emergency biscuit with a family next door for dinner, and that's all they had."

Used by permission of Victor Xu.

THINK *Critically*

1. What elements of this human interest story make it effective for a high school newspaper?

2. Think of several topics for human interest stories that currently relate to your school. Choose one of the topics and develop the story.

8.1 | Assessment

Understand Concepts

Determine the best answer for each of the following questions.

1. A story that focuses on how to make healthy choices when eating in a restaurant is an example of a(n)
   a. human interest feature.
   c. sidebar feature.
   b. informational feature.
   d. trend feature.

2. Common characteristics of feature stories include
   a. answers to the questions "how?" and "why?"
   b. brevity, humor and timeliness.
   c. details, in-depth coverage and point of view.
   d. facts, relevance and structure.

3. **True or False** A key component of a trend story is an explanation of how the trend developed.

4. **True or False** Feature stories are structured in the inverted pyramid journalistic style.

Write Now!

Practice your writing skills with the following activities.

5. For the next week, practice your observation skills. Look for events, trends, interesting people and other information that you come across that might make a good feature story. Make notes about your observations, and then create an outline of three story ideas.

6. Use the Internet to research a holiday celebrated in a non-English-speaking country that is similar to a holiday in this country. Write a broadcast feature for a high school audience that compares and contrasts the two holiday celebrations. As part of the feature, translate words specific to the foreign holiday celebration and teach your audience how to pronounce them.

7. Choose a major story from an online news site, such as CNN or MSNBC, that has sidebars. Print out the main story and highlight the primary facts. Then print out the sidebars. Write a paper that details how the sidebars are relevant to the main story and the structure of each sidebar. Detail the central point of each sidebar; explain how anecdotes and quotes help the story come alive; and describe the beginning, middle and end. Show how each sidebar uses any or all of the elements of news — has impact, is unexpected, has conflict, is about someone prominent, and has proximity to your school or community. Before writing your final paper, write a draft, and then, using correct copy editing symbols, edit your paper for clarity, engaging language and correct English grammar. Send your draft and paper to your teacher electronically.

Narrative Stories

Goals

- Describe narrative writing.
- Describe how to write a narrative story.

Key Terms

- narrative 207
- narrate 208
- lead 210
- body 211
- kicker 212

Narrative Writing

Feature writers often use narrative form, no matter what type of feature they are writing. Writing a **narrative** is different from writing news because it uses techniques of oral storytelling — that told by a narrator. Narrative storytelling is engaging, creative and compelling. It is a story written from the narrator's perspective. Like a news story, a narrative feature story also is accurate, factual, precise and, therefore, journalistic. But narrative style requires a little more room for the lead than a news story needs so the writer can draw the reader in. Narrative stories are likely to need more space than a news story so the writer has room to spin a good tale. Here's the lead on a narrative feature written by Nick Sortal, a reporter at the South Florida Sun-Sentinel.

> The sun isn't up yet, but Donald Miller locks his second-story apartment and eases downs the stairs to the ground floor. It takes a few seconds to get the morning creaks out.
>
> He's an 82-year-old man going on a 10-mile walk.
>
> "Gonna be a nice one today," he says, but you get the feeling that's his line every day before going around and through Plantation Central Park. Because he's consistent.

Every complete sentence has a verb, which is a word that shows action or a state of being. Action verbs are useful for journalists because they show what the subject is doing in the sentence. For example, in the sentence "John wrote a great feature," the verb *wrote* shows John's action.

Action verbs can describe physical actions, such as "John wrote," or mental actions, such as "John thought."

Journalists use action verbs to move the story along with impact and interest. Good journalists choose specific action verbs to add to the mental image they want the reader to get. To write "John pondered" produces a different image than to say "John thought." To say, "John wrote the story" produces a different image than to say, "John sweated over the story."

He has walked every day this year, he says, and in each of the past 17 years he has at least walked the equivalent of Maine to San Diego.

Just for the fun of it.

From Nick Sortal, "A Walk in the Park," *South Florida Sun-Sentinel*, 12/30/2003. © 2003 Nick Sortal and used with his kind permission.

The five-paragraph descriptive lead is tightly written and filled with detail. It sets the reader up to want more of the story. Descriptive and other alternative leads you can use to begin a story were discussed in Chapter 4. Feature stories of every genre — entertainment, human interest or any other — are opportunities to use those leads.

Narrative storytelling in journalistic writing was also discussed in Chapter 4. Narrative stories are told chronologically. "Narrative" comes from the word **narrate**, which means to tell a story in detail. Note how Sortal narrates in these paragraphs from his story on Miller.

He wears the same blue-gray pants, Kmart T-shirt and white visor. When they deteriorate, he replaces them with the most economical replicas.

He likes it simple.

His walking record was 5,300 miles when he was 72. But even this year, admittedly slowing down and going easier on weekends, he'll stroll more than 3,500. The 17-year grand journey: about 74,000 miles.

He's not a slave to his route. He's not beholden to time. He does not have a family to report to. He even is free enough to step on the sidewalk cracks.

On this day, to get in another mile, Miller doubles back three times along Nob Hill Road. Jack Fisher, a crossing guard for nearby Central Park Elementary School, starts his shift at 7 a.m. and the pair often discuss the Dolphins, the Marlins, the Heat — and the heat.

From Nick Sortal, "A Walk in the Park," *South Florida Sun-Sentinel*, 12/30/2003. © 2003 Nick Sortal and used with his kind permission.

Fisher has stood at this corner for five years, watching Miller walk through the rain, usually without a jacket, and the humidity, still in his long pants.

"I think the walking keeps him going," says Fisher, also 82. "He's here every single day. Unbelievable."

By 8 a.m. Miller has taken a shady route past a dozen developments, catching Broward Boulevard and heading east. He pulls on his visor as the maintenance crews fire up their mowers and the rush-hour crowd accelerates through yellow lights. His story unfolds with each step.

From Nick Sortal, "A Walk in the Park," South Florida Sun-Sentinel, 12/30/2003.
© 2003 Nick Sortal and used with his kind permission.

Sortal goes on to tell more of Miller's life story as the walk continues and the reader meets more of Miller's acquaintances along the way. Then Sortal ends the story with a kicker quote from Miller and a summation of his own.

"I don't like staying around much in my apartment," he says. "I like to get out and see what the rest of the world is doing." Which is why the next day, before sunrise, he'll be up and ready, eager to do it all over again.

From Nick Sortal, "A Walk in the Park," South Florida Sun-Sentinel, 12/30/2003.
© 2003 Nick Sortal and used with his kind permission.

Sortal's story has all the characteristics of a good feature: It has facts (miles Miller walked, clothes he wears, people who see him). It has detail and precision (where he goes, what time he leaves, where he buys the clothes). It has narrative style (Sortal sets up the story and tells it in chronological order with a beginning, middle and end). Finally, it has dialogue or quotes (Sortal talks to people who know Miller as well as to Miller himself).

checkpoint ✓

Describe narrative writing.

Write a Narrative Story

Narrative writing is different from oral storytelling because oral storytellers don't have to be as organized as writers. Narrative writers must develop a strong beginning and a descriptive middle, and wrap it all up in the end. The characters in the story come to life because the writer uses detail to let the reader into that life.

THE LEAD

The **lead** opens the story. Look at how Sortal begins this story about a woman whose son was the first from his area to die in the Vietnam War. Sortal tracked her down 34 years later because mothers were losing sons in Iraq and going through the pain she had experienced.

> News traveled slower during America's last unpopular war.
>
> A story buried in the July 1, 1970, newspaper reported that eight unidentified men, aboard two helicopters, were shot down in Cambodia the day before. It took two more days for the man in the car with the U.S. Army license tag to pull into Beulah Kellam's driveway in Pembroke Pines.
>
> At 7:10 a.m. July 3, he rang the doorbell. He looked at his clipboard, confirmed that the woman at the door was Donnith Fletcher's mother, and began, "I'm sorry, but it's my duty to inform you . . ."
>
> The past year has rekindled those memories and she feels a little pang each day the TV reports more young Americans dying in war.
>
> From Nick Sortal, "Price of Freedom," South Florida Sun-Sentinel, 6/28/2004. © 2004 Nick Sortal and used with his kind permission.

He opens with a simple sentence. His second and third paragraphs are filled with details.

> It took two more days ... the car with the U.S. Army license tag . . . at 7:10 a.m. . . . he looked at his clipboard.
>
> **Source:** Nick Sortal, "Price of Freedom," South Florida Sun-Sentinel, 6/28/2004. © 2004 Nick Sortal and used with his kind permission.

His fourth paragraph tells the reader why this story is relevant today.

> The past year has rekindled those memories and she feels a little pang each day the TV reports more young Americans dying in war.
>

THE BODY

The **body** — the middle — of the narrative is where the writer develops the story with details and quotes. This is part of the body of Sortal's story on the Vietnam War soldier's mom.

> Donnith Fletcher left for Vietnam from his Army training post in Oakland, Calif., on Oct. 3, 1969, and wrote often to his family, reassuring that he'd be back soon.
>
> Beulah believed it. On June 29, 1970, Beulah saw the 6 p.m. news and smiled when the anchorman said U.S. troops were leaving Cambodia and the most dangerous part of her son's stint was over.
>
> "I was so relieved," Beulah says. "I thought he was out of there."
>
> But he wasn't. Fletcher and others stayed back, about two miles inside Cambodia.
>
> On June 30, Fletcher and seven others were shot down and killed. The soldiers were on helicopters Nos. 3,862 and 3,863 to be reported shot down or missing during the Vietnam War, and Beulah never did find out details — such as who did the shooting or what exactly her son was doing. They were among the 58,000 Americans who died in the 11 years of the U.S. involvement. Beulah says she barely remembers the minutes after the Army official told her Donnith had been killed. She had seen the Army car pull into the driveway, but it was morning and she was groggy.
>
> "I thought they were coming to tell me he was coming home," she says. "I really thought it might be good news." Donnith, 21, was buried July 10 at Fred Hunter's Memorial Gardens in West Hollywood, a mile or two from Beulah's home, his McArthur High School and their church. The military delivered a posthumous Purple Heart.
>

He continues to use details: "Beulah saw the 6 p.m. news and smiled . . . the Army car pull into the driveway . . . she was groggy." He uses his quotes sparingly, but picks the quotes with emotion. "I thought they were coming to tell me he was coming home," she says.

THE KICKER

In the **kicker**, the ending of the story, Sortal continues to tell Beulah's story — she is widowed and finds love again with a man as patriotic as she remains. But Sortal brings the story back around in the end to the reason he wanted to tell her story to begin with. His last sentence is a quote from Beulah.

> "If this country and our freedoms aren't worth fighting for, why are we here?" she says.
>
> **Source:** Nick Sortal, "Price of Freedom," South Florida Sun-Sentinel, 6/28/2004. © 2004 Nick Sortal and used with his kind permission.

checkpoint ✓

What are the three parts of the narrative story?

///// *Why is the quote from Beulah in Nick Sortal's story an effective kicker?*

jbrizendine/iStockphoto.com

8.2 | Assessment

Understand Concepts

Determine the best answer for each of the following questions.

1. Writing a narrative story differs from writing a news story because a narrative
   a. uses storytelling techniques.
   b. is written in the inverted pyramid style.
   c. uses action verbs.
   d. is fictional.

2. The body of the narrative story is developed with
   a. facts and figures.
   b. details and quotes.
   c. explanations provided by experts.
   d. quotes and opinions.

3. **True or False**   Chronology is important to the structure of a narrative story.

4. **True or False**   The narrative writer develops the story with details and quotes in the body of the story.

Write Now!

Practice your writing skills with the following activities.

5. Research Internet news sites to find a narrative story. Download the story and highlight the lead in one color, the body in another and the kicker in a third color. Write an analysis of the story. Include details about how the lead pulls in the reader; use direct and indirect quotes from the story to show how quotes and other details develop the story and make it interesting to the reader; and explain how the kicker brings the reader back to the beginning. Write a draft of your analysis, and then, using copy editing symbols, edit your analysis for clarity, engaging language and correct English. Email your draft and final analysis to your teacher.

6. Use the Internet to locate information sources such as persons, databases, reports and past interviews to gather background information on a person in your community you would like to interview. For example, you might interview the principal at your school, a council member or the mayor, a prominent business person, or a community volunteer. Evaluate and confirm the validity of background information from a variety of sources such as other qualified persons, books and reports. Use your research to prepare for, and obtain, an interview with the person you have chosen. Plan and write relevant questions before the interview. Turn your interview into a narrative story. Be sure to include all characteristics of a narrative. Incorporate direct and indirect quotations. Your audience is the reader of the local newspaper.

8.3

Personality Profiles

Goals

- Identify what you need to write a good profile.
- Describe celebrity profiles.

Key Terms

- profile 214
- biography 214
- celebrity 215

FOCUS

Stories about people and the circumstances of their lives fill the mainstream media. But how well can one get to know a person in a newspaper story? The best way is through personality profiles, and you'll find them tucked in all parts of a publication — the business and sports sections, lifestyle and entertainment, even news.

Profiles

Profiles are feature stories about people. They can be ordinary people or they can be celebrated people — movie actors, athletes and rock stars, for example. Profiles bring people to life and give readers a glimpse of their character or personality. A profile is not a biography. A **biography** is an account of a person's life. It can be a short piece limited to significant milestones and accomplishments, or it can be a comprehensive review of all aspects of a person's life. A profile has a more limited focus and includes biographical details to help tell the story.

All profiles, whether they are about an ordinary person or a celebrity, require good preparation. You should learn as much as possible about your subjects before you interview them. Country music singer Martina McBride once told a class of journalism students that the only thing that annoys her when she meets with interviewers is being asked questions about her background or career history that are easily answered in the reams of material that have been written about her. She thinks it shows that a reporter is not prepared, and she may be correct.

Of course, not every profile subject is as well-known as McBride. Reporter Nick Sortal had been watching Donald Miller walk for about five years. It may have been unintended research, but he knew things about Miller before he approached him about an interview. "He walked for hours. He wore the same shirt and pants every day. I'd wave, he'd wave back, and I continued with my bike ride or jog," Sortal says.

To write a good profile you need the following:

- **The cooperation of your subject**   Imagine a teacher at your school wins a national teaching award. To write a profile you will need an interview and some time to observe the teacher in the classroom. The teacher will have to OK the observation and give you the time you need for interviewing.

- **Input from people around the subject**   If you are writing about a teacher, you will want to talk to colleagues, students, friends, relatives and the principal, at least. To write about a student you'll want to talk to friends, family and teachers. Miller, the walker, lived alone but Sortal talked to all the folks Miller met along his walking route.

- **Background and biographical material**   In the case of celebrities, you may find many other stories, even books, have been written that you can use for research. You may want to verify details with your subject but you don't want to use up all your time talking about the past or well-known facts about his or her life. With non-celebrity profile subjects, you may need to depend on them or family members and longtime friends for information about the past.

Use the tips about interviewing discussed in Chapter 6 to interview the subject of your profile.

 *Imagine this teacher just won a statewide teaching award. List the people you would interview to write a good profile of her.*

check point ✓

What do you need to write a good profile?

Celebrity Profiles

"Celebrity" is a relative term. It comes from the word "celebrate." A **celebrity** is a celebrated person, a person of note. Who are the people of note in your school? Successful athletes? Debate team winners? Gifted musicians? Radio personalities? Prom queens? Who are the names that everyone knows and those whose names should be known?

WHO IS A CELEBRITY?

As editors and writers on your school publication, you decide who will make a good story and whether they are celebrities in your school. Maybe it's the lead of the high school musical, or a musician who practices in a garage every night with his band mates. Maybe it's a successful alumna who is coming to speak at an assembly. There are plenty of worthy people about whom the staff might write profiles and who in your world may qualify as celebrities.

Because they are feature stories, profiles of celebrities are a staple of feature, entertainment and sports sections. Writing them requires a little different approach just because the subject is well-known.

For your school publication, you probably can arrange an interview directly with the person about whom you want to write — for example, the musical lead or the star athlete. In the professional journalism arena, an interview with a celebrity or high-profile person often is arranged through a press representative, also called a press agent, publicist or publicity agent.

There are press representatives for individuals, teams, bands, movies and television shows. Politicians such as mayors and governors have press representatives, as do presidential campaigns and government committees. Reporters who write celebrity profiles regularly are used to negotiating with publicists — sometimes more than one — over the amount of time they will get with the celebrity, the place they will meet, and other details.

"I learned early on to treat each and every publicist with respect and courtesy even if they are obviously not as keen on being cordial to others as you are," says USA Today film writer Susan Wloszczyna (pronounced wuh-ZIN'-uh). "Personal publicists see their job as protecting their client and they cherry-pick which (news and feature) outlets will give them the most bang for their buck — or rather, time."

Some press representatives try to get reporters to give them their questions for the celebrity in advance. Reporters generally don't agree to give specific questions to them, but they will tell the press representative the topics they might want to cover.

Wloszczyna says she does research from articles and biographies and always writes a list of questions for interviews, whether in person or on the phone. "While reminding me what to make sure to ask, it also allows room for spontaneity without going totally off topic." You may not have biographies to use in your research on local or school "celebrities," but you may find previous newspaper or Internet articles on them. Also, you shouldn't go to interview the star of your high school musical without knowing whether she has had other leading roles or parts elsewhere. Developing a detailed list of questions from your research will help you get what you need for a good story and show your subjects you have a respect for their interest.

Source: Personal Interview with Susan Wloszczyna

PEOPLE WHO KNOW THE CELEBRITY

Just as you will look for people to interview who know your profile subject, professional profile writers want input from people who know the celebrity well. Getting it can be difficult,

///// *List all the students at your school you would consider celebrities. Explain why each qualifies as a celebrity.*

Photodisc/Getty Images

however, because celebrities want to control who will talk about them. One reporter in the midst of writing a profile on Julia Roberts some years ago found a phone number for the actress's mother, who lived in the suburbs of Atlanta. The reporter left a phone message for Roberts' mom, but the return call came from Roberts' press representative. The reporter was told that Julia's mother would not cooperate with the story.

However, there are just as many cases of longtime friends or family who are willing to talk about their famous connections. When they do, it can be insightful.

In this USA Weekend profile of actor George Clooney, both his father, Nick Clooney, a broadcaster, and his famous aunt, singer Rosemary Clooney, with whom George lived when he first went to Hollywood, spoke candidly about George.

Rosemary says she always knew George would end up entertaining audiences for a living. "He was the youngest of all the children (including her five), so he had to work a little to get the attention, which was his main goal in life."

Yet neither Rosemary nor Nick wanted George to pursue acting. Nick, now 61 and a host of cable's American Movie Classics channel, thought he could steer George back to broadcasting, his son's first career choice and the one Nick saw as safer. "I was afraid that even with talent he wouldn't be able to break through and succeed. What I shortchanged him on was his absolute dedication."

Nick recalls a painful parental moment when, worried for his son, he tried to persuade him to return home to Augusta, Ky. "Come back, finish school, and when you're finished you'll have (broadcasting) to fall back on," he fairly pleaded in a phone call to California. "There was this long pause. Then he said, 'Pop, if I have something to fall back on, I'll fall back.'"

Source: From USA WEEKEND Magazine. Used with permission.

Through those anecdotes and memories of his family members, Clooney becomes more real. You can imagine him as a child trying to get attention, and later, as a young adult, trying to tell his father he won't come back.

If family or friends won't cooperate, colleagues such as teammates in the case of sports personalities, fellow actors in the case of movie or television actors or band mates in the case of musicians can offer anecdotes and quotations. It's worth the pursuit of outside voices to give the personality profile some outside perspective.

checkpoint ✓

Who are celebrities?

8.3 | Assessment

Understand Concepts

Determine the best answer for each of the following questions.

1. Arrangements for an interview with a high-profile person are often made through a(n)
   a. celebrity negotiator.
   b. editor.
   c. friend or family member.
   d. press representative.

2. **True or False**   "Profile" is another name for a biography.

3. **True or False**   When writing profiles, you should learn as much as possible about your subjects before you interview them.

Write Now!

Practice your writing skills with the following activities.

4. Identify a student in your school as an appropriate subject for a personality profile. Plan and write questions for an interview with the person, and then secure the interview. Also be sure to interview friends and family of the person. Write a profile feature that would be suitable for your high school magazine. Include direct and indirect quotes from the person and from friends and family. Before writing your final paper, use a computer to write a draft, and then use the track changes function on your word-processing software to edit the draft. Check for clarity, engaging language and the correct use of English grammar and mechanics. Send the original draft, the edited draft and the final profile to your teacher electronically.

Popular Actresses Win Libel Lawsuits Over Weight Reports

Celebrities often complain that news and gossip outlets get their facts wrong, but they rarely sue over errors. However, two of Hollywood's most popular actresses decided they would not allow false allegations about their weight and health to go unanswered.

Kate Hudson, who is American and lives in the United States, and Kate Winslet, who is English and lives in Britain, were successful when, in separate cases, they sued publications that wrote false statements about them. Both popular, successful actresses said they didn't want false reports about their appearance and diets to have a negative impact on young women. Both actresses sued in Britain, where libel laws are more favorable to public figures than those in the United States because in Britain the defendant (the news organization) must prove that what they published is true.

Hudson sued the American tabloid The National Enquirer, which is sold in Britain, for suggesting she had an eating disorder and calling her "painfully thin." The Enquirer wrote that Hudson's mother, the movie star Goldie Hawn, was concerned about her daughter and begging her to eat. Hudson won undisclosed damages and an apology from The Enquirer.

She said she sued because she didn't want impressionable girls to think she was starving herself. She was worried about the impact of such reports on young women and "I just couldn't let someone accuse me of something that serious — and such a blatant lie."

In Winslet's case, she sued the British version of the international fashion magazine Grazia for falsely reporting that she had visited a diet doctor in Los Angeles. Winslet has been openly critical of what she sees as Hollywood's obsession with being thin. She also was awarded an undisclosed amount in damages and an apology.

Winslet said she believes "very strongly that 'curves' are natural, womanly and real. I shall continue to hope that women are able to believe in themselves for who they are inside, and not feel under such incredible pressure to be unnaturally thin."

THINK *Critically*

1. Why did actresses Kate Hudson and Kate Winslet sue the publications that wrote about their weight?
2. Why did the women decide to make a stand on the weight stories?

CHAPTER 8 | Assessment

Review Journalism Concepts

8.1 Types of Features

Most features fall into three categories — human interest, informational or trends. Human interest is a catchall category for stories that are unusual, offbeat or the result of keen observation. Informational features provide information. Trend stories often are the result of observation. A trend is a current style or preference. Features sometimes are written as a sidebar, or secondary story, about current news.

Features have three main characteristics in common — facts, relevance and structure. Like news stories, feature stories are factual. They are not the writer's opinion. A feature story may not be as timely as a news story, though some are, but it will have relevance to your readers. It might grow out of a news event. It might be a topic of importance to your readership because of location. Or it might concern a timely topic. A feature story has a beginning, middle and end. Anecdotes help bring the story to life; quotes or dialogue reveal character and provide exposition; pacing makes the story easy to read.

8.2 Narrative Stories

Writing a narrative is different from writing a news story because a narrative uses techniques of oral storytelling. Narrative storytelling is engaging, creative and compelling. It is a story written from the narrator's perspective. Like a news story it also is accurate, factual, precise and, therefore, journalistic. The characteristics of a good feature story are the use of facts, an emphasis on detail and a narrative style that uses chronological order and dialogue or quotes to tell the story.

Narrative writers must develop a strong beginning, or lead; a descriptive middle, or body; and a kicker to wrap it all up in the end. The characters in the story come to life because the writer uses detail to let the reader into that life.

8.3 Personality Profiles

Profiles are stories about people. They can be ordinary people or they can be celebrities. Profiles bring people to life and give readers a glimpse of their character or personality. A profile is not a biography.

You need three things to write a profile: cooperation from your subject, input from people around the subject and background and biographical material.

Celebrities are celebrated people. They can also be described as people of note. There are celebrities within most groups, such as schools and communities. Some celebrities are more famous than others.

Develop Your Journalism Language

Write the letter of the term that matches each definition. Some terms will not be used.

_____ 1. Catchall category for stories that are unusual, offbeat or just the result of keen observation

_____ 2. Celebrated person or person of note

_____ 3. Current style or something in vogue

_____ 4. Secondary story

_____ 5. Story that provides information and uses experts to help explain the story

_____ 6. Feature story about a person

_____ 7. To tell a story in detail

_____ 8. Story that has the elements of a news story and is engaging, creative and told from the writer's perspective

_____ 9. The end of a narrative story

a. biography
b. body
c. celebrity
d. feature story
e. human interest story
f. informational feature
g. kicker
h. lead
i. narrate
j. narrative
k. profile
l. sidebar
m. trend

10. An emotional aspect that makes you smile, laugh or cry is a characteristic of a
   a. human interest story.
   b. personality profile.
   c. sidebar.
   d. trend feature.

11. The beginning of a narrative story is called the
   a. summary.
   b. narrative.
   c. lead.
   d. kicker.

12. An informational feature story often can be described as a __?__ story.
   a. filler
   b. formula
   c. how-to
   d. what-if

13. In narrative writing, the narrator
   a. creates the characters.
   b. is a character in the story.
   c. offers an opinion.
   d. tells the story.

14. Narrative stories are told
   a. in chronological order.
   b. in installments over several days.
   c. in the subject's own words.
   d. through flashbacks.

15. This part of a narrative story is developed with details and quotes.
   a. body
   b. kicker
   c. lead
   d. summary

16. This type of story is about current styles, what's in vogue, particularly when it comes to popular culture.
   a. informational
   b. trend
   c. celebrity profile
   d. human interest

Think Critically

17. In which section of a print or online newspaper will you find feature stories?

18. Why do you think Nick Sortal, feature reporter for the South Florida Sun-Sentinel, advises reporters, "First, get out of the newsroom; then, get out of the car. And, preferably, go somewhere you haven't been before. You'll likely end up with a good story."

19. Brainstorm a list of human interest stories you could write for your school paper. Choose one and write a one-paragraph explanation of the story's emotional appeal.

20. Name an informational feature story idea on a school-related topic that interests you. Write a list of sources you would use in writing this story.

21. Identify a trend in your school. How would you go about writing a story about this trend?

22. How is narrative writing different from a writing a news story?

23. How is narrative writing similar to writing a news story?

24. What is the purpose of a personality profile?

25. Explain how the central point of a feature story is unveiled. How is this different from a news story?

26. Explain how a feature story might be relevant to readers in terms of an event.

27. Explain how a feature story might be relevant to readers in terms of a location.

28. Explain how a feature story might be relevant to readers in terms of a time.

29. Why is "celebrity" a relative term? Explain your answer in terms of your school setting.

30. Why do reporters hesitate to provide a celebrity with a list of questions in advance of an interview?

31. What does a reporter hope to get from an interview with someone who knows a celebrity?

Make Academic Connections

32. **HISTORY**   Choose a famous journalist from history such as one of the following: Walter Cronkite, Edward R. Murrow, Joseph Pulitzer, Benjamin Franklin, Tom Wolfe or David Halberstam. Use the Internet to search reports, articles and the journalist's work to gather background information on the journalist. Evaluate and confirm the validity of the information from a variety of sources. Write a profile feature about the journalist that identifies the historical events that shaped the reporter's work. Incorporate direct and indirect quotes. Your feature should be appropriate for a national news magazine.

33. **TECHNOLOGY** YouTube encourages professional and citizen journalists to use technology to publish information in video format. Study several videos on YouTube, and then as a reporter create a video that could be uploaded to YouTube that answers this question: How might videos on YouTube change the way mainstream media journalists report the news?

34. **SCIENCE** Locate a feature story about science. Write a short critique of the story. Identify examples of the characteristics of a feature described in this chapter.

35. **WRITING** Plan a paper describing how feature writing can be used to help readers understand complex issues and information. Write a draft, and then, using copy editing symbols, edit your draft for clarity, engaging language and the correct use of English.

36. **MUSIC** Use the Internet to locate a personality profile of a celebrity musician. Rewrite the profile, adding research information from other sources such as past interviews and articles. Evaluate and confirm the validity of the information from a variety of sources. Also add any information you think is appropriate, such as a link to the artist's website or an audio clip of the musician. Write the profile in feature style, for your school website.

37. **RESEARCH** Choose a major news story from a national or local newspaper. Research to determine topics that would be appropriate for a sidebar for the story. Using your research, write the sidebar for the story.

38. **GEOGRAPHY** Find a feature story in a newspaper that depends on location for relevance. Write a short paragraph explaining why this feature is appropriate for the newspaper, where it was published and why it might not be appropriate for another publication.

Writing Portfolio Activity

39. Choose a celebrity in your school and write a personality profile. Make journal entries describing the planning, interviewing and writing process.

AP Stylebook Workshop

Rewrite the sentences to conform to AP style.

40. The county budget for next year is approximately $45 million dollars.

41. The organization hopes to raise two million dollars at this year's gala.

42. It is not unusual for a recent medical school graduate to owe more than a hundred thousand dollars in student loans.

CREATIVITY AND INNOVATION: Characteristics of a Good Reporter

Reporters come from all over the world. They have different personalities, values and reasons for becoming reporters. Still, good reporters have common characteristics. They are passionate about their work. They believe they have a calling to find and report the stories and keep their readers and listeners informed. They also have honed their skills. To become a good reporter, you need

- Good reporting skills
- Ways to continually improve your skills

GOOD REPORTING SKILLS

Creativity and innovation   Reporters must think on their feet. They need to act quickly when a story breaks and be able to think creatively. They must be able to analyze and evaluate the situation and their approach to the story and constantly seek to improve their creative efforts.

Communication skills   Reporters must develop and communicate ideas effectively, both orally and in writing.

Listening skills   Reporters must clearly hear what others are saying, including other reporters, editors and the people they interview.

Writing skills   Reporters must write clearly and concisely, using proper grammar, sentence structure and punctuation.

Speaking skills   Reporters must speak clearly so the people they interview understand them. Broadcast reporters must be poised and able to communicate orally to large audiences.

Interpersonal skills   Reporters must work as a team with others and interview people politely.

Curiosity and awareness   Reporters should always be eager to know about someone or something and to obtain more information. They must be aware of what it going on around them, see patterns in life and recognize when those patterns are altered.

Self-direction   Reporters must take direction from editors and publishers. However, reporters may be in the field and come across a breaking story. They must be able to get the story without being told what to do.

Self-confidence   Reporters must believe in their abilities and communicate their confidence in their abilities to their readers and listeners. They must have the confidence to act on creative ideas to make a useful contribution to their area of journalism.

WAYS TO CONTINUALLY IMPROVE YOUR SKILLS

Reporters are lifelong learners. Most continue their education through seminars and conferences given by news organizations. Reporters are avid readers of a variety of newspapers, magazines and websites as well as publications in their specific area of interest.

THINK *Critically*
List these skills that all reporters have, and then rate yourself on each skill. Which ones do you need to improve? How do you plan to improve your skills?

REAL PEOPLE REAL CAREERS

Susan Wloszczyna | Pop Culture Maven

Susan Wloszczyna (pronounced wuh-ZIN'-uh) always was a movie fan. She said, "I think I was 3 when I saw my first, 'Sleeping Beauty.'" In school she liked all the arts and tried to participate in some way. She wrote reviews of all sorts for her junior and senior high school papers. At Canisius College in Buffalo, N.Y., she majored in English but took art history and film criticism courses to "sharpen my ability to do critiques." She became feature editor at the college newspaper while doing a regular column and reviews. She went to graduate school at Syracuse University to get a degree in journalism and worked at several small New York papers before landing at USA Today.

© Photo courtesy of Susan Wloszczyna

Today Wloszczyna is a pop culture maven who constantly scans the Internet, magazines and newspapers to spot what or who is capturing people's attention. She also goes to movies and watches TV looking for trends not yet spotted. She said, "It is all a matter of being aware of what is going on in the world, and being willing to go beyond the obvious to see what others in the media haven't seen yet."

GETTING THE SCOOP

Once she has an idea for a story, Wloszczyna begins to research. She interviews people and immerses herself in a topic she does not know much about. She also contacts celebrities through their publicists to set up phone or in-person interviews. Then she looks for experts beyond Hollywood — authors, professors or other specialists — for comment on the story.

Most of her stories are features, and she looks for certain elements to write them well. She said, "The energy of a story doesn't just come from my writing but also the people I pick to quote, the quotes I choose to use and what I decide to leave out. If it is not supporting the theme of a story or is repetitive, get rid of it. Learn to NOT use a source if they aren't needed or say something in a less interesting way than someone else."

Wloszczyna has met plenty of movie and television stars and has had some good, bad and unforgettable experiences with them. Jack Nicholson, by force of personality, began taking over a joint interview with Diane Keaton. She got them both on track. Bill Murray, arriving two hours late for his interview for his 2004 movie, "The Life Aquatic with Steve Zissou," was difficult. Still, she wove a great story about the mercurial Murray by using his own behavior and comments from co-stars to illustrate his acting ability and character.

Source: Personal interview with Susan Wloszczyna

THINK *Critically*

1. What courses could you take in your school to become a better entertainment or pop culture writer?
2. Where would you find stories about pop culture and entertainment in your area?

Editorials and Columns

Sunscreen: A Column with Lasting Impact

Do an Internet search on "Mary Schmich" and you will find a column written a decade ago that has lived long past its initial impact, thanks to an Australian movie director and the Web. Schmich, a columnist and blogger for the Chicago Tribune, was walking to work along Lake Michigan one sunny day in May while thinking about what to write. "I was on my third column of the week and I was feeling dry," she says. She saw a woman sunbathing and thought, "I hope she's wearing sunscreen." That idea turned into her column, which began:

"If I could offer you only one tip for the future, sunscreen would be it. The long-term benefits of sunscreen have been proved by scientists, whereas the rest of my advice has no basis more reliable than my own meandering experience."

As she kept writing lines such as "The real troubles in your life are apt to be things that never crossed your worried mind, the kind that blindside you at 4 p.m. on some idle Tuesday," she got emotional. "A lot of writing is stuff that has been stored up in you," she continued.

Schmich's "Wear Sunscreen" column is personal and poetic. It caught the attention of film director Baz Luhrmann, whose video version is on the Web. Schmich says she's had offers to do another version for lots of money but she's turned them down. Why? "That (column) worked because it came from someplace true."

THINK *Critically*

1. Why did Mary Schmich's idea for a column on life lessons work?
2. Do you have any good ideas for a feature column?

Write Editorial Opinion

Goals

- Define editorials, distinguish facts from opinion and identify five types of editorials.
- Describe how to write an editorial.

Key Terms

- editorial 227
- subjective writing 227
- fact 228
- opinion 228

FOCUS

As you browse your favorite news website you may find a blog in the politics, news or sports area of the site that reads differently from the other content. It may include a picture of the blogger and may be labeled as editorial, opinion or view. You notice that the style breaks many newswriting rules because it is different from a news report. The blogger may be calling for action, asking readers to think about a local issue or just voicing an opinion about an issue. Editorial opinion has no place in news stories, but it does have its own place on many websites, in print publications and on some broadcast stations.

What Is an Editorial?

Newspaper editorials are so important they appear on a page of their own. **Editorials** are the voice of the newspaper. They are one place where **subjective writing** — that which expresses a point of view and is not concerned with being impartial — is allowed. Usually the editorial is a reaction to news or a community event or issue. The purpose of an editorial is to influence the reader.

For most of your writing life, whether in English, history, science or journalism classes, you have had to use facts obtained through research to make your argument or case. That's a good thing, because as an editorial writer you will need facts to make an argument to support your point of view. Editorial writing is subjective and thought of as opinion. The opinion, however, is supported by facts. Part of the editorial writer's job is to get the facts.

EDITORIALS AND RESEARCH

Research is your first step in good editorial writing. You may interview people who know the topic you are writing about. You may draw from written information — your own publication's stories, surveys or polls on the topic, reports done for government agencies. You need as much background information as you can get. You need to know the topic well, to become an expert yourself, before you can write an editorial that will persuade others to accept your point of view.

You will review many facts as you research and begin forming an opinion. You need to know the difference between fact and opinion. **Facts** are truths, information that can be proved. **Opinion** is a point of view, your way of interpreting information, one side of an argument.

For example, if you were writing an editorial about the coming flu season, your research might turn up this fact: "The Centers for Disease Control in Atlanta predicts a flu epidemic." Once that fact is established, you might decide to write that local health clinics should get ready for the flu season and provide free shots to children and seniors. That is opinion.

What if you are writing about the high cost of movies in your community? In your research, you find that the cost of movies is higher than ever before. That's a fact. You then write that movies do not seem any better than they were in previous years. That's opinion.

TYPES OF EDITORIALS

Just as there are different types of news stories, there also are different types of editorials. They include those that persuade, explain, praise, criticize and entertain. You might find yourself writing any of these in your school publication.

- **Persuade**   These editorials use facts and argument to convince or persuade readers to think as the newspaper does on a particular issue. They take a firm stand on an issue or person. They are editorials like those that promote a worthy candidate or action. They often ask the reader to get involved. You could write a persuasive editorial telling students why they should vote for student council candidates or recommending they get involved in a schoolwide charitable effort.

- **Explain**   These editorials give readers insight and facts and explain a complicated issue. You might write such an editorial to explain a new dress-code policy, or why the school board is considering closing your school.

- **Praise**   These editorials praise a person, a board, an event or a community reaction. You might write such a praising editorial after your school community pulls together to help victims of a natural disaster such as the earthquake and tsunami in Japan, or raises money for a disease affecting young people.

- **Criticize**   These editorials take issue with decisions, reactions, policies or people. You might write a critical editorial after an administration decision with which the newspaper staff disagrees.

- **Entertain**   These editorials may be hardest to write because it's not easy to write with humor. You may use humor to write about issues that warrant entertaining — the cafeteria food, perhaps?

Write the Editorial

An editorial that is the voice of the newspaper usually is written by one person to represent the editorial board or staff opinion, but it doesn't have a byline or signature. It uses the first person, the "we" voice. Opinion columns that do not represent the point of view of the editorial board or staff are signed, showing they represent the opinion and voice of that person. Opinion columns usually are written in the first person, using the pronoun "I." Editorial and opinion column writers are putting the credibility of themselves and their publication on the line with each column.

FIND THE TOPIC

The most important part of editorial writing is picking a topic. One way to do that is to survey the stories in the issue of the newspaper on which you are working. If you can connect an editorial to a news event, it will be more relevant to the reader.

Once you choose your topic, try to summarize the point you want to make in one or two sentences. It will help you focus and do further research that stays on point.

Suppose the length of lunch periods is an issue at your school and you have been given the job of writing an editorial in support of a lunch period that is 10 minutes longer — 40 minutes instead of 30. A news story on the front page details the proposal, which comes from the student council. The administration is reviewing it. Your first sentence might be:

> The administration is reviewing the student council's worthy proposal to extend our lunch period by 10 minutes.

Note the use of the word "worthy" in that first sentence. From the start you are signaling to the reader that this editorial supports the idea of an extended lunch.

FOLLOW THE STRUCTURE

Editorial writing, like news writing, calls for structure. In editorial writing that structure is: introduction, reaction, details and arguments, and conclusion.

Your introduction will lay out the issue, concern or problem. In your editorial on longer lunches, your introduction could read:

> The administration is reviewing the student council's worthy proposal to extend our lunch period by 10 minutes. This is good news for students who have been wolfing down food between tightly scheduled classes.

Reaction means the newspaper's reaction as well as that of others. On the longer lunch topic, reaction might be as follows:

> Students support the idea of longer lunches because it gives them a true break between morning and afternoon classes. It allows real time to step outside for fresh air, catch up on a homework assignment, or socialize with friends they don't see in class. Teachers and staff like it because it gives them a break, too, and allows time to run an errand at lunch.

The details-and-arguments part of the editorial is where the writer more fully explains the issue and is careful to make note of both sides of the issue. In this editorial, the writer notes that academics won't be affected.

> The student council's proposal calls for taking five minutes from the morning break time and five minutes from afternoon free periods to make the lunch hour 10 minutes longer. The administration has been concerned that academics would be affected. But this proposal means no class time is lost. The council has been considering the idea since September because students have been complaining that they don't have enough time even to eat during lunch.
>
> Any student who stays to talk to a teacher after the last morning class loses precious lunch time and may have to eat in as little as 10 or 15 minutes. Some students don't get time to eat at all.

The conclusion comes at the end. It restates the idea and the editorial's point of view, and issues a call to action.

> The student council made a responsible recommendation that gives teachers, staff and students a lunch break worth having. We urge the administration to adopt it quickly.

By following this structure, editorial writers clearly present facts, analyze the situation for readers, assess the reaction of the community and offer a recommendation.

checkpoint ✓

How do you structure an editorial?

AP Stylebook Concepts

AP style includes guidelines for the treatment of composition titles. Three general guidelines apply to most composition titles:

- Capitalize the principal words, including prepositions and conjunctions of four or more letters.
- Capitalize an article or word of fewer than four letters when it is the first or last word in a title.
- Put quotation marks around the names of all such works except titles of newspapers, the Bible and books that are primarily catalogs or reference material.

The following types of compositions are covered by these guidelines:

Books	Movies	Poems	Television episodes
Computer games	Operas	Songs	Television programs
Lectures	Plays	Speeches	Works of art

Examples of composition titles used in a sentence:

- Margaret Mitchell, a former newspaper reporter, won a Pulitzer Prize in 1937 for "Gone With the Wind."
- "Where No Man Has Gone Before" is the title of a "Star Trek" episode from the show's first season.
- Martin Luther King Jr. delivered his "I Have a Dream" speech on Aug. 28, 1963.

Should Newspapers Endorse Candidates?

In the newsrooms of multimedia outlets there has been debate about whether news organizations should endorse presidential candidates.

On one side of the argument are journalists who say that when a newspaper endorses a candidate it automatically makes the outlet's news coverage suspect, no matter how hard reporters work to be fair. Some say that readers even resent being told for whom they should vote.

On the other side are journalists who say that endorsements are one of a newspaper's most important responsibilities. They contend that the reporters and editors who have spent hours talking to candidates and researching issues are sharing some of their unique insight with readers, not telling them how to vote.

Whichever side you are on, the fact is that newspaper endorsements of presidential candidates don't seem to have much effect on voters. In the 2008 presidential election, some speculated that Oprah Winfrey's endorsement of Democratic candidate Barack Obama was more influential than any particular news media endorsement.

Because more voters are using a variety of platforms and media to get their news and information, news organizations are becoming savvy about how to present endorsements. As an alternative to endorsements, some news organizations are making available on the Internet audio recordings of their editorial board's interview with the candidates. Or, instead of doing standard interviews with candidates for endorsement purposes, news organizations hold debates that can be streamed onto a website.

Your school news organization may be debating whether to endorse candidates, too. Each school year you are likely to face student government and class officer elections. Do you have an editorial board to interview all the candidates? Are there alternatives to endorsements you should consider?

THINK *Critically*

1. Do you think news organizations should endorse candidates? Why or why not?

2. What are some ways news organizations can inform readers without endorsing candidates?

9.1 | Assessment

Understand Concepts

Determine the best answer for each of the following questions.

1. Editorial writing is always
   - **a.** creative.
   - **b.** objective.
   - **c.** reactive.
   - **d.** subjective.

2. An editorial writer lays out the issue, concern or problem in the
   - **a.** introduction.
   - **b.** reaction.
   - **c.** details.
   - **d.** arguments.

3. **True or False**   An opinion column expresses the opinion of the newspaper's editorial board or staff.

4. **True or False**   Editorial writing is always based on facts.

Write Now!

Practice your writing skills with the following activities.

5. Find the editorial page of a local or national newspaper. Choose an editorial and label the parts. Write a summary of the editorial and describe the details of the introduction, reaction, details and arguments and conclusion.

6. Choose an issue that concerns your school. Write an editorial suitable for your high school newspaper that persuades or explains. Use the correct journalistic style and structure for the editorial. Once you have completed your research, write a draft of your editorial on a computer, and then use the track changes function to edit your copy. Send your original draft, the edited draft and the final copy to your teacher electronically.

7. Choose two or three online news organizations. Read the news stories and editorials you find about the current U.S. president. Write an editorial suitable for your high school online news site that either praises or criticizes an action taken by the president.

8. You are the editor of your high school newspaper. A student submitted an editorial with the intent to entertain. The editorial is about new drivers who speed. Recently three students were seriously harmed and one killed in an accident where speeding was the major factor. Write a paper that explains whether you think this is the appropriate time to print the editorial. In your paper, distinguish between responsible and irresponsible media action. Before beginning your final paper, write a draft, and then edit your paper using proofreading symbols. Check your paper for clarity, engaging language and the correct use of English. Submit your original draft, the edited draft and your final paper.

9.2

Write Columns

Goals

- Identify the types of columns.
- Describe how to find your own writer's voice.
- Distinguish blogging from column writing.

Key Terms

- column 234
- voice 234
- op-ed 235
- blog post 238

FOCUS

Throughout this text, you have been told that journalists are objective, open-minded and able to look fairly at both sides of a story. Fairness, accuracy and truth remain important to column writers, too, but columnists have license to use opinion and to ask readers to understand a story through the columnist's point of view. Blogging has added a new dimension to writing from a point of view.

What Is a Column?

A **column** is a regularly appearing article that expresses the opinion of the writer, called a columnist. Columns can be found throughout most newspapers. A column is a privileged piece of real estate in any publication and many journalists would like to have one. There are several types of columns, but what they all have in common is point of view. Columnists are permitted to be opinionated and to develop their own **voice**, or style of writing. News writers are not columnists.

Some columnists write for the editorial page, where they offer opposing viewpoints on issues and events in which the paper takes interest, or they put their own spin on local, national or world events. Feature columnists write about general topics, often reporting trends or human interest stories within the column and offering insight or opinion. Beat columnists are those who have some expertise, like sports, and they appear in that section. Some news organizations also have humor columnists who write about the world in an entertaining way.

EDITORIAL OPINION COLUMNS

Editorial opinion columns are packaged with the editorials because they have a strong and consistent point of view on local, state and national issues. Opinion columns are different from editorials because they are signed or bylined and are the opinion of the writer. Opinion columns don't speak in the voice of the publication. Opinion columns can be written in less formal language than the editorial and often they have more space. Yet they rely upon the same writing structure as an editorial, with an introduction, reaction, details and argument, and conclusion.

An editorial opinion column might support the newspaper staff's editorial, or it may argue against it. Many newspapers go to some lengths to offer a variety of opinions on their editorial pages. The **op-ed** page is the newspaper page, often opposite the editorial page, devoted to editorial opinions. "Op-ed" is also another name for an opinion column on the op-ed page.

FEATURE COLUMNS

When Mary Schmich, the Chicago Tribune columnist who wrote the "Wear Sunscreen" column, first arrived at the Tribune, she told the feature editor she would like to write a column, as she had in her previous job. "She (the editor) laughed and said, 'You and everybody else,'" Schmich says. Instead, Schmich became a national reporter on the news desk, where she says, "I came to understand how little I understood about the world." By the time a column was offered to her, Schmich had covered many big national stories. "I knew so much more and was so much less certain."

The art of writing a feature column is one that takes time to develop. Experience is part of what it takes to see good stories in odd places and do the reporting that columnists must do. Feature columnists like Schmich, who writes three times a week, usually come up with ideas of their own. They are interested in what people talk about, but when they write on topical issues they want to have something to add to the conversation. They may have an opinion on a news event, but they don't want to rant. They have to offer researched, educated argument. Feature columnists look to inform, entertain or challenge their readers.

BEAT COLUMNS

There is no end to the number of columnists a newspaper could employ because there are so many topics and beats in which writers have expertise. Think about how many there may be in your local newspaper. There may be columnists on food, religion, real estate, television and celebrity. There probably is a sports columnist who writes about games, the people who play them, teamwork, strategy and some of the same topics sports reporters cover. The difference is that columnists can insert opinion or analysis that a beat reporter cannot. Television or media columns have become popular in many publications because the writers can cover in columns some of the background information they wouldn't put in a news story. This might include behind-the-scenes gossip on what shows networks are considering or which executives have been moved and for what reasons.

/////// *What qualities should the columnists for your school newspaper have?*

Think about how your school publication is set up. Could you use a sports columnist? How about a people column, about the people making news at your school? Is there a staff member who could write a regular column on student life?

Of course, your sports writer should know sports, your people columnist should be plugged into what's happening on campus, and your student life writer should be your keenest observer. If you have the right columnists, readers develop a relationship with them and look for them in each issue. Good columnists help draw readers into the publication and into the section in which they are found. The New York Post calls its gossip column "Page Six," because that's where it is found. It's the first page many readers turn to every day.

HUMOR COLUMNS

Being funny isn't easy. Being funny on schedule and in print is even harder. Even Dave Barry, master humorist and columnist for The Miami Herald, says a humor writer's own humor doesn't seem funny to the writer when the column is completed. He says he always shows his columns to his wife and lets her judge whether they are funny.

Barry says that humor writing takes pacing. Pay attention to the monologues of well-known comedians like David Letterman or Jay Leno. They don't take long to get to their humorous point. Barry also says he spends a lot of time writing. Columnists often make their work look easy, but humor writing takes as much time as any other good writing. Just because people are funny in personal conversation doesn't mean they will be funny in print.

EDITORIAL CARTOONS

Editorial cartoons are another way to provide commentary on issues. A cartoon can go with the day's editorial to underscore the point or be a comment on another issue. Editorial cartoonists often use one symbol or caricature to represent a specific person. Typically, editorial cartoons are simple and on one topic. Cartoonists can add much to gray editorial pages.

How does a column differ from a news story?

Find Your Voice

Columnists are allowed to have a "voice," or their own personal way of saying what they want to say. Mary Schmich says her "Wear Sunscreen" column came from her heart and her head, and she spoke to her readers in the voice she always uses with them.

A writing voice may be different from the voice you use in conversation, but it can't be forced. It still must be you. Writing the way you talk is a good way to start. It's simple. It's relaxed. It will feel natural to you and to your readers.

John Grogan, a longtime columnist turned best-selling author, says that "voice is about getting confidence and finding what's inside. Try and be as honest and candid as you can with what you're feeling … and don't overthink what you want your audience to think of you. Readers can sniff out someone who's being insincere a mile away."

Some inexperienced writers think writing with voice is an invitation to use slang or pay less attention to grammar and style. They get so breezy and folksy, or so hung up on sounding cool, that they don't pay attention to the language itself. Beware of those mistakes. Read your copy to friends and family who can tell you if it sounds like you or someone fake.

Writers find their voice by continuing to write. No one can tell you how to express yourself. There are certain tricks, however. Writers who have voice and personality try not to use cliches. They want to be fresh, ahead of the issue, or the talk of the town. And, once again, specificity in writing helps both the reader and the writer. Don't use a vague word when you can use a specific one.

checkpoint ✓

What is voice?

◗ grammar tip

An adjective modifies a noun or pronoun. In the sentence "This is a new textbook," the word "new" is an adjective that describes — or modifies — the condition of "textbook."

Adjectives usually answer one of four questions about the noun or pronoun: What kind? Which one? How many? How much? In the sentence above, the question "What kind?" is answered.

The first adjective you choose may not be the best, so keep digging until you come up with an original — and descriptive — adjective.

Blogging

Blogs are many things columns are not. Yet sometimes a blog is just like a column or even an extension of a column that exists in print. USA Today's daily Lifeline, called Lifeline Live at usatoday .com, is an extension of the newspaper column, filled with short items about entertainment and celebrities. The difference is that Lifeline Live usually has more items per day and the items are posted as they happen. For the print Lifeline, items are assembled throughout the day and edited to fit a finite space at the end of the day for presentation in the morning paper.

Bloggers, whether attached to a publication or independent, are similar to columnists in that opinion and point of view are OK in the pieces they write. A reputable blogger, much like a good columnist, uses facts to support opinions.

If your school newspaper has a website, you may see an opportunity to write a regular blog. Like a columnist, you will want to develop a dependable voice that will keep your Web readers coming back. You can show attitude or personality in a blog, but keep in mind the audience you aim to attract. Blogs, unlike columns, get immediate reaction. Readers can post comments to which bloggers often respond. Thus blogs can be far more influenced by readers than a column can. In fact they can become what the readers want them to be.

All **blog posts**, or entries, begin with an idea, and it is a blogger's job to come up with good ones. Like a columnist, a blogger will want to add something fresh to an idea that many others are writing about. As Schmich, the Chicago Tribune columnist, says, "In the Internet age you cannot hold onto your thoughts very long. You run the risk of seeming late, seeming derivative or seeming to copy." In other words, when you have a good idea, develop it, report it, write it and do it fast.

Blogs may have several posts a day, or be a longer post written like a feature column. Bloggers write their entries in chronological order but the blog is read in reverse chronological order. Each entry has to attract readers and move them to the next one. A descriptive headline helps, as do boldfaced names or phrases in the entry. Another plus for blogs is that links to other blogs and websites may be added, providing more resources for the Web reader.

////// *Name some advantages and disadvantages of writing a blog for your school paper's website.*

© Photodisc/Getty Images

*check*point ✓

What do bloggers and columnists have in common?

9.2 | Assessment

Understand Concepts

Determine the best answer for each of the following questions.

1. Columns on specific topics such as sports, entertainment, food or religion are types of
   a. beat columns.
   b. editorial opinion columns.
   c. feature columns.
   d. humor columns.

2. What is the major difference between news stories and columns?
   a. length
   b. location
   c. point of view
   d. subject matter

3. **True or False**   Editorial cartoons have a point of view.

4. **True or False**   Compared to other types of opinion columns, humor columns are the easiest to write.

Write Now!

Practice your writing skills with the following activities.

5. Find an opinion column in a local, national or online newspaper. Read several columns by the same writer. How would you describe the writer's voice?

6. Choose a subject that interests you and would be of interest to other students in your high school or other people in your age group. Using one of the free blog services on the Internet or your school website, write an online blog. Publish both versions. As with any online post, do not publish any personal information or information that is harmful to other students.

7. Finding your voice comes from writing consistently and often. Choose something that interests you, such as theater, art, music, fashion or sports. From a local, national or online newspaper, read several columns until you find a columnist you like who writes in your subject of interest. Using a computer and word-processing program, rewrite the column using your own voice and adding your own experiences. When you turn the column in to your teacher, attach the original column to the one you wrote.

Write Reviews

Goals

- Describe reviews and how to write them.
- Explain who writes reviews.

Key Terms

- review 240
- reviewer 240
- critic 242

review 240

FOCUS

It's Friday afternoon and you and your friends are trying to decide which movie to see tonight. The problem: Four new films are opening, and the group can't agree on one. You see a possible way to get consensus. You open up your smartphone and go to your local news website. You click on its entertainment section and there you have what you need — reviews of each of the movies you and the group are considering.

You read them aloud, realizing quickly that the reviewer, who works for the site, doesn't think much of two of the movies. The reviews are full of praise for the other two, however, so the group gives each one further thought. You click through a few entertainment apps to see what other reviewers say, and within a few minutes the group has decided the clear winner. You order your tickets online early because you figure that with good reviews like the ones you've just read, your choice will be the popular one this weekend.

What Are Reviews?

Reviews are the views or opinions of the writer about entertainment and art or new or existing products and services. As with column writing and editorial writing, reviewing is subjective, not objective. Entertainment and arts coverage includes many reviews — of books, movies, television shows, music, fashion, plays and concerts and also of the writers, actors, models and musicians. Reviews also are written about new and existing products and services. For example, cars and trucks, restaurants, appliances, cleaning products, software programs and roller coasters are all subject to review. Most media outlets label their reviews so consumers are aware they are reading the writer's opinion.

HOW TO WRITE A REVIEW

Reviewers, the people who write reviews, should know the medium they are writing about. In fact, it helps if they like it. You don't want to make someone who hates movies the newspaper's movie reviewer. Readers deserve a reviewer who will look at a movie in the same way they will and answer questions they want answered. Is it violent? Frightening? Sappy? Is it a good date night movie? Is it worth the price of admission?

Reviews need information as well as opinion. A plot summary is important, though it shouldn't give away too much. It also is helpful to compare the work to the artist's previous projects, or others like it. Here's an excerpt from a review in USA Today on the weekend that Cate Blanchett's movie "Elizabeth: The Golden Age" was to open. The reviewer helps readers put the movie in context by mentioning that it was directed by the same man who directed the movie "Elizabeth," also starring Blanchett. It also lets readers know what the reviewer thinks: that the first film was better, that the actress is terrific — "Blanchett is as superb here as she was the first time around" — yet the movie is not — "But she can't save the film . . ."

> This second "Elizabeth" is directed by Shekhar Kapur, who also directed the first and better film. Blanchett is as superb here as she was the first time around. But she can't save the film, which focuses on pomp and pageantry to the detriment of substance and historical accuracy.

© Photodisc/Getty Images

///// *How important do you think reviews are to the commercial success of a movie?*

Reviews need details, not generalities. Don't tell readers that the John Mayer concert you attended was "fantastic." Provide details. Say, "Mayer played for more than two hours without missing a note. He included all his hits to please the crowd, but introduced some equally interesting new works for a new album. Plus, he charmed the audience with his banter." Now the reader knows what the concert was like.

In general, reviews should not contain effusive words such as "fabulous," "terrific," "enthralling" and "stunning." Use examples — lines from the book if it's a novel you are reviewing, a telling scene from the movie you like, the worst line in a situation comedy — to place the reader there. If your first inclination is to declare the work "fantastic," dig deeper. Ask yourself why you think it so. What or who makes it worth going to the concert, listening to the recording artist or reading the book, and why?

Reviews give readers information with which they can make choices that affect their time and money. We live in a media-savvy world with too many options for entertainment. Reviewers do a heightened and more professional version of what we all do when we text or email quick opinions to each other. The difference is that reviewers may make comparisons, look at strengths and weaknesses, evaluate performances and suggest whether the product or performance lives up to expectations. In reviewing student works, however, be fair. Students should not be held to the same standards as professionals. It's a good idea to look for both good points and bad.

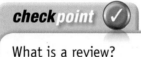

checkpoint ✓

What is a review?

Who Writes Reviews?

Writers who specialize in reviewing arts and entertainment are called reviewers or critics, often interchangeably. There are differences, however. Reviewers may take a subjective view of the work they are assigned to review. They will use the principles of good reviewing when writing about any work. A **critic** is a reviewer who places a work in the context of the whole field. Being a critic requires a scholarly approach. A movie critic, for example, also will know the history of film and be able to talk about any film in that context. If you want to be a critic you need to become a student of the medium you like. If you want to be a television critic it takes more than watching current TV shows. You need to know the history of television, have a working knowledge of classic shows and actors in them, and know the major influences on television shows of today.

Fans of the arts and entertainment often depend on reviewers and critics to help them make choices about the books they will read, the songs they will download, and the movies or television shows they will watch. Readers often develop favorite critics because they find they have similar tastes.

Your student publication is more likely to have reviewers than critics because it takes experience and study to become a critic. However, there may be experts in your school to whom you can reach out. You may tap a musician, for example, who knows theory and every genre, from classical to hip-hop. Or you may recruit a creative writer who has studied the American novel and would make a good book reviewer.

WHAT TO REVIEW

Your school probably has more entertainment news to report and review than you think. Is a hot local band booked to play at a school dance? You can write a news story announcing the booking — and a feature story on the band, and then review the band's performance.

When casting is announced for the school's annual musical, you may have a story in who gets each part. Is the director a creative genius? You may have a feature in the director's way of dealing with the cast. After opening night you should have a review.

Is the school chorus going to the state finals? Assign a reporter to write about the competition and the experience. Send a reviewer along to write about the performance of your chorus in the context of the competition.

School newspapers need not limit reviewing to the walls of the high school. If everyone is going to the opening of a new movie, it can be a review for your publication. If the lunch table talk is all about a new TV show or indie band, there may be a story in what everyone finds so appealing and a review in the band's next appearance or the show's premiere.

check *point* ✓

Who writes reviews?

////// *Name the events or performances given by groups or individuals at your school that the school paper could review.*

Digging Deeper

"So long Harry, your canon's still a blast"

With the July 2011 release of "Harry Potter and the Deathly Hallows Part 2," the movie series based on J. K. Rowling's highly successful books about the life of boy wizard Harry Potter draws to an end.

The much-anticipated and final installment in the series meant that directors, actors, producers and screenwriters were under pressure to deliver what Harry Potter fans had come to expect: a magical movie that brought the book to life. As the movie debuted, reviewers around the world rushed to give readers their opinions.

Access www.cengage.com/school/langarts/journalism, and click on the link to Chapter 6. Read Kate Muir's review of "Harry Potter and the Deathly Hallows Part 2," and then answer the questions below.

THINK *Critically*

1. Some reviews contain statements called "spoilers" that can give away crucial parts of the plot and possibly reveal the outcome of the movie. Find a "spoiler" statement in Muir's review. If you have seen the movie, write a paragraph explaining how the spoiler occurs in the movie. If you have not seen the movie, write a paragraph speculating on what the spoiler might mean.

2. Consider this quote from Muir's review: "Professor Snape will not be remembered fondly, but he will never be forgotten, [he is] as high-handed as he is handsome." Does this quote reflect Muir's personal opinion? Why or why not?

3. Consider this quote from Muir's review: "While Emma Watson has grown into a convincing Hermione, and Daniel Radcliffe is a steadily improving Harry, Rupert Grint as Ron seems to have regressed into some sort of gap mouthed, doughy yokel. His chemistry with Hermione is non-existent when they brave their first damp kiss." Go online and search for other reviews. Did other reviewers agree with Muir's assessment of the actors' performances? Were Muir's comments on their performances based on personal opinion or fact? Write a brief paragraph stating your findings. Be sure to correctly cite any reviews you quote.

4. Think about a movie you were very excited about seeing. Did a negative movie review ever prevent you from seeing the movie? Write a brief paragraph explaining your answer.

Source: Muir, Kate. "So long Harry, your canon's still a blast; the final Harry Potter is more subtle but still thrills. Kate Muir says Hallows and goodbye." Times [London, England] 15 July 2011: 44. Global Issues In Context. Web. 6 Aug. 2011.

9.3 | Assessment

Understand Concepts

Determine the best answer for each of the following questions.

1. Which of the following should you avoid including in a review?
   a. details
   c. opinion
   b. generalities
   d. information

2. **True or False** Student reviewers should hold student artists and performers to the same standards as professionals.

3. **True or False** A movie review is based on interviews with others who have seen the film.

4. **True or False** A critic often takes a scholarly approach when reviewing a play.

Write Now!

Practice your writing skills with the following activities.

5. Search the Internet to find an area that interests you such as music, books, art, movies and so on. Find two reviews about the subject written from different perspectives. Use a computer to write a paper that compares and contrasts the reviews. Incorporate direct and indirect quotes from the reviewers in your paper. Then listen to the music, read the book, see the piece of art or attend the movie. Write your own review as an addition to your paper. Your review should be appropriate for a high school audience. Before beginning your paper, write a draft, and then, using appropriate copy editing and proofreading symbols, edit your paper for clarity, engaging language, and the use of the conventions and mechanics of written language. Attach your draft with edits to your final paper before turning in the paper.

6. Many reviews written on behalf of the maker of the product are actually advertisements — or "advertorials" — for the product. Search the Internet to find a product review for a product you use regularly. Pay attention to the website where you found the review. Is the review on the product maker's website or is the review written by an independent writer? Is there any mention on the review that this is an advertorial? Does the review give a fair assessment of the product, or is the editorial content written to highlight only the product's advantages? Do you think it is responsible or irresponsible media action to have advertorials on sites other than the product makers' sites? Write an in-depth news feature suitable for a high school broadcast on your findings and your opinion about the responsibility of the media with regard to advertorials. Deliver your broadcast in class.

CHAPTER 9 | Assessment

Review Journalism Concepts

9.1 Write Editorial Opinion

Editorials are the voice of the newspaper and use subjective writing. This means the writing expresses a point of view and is not concerned with being impartial. Usually the editorial is a reaction to news, or a community event or issue. The purpose of an editorial is to influence the reader.

An editorial writer uses facts to make an argument to support a point of view or an opinion. Facts are truths, information that can be proved. Opinion is a point of view, a way of interpreting information, one side of an argument.

Types of editorials include those that persuade, explain, praise, criticize and entertain. Regardless of the type of editorial, the structure of an editorial includes four parts: introduction, reaction, details and arguments and conclusion.

9.2 Write Columns

A column is a regularly appearing article that expresses a point of view. Columnists are permitted to be opinionated and to develop their own voice, or style of writing. Types of columns include editorial opinion columns, feature columns, beat columns and humor columns. Although they are not columns, editorial cartoons also express a point of view.

A writing voice may be different from the voice you use in conversation, but it can't be forced. Writing the way you talk is a good way to start. It's simple. It's relaxed. It will feel natural to you and to your readers. Writing with voice is not an invitation to use slang or pay less attention to grammar and style.

Sometimes a blog is just like a column or even an extension of a column that exists in print. Blogs, unlike columns, get immediate reaction. Readers can post comments to which bloggers often respond. Thus, blogs can be far more influenced by readers than a column can.

9.3 Write Reviews

Reviews are the views or opinions of the writer. As with column writing and editorial writing, reviewing is subjective. Entertainment and arts coverage includes many reviews of works such as books, movies and music. Reviews need details and should not contain effusive words.

Reviewers, the people who write reviews, should know the medium they are writing about. Writers who specialize in reviewing arts and entertainment are called reviewers or critics, often interchangeably. There are differences, however. Reviewers take a subjective view of the work they are assigned to review. They will use the principles of good reviewing when writing about any work. Critics take a more scholarly approach. They place whatever work they are looking at in the context of the whole field.

Develop Your Journalism Language

Write the letter of the term that matches each definition. One term will not be used.

_____ 1. Type of writing that expresses a point of view and is not concerned with being impartial

_____ 2. Regularly appearing newspaper article that expresses the opinion of the writer

_____ 3. Newspaper page, often opposite the editorial page, devoted to a variety of opinions

_____ 4. Person who writes reviews

_____ 5. Point of view

_____ 6. Reviewer who places a work in the context of the whole field

_____ 7. The voice of the newspaper

_____ 8. Information that can be proved

_____ 9. Views or opinions of a writer about entertainment and art or new or existing products and services

_____ 10. Writer's style of writing

a. blog post
b. column
c. critic
d. editorial
e. facts
f. op-ed
g. opinion
h. reviewer
i. review
j. subjective writing
k. voice

11. Which of the following does NOT describe an opinion?
    a. a point of view
    b. information that can be proved
    c. one side of an argument
    d. your way of interpreting information

12. Editorials that _____ use facts and argument to convince readers to think as the newspaper does on a particular issue.
    a. criticize
    b. explain
    c. persuade
    d. praise

13. Editorials and opinion columns are written in the
    a. first person.
    b. second person.
    c. third person.

14. A sports columnist is an example of a
    a. beat columnist.
    b. feature columnist.
    c. humor columnist.
    d. topic columnist.

Think Critically

15. What is the purpose of an editorial?

16. After you choose a topic for an editorial, what can you do to help focus and keep your research on point?

17. Name the elements used to structure an editorial.

18. What is the details-and-argument part of an editorial?

19. What should the conclusion of an editorial do?

20. What do feature columnists try to offer readers through their columns?

21. How does a beat columnist's work differ from the work of a beat reporter?

22. How do writers find their voice?

23. How does the work of a reviewer differ from the work of a critic?

24. Why do some readers have favorite reviewers or critics?

25. Identify two ways that a reputable blogger's work is similar to that of a good columnist.

26. Explain how an editorial breaks many news-writing rules.

27. Even without looking at the byline, how might you identify the work of a particular columnist?

28. Explain the role of facts in an editorial.

29. Identify a topic that might be appropriate for each of the five types of editorials.

30. Why is a column considered a privileged piece of real estate in a publication?

31. How do editorial opinion columns differ from editorials?

Make Academic Connections

32. **COMPUTER SCIENCE** Use the Internet and a search engine, such as Bing, to find an editorial about a subject you find interesting. Identify the main point of the editorial and describe why you agree or disagree with the writer.

33. **CAREERS** Find the email address for a columnist for a local or national newspaper. The address may be on the "Contacts" screen of the news organization for which the columnist writes. Send a well-planned, respectful email to the columnist asking a specific question about a career as a columnist. Consider questions about what kinds of reporting the columnist did before getting a column, where the columnist gets ideas, or why the columnist enjoys writing a column. Share information from any response that you receive on your school's website or in an email to your classmates.

34. **ART** Use library or Internet resources to find and make copies of 10 editorial cartoons, all focused on the same subject but published in different newspapers. Use the editorial cartoons to create a display that highlights the

similarities and differences in the messages and the art. In a short report, describe the editorial cartoonist's point of view for each cartoon and characterize the cartoonist's voice. Exhibit your report with your display.

35. **PERFORMING ARTS** Choose an area of interest such as theater, music or dance. Find and read reviews about recent performances in your community. Study the writing and content of the reviews. Attend a performance and write a review.

36. **WRITING** Choose an issue concerning your school, such as an upcoming tax levy, the scholastic level of your school compared with that of other schools in your state, too much or too little emphasis on sports or physical activity, cafeteria food or any other topic of your choice. Write an editorial on the issue. Use a variety of sources, including interviews, to research the topic and to be sure you have used facts to back up your opinion. Incorporate direct and indirect quotations. Use a computer to write a draft of the paper, print out the draft, and then, using proofreading symbols, edit your editorial for clarity, engaging language, and the use of the conventions and mechanics of written language. Submit the final editorial for publication to your high school newspaper or website.

37. **ETHICS** As editor of your high school paper, you must distinguish between responsible and irresponsible media action when a student submits a review panning the high school play. The reviewer thought the play was generally well-done but she does not like the lead actor's performance. Write an opinion about whether or not to print the review.

Writing Portfolio Activity

38. Choose a columnist from a local or national newspaper. Read 10 recent columns and write a journal entry describing your reaction to those columns. Consider the following questions as you write: How are the columns similar? How are they different? How would you describe the writer's voice? What emotions did you have while you were reading the columns? What is your level of interest in reading this writer's column in the future?

AP Stylebook Workshop

Correct the following according to AP style, if needed.

39. The room was filled with the voices of family and friends singing happy birthday to you.

40. The national anthem was played before the start of the game.

41. Long Day's Journey into Night was first produced three years after the death of playwright Eugene O'Neill.

42. Although it was not written for Casablanca, the song As time goes by is a key element in the movie.

CRITICAL THINKING AND PROBLEM SOLVING: Excel as a Journalist

Every year several new journalists become part of print, online and broadcast news organizations. How do you excel and stand out among the new reporters as well as among seasoned journalists?

Your journalism skills separate you and show you have been properly educated and prepared for the complex environment of today's news world. To excel, you must have the ability to

- Reason effectively
- Use systems thinking
- Make judgments and decisions
- Solve problems

REASON EFFECTIVELY

Although your editor will assign you stories, you will be on your own to obtain the information in the field. You are expected to use your reasoning skills, such as inductive and deductive reasoning, to know what research is important to the story, whom you should interview and what questions to ask. You must know which photo best illustrates the story and which video to shoot.

USE SYSTEMS THINKING

In today's multimedia news organizations, reporters are expected to be able to analyze the elements of a story — the copy, photos and video — and see how they all fit together to produce the entire package. You must be able to see the whole picture and at the same time see the individual components of the story and how they fit into the whole.

MAKE JUDGMENTS AND DECISIONS

When deadlines are approaching, you must be able to analyze and evaluate the information effectively and decide what information to give the reader and what to leave out. This ability to quickly make judgments and decisions comes with experience. The reporter who excels learns quickly and uses the resources of past experiences and knowledge.

SOLVE PROBLEMS

Problem solving often requires being innovative. In the field, you must be able to think quickly and ask significant questions that clarify the different points of view. You must be able to deal with equipment problems, adverse weather and other obstacles that may call upon your resources and ability to find innovative solutions to get the story.

THINK *Critically*

Spend some time thinking about what type of reporter you aspire to be. Write a journal entry that discusses which of the characteristics mentioned above you think you have and which you think you need to develop. Discuss the ways you could develop these characteristics.

REAL PEOPLE REAL CAREERS

John Grogan | From Newspaper Column to the Movies

If you have seen the heartwarming movie "Marley & Me," the tale of a precocious Labrador retriever and his loving family starring Owen Wilson and Jennifer Aniston, then you might want to meet John Grogan, who started telling stories about Marley in his newspaper columns.

Grogan included many of Marley's misadventures, along with other personal stories, in his columns for the South Florida Sun-Sentinel and The Philadelphia Inquirer. Later, he turned his many stories about his dog into a best-selling book, also titled "Marley & Me," which sold 3 million copies.

Grogan didn't start out as a columnist. He studied journalism at Central Michigan University and Ohio State University. He wrote police stories in Michigan and county transportation stories in Florida. "A columnist is looking at the world through his own prism," Grogan says, "so the more experience you have, the more multifaceted your looking glass will be, and the more perspective you'll have to share."

During his years as a newspaper columnist, Grogan began his day by reading local newspapers, clipping stories and circling asides buried deep in the copy. More important, he got out of his air-conditioned office in Florida or Philadelphia, hopped in his car, and drove around in search of a slice of life to serve up to his readers.

Writing a best-seller gave Grogan options for a different kind of life. These days, thanks to "Marley & Me," he no longer writes a column. He left his job at The Philadelphia Inquirer in 2007 when the Inquirer, under financial pressure, was laying people off. Grogan has turned his attention to writing books full time. He still lives in Pennsylvania with his wife, Jenny, and their three children. He has a new Labrador named Gracie, who, compared with Marley, is a much calmer canine.

ADVICE TO ASPIRING COLUMNISTS

Grogan thinks confidence is important. For him, as for most other columnists, the biggest hurdle at first "was having the confidence that anybody really cares what you think about things." But as time went on, he got his voice, which helped him navigate the process of creating a column.

While addressing local and national interests is important, Grogan says, a columnist should look inward and not "go through life thinking nobody cares about your experience. A lot of my favorite columns and my readers' favorite columns were ones that were my own personal experience." He calls each column "a little piece of storytelling with a beginning, middle and end."

He advises aspiring columnists to study fiction-writing techniques. "I think the most important element about being a good columnist is being a good storyteller and getting out in the community you cover and experiencing that life."

Source: Personal interview with John Grogan

THINK *Critically*

1. How does experience help columnists find things to write about?
2. How can a columnist learn to tell a good story?

10

Sportswriting

A Baseball Lifestyle: Where's the Glamour?

Mel Antonen once waited 11 hours for an interview with baseball great Roger Clemens — which he eventually got. A baseball writer and radio/TV commentator for 30 years, Antonen travels to cover baseball games for nine months of the year — spring training through the World Series. It's not as glamorous as it may sound.

Reporting on major league baseball is a lifestyle, one that can be difficult on friends and family members because baseball writers are on the road most of the year. Beyond the travel, though, Antonen says it's also "a lot of hours of phone calls and waiting around." These days it is also a lot of hours of using Twitter to send reports to followers from the moment you arrive, hours before game time, until the lights are turned off in the ballpark.

"Baseball writing is a small part of journalism," Antonen says. To do it well, "you have to be in love with journalism."

THINK *Critically*

1. Why do you think a major league baseball writer says his job is "a lifestyle"?
2. Why might a writer have to wait hours to interview a player?

Write Sports News Stories

Goals

- Describe the two types of sports stories.
- Explain how to write the sports story.
- Explain the need for objectivity in sports stories.

Key Terms

- sportswriting 253
- game story 253
- highlights 253
- preview story 255
- jargon 257
- objectivity 258

FOCUS

Robin is on her high school soccer team. Every day when she comes home from school, she grabs the local newspaper and checks out the sports section to see if her team is mentioned. She also reads stories about professional soccer teams as well as stories about teams at competing high schools.

When you open your high school newspaper or a local paper, do you, like Robin, first turn to the sports section? People who like sports want to keep up with the latest news about their favorite teams, players and events that affect the way the team performs. Journalists who write, edit and take photographs or videos for the sports section for a news organization are responsible for keeping Robin — and all readers of the sports section — up-to-date on the latest sports news.

Two Types of Sports Stories

Sportswriting is the reporting and writing of stories about the many different sports events and the people who play them. There are two major types of stories — the game story and the preview story, the more prevalent of which is the game story.

THE GAME STORY

Game stories are exactly what they sound like, stories about individual games — news stories about the contest and conflict between two teams. Game stories include all the **highlights**, or important moments, of the games and, of course, the final score. Sports writers often write game stories with a summary lead very similar to a news summary lead. They get straight to the central point — which team won. For example:

> The Hamilton High Tigers won the state championship Saturday afternoon, beating rival Jefferson High by one run, thanks to Taylor Wright's ninth-inning homer.

Some will argue that the news of the game is often old by the time it appears in a newspaper, or even on a news website, because many people attended the event, watched it on TV or heard it on the radio. They favor a feature-style approach to writing about the game. For example:

> The rivalry between Hamilton and Jefferson high schools was as intense as ever Saturday afternoon when the state championship was still at stake in the bottom of the ninth inning. Then senior Taylor Wright sent a curve ball soaring far out to left field and easily rounded all four bases for a game-winning home run.

Whatever their approach to the lead, sports reporters who are writing game stories attend the games. They take careful notes, witness all the plays, and interview players and coaches about important moves or strategies. They conduct those interviews on the field or in the locker room, getting useful quotes to add explanation and dimension to the story. They also compile statistics of the game with an eye on records that could be set or broken, and they keep track of injuries to follow up on. Often, game reporters are tweeting throughout the game as well, giving their followers a play-by-play report as the game goes on.

///// *Why might some sports writers favor a feature approach over a news approach to writing about a sporting event?*

PREVIEW STORIES

Preview stories are a staple of sports sections on every platform — in print, on the Web and on broadcast stations. A preview story does not focus on one game but takes a broader look at how a team may be expected to perform for a season. Previews are produced when it is an appropriate time to look ahead — usually at the start of a season in any sport. These stories usually include interviews with coaches and players and a look at statistics from previous seasons. They set the scene for fans, who may be ever hopeful with the promise of a new start.

checkpoint ✓

How do the two types of sports stories covered by news organizations differ?

Write the Story

In writing a game story, the reporter covers the conflict that happened in the arena of the game. Sports writers must cover the same basic journalistic elements in their story as do news writers — who, what, when, where, why and how. Sports writers also add to their stories supplemental points, such as unusual or exciting game points made, significant events in a player's life, or weather that may affect a game, for example.

ELEMENTS OF A GAME STORY

Here is a checklist of points that every game story should include.

SCORE   The final score should be in your lead paragraph, because it is the most important point — the central point — of your story. For example:

> The Bears beat the Lions 14-7 . . .

WHEN THE GAME TOOK PLACE   This also should be in the lead paragraph:

> The Bears beat the Lions 14-7 today . . .

WHO PLAYED   Team names and any pertinent history, such as long-term rivalries, belong at the top. For example:

> The Bears and the Lions, rivals since the 1960s . . .

WHAT GAME THEY PLAYED   Don't assume it's obvious that your story is about hockey, basketball or baseball. Name the sport:

> The Bears and the Lions, football rivals since the 1960s . . .

WHERE THEY PLAYED   This can be covered at the top or within the body of the story. Unless the venue is important to the story, a few words can cover the where:

> The Bears beat the Lions 14-7 today at North Stadium . . .
>   The Bears and Lions, football rivals since the 1960s, met in North Stadium today . . .

WHY AND HOW   These are covered in the details of the game.

KEY PLAYERS   These are the stars of the show in any game story and should be featured in the story:

> Benjamin Hall scored the tie-breaking free throw, the third time this season he made a tough shot under pressure.

KEY PLAYS   These are the significant moments in the game — perhaps the game-changing basket, touchdown or goal — that should be noted and explained.

STATISTICS   The most important ones can go in the story — a record broken, for example — while others may go in a sidebar or other breakout box.

INJURIES   Note if a player is hurt in the action and follow up to get details of the injury, looking at whether it might affect future play.

QUOTES   Interview players and coaches from both teams.

SIGNIFICANCE OR CONTEXT   Explain the meaning of the game — whether it ends chances for the playoffs, for example, or puts the team in the running for a championship:

> Saturday's win means the Lions will go to the state championship in Lansing this year.

OTHER Look at the crowd, the weather, the parking lot for tailgating parties, the crazy outfits the fans wear. All can add color to your story.

WRITE IN PLAIN, GOOD ENGLISH

Once you've reported all the elements, it's time to put your story together. The cool thing about sports stories is that, for the most part, they should be fun to write and fun to read. A few do's and don'ts:

Do make your story as exciting as the game by providing your readers with the high and low points while minimizing or skipping the boring and unimportant parts.

Don't write your game story chronologically. Start with the good stuff. Look for the drama in the game and write colorfully. Perhaps a story can be built around a significant play — a missed catch or lost touchdown that set the tone or turned the game around.

Do use language that your audience will understand. Avoid sports **jargon**, words only sports fans use, and cliches. Of course, you will have to use sports terms, but beware of overused, hackneyed words such as "hoopster" for "basketball player," "puckster" for "hockey player" and "grappler" for "wrestler."

As William Zinsser says in "On Writing Well," the best sports writers "avoid the exhausted synonyms and strive for freshness elsewhere in their sentences." They write in plain, good English, not "sports English."

Don't be a cheerleader in your writing. When you write about any team, even those from your high school, do not use the word "our" as in "our Bears" or "we" as in "we won." The Bears may win on their own, without being yours or ours.

checkpoint ✓

How is sportswriting like news writing?

Objectivity in Sportswriting

Some young writers grow up being fans of certain sports — baseball, for example — and think they would enjoy a job as a sports writer. Being a fan, however, is the last quality an editor wants in a sports writer. Editors want sports writers who are objective and can report the facts of the story without showing favoritism to one team.

NO CHEERING IN THE PRESS BOX

Ask any sports writer about that motto "No cheering in the press box," and you'll probably also hear some variation such as, "If you want to have fun, go buy a ticket." Both phrases speak to the professionalism expected among the writers covering games and other sporting events. More specifically, the phrases get at an important rule of sports journalism: Writers are objective observers, not cheerleaders for one team or player.

It may be hard to imagine covering one of your high school's sporting events without rooting for your team. But that is what sports writers are expected to do — to be objective. **Objectivity,** or being objective, is the talent of remaining disinterested, or impartial. In journalism objectivity means gathering and presenting facts without judgment. For sports writers that means reining in the emotion and watching an event to collect the facts you need to tell a story well. When you are in the press box you are there to do a job, a job that requires you to look dispassionately at all sides and present the facts to your readers as best you can.

Does that mean all sports writers feel no allegiance to particular teams? Of course not. Sometimes they feel allegiance to the teams they are covering, or to teams from the places where they grew up, or perhaps their college teams. The "no cheering in the press box" rule doesn't dictate feelings, only behavior. Think of it as a code of conduct for the sports journalist.

Why is it so important? Obvious cheering creates questions about the sports writer's credibility and, as a result, the news or sports organization's credibility as well. A journalist's credibility is the most important part of his or her reputation, and news organizations want to hire people whose credibility is impeccable.

Think about the analogy of a news reporter covering your town's city hall. What if the reporter were an obvious fan of the mayor? Would you be able to trust the stories about the mayor's new policies?

check *point* ✓

Why must sports writers remain objective in their stories?

AP Stylebook Concepts

The AP Stylebook includes a section on "Sports Guidelines and Style." It includes entries for individual sports and information about how to list scores, winners and league standings.

Use figures for scores, inserting a hyphen between the totals of the winning and losing teams:

The Marshall High Red Hawks defeated the Centerville Cruisers 6-4.

AP also gives spellings for sports-related terms, which may differ in spelling from ordinary usage. Following is a list of baseball-related words and phrases spelled in AP style:

left-hander (noun)	playoff (noun, adjective)	put out (verb)
line up (verb)	play off (verb)	RBI (singular)
lineup (noun)	putout (noun)	RBIs (plural)

Sports Writer Sued for Game Tweet

Can you imagine being sued for something you wrote on your Twitter feed? Most of us think of those 140-character updates as a place to share a thought or link, or just update friends on what we are doing.

But Twitter is now an important reporting tool, and journalists must take the same care in writing a tweet as they take when writing full stories that will post to their news organization's website. Case in point: An Associated Press sports writer was sued by a National Basketball Association referee, who said the writer went too far in a tweet sent during a game the writer was covering.

In a tweet sent to his followers from a Minnesota Timberwolves game in Minneapolis in 2011, the AP writer Jon Krawczynski criticized a questionable referee call and then wrote that the referee promised he'd give points back to the Timberwolves in another call as the game continued.

The referee, Bill Spooner, said Krawczynski's tweet was false. He was disciplined by the NBA, nonetheless. Spooner subsequently sued AP and Krawczynski for $75,000 in damages. Krawczynski and the AP stood by the story — or, in this case, the tweet.

The lawsuit raises important questions for sports writers everywhere because Twitter is part of reporting most sporting events. It's an attractive platform for reporting game stories because it allows for up-to-the-minute reporting of even the smallest details. But tweets are posted in seconds, generally without review by editors. Because tweeting also lends itself to informal writing, it is easy to slip into an opinionated voice.

Should sports writers (and others) have a set of standards to tweet by? Should reporters who cover events — whether sports or other news events — be entitled to an opinion in their tweets? The NBA referee's suit wasn't settled at the time of publication, but regardless of the outcome, the lesson is clear: Accuracy and truth must prevail in every sentence journalists write.

THINK *Critically*

1. Why do sports writers use Twitter to report athletic events?

2. Do you think a writer should be subject to lawsuits for what he or she writes in a tweet?

10.1 | Assessment

Understand Concepts

Determine the best answer for each of the following questions.

1. A sports story that reports the news of a single game is called a
   _____ story.
   a. highlighted   c. game
   b. sample   d. preview

2. Which is something you want to do in a sports story?
   a. use jargon
   b. make the story exciting
   c. write the story chronologically
   d. be a cheerleader for one of the teams

3. A sports story that includes statistics from previous seasons is called a(n)
   _____ story.
   a. preview   c. game
   b. update   d. stat

4. **True or False** Game stories include all the highlights, or important moments, of the games and the final score.

5. **True or False** For game stories, you want to interview players and coaches from both teams.

Write Now!

Practice your writing skills with the following activities.

6. Choose a game story or preview story from your school or local newspaper. Using a computer, research and write a sidebar related to the original story. Attach the original story to your sidebar when you turn in your story. Identify the original as either a game or a preview story. Your sidebar's audience should match the audience of the original story.

7. Choose a sports preview story you would like to do for your high school newspaper. The story should include at least one interview. Once you have chosen your topic, read back issues of your school newspaper and the archives of the school website to gather background information and prepare for your interview(s). Evaluate and confirm the validity of the background information. Plan and write relevant questions for your interview(s). After conducting the interview(s), write a draft of your story, incorporating both direct and indirect quotations from the interview(s) as well as additional research. Edit the story using proofreading symbols. Be sure to edit for clarity, engaging language, and the correct use of English. Attach your draft to your final copy.

Write Sports Columns, Profiles and Features

Goals

- Discuss writing the sports column.
- Discuss writing a sports profile and features.

Key Terms

- column 261
- weblog, or blog 262
- insider 263
- independent sports blogger 263
- profile 264
- feature 265

FOCUS

When Jessie signed up to be a sports reporter for her school's newspaper, it was not because she wanted to sit in the bleachers watching football or baseball games. She did, however, want to write about the young men and women who were playing those games. A swimmer herself, Jessie knows about the dedication a sport can demand. As a storyteller, she knows there's often a good story behind the athletes who excel. Jessie made it her goal to become the newspaper's top sports reporter, which led to her writing her own sports column.

Write a Column

Imagine it's the biggest game of the year — the contest between your high school and its arch rival, the high school across town. All of your friends are going to the game Friday night, and plans are in the works for dressing in school colors, painting faces and making banners to support your team. You, however, are assigned to cover the game for your school news website, which means as a reporter you should remain objective and non-judgmental. Is that possible when you attend the high school whose game you are covering?

Jessie is lucky. As a column writer, she gets to add her opinion, something she could not do as a reporter. As with news stories, most sports stories should be objective. There is no room for a writer's opinion in most of the stories you read in a sports section. Columns, however, are different.

Columns — and there are plenty of them in sports pages — are stories that require opinion and emotion. A column is the place in the sports section where a writer may get mad about a losing season, the poor performance of a player or a referee's call. In a column, a writer may rally the readers around a cause or a player — or just write optimistically about the possibility of a winning future. Columns are found in the sports pages of print newspapers and as part of online news organizations' coverage.

ELEMENTS OF A SPORTS COLUMN

To write a good sports column, include the following elements:

State your opinion clearly in the lead.

> The Lions' losing streak won't end until team owners do what they must — fire head coach Stanley Smith.

Provide facts, figures and quotes to back up your opinion and further make your point.

> Since Smith took over the team at the beginning of last season, the Lions have not won a game, and watching practice this week, it is clear he is doing nothing to address holes in the defensive line. "I'm concentrating on our offense," Smith said.

Build to a strong conclusion and use words readers will remember.

> Until Smith is relieved of duty, fans will be forced to watch a bunch of losers. The team deserves better than Stan Smith's lack of leadership.

BLOGGING

Sports journalists are also writing **weblogs**, or **blogs**, which are a writer's personal opinions about a subject and published on the Internet for public reading. Blogs have become an important part of the sports media landscape in the 21st century. There are mainstream media blogs, hosted on the sites of news organizations; there are blogs hosted by the professional sports teams and athletes themselves; and there are independent blogs established by people who just want to write about the sports they love or hate.

Keith Langlois writes about the Detroit Pistons for the Detroit Pistons. He is a writer-editor for Pistons.com, the website owned by the Detroit basketball team. He uses blogging and Twitter to keep fans up-to-date on all the news about their NBA team — and, indeed, Piston fans are his audience. Langlois knows his credibility would be suspect if he did not cover the Pistons accurately and without cheerleading. However, he says, "I write about the team a little differently than I would if I were at a newspaper."

He was lead sports columnist at a suburban Detroit newspaper before he took the job with Pistons.com so he knows the meaning of objectivity. He says he now writes "from a less objective standpoint." His nearly 30 years of journalistic experience means he has a solid background in reporting and editing. He knows how to write objectively, but he also knows how to write for his audience — Piston fans.

Langlois also knows how to write profiles on favorite players and interviews with the top team managers. Even as an employee of the team-owned website, Langlois doesn't hesitate to ask tough questions. For example, if the team is on a losing streak, he'll ask why and what needs to be done to change the losing streak to a winning one.

Before hiring Langlois, the Pistons' management commissioned a study of the website. They learned users were hungry for news. Langlois takes that seriously and keeps the website up-to-date with all the latest news about the team and its players and coaches.

Langlois might be called an **insider** — he has access to the team and its managers. But plenty of bloggers who do not work for a sports team write on sports topics. Some work for the mainstream media, while others are **independent sports bloggers**, who set up their own blogs on the Internet.

Bloggers affiliated with a sports section on a mainstream media site also usually have access to the people and information they need because of their news organization credentials. They may be objective in reporting and writing, but bloggers write on a variety of topics and generally are permitted to use their "voice" and be opinionated in their blogs.

Independent sports bloggers can be unabashed cheerleaders for a team. Most independent bloggers do not strive for objectivity like bloggers affiliated with news organizations. Rather, they build readership with fans as a fan of the team themselves.

In 2005, Jason Fry set up "Faith and Fear in Flushing," a blog about the New York Mets. Fry, a Wall Street Journal reporter, began the blog as an experiment. He says he never thought he'd be a sports writer because he was too much of a fan.

His blog has allowed him to be both — a fan and a sports writer. With a number of years of successful blogging behind him, he is considered an established blogger and is granted access by the Mets to the same opportunities as writers for mainstream media outlets. Yet, he's independent of any media outlet.

Why is it appropriate for writer-editor Keith Langlois to use a "less objective" standpoint in reporting on the Detroit Pistons for Pistons.com than he did as a columnist for a suburban Detroit newspaper?

check point ✓

How is writing a sports column or blog different from writing a sports news story?

Sports Profiles and Features

For clear, well-structured sentences, do not use double negatives. Words such as "not," "nothing" and "no" are negative words — words that deny or say no. Unncessary negative words simply clutter a sentence. For example: "The story never told us nothing about the game." It's easy to correct this sentence by writing, "The story never told us anything about the game." The second negative word, "nothing," was changed to "anything," which makes the sentence clearer for the reader.

When looking for negative words, watch for contractions, such as "couldn't," "wouldn't," "didn't" and so on, that are made up of "could" and "not," "would" and "not," "did" and "not" and so on. Also, pay attention to words such as "nobody" and "no one," which contain "no."

Profiles, stories about people, along with feature stories, help round out the coverage found in most sports sections, whether in print or on the Web. Profiles may give readers some behind-the-scenes information or a glimpse of the athletes as they exist off the court or field. Profiles involve interviews with the athletes and the people around them.

SPORTS PROFILES

Sports writers often spotlight key players by writing about their records, how they train and how they live when not involved in their sport. Profiles of sports figures should also include information about their backgrounds, dedication and sacrifice.

Sports profiles may focus on the athlete's involvement in community activities or events. The story also should include information about an athlete's family and personal life; that is, the private side of a public individual. Good profiles of athletes often take readers behind the scenes, explaining why the successful athlete pursued his or her dream and who helped make it happen.

The basis of a sports profile is the questions you ask. Here are 11 topics to address in profiles on high school athletes:

1. The sport they play and what it takes to play it

2. When they began playing the sport — especially whether there were signs when they were younger that they would excel at the sport

3. How much training they put into they sport before they got to high school. Any awards or indication that they would become so good

4. How much training time they put in while playing on the high school team

5. Outside interests: For example, do they have a job? Do they belong to other clubs or organizations?

6. How they manage schoolwork while training

7. How they manage friendships

8. Family obligations and support: Does the family come to all the games?

9. What parental support have they had for the sport since they became interested in it?

10. Do they have a mentor or someone they look up to in their sport?

11. Professional aspirations, if any

SPORTS FEATURES

You read about feature stories in Chapter 8. You learned that **features** have all the journalistic elements of a news story but are written like a non-fiction story. They have a beginning, middle and end and often describe a person or place. You probably remember that a feature can be a human interest story, an informational story or a trend story.

Human interest stories are offbeat, often the result of keen observation. For example, let's say you attend a minor league baseball game and see a former classmate hit a home run. You know that both your high school newspaper and the local paper have already run profile pieces on the player, so you need a different angle. As you watch the excited reaction of the crowd, an idea forms. You decide to do a feature on fan loyalty, a feature that you sell to the local newspaper.

Informational features are those in which you call on the experts. These stories are often "how-to" stories. For example, you might do a story on how to become a good soccer player. Experts you could interview would include the soccer coaches at your high school and some of the key players. You might also interview coaches and players at other schools for a broader view. You could even try to interview a professional soccer player, which would give you a better chance of getting your story published.

////// *Who in your high school might be a good subject for a sports profile? Why?*

Trend stories — like human interest stories — are often the result of keen observation. When looking for trend stories, look for what's popular in sports and what the current movement is. For example, are there certain words related to sports that have become so trendy they are used in non-sports conversation? Is it a trend for students in your high school to wear team shirts or team colors the day of a big game? Has a particular sport, such as swimming, become the latest trend in your school?

Sports writers use all three categories of features — human interest, informational and trends — when writing sports stories for their news organizations, sports organizations and blogs.

checkpoint ✓

What are two types of stories that help round out the sports coverage in news organizations?

Digging Deeper

Reporting a Sports Milestone

When Derek Jeter reached 3,000 career hits in July 2011, sports writers around the world reported the milestone. Tyler Kepner wrote one such article for the International Herald Tribune entitled, "Yankees' Jeter goes deep — into the record books; Shortstop's home run gives him 3,000 hits, first from team to do so." Read this article by accessing the Gale Journalism eCollection at www.cengage.com/school/langarts/journalism, and clicking on the link to Chapter 10. Then answer the questions, below.

THINK *Critically*

1. Into which of these sports story categories would you place this article: game story, preview story, column, profile, or feature? Justify your answer with examples from the article.

2. Identify the baseball statistics in the story.

3. Write an article about an athlete in your school or a professional athlete who achieved a sports milestone or set a record.

Source: Kepner, Tyler. "Jeter Streaks Above 3,000, And It's a Blast." New York Times 10 July 2011: A1(L). Global Issues In Context. Web. 12 Sep. 2011.

10.2 | Assessment

Understand Concepts

Determine the best answer for each of the following questions.

1. Keith Langlois might be called a(n) _____ because he has access to the Detroit Pistons and the team's managers.
   a. independent sports blogger
   b. profiler
   c. insider
   d. outsider

2. Which refers to a story about what's currently popular in sports?
   a. weblog story
   b. trend feature
   c. human interest story
   d. informational feature

3. **True or False**   Column writers should inject their opinions and emotions into their columns.

4. **True or False**   Facts, figures and quotes should be included in a sports column.

Write Now!

Practice your writing skills with the following activities.

5. Use the Internet to find a sports team in a foreign country. If English is your second language, choose a team from your country of origin and read about the team in your native language. If English is your first language, choose a team from an English-speaking country, such as England, Australia, Scotland or Ireland. Research background information on the team using articles and past interviews of team members, coaches and managers. Evaluate and confirm the validity of the background information from a variety of sources such as books, news articles, other columns and reports. Using a computer, write a column about the team. Send the column to your teacher electronically.

6. Choose a topic for a sports feature from among the teams, athletes or coaches in your school. Plan and write relevant questions for an interview or in-depth research on the subject. Write a draft of your feature. Identify the type of feature it is. Revise and edit your draft using proofreading symbols. Attach your draft to your final copy and turn them both in to your teacher.

CHAPTER 10 | Assessment

Review Journalism Concepts

10.1 Write Sports News Stories

Two types of sports stories are game stories and preview stories. Game stories are exactly what they sound like, stories about individual games — news stories about the context and conflict between two teams. Game stories include all the highlights, or important moments, of the games, including the final score. Sports writers often write game stories with a summary lead very similar to the news summary lead. A summary lead gets straight to the central point — which team won. The other type of sports story is a preview story, which takes a broader look at how a team may be expected to perform for a season.

Writing the game story is like writing a news story about the conflict that happened in the arena. Sports writers, like news writers, must cover the basics of the story — the who, what, when, where, why and how — as well as supplemental points such as significant events in a player's life or unusual weather conditions. Sports writers must avoid jargon and remain objective.

10.2 Write Sports Columns, Profiles and Features

In addition to sports news stories, journalists also write sports columns, profiles and feature stories. While news stories require the reporter to be objective, columns require opinion and emotion. Columns are found in the sports section of print newspapers and are a part of online news organizations' coverage. Elements of a sports column include stating your opinion clearly in the lead; providing facts, figures and quotes to back up your opinion and further make your point; and building to a strong conclusion, using words readers will remember.

Sports journalists also write weblogs, or blogs, which are a writer's personal opinions about a subject and published on the Internet for public reading. There are mainstream media blogs, hosted on the sites of news organizations; blogs hosted by the sports teams and athletes themselves; and independent blogs established by people who just want to write about the sports they love or hate.

Profiles (stories about people) and features (stories written like a non-fiction story) help round out the coverage found in most sports sections, whether in print or on the Web. Profiles may give readers some behind-the-scenes information or a glimpse of the athletes as they exist off the court or field. Profiles involve interviews with the athletes and the people around them. Features have all the journalistic elements of a news story but are written like a non-fiction story. They have a beginning, middle and end and often describe a person or place. You probably remember that a feature can be a human interest story, an informational story or a trend story.

Develop Your Journalism Language

Write the letter of the term that matches each definition. Some terms will not be used.

_____ 1. The talent of remaining impartial; gathering and presenting facts without judgment

_____ 2. A sports story that requires opinion and emotion

_____ 3. News story about a single game

_____ 4. A writer's personal opinions about a subject, published on the Internet for public reading

_____ 5. Important moments in a game

_____ 6. Columnist who has access to a sports team and its managers

_____ 7. Sports writers who set up and write their own sports stories on the Internet

_____ 8. A story that gives a broad view of how a team may be expected to perform for a season

_____ 9. Stories about people

_____ 10. The reporting and writing of stories about the many different sports events and the people who play them

a. column
b. features
c. game story
d. highlights
e. independent sports bloggers
f. insider
g. jargon
h. objectivity
i. preview story
j. profiles
k. sportswriting
l. weblog, or blog

11. If you write a game story with _____, your readers will not be able to tell which of the teams you prefer.
    a. balance
    b. subjectivity
    c. dominance
    d. objectivity

12. You should avoid using words such as "hoopster," "puckster" and "grappler" in your sports stories because they are
    a. words not used in sports.
    b. only used in the locker room.
    c. jargon.
    d. plain English.

13. Which of these elements would you find in a preview story?
    a. a play-by-play report as the game takes place
    b. an interview with coaches and players about the new season
    c. tweets during the game to update followers
    d. locker-room or on-the-field interviews

14. Which would you find in a game story?
    a. a look ahead at the upcoming season
    b. a story about new players
    c. setting the scene for fans hopeful for a new start
    d. a focus on one game with highlights of that game

Think Critically

15. Why do sports writers often write game stories with a summary lead?

16. Which sports stories are more prevalent — game or preview stories?

17. Do sports writers who write game stories have to attend the games? Why?

18. Why do sports writers who write game stories compile statistics of the game?

19. When is it most appropriate to write preview stories? Why is this the most appropriate time?

20. Why should the final score be in the lead paragraph of a game story?

21. Is being a fan a good idea for a sports writer? Why or why not?

22. Do the best sports writers write in sports English or plain English? Explain your answer.

23. Should you be a cheerleader for your home team when writing about it for your high school newspaper? Why or why not?

24. Which would you rather write — a game story, a preview story or a column? Why?

25. Can an independent sports blogger also be an insider? Explain your answer.

26. Why do you want to interview an athlete's family for a profile?

Make Academic Connections

27. **WRITING** Use the Internet to research a sports figure who has accomplished much in his or her career. Access a sports hall of fame, such as the football hall of fame, the baseball hall of fame or a sports hall of fame in your city, town or state. Choose one of the people you read about. Once you have chosen your subject, read reports, articles and past interviews to gather background information. Evaluate and confirm the validity of the background information from a variety of sources such as qualified persons, books and reports. Plan, draft and write a sports profile story about the person that is suitable for publication in your high school newspaper or news website. Include information such as his or her hometown, sports history and accomplishments and why the person was chosen to be in the hall of fame. Once you have completed your draft, revise and edit your copy using proofreading symbols. Attach your draft to your final paper when you turn in your paper.

28. **HISTORY** Explore the history and development of American sports journalism through people and events. Use the Internet to research the major people and events of a specific sport, such as golf, or a specific event, such as the Masters. Write a feature story, suitable for a high school broadcast news program, which explains the sport or event, the major figures through the history of the sport or event and how the event played out against other historical events in the world, such as the Olympics during a war. Incorporate direct and indirect quotes in your story. Be prepared to deliver your broadcast feature in class.

29. ETHICS You are the editor of your high school newspaper. You are on deadline when a reporter comes to you with a story about your school's top basketball athlete, who was seen driving under the influence of alcohol after a party last night. You know that if this information is printed, the athlete will be suspended. Your school is set to play a major game Friday night that will determine which team goes to the state semifinals. What do you do? Would it be responsible or irresponsible media action to print the story?

30. READING Choose a traditional newspaper that also has an online version. Read a sports story in print and then online. Write a report that compares and contrasts the two versions. Include information on the photos, audio or other elements. Rewrite both stories for a high school audience. Add a note that explains what elements, such as photos, you would add to each version.

31. ART Make a bulletin board that illustrates the information in this chapter and allows students to add stories and information. For example, in one section of the bulletin board, have the title "Game Stories," with the definition. Allow room beneath this title. Every time a classmate has a story published, clip it and add it to the bulletin board.

Writing Portfolio Activity

32. Use a computer to create a spreadsheet with columns titled Game Stories, Preview Stories, Blogs, Columns, Profiles, Human Interest Features, Informational Features and Trend Features. Read several back issues of the sports section of your high school newspaper and the archives of the online sports news. Look for examples of each category of story. There will be some overlap, so stories will be in more than one category. For example, a profile could also be a blog. What is missing that you might write about that would be of interest to other students in your school? Make a list of possible stories. Add the spreadsheet and list to your portfolio.

AP Stylebook Workshop

Use copyediting symbols to make the following sports-related terms conform to AP style. The correct form of each term is listed on page 258.

33. lefthander

34. put-out (noun)

35. line-up (verb)

36. play-off (noun)

37. rbi

38. RBIS

SOCIAL AND CROSS-CULTURAL SKILLS: Work in Diverse Teams

Today's reporters need to understand the world and be able to work effectively in diverse teams. Even in your high school, working in diverse teams may be a necessity. In your school, and in the larger world, it will help you to develop — and use — good social and cross-cultural skills. To succeed as a reporter in the 21st century, you will need to

- Interact with others
- Work in diverse teams

INTERACT WITH OTHERS

Two of the strongest abilities a reporter can have are to know when it is appropriate to listen and when it is appropriate to speak. When sitting in an editorial meeting, you must be able to speak up when it is appropriate, but how do you know when that is? You know by using good listening skills and by having confidence in what you have to add to the conversation.

When you listen, you know what has been said and what still needs to be said. If you do not use good listening skills, you may repeat what someone else has added to the meeting, which does not demonstrate that you have the ability to interact effectively with others.

You also need to speak with confidence, which comes from believing in what you are saying. You must first convince yourself before you can convince others that your idea for a story is sound.

To be known as someone who interacts effectively with others, you must also conduct yourself in a respectable, professional manner. You must be confident, but not arrogant.

WORK IN DIVERSE TEAMS

Journalists work with people of different social and cultural backgrounds. To work together effectively, you must be able to respect social and cultural differences and be able to communicate with people who are different from you.

You also must be able to listen to and respect other people's ideas and values. On your high school newspaper staff, you may have students who come from different areas of the city or from other countries. To work effectively with them, you need to develop and use good cross-cultural skills. Always respect yourself and your co-workers.

Keep your mind open. Do not reject ideas immediately. Take time to listen respectfully to the other person. Whether working with one other person or several, work as a team. Use the social and cultural differences among you to create new ideas, which will increase both innovative ideas and the quality of your work.

THINK *Critically*
Spend some time thinking about how effectively you work with others. Write down at least three ways you can improve your social and cross-cultural skills.

REAL PEOPLE REAL CAREERS

Marc Carig | Sports Reporter and Blogger

Marc Carig says he has only had one career goal since attending community college — to become a sports writer. But even at the student newspaper, "I wrote far less about ball games than I did about local government and school administration, which taught me to pay attention to detail. It's a skill I use every day while covering the Yankees."

Carig covers the New York Yankees for the Star-Ledger of Newark, N.J., and he calls it "a daily challenge. It's nerve-racking because there is an element of pressure to get information first, or to best provide context with whatever news might be breaking at the time."

As a beat writer, Carig goes where the team goes. "It's three months of sweating under brutal late-night deadlines, of dry room-service hamburgers, of 4 a.m. wake-up calls to make your flight to the next city." It's a grind, but it's also exhilarating, he says.

Carig uses Twitter for some of his reporting and he also writes a blog about the Yankees. He gets ideas by talking to "as many people as I can around the team, whether it's the clubhouse attendants or the general manager. You never know what may pop up in conversation."

MULTIMEDIA SKILLS ARE IMPORTANT

Born and raised in California, the son of first-generation Filipino immigrants, Carig went to a community college and then worked at a small paper while he saved money to finish his degree at the University of Nevada. The program emphasized the importance of multimedia skills and Carig says he uses them every day "even though I work at a newspaper. It's not unusual now for reporters to edit audio and video for their websites."

Carig uses an RSS reader to keep track of what other writers are covering on the Yankees beat. He estimates it saves him hours. But within the RSS feed he has a feed called "writers" to help him keep up with the writers he most admires. "If you want to do great work, expose yourself to great work," he says. "If you are a photographer, keep an eye out for images that stay with you. If you're a page designer, find great pages and figure out why they work. If you're a writer, read until your eyes get tired."

Source: Personal interview with Marc Carig

THINK *Critically*

1. How do you think covering local government might be helpful experience before covering a team like the Yankees?
2. Why do you think you should expose yourself to great work if you want to do great work?

11

Television and Radio Broadcasts

| 11.1 | **Write for Broadcast** |
| 11.2 | **Write a Newscast** |

Cable Network Changes TV Landscape

At 5 p.m. on June 1, 1980, a businessman named Ted Turner forever changed the way consumers would see television news. He launched Cable News Network, CNN, the first 24-hour all-news network. Today you take for granted your ability to get news anytime — on computers, iPads and smartphones, as well as television and radio. Before CNN launched, most broadcast news was seen on the evening programs of the three largest networks. Today CNN alone reaches more than a billion people worldwide. Two other national cable news networks — MSNBC and Fox News Channel — were inspired by CNN's success.

CNN's daily newscast model was based on talk radio. Stories would be repeated during the day, with updates if they were needed. It soon became an important news source. In 1981, CNN was the first television network to report that President Ronald Reagan had been shot outside a Washington hotel. In 1986 it was the only network covering live the doomed space shuttle Challenger's liftoff. By 1991, CNN proved itself must-see TV with its coverage of the Gulf War and reports "live from Baghdad."

THINK *Critically*

1. What did CNN do that hadn't been done before?
2. On what did CNN base its news model?

Write for Broadcast

Goals

- Understand how writing for broadcast differs from writing for print.
- Write a broadcast news story.

Key Terms

- broadcast 275
- scripts 276
- umbrella lead 277
- chronological order 278
- newsreader 279
- anchor 280
- teleprompter 280

FOCUS

Alicia wakes every morning not to a blaring alarm clock but to the news on National Public Radio's "Morning Edition." She gets breakfast in the kitchen while the anchors of a national television morning show tell her the news that happened overnight. She gets into her car to drive to her downtown office while keeping the radio tuned to an all-news station that gives traffic and weather reports every 10 minutes. By the time she gets to work she feels as if she's as informed as she needs to be, thanks to the familiar voices of her favorite broadcasters.

Broadcast

A **broadcast** is a radio or television program. When used as a verb, "broadcast" refers to the transmission of programming or information on radio or television. The language of broadcast news is the language of the spoken word. Writing for broadcast is different from writing for print precisely because the information must be spoken. That requires a different story structure and language rhythm. Listen to radio and television newscasters to hear how they speak when they read the news.

LEARN THE LANGUAGE OF BROADCAST

Broadcast news is part of the fabric of your life because you have so many opportunities during a day to hear it. Like Alicia, you may wake up to a clock radio set to an all-news station, eat breakfast or dinner with a TV tuned to a news show, hear news and traffic updates in your car while commuting to and from work or school, or catch a news video on your computer during the day. It's hard to go a day without hearing a news broadcast somewhere. As listeners, you've become familiar with the language of broadcast.

Writing for broadcast means writing for listeners. Broadcast writing must be shorter and more concise than the writing a print news outlet requires.

////// *Why do you think broadcast news stories such as those you hear on the radio need to be shorter than stories printed in newspapers?*

Scripts, as the written broadcast stories are called, often are no more than 30 to 60 seconds long. Broadcast writers think about how much listening and viewing time they will have, whereas print reporters think about how much space they have. Like their print counterparts, broadcast writers look for a central point on which they will structure the story, but unlike print reporters, broadcast writers have to focus their stories right from the start. And as you'll see in the examples below, broadcast scripts deviate from AP print style in several ways.

LEADS

There are several types of broadcast leads, but the five-W's-and-an-H summary news lead that print reporters use is too long for broadcast. The most important point of the story comes first, followed by the rest. The lead should tell one or two facts to interest the listener.

A local man is 2 million dollars richer this morning.	Lead

Thirty-five-year-old Paul Hayes won the Texas state lottery yesterday. He says he plans to pay off his house and buy himself a new truck.	Story

Broadcast leads can be updated many times after a story is originally written, so the lead about the lottery winner could change by the afternoon.

A local man who won 2 million dollars in the lottery received congratulations from the governor today.	Lead

Thirty-five-year-old Paul Hayes says Governor Williams called him at home this afternoon to wish him well. The governor also joked with Hayes about paying his taxes.	Story

Broadcast writers sometimes use a feature approach to leads so listeners want to hear more.

> Teenagers are taking over local beaches and boardwalks.

Lead

> Beach Week, the annual rite of passage for graduating high school seniors, begins today. That means thousands of teens from inland towns and cities will move into rental houses for a week of sun, surf and post-graduation relaxation.

Story

Like print reporters, broadcast writers may have to summarize two or more related stories in one lead before telling the individual stories. This technique is called an **umbrella lead**.

> Five people were hurt in separate fireworks incidents on Independence Day.

Lead

> Two brothers, eight and nine years old, have second-degree burns after playing with a bottle rocket.
>   Three men in their 20s also were treated for burns after the fireworks they lighted in a downtown park backfired. Police say the fireworks were illegal and they are investigating.

Story

BODY OF THE STORY

Print reporters write in an inverted pyramid style, putting the most important facts in descending order of importance so the reader can leave the story at any time and still have some information. Broadcast reporters write so that every sentence must be heard. The most important information goes first. The next sentences back up the first sentence and give information pertinent to it. For example, in the story about Beach Week, the reporter found a way to get listeners' attention while getting the most important point across.

> Teenagers are taking over local beaches and boardwalks.

The next sentence backs up the first with more specifics and context.

> Beach Week, the annual rite of passage for graduating high school seniors, begins today.

The third sentence supplies meaning.

> That means thousands of teens from inland towns and cities will move into rental houses for a week of sun, surf and post-graduation relaxation.

Some broadcast stories lend themselves to being told in **chronological order,** the order in which things happened. The lead will be the most important element of the story, but the rest of the story is related as it occurred.

> A father and his missing son were reunited this afternoon after an 18-hour search. The youngster was found wandering a little-traveled hiking path, dazed and dehydrated, but otherwise in good health.

The lead tells listeners that a missing boy has been found and he's OK. Now the writer can go on with a chronological narrative.

> John Johnson and his 13-year-old son, Luke, were hiking in Woodland State Park when they accidentally got separated at about four o'clock Saturday afternoon. Johnson scoured the hiking trails for two hours without finding Luke. He called park rangers for help when it began to get dark.
>
> Rangers and volunteer searchers looked for the boy through the night but it wasn't until ten o'clock this morning that Luke was spotted on the meandering trail six miles from where his father had last seen him.

check_point_ ✓

How do broadcast news stories differ from print stories?

Write a Broadcast Story

Writing for listeners and viewers requires attention to the way they will process your words. Broadcast writers need their listeners to understand the story the first time because the listeners may not get a chance to hear it again. **Newsreaders** — anchors, disc jockeys and correspondents — deliver the stories to the listeners and viewers.

WRITE FOR LISTENERS AND VIEWERS

Here are some guidelines.

- **Write the way you talk.** Make your story conversational. Listeners want to feel as if they are part of the conversation, not that the newsreader is preaching to them.

- **Write simply.** Write short sentences, no more than 15 words. Break your long sentences into two.

- **Go with the clarity of subject-verb-direct object order.** The marching band (subject) is rehearsing (verb) the new fight song (direct object).

- **Use one idea per sentence.**

> Tim Jones is running for class president. The November election includes ten candidates.
>
> Good

> Tim Jones is running for class president in the November election, which includes ten candidates.
>
> Not so good

- **Use short words with those short sentences.** This is no time to show off your extensive multisyllabic vocabulary. Say "use," not "utilize," and "help," not "assist."

- **Use the active voice** and put words you want to stress at the end of the sentence, where the newsreader will emphasize them.

- **Don't start with a question or a quote.** That may work in print but it does not in broadcast writing. Listeners may end up confused.

- **Identify the speaker before what is said.**

The president says the economy is fine.	Good

The economy is fine, says the president.	Not so good

- **Hit the highlights only.** You won't have time for more.
- **Use titles before names and shorten long titles.** Titles cannot be easily said aloud after a name. "Richard Edwards, superintendent of Washington County Schools," should become "Schools Superintendent Richard Edwards."
- **Leave out ages, middle initials and addresses** unless they are important to the story.

WRITE FOR THE ANCHOR

All the elements of writing for your listeners and viewers make your broadcast story easier for an **anchor**, the main news presenter, or reporter. Anchors read the newscast script from a teleprompter located near the camera. A **teleprompter** is a device for displaying a script or prepared text so that the speaker or performer does not have to look down. The name TelePrompTer was trademarked in 1951, but the lowercase version is widely used to mean any similar device.

/////// *What are the major differences between writing for broadcast and writing for print?*

Follow these tips to make your copy anchor-friendly.

- **Spell things out phonetically.** Announcers or anchors may need help in pronouncing a name or place. Many writers put pronunciations in brackets and all capital letters so places and people are identified correctly. Alternatively, you can use lowercase letters for unstressed syllables and uppercase for stressed syllables. For example: Jesus Martinez [hay-SOOS' mar-TEE'-nes].

- **Hyphenate words that go together.** It shows newsreaders where they may or may not take a breath. For example, "The monster-truck event" or "the young-urban-professional." The hyphens help the newsreader see that "monster-truck" should be said as one, and "young-urban-professional" should not be said as "young, urban (breath) professional."

- **Hyphenate numbers that go together.** Addresses, years and telephone numbers in particular need hyphens so the reader knows how to say them. Examples: "The suspect was found at 15-33 Main Street. He was born in 19-64."

- **Spell out numbers up to and including 11.** "The gardener has ten zucchinis, 24 tomatoes and eleven heads of lettuce."

- **Use numerals and words for big numbers.** Write them in a way that is easiest for your anchor to read without stumbling. "Bank robbers got away with 4 million dollars."

- **Spell out signs and symbols.** "He gave 100 percent of his time to the charity." "Her home is worth 250 thousand dollars."

> Why do broadcast writers need to make their listeners understand the story the first time it is read?

AP Stylebook Concepts

AP style includes guidelines for the treatment of names and call letters of radio and television stations.

- Capitalize the call letters.

  Example   WHIO

- Use a hyphen to separate the type of station (radio or television) from the call letters.

  Example   WHIO-TV, WHIO-FM or WHIO-AM

- Do not capitalize "radio station" or "television station."

  Example   television station WHIO

- However, for official government stations, capitalize "Radio" or "Television" before the station name.

  Example   Radio Moscow

11.1 | Assessment

Understand Concepts

Determine the best answer for each of the following questions.

1. What kind of lead is used when a broadcast writer needs to summarize multiple related stories in one lead before telling the individual stories?
   - **a.** summary
   - **b.** chronological
   - **c.** pyramid
   - **d.** umbrella

2. Which of the following is not a guideline for writing a broadcast story?
   - **a.** Write the way you talk.
   - **b.** Use complex sentences.
   - **c.** Use the active voice.
   - **d.** Hit the highlights only.

3. Some broadcast stories lend themselves to being told in the order in which things happened. This order is called
   - **a.** alphabetic.
   - **b.** chronological.
   - **c.** consecutive.
   - **d.** typological.

4. **True or False**   Writing for broadcast is different from writing for print.

5. **True or False**   When writing for broadcast, starting a story with a quote is a good idea.

Write Now!

Practice your writing skills with the following activities.

6. Contact your local television news station to request a bio on your favorite anchor or reporter. Also, use the Internet for additional research. Use reports and past interviews, for example, to gather background information. Evaluate and confirm the validity of the background information from a variety of sources such as other qualified persons and reports. Plan, draft and then write a composition that describes the person and his or her background and discusses why you like this person. Include stories he or she has reported on, his or her delivery and other aspects of the reporting that impressed you. Also, include direct and indirect quotations in your paper. Edit your paper for clarity, engaging language and the correct use of English.

7. Use the broadcast journalist and the information you gathered in exercise 6 to write an appropriate story for broadcast about this journalist. Be prepared to deliver your story in class in a broadcast story format. Practice delivering your story in front of family members or friends before attempting to deliver the story in class.

To Link or Not to Link

If you are writing an in-depth story for your school website about a new movie theater opening in town, would you provide readers a way to find the theater's home page from your story? Would you provide readers a link — words in the story text that connect the readers to a story on a different website? Would you link readers to the local newspaper's website story on the same topic as your story? Do you owe links to your readers? Is it unethical to omit a link that may help your readers?

When you read an in-depth story on the website of a local or national news organization, you may see links (hyperlinks) that take you to more information on the topic — whether it is a home page for an organization or a story on the topic by another media group. While links are commonplace all around the Web, and particularly in blogs that aggregate news, some media organizations are still reluctant to link to information that is not on their site.

The "ethic of the link," says Jay Rosen, a New York University professor who writes the media blog Press Think, is what the Web is all about. Rosen says "the link is the way we make the Web a place to connect people and knowledge."

In the early days of the Internet, news organizations reacted to the rise of the Web by repurposing their print stories and photos for their websites. These news organizations did not want to send Web readers away from their sites, so they rarely linked to additional information on another site.

As Rosen puts it, "When they gave birth to their first websites, their sites were actually anti-Web because they didn't understand or accept the ethic of the link."

Of course, today news organizations understand that it can be helpful to Web visitors to link to additional information on a topic, even if it is on another website. Still, some news organizations remain reluctant to do so because it can mean losing a visitor who might have continued to other news or feature pages on their own sites.

THINK *Critically*

1. Why could it be helpful to link from your story to pertinent information that is not on your website?

2. Why do some online newspapers resist linking to outside sources?

Write a Newscast

Goals

- Define newscast.
- Write a newscast for television or radio.

Key Terms

- newscast 284
- news director 285
- producer 285
- transition 285
- kicker 286
- sequencing 286
- pan 286
- sound bite 287
- chyron 287
- lead-in 288
- slug 289

FOCUS

Scott Pelley, Diane Sawyer and Brian Williams anchor evening newscasts for the three largest broadcast news organizations, CBS, ABC and NBC. Although being a television news anchor is still prestigious, it is less so than it was before the onset of Internet news. Nightly news broadcasts are competing for a shrinking audience that has family obligations, work to do, social activities and volunteer commitments. Plus, thanks to technology, including cable television networks such as CNN and MSNBC, anyone interested in keeping up with the news is likely to have heard it already. As television news moves further into the new century, its biggest challenge will be retaining an audience.

What Is a Newscast?

A **newscast** is a compilation of visual or audio broadcast stories. Just as a newspaper has a managing editor making decisions about which stories will get prominent play, local and national broadcast outlets have managing editors who determine which stories will be included in a newscast. Depending on the media outlet, the newscast might include a mix of local, national or international stories.

Newscast stories come from in-house and from news services. When producing their own stories, news directors at the broadcast news outlets assign their reporters the stories. There also are opportunities for reporters to develop their own story ideas. Broadcast outlets also subscribe to news services such as the Associated Press and Reuters. These services provide complete stories as well as video and audio segments that can be incorporated into stories.

CREATE THE NEWSCAST

Local and national news programs usually are no more than 30 minutes long, including commercials. Some radio newscasts are as short as five minutes long. Clearly, broadcast reporters and writers have little time in which to tell their stories.

A broadcast **news director** is responsible for all news programming for a broadcast media outlet. The news director is at the hub of the newsroom, keeping a list of the stories the staff is working on for the nightly newscast. A broadcast news director is similar to a city or metro editor at a newspaper. The news director needs to keep track of which stories will be ready in time for broadcast. The news director depends on reporters and producers to provide updates on their stories throughout the day. A **producer** is responsible for coordinating and organizing news coverage. Producers are similar to newspaper editors. They work closely with reporters and are responsible for getting the story edited to length and in on time.

As the day progresses, the news director — sometimes working with the anchors — makes decisions about which stories will get the most time in the broadcast. The news director also gives direction to the producers and reporters who are working on the stories. Related stories will be packaged together, with **transitions**, or connecting words, written for an anchor to say between stories.

The anchor or announcer will read aloud all the copy for the newscast to get familiar with the words before the newscast goes live. This ensures that the timing of each story is accurate and the words that should be emphasized are marked on the copy.

////// **In creating the newscast, what are the responsibilities of the news director?**

Personal pronouns take the place of nouns that name persons. These pronouns include:

I, me, my, mine, we, us, our, ours, you, your, yours, he, him, his, she, her, hers, it, its, they, them, their and theirs.

When using personal pronouns, you must be clear about to whom you are referring. In print news, the reader can refer back to a person's name for clarity. In broadcast reporting, the listener has to understand you the first time.

If you are talking about two people, refering to them as "they" will be clear to your listener. But if you are talking about two men and refer to one of them as "him," how will your listener know which man you mean?

When using personal pronouns in broadcasts, make sure it's clear to whom you are referring. For clarity, you may have to repeat a person's name rather than use a pronoun.

ORGANIZE THE NEWSCAST

Like the front page of a newspaper, a newscast needs organization. Stories are grouped together in logical ways so viewers or listeners know what to expect. Some local stations have a policy about presenting local news before national and foreign, so all local stories will be told before moving on to national ones. However, the news director will decide which story is the lead, or most important, which is the second most important, and so on.

The trick to putting together a newscast is first to find the story that will engage viewers or listeners immediately so they will stay with the newscast. The second step is to write transitions that are conversational and promising. The transitions need to move the viewer or listener from one story to the next, allowing little or no time for them to change channels, or turn the newscast off. Third, newscasts often end with a **kicker**, a feature such as good news or a human interest story.

check point ✓

What is a newscast?

Write the Newscast

A newscast is only as good as the stories in it. Good broadcast journalism, like good print journalism, requires getting all the facts, doing interviews and writing clearly. When writing for broadcast, however, reporters have to take into consideration the video and audio elements they have obtained.

PICTURES

"Let's go to the video!" All sportscasters say this line at some point in their careers. They will start a story about the big game with who won, and may then explain some key moves. The video, however, shows viewers what happened.

Pictures don't always tell the story better than the words, but in television news they will come close. Having a variety of pictures that make a story move smoothly is called **sequencing**. A sequence has three parts: a close-up, a medium shot and a wide shot. There are variations on the basics, too, such as a **pan**, which means moving the focus from one side to another.

A reporter will write copy to the various shots in the sequence. For example, imagine you've been assigned to do a story on a St. Patrick's Day parade in your town. You have a wide shot of the parade as it begins, which pans to a medium shot of drummers in a marching band and a close-up of a young Irish dancer you interviewed. Your story begins with the wide shot of the parade.

Thousands watched and cheered the annual St. Patrick's Day parade this morning.

Then you write to the medium shot and the close-up.

There were green floats, marching bands and, of course, Irish dancing.

Your next sequence is from the interview. You have a wide shot of your dancer dancing in a group, a medium shot of her dancing alone, and a close-up of her head and shoulders as she talks to the camera. You use the wide and medium shots to set up what you want to say about Irish dancing and the young dancer speaking. You use the close-up shot for a **sound bite**, a short segment showing the source speaking. You use a **chyron**, words superimposed on the screen, to tell viewers her name and age. The words superimposed on the screen also are called lower-third graphics or lower thirds. "Lower-third graphics" refers to the graphics that appear in the lower third of the screen. Videographers generally try to frame their shots so that nothing critical appears in the bottom third of the screen, where it might be obliterated by words.

You've focused on the young Irish dancer because you wanted to put a human face on your story. She talks about preparing a dance for the parade and how much it means to her to be part of the parade. That's a story with emotion and meaning, not your typical parade story.

© Photodisc/Getty/Images

/////// *Imagine this is one of the pictures in a sequence for a story about participants in a parade. Which part of the sequence do you think it would be?*

AUDIO

The challenge for radio reporters is to use sound to create a picture for the listener. Radio reports are often even shorter than those on television, so radio reporters need to be able to digest material quickly, summarize it accurately and be comfortable with brevity.

If a radio reporter were doing the St. Patrick's Day parade story described in the section on television broadcast, it might begin with a few seconds of sound — festive music and cheering, the whine of bagpipers and the boom of drums. All those sounds would help set the scene of the report. The lead of the story could be the same.

> Thousands watched and cheered the annual St. Patrick's Day parade this morning. There were green floats, marching bands and, of course, Irish dancing.

But now you need to introduce the dancer you interviewed because the listener can't see her. Describing her helps the listener picture what's happening.

> For 8-year-old Colleen McDonald it's a special day. She has been practicing a dance for the parade since last summer. It's an Irish dance, done in a colorful costume, arms at sides, steadfastly straight.

Here you might add sound to evoke another picture — one of a dancing girl. The click of heels on the pavement, the swish of her dress could be good — and a sound bite from Colleen could go here, too.

PREPARE YOUR COPY FOR BROADCAST

Once all the stories that will be part of the broadcast are ready, a news writer writes copy to go before the reporters' segments — lead-ins. A **lead-in** is the anchor's introduction to the story. Lead-ins are written like the lead of the story but they should not repeat or steal from the reporter's lead. Lead-ins are written after the story is complete so they accurately reflect the story.

Writing for television and radio is different from writing for print. How a story appears on paper is different from how it appears on the teleprompter that the anchor or reporter reads in a studio. Your copy should be clean, without many extra markings that could confuse the newsreader, the anchor, disc jockey or correspondent delivering the report. If your copy starts to look sloppy from changes and edits, you need to make corrections and print out a clean copy.

Every radio or television station has its own standards for copy preparation, but the basics include:

- Copy should be double- or triple-spaced so it can be easily read.

- Type on one side of the page only.

- Use all capital letters or capitals and lowercase, but be consistent.

- Set margins on your page to 65 characters a line. That's the universal line measure for timing stories. Fifteen lines (of 65 characters) is about one minute of air time.

- Type one story per page only.

- Put a **slug**, or story name, in the upper left corner. Begin your story about six lines beneath the slug.

- Keep words and phrases that go together on the same line to make them easier for the announcer to read.

- Use three pound signs (###) or -30- to indicate the story is finished. Put -more- at the end of a page if a story continues.

- Circle anything that is NOT to be read by the announcer.

check point ✓

What elements make writing for broadcast different from writing for print?

Digging Deeper

The Bigger They Are, the Harder They Fall

The pressure to scoop other media outlets with hot-breaking news stories can lead many newspaper editors and reporters to commit unethical acts. And the bigger the media empire, the stronger the pressure to deliver big stories. Thus, many people were not surprised when the media empire of Australian media mogul Rupert Murdoch — one that controlled television, newspapers and radio around the world — fell under scrutiny for having committed illegal and unethical acts.

Some of Murdoch's editors and reporters working on the London paper News of the World were accused of illegally hacking into the cellphones of a 13-year-old kidnap and murder victim, families of 9/11 victims and British soldiers killed in Afghanistan. Other alleged hacking victims included Britain's royal family and former Prime Minister Gordon Brown. As the scandal unfolded more people were further implicated in taking money for tips and illegally accessing medical and financial records, including police officers and Murdoch's trusted News of the World editor, Rebekah Brooks.

With the investigation in its infancy, more of Murdoch's media outlets could face difficulties. Murdoch is well known for his unethical and ruthless business practices, and his empire faces sanctions in Britain. When the scandal broke, he shut down News of the World and news outlets around the world scrambled to report on the situation.

Access www.cengage.com/school/langarts/journalism and click on the link to Chapter 11. Read the transcript for "NBC Nightly News" in which news anchor Brian Williams interviewed NBC's London correspondent Stephanie Gosk about the scandal. Then answer the following questions.

THINK *Critically*

1. After reading the transcript of William's interview with London correspondent Stephanie Gosk, note in a brief paragraph the names of the people interviewed and mentioned in the sound bites and outline their role, if any, in the scandal. From the context of the transcript, did the people interviewed in the sound bites add important information to the interview? Why or why not?

2. Identify the lead-in to Brian William's story. Go online and research the scandal. Try to find other instances in which Murdoch has been accused of improprieties. Write another lead-in following the format you learned in Lesson 11.2 and using the information you discovered in your research.

Source: "Newscast: Rupert Murdoch scandal grows." NBC Nightly News [Transcript] 18 July 2011. Global Issues In Context. Web. 8 Aug. 2011.

11.2 | Assessment

Understand Concepts

Determine the best answer for each of the following questions.

1. A compilation of visual or audio broadcast stories is called a
   - **a.** broadcast.
   - **b.** newscast.
   - **c.** production.
   - **d.** script.

2. Who keeps a list of the stories the staff is working on for the nightly newscast?
   - **a.** anchor
   - **b.** engineer
   - **c.** news director
   - **d.** producer

3. The words the anchor says between related stories are called
   - **a.** ad libs.
   - **b.** connections.
   - **c.** exchanges.
   - **d.** transitions.

4. Having a variety of pictures that make a story move smoothly is called
   - **a.** arranging.
   - **b.** pacing.
   - **c.** progressing.
   - **d.** sequencing.

5. A video shot that involves moving the focus from one side to another is called a
   - **a.** pan.
   - **b.** stretch.
   - **c.** sweep.
   - **d.** zoom.

6. The anchor's introduction to a story is called the
   - **a.** lead-in.
   - **b.** opening.
   - **c.** overture.
   - **d.** preface.

7. What word appears at the bottom of a page to indicate the story continues on the next page?
   - **a.** continue
   - **b.** go
   - **c.** forward
   - **d.** more

8. **True or False**   A kicker is a short story used to kick off the newscast.

Write Now!

Practice your writing skills with the following activity.

9. You are the news producer for your high school broadcast station. List some possible news stories that you could cover in your high school in one day. Add events in the community that affect your high school, its staff or students. Write a few sentences for each story to show how it will be developed.

10. Choose a story from within your high school that you think is appropriate for a high school broadcast. Using the guidelines in this chapter, prepare the copy for a newsreader. Have another student in your class deliver your story to the class.

CHAPTER 11 | Assessment

Review Journalism Concepts

11.1 Write for Broadcast

A broadcast is a radio or television program. When used as a verb, "broadcast" means to transmit programming or information on radio or television. The language of broadcast news is the language of the spoken word. Writing for broadcast is different from writing for print precisely because the information must be spoken. Writing for broadcast means writing for listeners. Broadcast scripts must be shorter and more concise than print writing. The most important point of the story comes first, followed by the rest. Broadcast reporters write so that every sentence must be heard. Broadcast writers summarize two or more related stories in one lead — an umbrella lead — before telling the individual stories. Some broadcast stories are best told in chronological order, the order in which things happened. Broadcast writers need to make their listeners understand the story the first time it is read because the listeners may not get a chance to hear it again. Writers should follow established guidelines for writing for listeners and viewers. It is also important to make the copy easy for the newsreaders to read.

11.2 Write a Newscast

A newscast is a compilation of visual or audio broadcast stories. Broadcast news outlets produce some of their own stories, including visual or audio elements, as well as subscribe to news services such as the Associated Press and Reuters. Nightly news programs are usually no more than 30 minutes. Radio broadcasts are as short as five minutes. The broadcast news director is responsible for all news programming for a broadcast media outlet. The job is similar to that of a city or metro editor at a newspaper. A producer is responsible for coordinating and organizing new coverage. Producers are similar to newspaper editors who work closely with reporters. Throughout the day, reporters and producers give the news director progress reports on their work so the news director knows what will be ready in time for the broadcast.

Broadcast news must take into consideration the video and audio elements of the stories. In television, having a variety of pictures that make a story move smoothly is called sequencing. A reporter will write copy to each shot in the sequence. Radio reporters write much like television reporters do except the radio reporter has to use sound to create a picture for the listener. Every radio or television station has its own standards for copy preparation, but there are basic guidelines common to the broadcast industry.

Develop Your Journalism Language

Write the letter of the term that matches each definition. Some terms will not be used.

_____ 1. Anchor's introduction to the story

_____ 2. A compilation of visual or audio broadcast stories

_____ 3. A "good news" or human interest story at the end of a news broadcast

_____ 4. Also known as lower-third graphics

_____ 5. Main news presenter

_____ 6. Move the camera's focus from one side to another

_____ 7. Order in which things happened

_____ 8. Person responsible for all news programming for a broadcast media outlet

_____ 9. Person responsible for coordinating and organizing news coverage

_____ 10. Short comment suitable for broadcast

_____ 11. Story name

_____ 12. Summary of multiple related stories in one lead used before telling the individual stories

_____ 13. Showing a variety of pictures to make a story move smoothly

_____ 14. Written broadcast stories

_____ 15. To transmit programming or information on radio or television

a. anchor
b. broadcast
c. chronological order
d. chyron
e. kicker
f. lead-in
g. news director
h. newscast
i. newsreader
j. pan
k. producer
l. scripts
m. sequencing
n. slug
o. sound bite
p. teleprompter
q. transition
r. umbrella lead

16. The role of a producer in creating a newscast is similar to the role of which person working for a newspaper?
   a. columnist
   b. editor
   c. reporter
   d. publisher

17. When writing for a newsreader, how many stories should appear on a page?
   a. as many as will fit
   b. one
   c. two
   d. three

18. What symbol appears at the end of story to indicate the story is finished?
   a. # # #
   b. ///
   c. %%%
   d. ***

19. Where do you put a slug?
   a. upper right corner
   b. lower right corner
   c. upper left corner
   d. lower left corner

Think Critically

20. Compare and contrast the structure used for writing a print story and a broadcast story.

21. Explain what it means to spell out a name phonetically.

22. Give a specific example of a situation when an umbrella lead might be appropriate.

23. Name two ways in which writing for broadcast differs from writing for print.

24. What is included in the lead of a story told in chronological order?

25. What type of story is told in chronological order?

26. While print reporters think about how much space they have to fill, what do broadcast writers think about?

27. Why don't broadcast news writers use the five-W's-and-an-H summary news lead?

28. Why do broadcast writers sometimes use a feature approach to leads? Are these stories always aired first? Why or why not?

29. Why is it important for broadcast writers to make sure their listeners understand the story the first time it is read?

30. Explain why videographers try to frame their shots so that nothing critical appears in the bottom third of the screen.

31. How many lines of how many characters equal about one minute of air time?

32. Identify the overarching motivation behind the order of stories in a newscast.

33. How do radio reporters create a picture for the listener?

34. What is a slug?

35. Why is it important to set the margins correctly when preparing copy for a newscast?

36. Why is the copy for a newscast double- or triple-spaced?

Make Academic Connections

37. **ART**   Using computer graphics and other art supplies, create a graphic that could be used during a newscast to introduce a particular kind of story. For example, many stations have a graphic for breaking news, a continuing story or special reporting such as investigative reports.

38. **CAREERS**   Investigate the educational requirements for a specific job in broadcast journalism. Also, look for information about opportunities for advancement. Prepare a short presentation about your findings.

39. **COMMUNICATION**   Create a poster of tips for creating anchor-friendly copy. Include examples.

40. **COMPUTER SCIENCE**   Using the basic information about copy preparation, create a handout with computer software that illustrates all the points.

41. **HISTORY**   Use the Internet to research the history of broadcast news. Make a timeline that identifies the history and development of American broadcast journalism through people and events. Choose one journalist and an important event reported by this journalist. Plan, research and develop a paper that discusses the event, the coverage by the journalist and why you are impressed with how this journalist handled the stories. Evaluate and confirm the validity of the background information on the journalist and event from a variety of sources such as past interviews, other persons or reports. Include direct and indirect quotes in your paper. After you have written a draft of your paper, use appropriate proofreading symbols to edit your paper. Be sure to edit for clarity, engaging language and the correct use of English. Turn in the edited copy along with your final paper.

42. **PERSONAL FINANCE**   Use the Internet and personal interviews to research the incomes of starting broadcast reporters in your local market. Use computer software to create a spreadsheet to make a budget that illustrates living within the income of a beginning broadcast reporter. Include such necessities as rent, food, medical and dental expenses, clothing and transportation such as public transportation or the cost of a car payment, gas and upkeep. Also include entertainment expenses.

Writing Portfolio Activity

43. Look for opportunities within your school for a broadcast news story. Develop a story and write a script suitable for a television audience that will take between two and three minutes to deliver. Deliver the broadcast in your class while being recorded. If English is your second language, you may deliver the broadcast in your native language while another student acts as interpreter, and then deliver the same broadcast in English. Submit your script to your instructor for evaluation and feedback. When returned add both the video of your broadcast and your script to your portfolio.

AP Stylebook Workshop

Correct the following according to AP style.

44. Radio Station WXYZ held a fundraising event at Gateway Park to benefit the local homeless population.

45. WXYZ-fm's affiliate, WXYZ-tv, co-sponsored the fundraising event.

46. Staff members of Gateway High School Radio Station whgh also participated in the event.

LEADERSHIP AND RESPONSIBILITY: Leaders in Broadcast Journalism

Successful broadcast journalists understand the skills needed for leadership and for assuming responsibility. As you learn and grow in your career as a broadcast reporter, you may have aspirations to become a news anchor or producer. If so, you will need to be able to

- Guide and lead others
- Be responsible to others

GUIDE AND LEAD OTHERS

Guiding and leading others requires the use of interpersonal and problem-solving skills. Interpersonal skills involve the relationships you have with people. To lead people, they must believe in you and your leadership. You will need to be able to influence others' opinions and guide your staff toward a goal.

Good leaders leverage the strengths of their team to accomplish the goal that is best for the team and the station. For example:

A recent survey shows that one of the reporters on your staff is very popular. This popularity is due to good, solid reporting. You think it is a good idea to try out the reporter as a weekend anchor. The problem is getting the whole staff to go along with the idea without jealousy or resentment. This is the newest reporter on the team, so some staff members might resent the newcomer getting to anchor before paying dues.

As the leader of the team, you need to inspire your team to accept and support the new reporter as the new weekend anchor. You can accomplish this by inspiring all staff members to do their best while allowing each person to shine in his or her own way. Assign a sports reporter to sports assignments, not to cover the local art show opening unless that reporter is also an expert on art or has knowledge of art. Also lead by example and demonstrate your own selflessness when dealing with other employees on the news staff. As your team members see that you are fair and bring out the strengths in each staffer, they will come to respect and trust you as a leader.

As the leader, you hold the standard for ethical behavior and the integrity of the news broadcast from your station. Never use your influence and power over staff members to hurt, harass or in any way influence them against their will or in an unethical manner.

BE RESPONSIBLE TO OTHERS

Leaders are always in the position of weighing the needs of the individual with the needs of the larger community. Using the example of promoting a new reporter to the position of anchor over more seasoned reporters, as the leader, you must think of the greater good of the station. Promoting the newer reporter may make a few staff members unhappy, but if the audience has made the popularity of this reporter clear — and the reporter is doing a good job — then the greater good is to promote this reporter. The decisions that leaders make will not always be popular with everyone.

THINK *Critically*

Take a few days to list qualities you think a good leader should have. Once you have completed your list, ask three adults to look at it and then to add any missing qualities of leadership. Next, put a plus sign beside each quality you have and a minus sign beside the qualities you have yet to obtain. Write a short paper that explains something you can do to increase your leadership qualities.

REAL PEOPLE REAL CAREERS

Andrea Roane | A News Anchor

Andrea Roane wasn't looking for a new career when a career in television found her. "It was one of those chance things," she says.

Roane, a native of New Orleans, was content as a young educator managing a high school for the performing arts in her hometown. Then she went on public television for a fundraising event. Her natural warmth and comfort with the camera must have been apparent because the public television station soon offered her a job as an education reporter. After a little "hemming and hawing" and thinking it over, she said yes and has never looked back. Now an anchor for WUSA, the CBS affiliate in Washington, D.C., Roane has been a television broadcaster — a producer, reporter and anchor — for nearly 30 years.

"I was a novice when I started," says Roane. She didn't know anything about how broadcasters do their jobs because she had not studied journalism. "I thought I'd have to memorize all the copy," she says. She had been a teacher of speech, theater and English. Her undergraduate degree is in speech education and her master's degree is in drama and communication. She earned both at what is now known as the University of New Orleans.

Roane says one of the hardest things she had to learn about writing for television was "how to boil it down to 1 minute and 30 seconds or 2 minutes. I went from teaching English and all its compound sentences to writing that short." She jokes that she is still learning to write for television and says the benefit of having a blog on her station's website is that she can expand on stories she has reported on the newscast.

Roane, who has interviewed people as notable and varied as Hillary Clinton and Michael J. Fox, is one of the most respected broadcasters in Washington. She has worked on every news broadcast from early morning to late night. She knows that "I read very well and I communicate," she says. "When I'm reading, people feel I'm talking to them."

ANCHORING A NEWSCAST

Being a television news anchor is not always glamorous. Roane gets up at 2:30 a.m. to be on the air for a 6 a.m. show. She gets ready at home, quietly, and gets to the station in time to read through copy that has already been written. She adds and subtracts to "make the copy speak like you do." She uses a teleprompter to read the stories on air but keeps print copies of the story at the anchor desk for those times something goes wrong. Computers run the teleprompter and the cameras, says Roane, and if something doesn't work right "you have to be able to recover." Roane works with a news producer who can speak into the earpiece she wears on the air. She's always prepared but notes that during the actual interview "it's about listening. I've had people say to me, 'You look at me when you're talking to me.' That's because I'm listening to what they say in the interview."

Source: Personal interview with Andrea Roane

THINK *Critically*

1. Why do you think Roane had trouble with writing for broadcast after being an English teacher?

2. What skills does Roane have that make her a good newscaster?

12

Online Publishing

Blogging from the Scene of Police Action

On a warm September day, news was breaking fast in Silver Spring, Md. A man with a gun had taken three hostages at a large downtown business. Almost immediately, news of the situation spread on Facebook and Twitter as people near the scene posted to those popular social media sites.

Meanwhile, TBD.com, a just-launched website with a mission to cover all local news in the Washington, D.C., area, was on top of the story. Reporters were posting to TBD's news blog as many details as they could get within moments of confirming them with authorities. Because information was coming quickly, they topped each blog post with the freshest facts, then rewrote and updated a separate news story several times throughout the afternoon.

Four hours after it began, the story ended with the safe release of the hostages and the death of the hostage taker. And the staff at TBD.com had passed its first test of using the blog to cover critical fast-breaking news.

THINK *Critically*

1. How did news of the hostage taking get out on social media sites like Facebook and Twitter?
2. Why was blogging an effective way to tell the hostage story?

Why Publish Online?

Goals

- Identify the reasons school newspapers are moving online.
- Explain the influence and reach of Internet publications.

Key Terms

- online publishing 299
- software tools 299
- tweeted 300
- news magazine 302

It's prom time at Edison High School and both the boys and girls who are planning to go to the big dance, as well as those who are not, are debating the high cost of this rite of passage. Should girls pay $500 for a prom dress? Should limousines be rented at equal expense?

Rafael listens to the talk swirling about the halls of the school and writes a story about the high cost of prom for the school's news website. Soon after his story is published, the debate begins on the Web as students post to Rafael and each other in the space provided for comments beneath his story. The story gets thousands of page views in a school of just 1,200 students. Publishing on the Web allows for interaction among readers and may encourage the building of community in a way that could not happen with a print publication.

Online Publishing

There's no doubt that **online publishing** — using the Web and its tools to get news and information to a targeted audience — is where high school news publication is going, just as it is in the professional world of journalism. "There's been a big push to do this in recent years and the floodgates have opened," says Aaron Manfull, media adviser at Francis Howell North High School in St. Charles, Mo.

Scholastic journalism associations are recognizing the trend and have added online categories to their award competitions. More and more students are interested in working on Web publications so they can learn to use **software tools**, computer programs that allow the user to write copy or design pages, among other uses. For example, WordPress is a software tool used for blogging and text management. Dreamweaver is a software program used for design.

PUBLISHING ONLINE SAVES MONEY

School budget cuts have forced the elimination of some high school newspapers because it costs money to print on paper. In Boulder, Colo., where one high school newspaper was $3,700 in the red, student adviser Jeff Likes proposed moving online. "The school has been publishing a paper for more than 100 years," Likes told Boulder's local newspaper, The Daily Camera. "It would be a shame to see the program disappear after that long tradition."

By moving the newspaper, The Owl, onto the Web, Boulder High School saved money and continued to publish — in fact, did so more frequently. Now it publishes every day, which is a more realistic experience for student journalists.

There is no doubt that moving online saves money. It can cost nothing to publish on the Web because some website platforms are free, though it's likely to cost a little something to get going. There are some limited costs to getting on a website platform such as WordPress or in securing domain names. And there may be some upfront costs for equipment such as video cameras, for example. But, on an annual basis, an online publication is far less costly than a traditional newspaper because there are no printing costs. A website certainly won't cost in the $5,000 to $6,000 range that some schools spend to put out a print product that comes out six or seven times a year.

EVERYDAY EXPERIENCE

The reality of most printed newspapers in high schools is that the news they print is outdated by the time it is circulated to readers. Sometimes it's outdated by weeks. More important, however, is the fact that the audience for the printed publication — students at the school — is not a group that is in the habit of reading print to get their news. Rather, 65 percent of high school-age students and young adults say they get their news from the Internet, according to a poll done for the Pew Center. Students, in other words, are more comfortable with online news and more likely to read news on a digital device than on paper.

With digital publication, journalism students are learning the ways of the professional world of journalism, where information is written, blogged or **tweeted** — posted on a Twitter account — as it happens. Sports stories, for example, can be blogged from the scene and readers can know the score seconds after a game finishes. When the high school newspaper is online, journalism students can write and post daily. There's no better way to teach aspiring journalists than to allow them to think, write, edit, design and publish every day.

Moving online also gives high school students the opportunity to branch out from the inverted pyramid style, and adapt that news style for the many

 What are the benefits to student journalists who publish their high school newspaper online?

formats professional journalists are using to present news to their followers — including Web articles, blog posts, video scripts, extended captions for slide shows and 140-character tweets. The learning taking place in the digital journalism classroom is more authentic, and in some ways more demanding, than that of the traditional print journalism class where students might take days or weeks to craft lengthy news and feature stories.

check *point* ✓

Why does publishing online cost less than print publishing?

Expand Influence

Whether you are writing from Boulder, Colo.; Anchorage, Alaska; or Portland, Maine, when your story is online, it may be read by the entire world. Of course, "may" is the key word here. It's unlikely that many people beyond your school and community will find your stories on the Web, but publishing online means the potential is there to extend and evolve your school newspaper's editorial influence and, perhaps, even your own voice.

A PRINT AND ONLINE MIX

Because the online publication can be seen by anyone who has access to the Internet, readership of your work can expand exponentially. Parents, neighbors and local advertisers have easy access, but so do grandparents, cousins and family friends who may live a distance away, or former students or Internet searchers who just happen to be interested in a topic covered by your school publication.

However, as high school teachers know, some parts of the community — including students, teachers and administrators — are reluctant to give up paper. They may like the permanence of print; students like seeing their bylines, stories and photos in a publication they can touch or save in a scrapbook. They also like the traditional late nights of getting the print publication off to the printing press, called putting it "to bed."

Some high schools have opted to continue a print publication in the form of a **news magazine**, which is a format that allows for more in-depth coverage of traditional news and features. News magazines are not published as often as news websites, which are published daily. Often the news magazine — with its more comprehensive information on a topic or theme of school-related stories — is paired with the online news site, which offers Web features such as a video or photograph of the day along with the news. With both a print publication and an online news site, the school community gets an in-depth look at issues around them as well as the day-to-day information they need to know what's going on — the best of both worlds.

checkpoint

Why is a mix of print and online publications good for the high school community?

AP Stylebook Concepts

AP style has specific guidelines for datelines, the line at the head of a newspaper article or website news story that specifies where, and occasionally when, the story was written. When writing a dateline for a news story, check your AP Stylebook to find out whether the city is a "stand-alone" city or a city that also requires the name of the state or country.

Many of the largest cities in the world — among them London, Moscow, Buenos Aires and, in the United States, New York, Miami and Los Angeles — require no state or country identification in a dateline. Most cities, however, require a state or country to make them more identifiable, such as Nashville, Tenn., or Grand Rapids, Mich. AP periodically reviews its list of stand-alone cities, so the list can change.

Who's Responsible for User Comments?

One legal question news organizations wrestle with as they expand what they offer on their website is: What is the organization's legal responsibility for comments users post to the site? The issue remains unsettled. At this writing, there has not been enough case law to make legal experts comfortable with any answer they give.

For now, courts have said that as long as the news organization does not review or edit a comment before it is posted to an online discussion board or blog, the organization is not responsible for its content. The organization may be liable, however, if someone brings attention to a potential problem after a comment is posted.

Most news organizations don't have the resources to set up a prior review of comments submitted to their blogs and sites. Even if they tried, it would take so much time to review comments, the comments would be of little value to the online discussions. So most organizations, for legal as well as logistical reasons, do not review or edit comments. Nor do they require users to register before they are allowed to comment.

Some news organizations, however, do remove posts that violate their guidelines and standards. Those are likely to be posts that are obscene, attack someone personally, provide personal information on someone, are blatantly commercial or are potentially libelous. In most cases, the post is returned to the user with a request to rewrite it according to the guidelines. That may not make the user happy, but it makes for more civil discourse. It also sends the message to users that the news organization takes its standards seriously.

THINK *Critically*

1. Why would a news organization remove a post from a blog or online discussion?

2. Why is a news organization not responsible for a post if the organization does not review the item before it's posted?

12.1 | Assessment

Understand Concepts

Determine the best answer for each of the following questions.

1. The least expensive way to publish high school news is
   a. in a print newspaper.
   b. as a news magazine.
   c. online.
   d. quarterly.

2. **True or False**   Using software tools such as WordPress or Dreamweaver will help you write copy or design pages online.

3. **True or False**   High schools should have either a print publication or an online website for dispensing the news, but they should not have both.

4. **True or False**   The news in most printed high school newspapers is outdated by the time the papers are circulated to readers.

Write Now!

Practice your writing skills with the following activities.

5. Research high school news websites. Use the phrase "online high school newspapers" to begin your search. Choose three sites to study. Plan, draft and use a computer to write a paper that compares and contrasts the sites. Your paper should describe what information is on each site, what you like most and least about each site and what you think works well and why. Use the track changes feature on your computer to edit the paper for clarity, engaging language and the correct use of English. Send the draft and the final paper to your teacher electronically.

6. Use the information in this text and on the Internet to identify the people and events involved in the development of online publishing in America. Use computer software tools to create a Web screen with a timeline that explains and illustrates your findings. Send your Web page to your teacher electronically.

7. Write a blog entry that justifies an online news site for your high school and persuades readers to support your idea. In your entry, describe the cost, the savings over a print newspaper, the advantages to aspiring journalists and to the student body and any other pertinent information. Edit your blog entry using proofreading symbols. Turn in your draft along with your final version.

Write for the Internet

Goals

- Describe how to write for the Internet.
- Explain how to write a news blog.

Key Terms

- Web writing 305
- digital journalism 305
- subhead 307
- real time 307

FOCUS

Sarah, a rookie reporter on the school newspaper, knows a good story when she sees one. In the gym are hundreds of new backpacks filled with school supplies to be sent to children who were displaced by a hurricane. Sarah shoots video of the sea of backpacks — all colors, sizes and shapes — and the workers loading them with pencils, pens, notebooks, binders and other supplies. She interviews the students who started the effort, the students bringing in backpacks, and the principal about the school-wide response.

Sarah talks to the news editor and together they review the video and audio as they work on a multimedia story for the newspaper's website. Sarah writes a short story for the front page of the website, accompanied by her edited video.

Sarah's editor is impressed. Her instincts to go for the story were good, and she proved herself a capable videographer, interviewer and Web writer. Now, there's one more thing left to do: write the story for the newspaper, which will come out in two days. Sarah gets right to work. Her editor has no doubt this story, too, will be right on.

Write for the Internet

Web writing is a hybrid, a combination of print and broadcast techniques. Broadcasters write for the ear and print reporters write for the eye, but Web writers do a little of both. They must keep in mind that ultimately their words go onto a screen, a medium far different from paper, television or radio.

KNOW YOUR AUDIENCE

In the early days of **digital journalism** — online journalism — writers and editors who worked for print publications simply posted a story on the

////// **What do writers and editors who work on Web publications need to understand about the reading habits of their audience?**

publication's website just as the story existed in print. Stories that were too long, with headlines that were clever but obscure, did not attract the attention of Web users. It took a while for print journalists to understand that writing and producing stories for the Web requires a different approach than it does for either print or broadcasting.

Writers and editors working online need to understand their audience just as well as print and broadcast journalists need to understand theirs. Web users are different from the news consumers of print, radio and television. Studies show that Web users tend to skip around, skimming sites rather than settling in to read everything on the site. However, when readers do settle in, they are likely to read 75 percent or more of a story, a higher percentage than print readers. Web users often are looking for particular information, not passively taking in all the news that's fit to print, and they use the computer interactively, so they want multimedia extras such as animated informational graphics, picture slide shows, video and audio.

PLAN YOUR STORY

Before the reporting begins, think about elements that will make the story attractive to Web users. Talk with audio and video producers in the newsroom for ideas. Think about the images and sound elements that might complement the story. If your story is about a new experiment the chemistry teacher is presenting, then you probably want to make a video. If you don't take a videographer with you, take a video camera and shoot your own video. It's better to collect all the elements at the same time than try to come up with audio or video after the reporting is done. If you wait, you may miss out on getting the audio or video. In addition to learning to use a video camera, you should learn to use a digital audio recorder and a digital still camera. Many of today's journalists know how to use a lightweight digital camera/video camera and they travel with digital equipment when on assignment.

WRITE TIGHT

There will always be long stories on the Web, but it is unlikely that they will be read in their entirety. This isn't because it's harder to see type on a computer screen than on a magazine page. It's because the behavior of readers on websites is different from the behavior of readers of print publications. While reading on the Web, readers' eyes flit about scanning for headlines and keywords. Readers look for photos and video, even if they don't watch the video.

In short, their behavior shows impatience. Good Web writers need to understand that. It's the key to getting read.

Your writing for the Web must be short, active and detailed. A few points to remember include the following:

- Each sentence should be simple and have one idea.

- Get straight to the central point.

- Don't bury your lead in flowery language or the Web user will click away quickly. Studies show you have about three seconds to grab a reader whose eyes are scanning the page with your article on it.

- Paragraphs should be short so they don't look overwhelming on the screen.

- Headlines should be direct, and not too clever.

- **Subheads**, smaller headlines within the body of the story, should be used to help the reader navigate the story and make it easy to read.

What does the behavior of Web readers show?

Blogging the News

Web logs, or blogs, started as personal journals or musings, like diary writing but online. They quickly became amateur websites with news, information and opinion on any topic imaginable. As the popularity of blogs grew, mainstream media outlets saw them as an opportunity to expand news coverage and interact with Web users. Now blogs are legitimate additions to a news organization's non-print outlets. Many news organizations use blogs as tools to report breaking or other deadline news because they can be updated in short bits of information in a matter of seconds and from the scene of a news event.

USING BLOGS FOR NEWS

News organizations with Internet sites have figured out a way to use blogs to keep readers up to date on big breaking news stories. In Southern California, where wildfires occur all too often, a San Diego newspaper set up a news blog to post information about the fires, evacuation plans, traffic detours, school closings and more. Readers add information, experiences and questions.

USA Today uses news blogs in its "Life" section to post reports in **real time** — while the event is taking place — such as placing reporters on the

grammar tip

In the Chapter 9 Grammar Tip, you learned that you can use adjectives to clarify the nouns in a sentence. These adjectives are called modifiers, and if they are misplaced in a sentence, you lose clarity. A modifier should always be as close as possible to the word it modifies. If the modifier is too far away from the word it modifies, it is called a misplaced modifier.

Can you find the misplaced modifier in this sentence?

> The Web editor is a short guy with a mustache weighing 150 pounds.

This sentence reads like the mustache, not the editor, weighs 150 pounds. To clarify the meaning, rewrite the sentence to read:

> The Web editor is a 150-pound short man with a mustache.

red carpets of the Oscar and the Golden Globe award ceremonies. In 2011, the paper sent a blogger to cover the wedding of Britain's Prince William to Catherine Middleton.

In today's competitive news world, most major news organizations have regular daily news blogs, a compilation of the day's news, political events, entertainers and entertainment, sports, and financial and business reports, with a focus on national and international issues.

News organizations of all sizes have used blogs to cover ongoing trials of public interest, meetings on controversial issues, weather disruptions or disasters, high-interest sporting events, and other areas of interest to readers. Writing for these blogs is less formal and more conversational than in print newspapers, and the blogs often allow for a writer's voice. News organization blogs usually convey reported information without the "spin" or opinion of non-news blogs.

HOW TO WRITE A BLOG

The rules and tips for news writing presented in other chapters of this book also apply to writing blogs. When you write a blog for a news organization you are expected to follow the rules of good writing for any medium. That means proper grammar, spelling, punctuation and style. However, blogs do have their own set of rules. Following are some guidelines specific to blog writing.

- Blog posts should be short and to the point. They should be as short as, or shorter than, the lead of a news story.

- Sentences should be simple and contain one idea. Use the subject-verb-direct object construction. Use active verbs and descriptive words.

- Omit all unnecessary words. (For example, in the previous sentence you could take out the word "all.")

- Understand what you are writing about. You can't write clearly about a topic you don't understand. Do your homework.

- Avoid using the first person. News blogs generally are not about the writer. Write for the reader. Answer questions you think the reader wants answered.

- Avoid expressing your opinion. News blogs are not editorials. Provide facts.

- Remember that Web users read in reverse chronological order. Make updates clear.

- When available and appropriate, add photos or video for interactivity.

 **check**point ✓

Name three guidelines for writing a news blog.

12.2 | Assessment

Understand Concepts

Determine the best answer for each of the following questions.

1. Smaller headlines within the body of a story are called
   a. banners.
   b. callouts.
   c. subheads.
   d. cutlines.

2. **True or False** Web writing is a combination of print and broadcast techniques.

3. **True or False** Digital journalism is simply posting a story written for the news organization's print newspaper onto the Web.

4. **True or False** To post blogs in real time, news organizations send reporters to live events.

Write Now!

Practice your writing skills with the following activities.

5. Rewrite a newspaper story as an online news blog post suitable for a high school audience. Scan the original news story and submit it along with your blog electronically to your teacher.

6. Watch a news broadcast of one of the major television networks. Count the number of stories and note the length of each one. Access the same network's online news site. Look for the stories from the broadcast. Write a paper that compares and contrasts the broadcast news delivery with the online format. Plan, draft and complete your written composition, carefully examining your paper for clarity, engaging language, and the correct use of English. When revising and editing your paper, use proofreading symbols. Turn both your draft and final composition in to your teacher.

7. You are the editor of your high school online news website. You overheard two teachers saying that a coach had been offered a coaching job at a college in another state. You have heard other rumors about this, but there has been no official announcement. You must decide whether it is responsible or irresponsible media action to report the rumors in your online editor's blog. Write about what you would do and why this is the action you would take.

12.3

Digital Storytelling

Goals

- Identify elements of a digital story.
- Explain a content management system.

Key Terms

- assets 311
- storyboard 311
- slideshow 311
- caption 311
- links 312
- content management system (CMS) 313

FOCUS

At North High School, the editorial staff of the school's news website is meeting over computers filled with copy, video, audio, informational graphics and photographs. The staff is choosing which components to post with each story. With a story on the new building, they decide to include a drawing of the interior to show the classrooms that will be added. To a story on the soccer team's win the night before, they add video of the winning goal. Still photos are included with the story on students who received scholarships at the awards banquet, and audio is added of the choir that performed at the banquet.

The editorial staff is satisfied. They make one last check, and then click on the "publish" button. Their online news is complete for another day.

Storytelling on the Web

Telling a story online affords the opportunity to use more than words. The Web is a multimedia environment and consumers who come to it for news and information expect to see video and picture slideshows (with and without sound) and to be able to easily and immediately interact with stories, neither of which they can do with print or broadcast.

Expectations for storytelling on the Web are different from print publications and journalists are constantly trying to figure out how to meet the readers' expectations, and even exceed them. At the same time, the devices many readers use to access information sites — smartphones or tablets like the iPad — are smaller than traditional computer screens, so designers are working to determine how to make stories work on smaller screens.

USE NON-TEXT ELEMENTS

Good digital editors and storytellers use a number of elements when they plan news and feature stories for the Web, and they have a variety of non-text elements with which to work. Among the elements, also called **assets**, that might be available are video, photographs, informational graphics and links to audio extras such as the voice of an important speaker delivering the main point or the encore performance of a band at a sold-out concert. They may not use all the assets for every story, but editors are likely to use at least some of them. Following are some of the basic assets available and how they may be used.

VIDEO   Video images can tell all or part of a news or feature story. For example, imagine you are telling the story of a three-way race for student council president. You might plan for a short text story to introduce the candidates, but use video interviews with each candidate to allow viewers to see them and explain their platforms in two minutes or less. Another option is to have a text introduction of the candidates and their platforms, and conduct video interviews of students from each grade in the school talking about the issues that are important to them and why. For such a news-feature story you want to plan ahead and have permission from the student candidates or voters to use their images on video. It also helps to **storyboard** — map out your plan for the story and the elements you will use for each piece — so you are clear about which aspects of the story will be covered by text, by video or by other media.

PHOTOGRAPHS WITH AND WITHOUT AUDIO   Photographs are as important in digital storytelling as they are in print. Online, however, you have the option to do **slideshows** of multiple photos. Slideshows can be an effective way to tell a story or to add elements that will enhance the story.

You can present slideshows in two ways: with or without audio, or sound. Slideshows with audio involve scripting and recording an explanation of each picture. The script tells the story as the user moves through the photos. The script must be simple and clear and match the photos.

You might choose to do a slideshow without audio but with extended captions that go into detail about the pictures. **Captions** are copy adjoining the photo that relate to the photo. With slideshows, captions tell the story as the user clicks onward.

Either way, it is helpful to storyboard your plan before you shoot or assemble photos, write a script for the sound recording or use the captions to tell the story you've planned. For example, suppose it is the 50th anniversary year of your high school. You might want to tell the story of the school in photos going back five decades to the year officials broke ground to build the school. First, determine what photos you have. Do you have photos of the first day doors opened? The first graduating class? Students in cars from another era? Homecoming and prom queens from important years past? Your school yearbook's archives might be a wealth of photos — and the yearbooks themselves could be a good source of information as you begin piecing the story together with photos.

By using a software program such as Soundslides, you may record a script to go with the photos. Or, you might decide to write a short caption underneath each photo. Whichever you choose, it is the ability to move through the photos, to see the story come alive in photo after photo, that makes slideshows a terrific storytelling tool.

INFORMATIONAL GRAPHICS   Informational graphics are as important in digital storytelling as they are in print newspapers. Charts, graphs, line drawings, timelines, maps and other types of graphics that illustrate the information in the copy add to the readers' understanding of the story. Using the story about the 50th anniversary of your school, you may want to include a drawing of the original school to accompany a story on the beginnings of the school. Or, with a story on how the enrollment increased over the years, you could add a chart that shows the progression over time.

LINKS   Hyperlinks or **links,** the words in Web stories that take you to another story or informational site when you click on them, are a way to supply context, background information, further explanation of the topic or even an opposing view within a story. Suppose in your Web treatment of the anniversary of the school you are writing a story about all the events that are scheduled to celebrate the anniversary. Within that story you might include a link to the main story about the history of the school. A user who wants that information will click on the link. You need not duplicate that explanation in the story about anniversary activities.

/////// *Why do online journalists use non-text elements such as informational graphics in Web stories?*

checkpoint ✓

What are three non-text elements that help digital journalists tell their stories?

Manage Web Content

Publishing on the Web requires a software program to manage all the information you produce. That software program is called a **content management system**, or **CMS**. Media outlets use many different content management systems. Your school is most likely to use a Web CMS — a content management system on the Web that you and other staffers will get into through your Internet browser. Reporters, editors, designers, photographers and any others involved in getting news onto the website may have access to your CMS to handle stories, headlines, photos, captions, video, promotional text and any other items or documents for publication.

Some content management systems are free. Even those that charge an initial fee, plus annual renewal, come nowhere near the average $600 per issue it costs to publish a print newspaper.

What can you expect when working with a Web-based CMS? Here are a few things you can expect:

- Your design and layout will be controlled by templates, though customization is possible.

- You will be able to build uniform pages so your website has a consistent look and feel.

- Different types of content can be organized and presented in a variety of ways.

- Your pages can be edited online and can go live immediately.

- Using a content management system may take a little training, but once you are familiar with the basics of your news site's CMS you will easily learn how to use any other CMS, which will be an important skill to take with you to a college or professional website position.

checkpoint ✓

What is a CMS and what does it do?

12.3 | Assessment

Understand Concepts

Determine the best answer for each of the following questions.

1. Which refers to the words in Web stories that take you to another story or informational site?
   a. links
   b. information centers
   c. assets
   d. captions

2. Which refers to copy near a photo that describes or discusses the photo?
   a. CMS
   b. slideshow
   c. caption
   d. storyboard

3. **True or False**   Readers' expectations for storytelling on the Web are different from those for print publications.

4. **True or False**   Content management systems are too expensive for most high schools.

Write Now!

Practice your writing skills with the following activities.

5. Research the type of content management system that is used in your school or for a local online news organization. Also, research other CMS systems. Find information through the Internet and sources such as people, databases, reports and interviews. Evaluate and confirm the validity of the background information from a variety of sources such as qualified people and reports. Plan and write questions for any interviews you conduct. Write a draft of a composition that compares and contrasts the system your school — or local news source — uses with at least two other systems. Include the names of the systems and the advantages and disadvantages of each. Cite your sources. Also, include direct and indirect quotes as appropriate. Edit your composition for clarity, engaging language and the correct use of English. Send your final paper to your teacher electronically.

6. Create a storyboard electronically for a story of your choice that is of concern to the students and staff in your high school. Once the storyboard is complete, demonstrate an understanding of the elements of news through writing the story and adding assets you want to be part of your story, as well as any sidebar stories. Add captions to any photos or slideshows.

Sports Blog Entry

By Brandon Sosna, Sycamore High School, Cincinnati, Ohio, "For seniors, it's one last hoorah, Posted Tuesday, 2 November 20– at 12:07 PM"

A loss to Colerain all but eliminated the SHS varsity football team from the chase for the postseason. However, there is still much on the line when SHS battles Mason.

The Battle for the Skies is a recently born rivalry between the two institutions. SHS has won two of the three meetings, all of which have taken place in the teams' final game.

Last year, Mason was victorious for the first time, winning a thrilling, low-scoring 10-3 affair.

This season, beyond the standard pride, there are more far-reaching implications.

With a win, SHS would catapult Mason in the Greater Miami Conference (GMC) standings and finish in fourth place. That would mark an amazing comeback from the tenth place finish the team endured a season ago.

SHS may be without quarterback Kyle Sess, who was injured early in the 45-7 loss at Colerain. Joey Bruscato played the rest of the game, completing five passes for 51 yards.

It is anticipated that Bruscato will get the nod on Senior Night, which would be a remarkable story for the journeyman quarterback.

The entire SHS football team will be playing with heavy hearts, after the passing of fellow senior and classmate Jose Cerda.

A source within the team said that the senior captains are planning on a commemorative pregame ceremony in his honor.

Used by permission of Brandon Sosna.

THINK *Critically*

1. Analyze this sports blog entry in terms of the "How to Write a Blog" guidelines on page 308 of this chapter.

2. Do you have a topic or area of interest that you would like to blog about? Assume you were assigned to write a daily blog on this topic. Write today's entry.

CHAPTER 12 | Assessment

Review Journalism Concepts

12.1 Why Publish Online?

Online publishing — using the Web and its tools to get news and information to a targeted audience — is where high school news publication is going, just as it is in the professional world of journalism. Students are increasingly interested in working on Web publications so they can learn to use software tools and computer programs that allow the user to write copy or design pages. Publishing online is advantageous for schools because it saves money (there are no printing costs), provides up-to-date information for readers and helps students learn the ways of professional journalists.

Some schools that have moved to online news have also added a news magazine, which allows for more in-depth coverage.

12.2 Write for the Internet

Web writing is a hybrid, a combination of print and broadcast techniques. In the early days of digital journalism, writers and editors for print publications simply published the same stories on the website. Today, they know better. Web stories are well-planned because in addition to Web users looking for particular information, they also want multimedia extras such as video and audio. Writing for the Web must be short, active and detailed. Each sentence should be simple and have one idea, and paragraphs should be short.

Blogs, which started as personal journals, are now used by all major news organizations. Updates to blogs are posted in real time as a way to keep readers up to date on big breaking news stories. Blogs are written tightly and are often interactive.

12.3 Digital Storytelling

Telling a story on the Web affords the opportunity for a multimedia environment. Web readers expect to see non-text elements along with the stories and to be able to interact with the stories. Non-text elements include video, photos, informational graphics and audio links. Web writing requires a storyboard — a mapped-out plan for the story and the elements, also called assets, to be used with the story. Video images can tell all or part of a news or feature story. Photos can be used with or without audio, or sound. Captions, copy that relates to photos, can be added to individual photos or to slideshows. Informational graphics include charts, graphs, line drawings, timelines, maps and other types of graphics that illustrate the story. When readers click on the blue, underlined links in a Web story, they are directed to related information.

A content management system, or CMS, is a software program that allows you to manage all the information you produce for your news website.

Develop Your Journalism Language

Write the letter of the term that matches each definition.

_____ 1. Posted on a Twitter account

_____ 2. While the event is taking place

_____ 3. Writing that is a combination of print and broadcast techniques

_____ 4. Using the Web and its tools to get news and information to a targeted audience

_____ 5. Online journalism

_____ 6. Words in a story that take you to another story or informational site

_____ 7. A mapped-out plan for the online story and the elements you will use for each piece

_____ 8. Computer programs that allow the user to write copy or design pages

_____ 9. Elements used with online stories

_____ 10. Copy that explains a photo

_____ 11. Multiple photos that tell a story

_____ 12. A software program that manages all the information you produce for online publication

_____ 13. Smaller headlines within the body of a story

a. assets
b. caption
c. content management system (CMS)
d. digital journalism
e. links
f. online publishing
g. real time
h. slideshow
i. software tools
j. storyboard
k. subheads
l. tweeted
m. Web writing

14. Which is a software tool used for blogging and text management?
   a. Dreamweaver
   b. WordProducer
   c. Reporter's Write
   d. WordPress

15. Which of the following is not a benefit of publishing a high school newspaper online?
   a. saves the school money
   b. provides a more realistic experience for student journalists
   c. gives student journalists experience with software tools such as WordPress and Dreamweaver
   d. confines student journalists to using the inverted pyramid style

16. Which piece of equipment would be helpful to have with you when working on a story about an event in your high school?
   a. a video camera
   b. a storyboard
   c. a CMS
   d. a link

Think Critically

17. Why are scholastic journalism associations adding online categories to their award competitions?

18. Why might high school students be more comfortable with online news than people of their parents' generation?

19. In what formats, other than the inverted pyramid style, does online journalism allow you to present the news?

20. Why have some high schools opted to have both an online publication and a printed news magazine?

21. Why is Web writing a hybrid?

22. Why might it be harder to plan a Web story than one for print?

23. Explain the saying that broadcasters write for the ear, and print reporters, the eye, but Web writers write for both.

24. How might a news organization's blog help readers during a natural disaster?

25. Why do you want to add captions to slideshow photos?

Make Academic Connections

26. **RESEARCH**   Research the background and career of an online news blogger from a major online news source such as CNN, MSNBC or The Huffington Post. Use the Internet to find information on the person through databases, reports and past interviews. As you gather background information and investigate the journalist, evaluate and confirm the information from a variety of sources such as other qualified persons, books and reports. Create a storyboard about the journalist that includes multimedia elements. Plan, and then write, the copy for the story and any side stories. Carefully edit the copy for clarity, engaging language and the correct use of English. Send your storyboard and final copy to your teacher electronically.

27. **TECHNOLOGY**   Choose a lead story in your local newspaper, and then record a story on the same topic from a broadcast news program. Use a computer and word-processing program to write the news story as a blog post for your high school newspaper.

28. **COMPUTER TECHNOLOGY**   Use a CMS to create an interactive slideshow about your family or an event in your life. Create and design the slideshow with a high school audience in mind.

29. **SOCIOLOGY** Survey 25 students in your high school to see which they prefer — an online news site, a print newspaper, a news magazine, or a combination of an online site and news magazine — to read the news about your school and its people and events. Use spreadsheet software to record the survey results. In online journalistic style, write an article that describes your findings. Explain whether you were surprised by the findings and why or why not.

30. **WRITING** Headlines for online stories should be direct, and not too clever. Write a headline for each of the following stories: an upcoming carnival at your school; a big win for a sports team; a celebrity coming to your school; a play review; students who formed a band will play at a local spot; new equipment arrives at the computer lab; scholarships are awarded to six students; a skunk got loose in the building; student wins a talent contest; new cafeteria food; and a story about riding the bus to school.

31. **ETHICS** You are the editor of your high school news website. A student submits an editorial that is full of offensive remarks about a certain group of students. You decline to publish the editorial, but the writer claims you are denying his First Amendment rights. Write a essay that explains what you would do. Distinguish between responsible and irresponsible media action.

Writing Portfolio Activity

32. Choose a subject that interests you and would interest other students in your school. Know your subject and what you are writing about. Plan an online news story for this subject. Your plan should include how you will include audio, video and or photos in your story. For example, you might choose high school drama. Your story could be about the plays that the drama department chooses to perform, the actors who perform in the plays or the people behind the scenes such as the stage crew. Submit your plan, online news story, and any photos, audio or video you may have to your instructor for feedback. Print your work and add to your portfolio.

AP Stylebook Workshop

Correct following datelines, if necessary, to conform to AP style. (Hint: For U.S. cities make an educated guess based on size and name recognition as to whether the state name would be required.)

33. London, England   Moscow, Russia   Buenos Aires

New York, New York   Miami, Fla.   Nashville, Tenn.

Grand Rapids, Mich.   Chicago, Ill.   Beijing, China

Cincinnati, Ohio   Mexico City, Mexico   Rome, Italy

Whether writing for a print newspaper, broadcast news, an online news organization or your own blog, you need to understand the medium in which you are writing and the purpose of your message. You need to know whether the message is to report the news, to entertain, to influence readers' beliefs or to advertise a product. You also need to analyze the

- Construction of the message
- Possible interpretations of the message
- Potential ethical and legal issues involved

CONSTRUCTION OF MEDIA MESSAGES

When writing a news story, you stick to the facts, but that's not true of writing for all types of media. Whether writing a blog to entertain, an editorial to persuade students to take an action or ad copy to influence students to buy a product, there are four tools you can use. These are factual content, logic and reason, appeals to emotion and creation of a mood.

Factual content helps convince readers of the truth of your argument. For example, assume you want to write an editorial to persuade students in your high school to participate in a walk to raise money for the local animal shelter. From your Internet research, you obtain facts from the Humane Society of the United States, and then you conduct a phone interview with your local shelter on the cost of feeding and housing animals.

These facts alone are not enough to persuade your readers to commit to the walk, so you explain their meaning through logic and reason. You might focus on one dog and show the costs of his care.

You also need to appeal to your readers' emotions. You might use a photo of the dog,

or obtain the endorsement of a top student leader in your school.

Finally, you will need to create a mood. You choose subjects, words and images that create pictures in your readers' minds. If you can convince your readers to feel strongly about the topic, they will act.

INTERPRETATION OF MEDIA MESSAGES

When interpreting media messages that others have written, you must evaluate the factual content, assess the writer's opinion, and evaluate the information in terms of what you already believe. In the case of an advertising message, you should recognize that the writer is trying to persuade you to form a favorable opinion about a particular product or service so that you will purchase it.

To evaluate the factual content of the message, make two lists: one lists the facts and one lists the opinions in the story. Then ask yourself if the information is true, and if the facts are complete, current and relevant.

In assessing the writer's opinion or point of view, ask yourself if the opinions are based on facts, and if the facts are based on logic and reason. Ask yourself if the writer's opinions are valid, or if the story is written with bias or prejudice. Trust yourself and evaluate the information against what you already believe.

ETHICAL AND LEGAL ISSUES

Always check to make sure the stories you write follow ethical and legal guidelines such as those you have read about in Chapter 1 and the Editorial Ethics and Legal Issues features in this textbook.

THINK *Critically*

Choose an editorial from a local paper and write an analysis of it. Use the information in this feature to guide your analysis.

REAL PEOPLE REAL CAREERS

Jonathan Strong | Online Reporter

Jonathan Strong purposely did not study journalism during his years at Wheaton College in Wheaton, Ill. Instead, he followed some advice he agreed with: Study something other than journalism to be well-rounded intellectually.

Photo courtesy of Jonathan Strong

"Reporting is conceptually simple," says Strong, who studied political science, "and the hard subtleties are learned by experience." Experience is something Strong's got plenty of. By the time he was 27, Strong was covering the U.S. Congress for the news website The Daily Caller. He had already worked for the websites Inside Washington and Inside EPA, and he was a staff aide to a Republican congressman from California. While he was at Wheaton, he worked for the school newspaper and its online publication.

"Because I have an insatiable curiosity, reporting was naturally something I always wanted to do," Strong says. "I didn't really have to plan for a career in it, in that sense."

COVERING CONGRESS

Asked what it's like to cover Congress, Strong says, "It's a blast. With 535 lawmakers maneuvering to advance their agendas and their own personal power in the most important city in the free world, the possibilities for news stories are seemingly endless."

Strong doesn't hesitate to ask tough questions of his interview subjects. He says, "Too many people shy away from confronting their subjects with the hard questions before they hit 'publish.' You have to give them their shot at responding."

He gets his best story ideas from talking to trusted sources on the phone, and — no surprise in the age of social media — he says he does get ideas from reader feedback. "It all depends on the story. There are some subjects readers care deeply about, others not. Sometimes I answer questions; it depends on the circumstances."

The changes in the journalism world are scary, Strong admits, but he's upbeat about his specific world. "Political journalism in Washington, D.C., is thriving. Be prepared for how highly competitive it is."

Source: Personal interview with Jonathan Strong

THINK *Critically*

1. Why would it be useful for someone wanting a career in journalism to major in something other than journalism in college?

2. Where can a beat reporter like Strong get his best story ideas?

In-Depth Reporting

The Washington Post Takes on the U.S. Army

One dreary February Sunday readers of The Washington Post woke to the first of two front-page stories on the Walter Reed Army Medical Center. Soon those stories would get the attention of the nation.

A Post investigation of the outpatient facilities run by hospital personnel revealed intolerable conditions. Wounded soldiers who had fought in Iraq and Afghanistan were being housed in rooms that had unhealthful mold, cockroaches and rat droppings. Lost or incomprehensible paperwork made getting care frustrating for both the soldiers and their families. Some soldiers got no care at all.

Two Post reporters spent more than four months interviewing dozens of soldiers, their family members, people in veterans' aid groups and Walter Reed staff. They did it without Army officials knowing about it. They gave the Army a week before publication to respond to all the problems the reporters had uncovered.

Reaction to the Post's stories came at the highest level. The U.S. Army secretary resigned. Congress set up hearings to investigate. Within days of publication, some soldiers saw better conditions at the hospital. The military began painting rooms, killing roaches and mice, removing mold, and paying attention to the bureaucratic problems that the wounded soldiers faced.

THINK *Critically*

1. Do you think the Post reporters should have asked permission to be in the Walter Reed outpatient facilities?

2. How did this story make a difference in the lives of the soldiers at Walter Reed?

In-Depth Reporting Defined

Goals

- Define in-depth reporting.
- Define the three I's of reporting.

Key Terms

- in-depth reporting 323
- investigative reporting 324
- Pulitzer Prize 325
- tip 325
- issue reporting 325
- general in-depth reporting 326
- documents 326
- data 326
- diverse sources 326

FOCUS

Olivia liked being a reporter for her school newspaper. Usually she covered student council meetings and other news that affected students. She was good at reporting the five W's and H, finding the right quotations and putting together a strong news story. One day during lunch in the cafeteria, Olivia overheard a conversation about students writing term papers to sell to other students. She decided to put her own writing talents to work in a story on cheating.

After interviewing students who had written term papers and the students who had bought them, Olivia interviewed teachers and talked to the school counselor to learn why students cheat. She also did research on the Internet, looking for information on cheating in high schools. Before long, Olivia realized she had more than a single news story.

In-Depth Reporting

Reporters have a natural curiosity. They like to dig into issues, investigate public concerns, and report on wrongdoing or social problems. Often, news stories bring up questions that can be answered only with time, energy and extensive research. Stories that provide more information than the five W's and H require **in-depth reporting**, or reporting that gives critical analysis and careful consideration to all details and aspects of a subject.

When writing in-depth stories, also called "long-form journalism," you use the same research and writing techniques as when writing breaking news stories or feature stories. You expand the news or feature stories by exploring the person, issue or topic in more detail. In-depth stories may take weeks, or even months, of research. Stories might uncover wrongdoing, such as cheating in schools; explore important issues, such as where to find, and how to apply for, college scholarships; or investigate a topic, such as where government spends tax dollars. In-depth stories are longer than regular news stories. They require the patience and perseverance of reporters who are willing to find the story, then analyze the information and meet the challenge of writing a story that diverts from the traditional inverted structure for more creative approaches to storytelling.

checkpoint ✓

What is in-depth reporting?

The Three I's of Reporting

In-depth reporting falls into three categories — investigative, issue and general in-depth reporting. All three types of stories require in-depth research and writing.

INVESTIGATIVE REPORTING

Investigative reporting requires journalists to ask questions about the regular news stories and dig deeper to uncover what is hidden beneath the surface. Investigative reporters go that extra step and often investigate wrongdoing.

Three decades ago, when investigative reporting was coming into its own, enrollment in journalism schools soared. Writers who were interested in telling good stories saw investigative reporting as the way to tell some of the best — and maybe even right a few wrongs along the way. One of the most famous of all investigative stories is Watergate, reported by Washington Post writers Carl Bernstein and Bob Woodward.

The Watergate story began in 1972 as a routine petty crime story, "a third-rate burglary," as one editor put it. The reporters wrote a series of stories that began with a break-in at the Watergate complex in Washington, D.C., which housed apartments and offices as well as a hotel. It also was the home of the Democratic National Committee headquarters.

The Watergate stories became the undoing of President Richard Nixon, a Republican. Faced with impeachment, Nixon eventually resigned on Aug. 9, 1974. The break-in was important politically because it occurred at the Democratic headquarters. Nixon tried to cover up the break-in, but the reporters continued their research. Eventually the investigation uncovered a series of illegal activities carried out by the president's staff.

Woodward and Bernstein were not trained investigative reporters. They may not have called what they were doing investigating. They were solid reporters who knew how to take the extra steps necessary to get the information they needed. They followed leads. They tracked down sources at home. They confronted government officials with information about their conduct. They did their job and did it well, and in May 1973 they were rewarded.

The reporters won the **Pulitzer Prize** for their Watergate stories. The Pulitzer Prize is to journalists what the Academy Awards are to actors. It is the top recognition journalists can receive from their peers.

Investigative reporting as Woodward and Bernstein practiced it occurs less often today. News organizations may not have the time or the staff to produce as many in-depth investigative stories as they would like. Yet, there are still fine examples of investigative reporting being conducted by organizations that have embraced the new electronic media. In Riverside, Calif., the Press-Enterprise's special reports on PE.com use slide shows, video and interactive animation to report on important investigations. The newspaper did one such

What is the significance of Bernstein and Woodward's Watergate story to U.S. history?

report on toxic cargo in railroad cars traveling through the Riverside area. Another story was about young lives cut short, an investigation into the number of children in the community who died in one year at the hands of other people.

At Newsday.com video and interactive maps are part of an online presentation of investigations. One story investigated the number of railroad stations on New York's Long Island with dangerously wide gaps between the platforms and trains.

Investigative stories often begin with a **tip** — a phone call or email from a trusted source or an interested reader. In the case of the Washington Post's report on Walter Reed Army Medical Center in the Case Study, the reporters heard from families whose soldiers were living in terrible conditions there. The reporters then followed up on what the families were saying.

For a look at some diverse ideas for investigative reporting, look at the news blog Extra Extra of the Investigative Reporters and Editors (IRE) organization.

ISSUE REPORTING

Issue reporting is in-depth reporting that looks at special issues of concern to society. Issue reporting also takes reporters who will go the extra mile, reporters willing to go beyond a story they may already have told and take it to another level. Canadian journalist Gregg McLachlan, who runs the website NewsCollege, says issues can be found all around us because people are always talking about issues.

Where can you find issues at your school? Listen at the lunch table. Do you hear students talking about how much homework they have? Is the amount of homework given to students nightly an issue at your school? Is the amount unreasonable when compared with what is given at other schools? Can you get students to log the hours it takes to complete their homework each night for a week or two so you have some real numbers?

Issue reporting can be done by news organizations of any size, including your school news organization. These stories add refreshing depth to the mix of news stories.

When considering whether a topic could be turned into an in-depth issue story, ask yourself these questions:

- Is this a story that needs to be told?

- Why should the public know about this?

- What kind of change might happen if I report this?

- How can I take this beyond a regular news story?

GENERAL IN-DEPTH REPORTING

General in-depth reporting covers all in-depth stories that do not revolve around investigation of a particular issue. These stories are just as hard-hitting as investigative and issue stories. Reporters must dig beneath the surface to report stories of substance. Many journalism schools call in-depth reporting "3D reporting: Documents, Data and Diverse human sources."

Documents refer to the paper trail everyone leaves. Tax records, licenses, death and birth certificates, and credit card and phone records are all resources you may be able to use in your story. **Data** are statistics and information that bring perspective to a story. You can use statistics to compare or contrast information. In a story about your school's rate of college acceptances, you might compare national statistics with the numbers going to college from your school. You also can use data to show overall trends or to help illustrate a point in your story.

Journalists can find information on documents and data on almost every subject on the Internet. Be sure to check the source of the information for reliability. While Wikipedia, for example, can be helpful for background and ideas of other sources, it is not considered a reliable source in many newsrooms. The most trusted sources are "official" government, news, business, association or educational websites.

Diverse sources are the people you need to interview who represent all sides of the issue on which you are reporting. Some stories have more than two sides. All sides must be part of your reporting for in-depth stories. Think broadly.

In-depth, issue and investigative reporting take time, talent and tools. Through this kind of reporting, the media fulfill their role of "watchdog" over the public interest. Sometimes this kind of reporting reveals wrongdoing, abuse or illegal practices. More often reporters help readers understand important social or cultural issues because they take the time to analyze information, as well as interview and reinterview sources to get a greater understanding of their subject. Here's how Murrey Marder, creator of the Watchdog Journalism project at the Nieman Foundation, describes this kind of reporting: "Watchdog reporting — when it is done well — extends basic reporting to a deeper level of intensity and thoroughness without hobbling deadline pressure."

Today, investigative, issue and in-depth reporting have blended. Issue stories require investigation and are definitely in-depth when they are told. Whatever they are called or however they are blended, the three I's of reporting generally result in a longer-than-traditional form that gives writers some room to tell a good tale.

checkpoint ✓

What are the three I's of reporting?

AP Stylebook Concepts

In a global world, you need to know the different time zones and how to refer to them in your copy. Time zones are neighboring regions that agree to the same time. The time zone you live in is your local time. When writing the name of the time in force in a particular zone in copy, you always capitalize the first letter of each word.

> Eastern Standard Time, Eastern Daylight Time

When referring to the zone itself, you capitalize only the regional reference.

> Eastern time zone, Eastern time

You can abbreviate the names of the time zones on first reference, but only when referring to zones within the continental United States.

> EST (Eastern Standard Time), EDT (Eastern Daylight Time)

Outside the contiguous United States, spell out all references to time zones.

> It is noon EST in Ohio and 8 a.m. Hawaii-Aleutian Standard Time.

Should News Outlets Pay for Information?

Checkbook journalism, the practice of paying sources for information, is an ethical issue for newsgathering organizations because it can make the objectivity and quality of the reporting suspect. Most reputable news organizations make it their policy and practice NOT to pay sources of any kind for information or interviews.

In most reporting situations, the idea of paying a source for information is unlikely to come up. For example, if you are sent to cover a car crash on a local highway you will want to collect statements from the police and medical authorities, as well as from eyewitnesses and the drivers involved, if possible. Through interviews at the scene and official reports of the incident later filed by police and medical personnel, you could put together a factual story for your publication's news blog. The police report of the accident is public record, general medical information can be made public (individual records are private), and witnesses are likely to talk to the news media without payment just to be helpful or to get their name in the story.

Let's suppose, however, that one of the cars involved in the crash was driven by a prominent personality in your community, a city council representative, and while you are reporting the story you find that the other driver claims the council representative was drunk. You approach that driver for an interview, but he declines to talk unless you pay him. You may think that he has good information and — if true — it would be an important angle to the story. If you were the only reporter to get the information it might even be a "scoop" — a story that no other news organization has. Yet, the fact that the driver is asking for payment should raise questions. Is he stretching the truth or making up "facts" just for the money? Is he someone who has opposed the council member's position on an issue and would benefit from damaging the council member's reputation?

While the incident above may seem far-fetched, questions about checkbook journalism are raised more often on sensational stories when broadcast or print organizations compete for an exclusive with key figures in a crime story, for example. Sometimes reporters and editors pay for what they call "licensing" fees to the key players for the right to air or publish their interviews; they say they are not paying for the information itself. As more news media compete on developing stories and each wants to provide fresher information than the competition, it's easy to see how the possibility of paying for information could be tempting. The question for reporters and editors is how to serve readers while maintaining the ethical standards requiring independence, truth and accuracy.

THINK *Critically*

1. Why is paying for information a practice most reputable news organizations avoid?

2. What questions should reporters and editors ask themselves when a source asks for payment?

13.1 | Assessment

Understand Concepts

Determine the best answer for each of the following questions.

1. The Watergate stories are a good example of which type of story?
   a. personality profiles
   b. issue reporting
   c. investigative reporting
   d. breaking news

2. A story that looks at the number of hours students in your school spend on homework every night is an example of
   a. hard news.
   b. issue reporting.
   c. enterprise reporting.
   d. investigative reporting.

3. Which refers to information and statistics that bring perspective to a story?
   a. data
   b. documents
   c. diverse sources
   d. gatekeepers

4. **True or False**   In-depth reporting requires more information than the five W's and H.

5. **True or False**   General in-depth, investigative and issue reporting are considered the three I's of reporting.

Write Now!

Practice your writing skills with the following activities.

6. Choose a topic concerning your school for an in-depth story. Gather background information from sources such as databases, reports and past interviews. Evaluate and confirm the validity of the background information from a variety of sources. Plan and write a draft of your story on a computer. Incorporate direct and indirect quotes and other research in your copy. Use the track changes function to edit your story for clarity, engaging language, and the correct use of the conventions and mechanics of written English. Send the draft and the final story to your teacher by email. In the email, indicate whether your story is an investigative, issue or a general in-depth story and cite why.

7. You are the editor of your high school news magazine. A reporter comes to you with an exciting story you want to print, but you learn the information was obtained by hacking into personal computers. Write a justification for your actions — yes, you would print the story, or no, you would not print the story, and why it would be responsible or irresponsible media action to print the story.

13.2

Use Reporting Tools

Goals

- Know the reporting tools available for in-depth reporting.
- Understand how to use reporting tools.

Key Terms

- FOIA (Freedom of Information Act) 331
- sunshine laws 331
- computer-assisted reporting 333

FOCUS

The newspaper in your community is about to celebrate 100 years of publishing. You are assigned to write an in-depth piece on the family behind the paper. How are you going to learn about them? Certainly you want to interview the family, employees of the newspaper and people who read the paper. Before beginning your interviews, however, you can learn a lot about the family by using the Internet to research public records.

Think for a moment about all the records that might say something about who you are. There's a birth certificate with your date of birth, legal name and parents' names. You may have a driver's license that shows your address, weight, eye color and even whether you wear glasses. You probably have a Social Security card with a government-issued Social Security number. This number is the key to all kinds of information about you, including where you have worked and whether you paid taxes. You also may have a passport, which shows where you have traveled. No matter who you are, you have a paper trail that reporters can search to learn more about you.

Reporting Tools

To do watchdog, or in-depth, reporting, you need to know what tools are available to you. There are a variety of public records accessible through state and federal agencies and computer programs available to help you analyze the documents and data you collect.

PUBLIC RECORDS

You may obtain public records two ways. You may make a direct request to the agency that holds them. If your request is denied, you may obtain them through following the procedures set down by the federal Freedom of Information Act.

The federal **Freedom of Information Act**, or **FOIA** (pronounced FOY-uh), became law in 1966. It says everyone should have access to federal public records. Though FOIA gets attention when journalists use it on big stories, it was not designed just for journalists. The law was designed so anyone who searches, including students, can obtain information.

That doesn't mean it is easy to get the information you want. FOIA requests for many agencies are available on the individual website of each agency. The Student Press Law Center is a helpful resource and offers a free FOIA letter generator to get access to state and local government records.

FOIA laws differ from state to state. Your newsroom may have a copy of the FOIA laws in your state. Some states have **sunshine laws**, which require open access for the media and a public representative to most government business and regulatory meetings. Both the federal and state FOIA laws allow people to access public information and many public records that affect life in the United States. Some of these records could become part of good in-depth or investigative work for your news stories.

FOIA helps reporters all around the country break significant stories. For example, reporters for the New York Daily News used FOIA to obtain information they used to report that the area around Ground Zero was contaminated with asbestos and other chemicals. Ground Zero is where the World Trade Center collapsed on Sept. 11, 2001, in a terrorist attack. Government officials claimed the area was free of asbestos and other chemicals harmful to human beings, but records said differently.

In recent years, FOIA requests have taken so long to process that journalists and others have complained that the law has become useless. Backlogged cases at some government agencies numbered in the thousands and people requesting information have had to wait years to obtain it. In 2007, Congress began talking about passing new laws to set timelines and penalty fees to break the backlog.

Obtaining Information From Government Agencies   Before using FOIA procedures to obtain the information or records you need, you should first try to obtain them directly from the government agency that handles the information or records. The best way to start is to informally ask for what you want. If you know specifically what information or records you want, and from which agency, call the public information, media relations or press office of the agency, identify yourself as a reporter, researcher or scholar and ask for copies of the information. The agency may agree to supply all or part of what you want at the time of your request. If you are turned down, try the agency's FOI (freedom of information) officer, who may tell you how to get what you want without filing a formal FOIA request. Make a point of telling any official with whom you speak that you intend to make a formal request if you cannot get help informally. Only a written FOIA request — not an informal, oral request — will place the agency under a legal duty to act.

● **grammar tip**

An interjection is a part of speech that expresses feeling or emotion. "Wow!" is an interjection. Interjections, when used effectively, can add richness to an in-depth story. However, if overused or used inappropriately, interjections distract from your story. Other common interjections include hey, oh, whew, aack, ugh, um, er, say, well, huh and hmm.

When expressing a mild feeling, such as hmm, you would usually set it off with a comma. For example, "Hmm, I see what you mean." When expressing a strong emotion, you most likely will use an exclamation mark. For example, "The only response from most of the students was, 'Wow!'"

Use interjections wisely and sparingly.

Obtaining Information Using FOIA Procedures If you are ready to file a FOIA request, you can write a letter explaining what you want as specifically as possible. (See the sample FOIA letter on page 334.) Writing a letter will preserve all your rights under FOIA. Each federal agency has an FOI officer. Think about which agency you want to address. If you want information on education, for example, you want to write to the FOI officer in the Department of Education. Some large agencies have separate FOI officers for subdivisions or regional offices. You can call the agency to learn to whom to address your letter. If you are unsure where to send the letter, address it to the agency or departmental FOI officer and ask that the letter be forwarded to the FOI officer in charge of the information you are requesting.

State requirements vary. Contact the state agency from which you want information to find out what needs to go into a letter.

///// Why is it important to put a FOIA request in writing?

How does the Freedom of Information Act help reporters?

COMPUTER-ASSISTED REPORTING

Computer-assisted reporting is the reporting that journalists do with data and documents that are stored electronically instead of on paper. Think of this type of reporting as an extension of traditional investigative reporting, with an emphasis on using public documents.

Done properly, computer-assisted reporting can raise your level of expertise as a journalist. You do not have to rely on anecdotes and quotes to make a point that can be made with solid data analysis. Here's an example:

> In 2007, Florida Today looked into a state law that set up specific zones in which drivers who speed would get higher fines. The trouble was that the zones they set up were not in the spots with the most speed-related crashes. How did the newspaper find out? It reviewed more than 1 million crashes in Florida from 2002 to 2005, information available in a computer database.

In St. Paul, Minn., the Pioneer Press analyzed three years of test scores from 731 elementary schools and found that 13 high-poverty schools were doing better than expected. The numbers made the point better than any quote from teachers or principals could.

Kent State University students in Ohio collected information on scholarships to determine that 207 athletes received a full ride to the school, but in the largest college, Arts and Sciences, no student received a full ride.

The National Institute for Computer-Assisted Reporting (NICAR) is a program of an organization called Investigative Reporters and Editors (IRE) at the University of Missouri. This program has a database library that helps journalists working on stories where data and documents might be helpful. It also has programs to download, training opportunities and examples of good computer-assisted reporting that might inspire you.

check *point* ✓

What is computer-assisted reporting?

SAMPLE FOIA LETTER

[Date]
Freedom of Information Act Officer
[Name of agency]
[Street address]
[City, State, ZIP Code]

Dear Freedom of Information Act Officer

Pursuant to the federal Freedom of Information Act, 5 U.S.C. # 552, I request access to and copies of reports regarding the specific information for which you are asking.

Please send the requested information in electronic format to your email address.

As a student journalist, I am affiliated with an educational institution. I request this information for a scholarly purpose and not for a commercial use.

I agree to pay reasonable fees for the processing of this request up to a maximum of [put dollar amount here]. Please notify me if the fees will exceed this amount before applying them.

If you deny all or any part of this request, please justify all deletions by citing the specific exemption that forms the basis of your refusal and notify me of appeal options available to me under the law. Please also release all segregable portions of otherwise exempt material.

If you have any questions regarding this request, please contact me by telephone at [your phone number].

I look forward to your reply within 20 business days. Thank you for your assistance.

Sincerely

Your signature

Your printed name
Street address
City, State, ZIP Code
Phone number
Email address

13.2 | Assessment

Understand Concepts

Determine the best answer for each of the following questions.

1. Which reporting tool is appropriate for obtaining information from a federal agency such as the U.S. Department of Defense?
   a. First Amendment
   b. FOIA
   c. sunshine laws
   d. Wikipedia

2. Computer-assisted reporting is performed by
   a. getting past gatekeepers.
   b. obtaining informal records through FOIA.
   c. researching public records stored electronically.
   d. using wire services.

3. **True or False** Only professional journalists can obtain information under FOIA.

4. **True or False** Sunshine laws protect state government agencies from allowing journalists to obtain information about meetings.

Write Now!

Practice your writing skills with the following activities.

5. Write a letter to a federal agency requesting specific information through FOIA.

6. Write a letter to a state agency requesting specific information through FOIA.

7. Use a computer to create a multimedia in-depth story that is suitable for a high school website. Your story should inform the audience about a situation that affects their lives. For example, your story could be about schools that have organic vegetable gardens, the reasons the schools started the gardens and the students responsible for working on them. Gather information through interviews (in person, electronically or by phone) and through researching databases, reports and interviews. Plan and write questions for your interviews and in-depth research. Evaluate and confirm the validity of the background information from a variety of sources. Incorporate direct and indirect quotes in the copy and video or audio components. Write captions for any photographs or illustrations. Write a headline for your story. Before submitting your multimedia story, carefully proofread and edit all the components. Submit your story electronically to your teacher.

Write In-Depth Stories

Goals

- Understand the structure of in-depth stories.
- Know how to present all sides of the story.

Key Terms

- structure 336
- transition 339

FOCUS

Have you ever found yourself involved in a long newspaper story before you realized how much time had passed? You started on the first page, and then jumped to an inside page and kept right on reading before you could even say, "I don't have time for this." Think about the last time you used the remote control to flip through television channels. Maybe you stopped at a news magazine show just as the correspondent began a compelling interview. The next thing you knew 15 minutes were gone and you hadn't stirred. That's the kind of tug writers of in-depth stories want to have on their readers and viewers. Powerful writing and interviewing that makes you say, "I do have time for this."

Story Structure

Writing an in-depth story involves the why and how of writing the five W's and H. But it is different from writing a traditional news story. You may have spent weeks, even months, interviewing, reporting and researching documents. You need more than the news story's traditional framework. In-depth stories require a different **structure**, or organization. Writing an in-depth story is like putting together a puzzle. Good in-depth reporters look for ways to get the story across clearly in words, graphics, photos, charts, audio, video and other means available. Reporters use every tool that adds to the story.

THE INTRODUCTION

The beginning of your in-depth story is likely to be several paragraphs long. Your goal is different from the goal you have as a news writer. With an in-depth story, you want to do more than provide the reader with the five W's. You want to draw readers into the story and keep them reading until the end. You don't need to answer all five W's in the first paragraph as you would for a traditional lead. The Washington Post's story on conditions for soldiers wounded in Iraq and Afghanistan who were recuperating at Walter Reed Army Medical Center began like this:

> Behind the door of Army Spec. Jeremy Duncan's room, part of the wall is torn and hangs in the air, weighted down with black mold. When the wounded combat engineer stands in his shower and looks up, he can see the bathtub on the floor above through a rotted hole. The entire building, constructed between the world wars, often smells like greasy carry-out. Signs of neglect are everywhere: mouse droppings, belly-up cockroaches, stained carpets, cheap mattresses.
>
> This is the world of Building 18, not the kind of place where Duncan expected to recover when he was evacuated to Walter Reed Army Medical Center from Iraq last February with a broken neck and a shredded left ear, nearly dead from blood loss. But the old lodge, just outside the gates of the hospital and five miles up the road from the White House, has housed hundreds of maimed soldiers recuperating from injuries suffered in the wars in Iraq and Afghanistan.
>
> **Source:** "Soldiers Face Neglect, Frustration At Army's Top Medical Facility" from The Washington Post, © 2007 The Washington Post All rights reserved. Used by permission and protected by the Copyright Laws of the United States. The printing, copying, redistribution, or retransmission of the Material without express written permission is prohibited.

Like the Post reporters, you can begin an in-depth story with descriptive scene-setting. Or you might decide to take the approach that a Florida Today reporter did in a story that ran just before a special session of the Florida Legislature on hurricane relief. The writer addresses readers directly because the topic is one readers can relate to:

> You might think, with thousands of blue tarps still covering your neighbors' roofs, that Florida insurers are buckling under record losses.
>
> You might have assumed — if you've dickered with an adjuster or fretted over your windstorm deductible — that property insurers must double their rates to survive.

> Or that insurers will drop policies and leave the state. Or that a state fund must cover a bigger share of disaster claims for companies to remain solvent.
>
> But none of that is true.
>

The writer helped readers get invested in the story about insurance by reminding them of experiences they have shared: tarps on roofs and dickering with an adjuster. Other ways to introduce a story include opening with an anecdote, a startling statistic or a question. Introductions can be creative or factual, depending on the story. Whichever introduction you choose, use one that captures your readers and makes them want to keep on reading.

THE NUT GRAPH

In Chapter 4 you learned that the nut graph, short for "nut paragraph," is the one that comes after your introduction and explains the reason you've written the story. It should explain who is affected and clue the reader into what the rest of the story is all about. In the Walter Reed story, the nut graph was the fourth paragraph.

> Not all of the quarters are as bleak as Duncan's, but the despair of Building 18 symbolizes a larger problem in Walter Reed's treatment of the wounded, according to dozens of soldiers, family members, veterans aid groups, and current and former Walter Reed staff members interviewed by two Washington Post reporters, who spent more than four months visiting the outpatient world without the knowledge or permission of Walter Reed officials. Many agreed to be quoted by name; others said they feared Army retribution if they complained publicly.
>

The nut graph of the insurance story was the fifth paragraph.

In fact, Florida's major property insurers managed to earn profits during the period that included hurricanes Charley, Frances, Ivan and Jeanne, securities filings and earnings reports show. Even as the industry announced record losses and called for higher rates, company executives told analysts they were strong enough to pay claims and still make money. And that's before any changes.

Source: From Florida Today. © 2007 Gannett Co., Inc. Courtesy of Florida Today.

THE MIDDLE

By definition, in-depth stories are longer. Writers need to pace the stories to keep readers interested to the end. Vary your sentence structure and don't write long sentence after long sentence. Use a short sentence after a long one, a short paragraph after a long paragraph. Use dialogue but vary the length of quotes and use the best ones you've got.

Part of your job is to move readers through the story, so look carefully at **transitions** — the words that take you from one paragraph to the next. One trick writers use is to raise a question in one paragraph that is answered in the next. Another way to transition is to repeat a word or phrase in the second paragraph that is used in the first. If your story has a lot of information, you can use bulleted lists within the copy to keep the reader moving along.

ENDINGS

In-depth stories need endings. News stories may stop without an ending. They contain information until the last paragraph, and they are written to be cut from the bottom up. In-depth stories require a wrap-up to give the readers closure. Many writers save a good emotional quote for the ending. At the end of the first day's story on Walter Reed, which was about 5,000 words long, the reporters used this quote:

///// *How do transitions help keep readers interested in the news story?*

"I hate it," said Romero, who stays in his room all day. "There are cockroaches. The elevator doesn't work. The garage door doesn't work. Sometimes there's no heat, no water. . . . I told my platoon sergeant I want to leave. I told the town hall meeting. I talked to the doctors and medical staff. They just said you kind of got to get used to the outside world. . . . My platoon sergeant said, 'Suck it up!'"

The ending is an example of coming full circle with the story. It began with a soldier in awful conditions and it ends with a soldier in awful conditions.

Quotations are not the only way to end stories, however. You may wrap up a story in your own words, though be careful not to be opinionated. Use a short sentence that restates the point or offers a conclusion. You also may end with a statistic, an anecdote, or a strong statement or question that leaves the reader thinking about the story.

checkpoint

How does the structure of in-depth stories differ from that of traditional news stories?

Present All Sides

Presenting all sides to an in-depth story can be a challenge, but it is part of your journalistic duty to be fair and accurate. First, you need to figure out what "all" means. How many parties are involved in your story? Suppose you decided to do an in-depth look at the homework practices at your school because students think it is an issue. You interview teachers, students and parents. You compare your school's practice with the practice of other local high schools. You look at national statistics on homework. You conclude that the majority thinks that your high school gives too much homework and that teachers should coordinate better so the homework load is more evenly spread.

After outlining your story, you begin your first draft by summarizing the various opinions from each group you interviewed — students, parents and teachers. You clearly describe the opinion of each group. You create a chart of what other local high schools are doing to go with the story.

After you read through your first draft, think about whether you've given everyone who should have a voice a chance to speak. What about your school's principal or academic dean? Should you interview him? What would he add to the story? Now is the time to do any fill-in interviews to strengthen your story. You may be nervous about telling the principal that you are writing about too much homework. However, it is only fair to give the principal a chance to say something on the topic because principals are ultimately responsible for school policies and practices.

The Washington Post reporters who worked on the Walter Reed series had their information collected and interviews done before they called Army officials to give them a chance to respond to their findings. They gave the Army a week to respond. The Army officials responded by criticizing the report, but they couldn't say they hadn't had a chance to respond.

Photodisc/Getty Images

////// *Why, as a reporter for a school news organization, would you want to interview the school principal for a controversial story?*

check *point* ✓

Why do journalists try to present all sides of in-depth stories?

13.3 | Assessment

Understand Concepts

Determine the best answer for each of the following questions.

1. A good way to pace an in-depth story is to
   a. interview all parties involved.
   b. open with a quotation.
   c. use charts and photos.
   d. vary the sentence structure.

2. Which is the term for the way a story is organized?
   a. transition
   b. structure
   c. tip
   d. nut graph

3. **True or False**   In-depth stories have a different structure than news stories.

4. **True or False**   With an in-depth story, you need to interview enough people so that you can present all sides of the issue.

5. **True or False**   You need to answer the five W's in the first paragraph in an in-depth story.

Write Now!

Practice your writing skills with the following activities.

6. Choose a topic of interest to you in your school or community that might be worth an in-depth story. Make a list of people you want to interview and the type of information you want to research. Explain what information you hope to obtain from each person. Plan and write relevant questions for each interview.

7. Choose an in-depth story from a news magazine, newspaper or online news source. Outline the story, and then rewrite the story for a broadcast suitable for a general audience. Be prepared to deliver your story in class as a broadcast with video or still photographs.

8. Choose a short news story from a print, online or broadcast news source that can be developed into an in-depth story. Look for related stories. Write several introductions to the in-depth story using each of the following types of introductions: a descriptive scene setting, an anecdote, a startling statistic and a question. Revise and edit your introductions using proofreading symbols. Turn in your edited copy along with the final draft.

Jose's Dream

Pulitzer Prize-winning investigative journalist Jose Antonio Vargas is working the biggest story of his career — the story of how, as a child, his grandfather brought him illegally to the United States to live.

Jose didn't find out he was undocumented until he was 16 and applied for a driver's license — the clerk told him that his green card was fake. Jose didn't want to return to the Philippines, live without his family and wait for 10 years before he could legally immigrate to the United States.

Jose stayed in the United States illegally, but he had help. The DMV clerk didn't turn him in and his high school principal helped him find a college scholarship that did not require proof of citizenship. His employer, the Washington Post, also kept quiet about his illegal status.

Tired of running, Jose recently risked everything and told his story to the media. He wanted to draw attention to The Dream Act, a piece of legislation coming before the House and Senate that offered a way to citizenship for people in his position.

The Dream Act is a bipartisan legislation that will help qualifying, undocumented youth who were brought to the United States as children, and who played no part in the illegal activities of older family members, become eligible for citizenship by completing a college degree or two years of military service. Access www.cengage.com/school/langarts/journalism and click on the link to Chapter 13. Read Maria Peña's EFE World News Service article about Jose, and then answer the questions below.

THINK *Critically*

1. There are two sides to every story. After you've read the article about Jose, go online and look for information outlining the position of groups who are opposed to The Dream Act. Write a paragraph in favor of the act's passage, and one against.

2. Jose's story can end one of two ways — The Dream Act passes and he will remain in the United States with his family, or he will be sent back to the Philippines, a country he barely remembers. Assume you have just written an in-depth story about Jose's predicament. Write an ending to the story in which Jose is able to remain in the United States. Then write an alternative ending in which Jose is sent back to the Philippines. What happens to him? Does he find family members? A job? Does he speak the language? What hardships might he face?

"Undocumented journalist joins fight for DREAM Act." EFE World News Service 28 June 2011. Global Issues In Context. Web. 8 Aug. 2011.

CHAPTER 13 | Assessment

Review Journalism Concepts

13.1 In-Depth Reporting Defined

In-depth reporting gives careful consideration to all details and aspects of a subject. The three I's of in-depth reporting are investigative reporting, issue reporting and general in-depth reporting. Investigative reporting requires journalists to ask questions about the regular news stories and dig deeper to uncover what is hidden beneath the surface. Investigative reporters go that extra step and often investigate wrongdoing. The most famous instance of investigative reporting is the Watergate story reported by Washington Post writers Carl Bernstein and Bob Woodward in the early 1970s. Issue reporting is in-depth reporting that looks at special issues of concern to society. General in-depth reporting covers all in-depth stories that do not revolve around investigation of a particular issue. Many journalism schools call in-depth reporting "3D reporting: Documents, Data and Diverse human sources."

13.2 Use Reporting Tools

To write in-depth stories, you need to know what tools are available. There are state and federal laws that make public records accessible and computer programs to help you analyze the documents and data you collect for your in-depth stories. The federal Freedom of Information Act (FOIA) states that everyone should have access to federal public records. There are FOIA laws in the states, but they differ from state to state. You can obtain information or records from government agencies by asking the agency for the information, or by writing a letter to the FOI officer at the agency. Computer-assisted reporting is a fairly new name for the reporting that journalists do with data and documents. It refers to the analysis of public records that are stored electronically.

13.3 Write In-Depth Stories

In-depth stories are structured differently from news stories, which require answering the five W's within the first paragraph. In-depth stories have an introduction, a nut graph, a middle and an ending. Introductions pull the readers into the story. The nut graph is a paragraph that explains why you wrote the story. The middle must be paced to keep the reader interested, and the ending wraps up the story and leaves the reader thinking about the story. In-depth stories require journalists to present all sides in order to be fair and accurate.

Develop Your Journalism Language

Write the letter of the term that matches each definition. Some terms will not be used.

_____ 1. Reward given for outstanding reporting

_____ 2. Reporting that gives careful consideration to all details and aspects of a subject

_____ 3. Refers to the paper trail everyone leaves

_____ 4. Refers to a story's framework

_____ 5. Allows you to obtain information and records

_____ 6. Helps reader move from one paragraph to the next

_____ 7. Information and statistics that bring perspective to a story

_____ 8. Reporting that could uncover a wrongdoing

_____ 9. People you need to interview who represent all sides of an issue

_____ 10. All in-depth stories that do not revolve around investigation of a particular issue

_____ 11. Information obtained through electronic sources

_____ 12. Reporting that looks at special concerns of society

a. computer-assisted reporting
b. data
c. diverse sources
d. documents
e. FOIA (Freedom of Information Act)
f. general in-depth reporting
g. in-depth reporting
h. investigative reporting
i. issue reporting
j. Pulitzer Prize
k. structure
l. sunshine laws
m. tip
n. transition

13. Watergate is an example of
    a. profile reporting.
    b. traditional news stories.
    c. issue reporting.
    d. investigative reporting.

14. The paragraph that explains why you've written the story is the
    a. nut graph.
    b. ending.
    c. introduction.
    d. fifth.

15. One of the highest honors a journalist can achieve is to be awarded the
    a. Academy Award.
    b. Pulitzer Prize.
    c. Emmy.
    d. Newspaper Recognition Award.

16. A story on the amount of homework students in your school are assigned is an example of
    a. issue reporting.
    b. off-the-record reporting.
    c. investigative reporting.
    d. conflict of interest reporting.

17. State laws that require open access for the media and a public representative to most government business and regulatory meetings are called the
    a. state legislative laws.
    b. Pulitzer laws.
    c. sunshine laws.
    d. open meeting laws.

Think Critically

18. How does being curious help reporters who write in-depth investigative stories?

19. What are the advantages and disadvantages of electronic news coverage of in-depth stories?

20. How does in-depth reporting fulfill the role of watchdog over the public interest?

21. You are the editor of the school newspaper. One of the reporters turned in an in-depth story on peer mentors. It's a good story, but you have just learned that some pages in the paper need to be cut. What do you do?

22. How does FOIA help you as a journalist?

23. Why is writing a letter to specific federal agencies to request information under FOIA more effective than making a phone call?

24. How is an in-depth story like a fiction narrative?

25. Why should you reevaluate who needs to be interviewed after you write the first draft of an in-depth story?

26. What is the most important difference between in-depth and regular news stories?

27. Do you think long-form journalism has a place in the media environment of today? Why or why not?

Make Academic Connections

28. **ETHICS**   In 2011, News Corp., the world's second-largest media conglomerate, was accused of hacking the phones of British citizens to obtain information for stories. As the scandal unfolded, the FBI in this country also investigated the company. Use the Internet to investigate the accusations against the corporation, and then write a paper that explains the accusations and your personal thoughts on the way the news organization conducted business. Plan and develop a paper that answers this question: Were actions taken by reporters and editors within the organization's different news entities responsible or irresponsible? Cite specific reasons and examples to justify your stance. Use the Internet to locate sources such as reports and past interviews and to gather background information. Evaluate and confirm the validity of the information from a variety of sources. Plan, develop and write a draft of an in-depth story. Revise and edit your article using proofreading symbols for clarity, engaging language and the correct use of English. Turn in your draft along with your final paper.

29. **CAREERS**   Research the careers of journalists who specialize in financial reporting. Create a fact sheet that includes information about what news organizations they work for, education needed beyond journalism, the types of news stories and in-depth stories they write, and possible starting job opportunities.

30. **SOCIAL STUDIES** Analyze an in-depth story that appears in a foreign newspaper or on the website of a foreign news organization. If English is your second language, choose a story in your first language. Write a report that addresses the following: How does this story meet the needs and interests of the news organization's readership? Would this story be of interest to the people of your community? Why or why not?

31. **HISTORY** Research the history of the country in the 1960s that brought about FOIA. Write an in-depth story that explains this period of U.S. history and the cultural environment in which FOIA was written.

32. **RESEARCH** Watch a television news magazine's report of an in-depth story. Analyze the show and write a report on how well the story was covered. Include what information you think is missing, if any.

33. **ART** Work as a class to create a wall chart that illustrates the elements of an in-depth story, including introduction, nut graph, middle and ending. Provide examples of each element. Use magazine cutouts, computer graphics and other art supplies.

34. **MULTIMEDIA** Write a plan that describes what you consider the ideal outlets of your school's multimedia, multiplatform news organization. Be sure to include an outlet for in-depth stories.

35. **WRITING** Choose a news story from your school publication or the local paper. Think about how you can turn this news story into an in-depth story for a high school news website. Make a list of the people you might interview and write the interview questions. Create a chart that lists the graphics, photographs and other visual elements that could be used with the story. Use the reporting tools discussed in this chapter to research your subject. Conduct the interviews and create the visual elements for the story. Analyze the data and information you have gathered and write the in-depth story for a high school website. Be sure to present all sides to be fair and accurate.

Writing Portfolio Activity

36. Choose a current news story and write a list of ideas from the story that could be turned into in-depth stories. Add to the list if the news story continues to develop over the next two or three weeks. Include the list in your portfolio.

AP Stylebook Workshop

Edit the following sentences to conform to AP style.

37. New York City is on eastern daylight time.

38. Cincinnati is in the Eastern Time Zone.

39. When it is noon EST in New York, it is 7 a.m. Hawaii-Aleutian standard time.

40. New Mexico is on mountain time.

INFORMATION LITERACY: Research Skills

Successful journalists know how to conduct research. So do successful students. The research skills you foster as a student journalist will serve you well in your other classes and in your future career.

To be a good researcher, you need to know how to

- Access and evaluate information
- Use and manage information

ACCESS AND EVALUATE INFORMATION

Good research skills require that you are able to access information efficiently and effectively and that you are able to critically and competently evaluate the information you find.

Why should you be efficient when accessing information? Research can take a lot of time, so you want to access the information you need without wasting time. Here are a few tips to help you:

- Keep an organized list of websites that you can use for research.

- Make friends with the local research librarian and other expert sources in the areas you normally write about. For example, if you write an online blog about the weather, your list of experts will include the local broadcast weather newscasters.

- Use note cards to organize your research.

- Schedule your research time and stick to the schedule as much as possible. You also need to be flexible enough to investigate a side topic if it is relevant to your story.

- Stay on task by keeping a notebook handy to write down websites that look interesting but are not on topic, and then go back at your leisure to visit them.

If a website, or source, is not yielding the information you need, go on to the next source on your list.

To have good research skills you must be able to critically evaluate the information you find. This means reading several websites or talking with several people about the topic to assure you have all sides to the story. It also means using what you already know about the topic and a good dose of common sense.

USE AND MANAGE INFORMATION

Once you have completed your research, you must use the information accurately and creatively in your story. Organize your note cards according to similar information and where that information will fit into the story. Outline your story, write a draft and then edit the story. Go over your research cards again to make sure you have included everything you want to include.

Always be ethical and respectful of copyright laws when using someone else's work. Give credit where credit is due and name the source.

Learning and practicing good research skills will go a long way in helping you as a student journalist and in your future career. Good research skills will also help you with your other high school classes. You can use the same skills in English, history, social studies and many other courses.

THINK *Critically*

Write a few paragraphs about something you could do today to improve your research skills. Include what steps you could take. For example, you could start a list of websites — with notes about the information on each site — that you use for research for your classes, including this one. Next, you could organize those websites by classes, and then by the information you obtain from them. You could add a cross-referenced index that would allow you to use the research from one story — or class — for another story.

REAL PEOPLE REAL CAREERS

Helen Thorpe | A Freelance Writer and Author

You never know where an idea for an in-depth project will come from. Helen Thorpe, whose book "Just Like Us" is about four Mexican girls growing up in the United States, began with someone else's story.

Photo courtesy of Helen Thorpe

"I read a local newspaper story about the fact that students without legal status were not eligible for driver's licenses in the state of Colorado," says Thorpe, who lives in Denver. "I remembered how cool you were when you got a driver's license, and wondered what it felt like to be one of the kids who couldn't, who didn't qualify. That's where the book began." However, it took years of reporting to develop and write.

"You can't be in a hurry," says Thorpe, who grew up in New Jersey and studied creative writing at Princeton University. "You have to be willing to actually get to know people, which is very different from parachuting in, asking a few questions and running away. You have to be honorable, willing to be real and worthy of trust."

Trust-building can be difficult, however, when you are writing about the legal status of immigrants or about others who might be vulnerable because of their legal situations. In Thorpe's case, two of the girls she writes about in her book were not legal residents; the other two were legal. She followed their lives for five years.

"The hardest times for me in the course of reporting 'Just Like Us' were the times when the girls went silent," Thorpe says. "Often, I wouldn't hear from them for a few weeks or occasionally a whole month or two. I learned to be persistent and to just keep sending along an email or a text, or to make another phone call. I tried never to make them feel badly about not responding. I knew their lives were hard and sometimes overwhelming. I tried to communicate that if and when they were ready to talk some more, I was there to listen."

ADVICE FOR ASPIRING WRITERS

Thorpe, who is married to Colorado Gov. John Hickenlooper, says she had to learn new habits of organization for a project the length of the book. She cautions that it takes perseverance to be a long-form writer. "If you really want to do it, you have to be willing to endure failure, and to learn from it, and not to give up," she says. "You just have to keep on writing."

Thorpe also advises, "Be kind to the people you write about. Malice, snarkiness, sarcasm — all those are variations on making fun of other people, and that's cheap drama. Go for the real stuff. Honor the people you write about, let their deepness shine through, put words to the truths they find hard to say."

Source: Personal interview with Helen Thorpe

THINK *Critically*

1. Why do you think Thorpe suggests that writers should not be in a hurry when writing a book?

2. Why do you think Thorpe warns aspiring journalists to be kind to the people they write about?

14

Photojournalism

Freezing a Moment in Time

There is something beautiful in news photographer Joe Rosenthal's picture "Raising the Flag on Iwo Jima." With its strong lines, off-center focal point and artful use of the "rule of thirds," it is a piece to admire. Those who saw it within 24 hours of its taking on Feb. 23, 1945, declared the photo "one for all time." The picture was reprinted in thousands of papers and was the face of a war bond campaign with 3.5 million posters printed. It was the model for the bronze statue in Arlington, Va., honoring U.S. Marine Corps veterans.

Rosenthal didn't start out to make history. A photographer for the Associated Press, he was in the Pacific to document World War II. He followed servicemen who climbed to the summit of Mount Suribachi on the island of Iwo Jima to raise a second, larger flag. He arrived at the top just as they were preparing to take down the first flag. He couldn't get both the lowering and the raising of the flags, so he decided to concentrate on the raising.

Rosenthal, who died at 94 in 2006, took 18 photos on Iwo Jima, one of them a posed shot of servicemen with the flag at the top of Mount Suribachi. Because of a mix-up in his communication with the AP photo editor, there was confusion about whether the famous flag-raising picture was posed. Rosenthal and eyewitnesses said it was not, and Rosenthal later said that if he had posed the photograph he would have "ruined" it. Because it is a true reflection of what happened, raising the flag on Iwo Jima has become an immortal moment.

> **THINK** *Critically*
> Why does it matter whether the picture "Raising the Flag on Iwo Jima" was posed?

What Is Photojournalism?

Goals

- Define photojournalism.
- Describe who is a photojournalist.

Key Terms

- photojournalism 351
- still photograph 351
- cutline 352
- video journalism 353
- videographer 353
- photojournalist 353
- found situation 354

FOCUS

Technological advances have changed 21st century photojournalism in three important ways. First, the equipment a photojournalist carries is lighter and easier to use than it was when Joe Rosenthal took his pictures on Iwo Jima. Second, it's fast. Images can be transmitted electronically straight from the scene of a news event in seconds, and then published equally quickly. Third, nearly everyone, it seems, has a camera in his or her pocket, and amateur photos taken by regular citizens become part of a news package presented by professional journalists.

Photojournalism Defined

Photojournalism is visual reporting of facts and truths. It is telling news and feature stories through photography and videotape and telling them with the same objectivity, accuracy and fairness required of all journalists. It is using pictures — sometimes one, sometimes more — to get across the essence or impact of those stories. If journalism is the first draft of history, then photojournalism is the visual documentation of history.

STILL PHOTOGRAPHY

When journalists talk about photojournalism they usually mean **still photographs**, one-frame images taken on film or digitally. The profession is changing and embracing new technologies, but still photography continues to play an important role in journalistic storytelling.

Still photos can freeze a moment in time, even an active one. The image mentioned in the beginning of this chapter is of men in the act of raising the flag. A photo allows a reader, or viewer, to linger over the moment, absorbing the meaning of it and the story it tells.

Still photographs grab the reader's attention. Photo editors and news editors look for compelling photos to put on front pages of the print editions or their home pages on the Web because photos will bring readers into the story faster than headlines.

Photojournalism is different from other types of still photography — studio photography, fine art photography, documentary photography and so on — because the images are timely, objective, and a fair and accurate representation of the event. They are never manipulated at the scene, in the darkroom or on a computer. Also, the images are used with **cutlines** — the words beneath the pictures generally written by editors from information supplied by photographers.

The photojournalism done after Hurricane Katrina devastated New Orleans in 2005, or the terrorist attacks on the World Trade Center in New York in 2001, is remarkable for the way it vividly showed the drama of each event. In the first few days after both events photojournalists documented the destruction, but as the stories continued for weeks after the initial events, photojournalists put a human face on tragedy that words alone could not. In single photos and photo essays, photographers worked like their reporter counterparts. They moved the story forward through images.

It doesn't take a disaster to produce telling photographs. High school photojournalists may find school events such as a chess team match, or an off-campus activity such as feeding the homeless at a soup kitchen, to be a good opportunity for telling a story through images.

Imagine, for example, a photo essay or a digital slide show on a high school glee club invited to participate in a statewide competition. To tell the story in images, your photographer will want to shoot glee club rehearsals at school, students packing for the trip, the travel by bus to the state capital, rehearsal on site, behind the scenes on concert day and, finally, the concert with competing glee clubs. The photo editor will want close-ups, wide shots, active pictures of glee club members singing, and quieter photos of the glee

///// How do photographs enhance the reporting of tragic events such as storms that destroy people's homes and livelihoods?

club members, perhaps as they rest on the bus, eyes closed, iPods lulling them to sleep. There are many photo essay possibilities in your school and community, but they may take some time and planning to achieve.

VIDEO JOURNALISM

Photojournalists now also work with the modern multimedia tools of computers and video cameras to tell their visual stories. **Video journalism** is the art of telling the story with video. A **videographer** is the journalist who shoots the story with the video camera.

Photographers new to the business today are expected to know more than how to produce terrific still photography. Most news organizations need photojournalists who can produce online slideshows, galleries, and video of their news and feature assignments. At many newspapers, the photography department now is called the multimedia department. Photographers (and often reporters, too) carry both still and video cameras, laptops and cellphones. They shoot for print publications, websites and, sometimes, a television station.

Recognizing that multimedia is the way the journalistic world is going, the National Press Photographers Association has divisions for both Web and TV news video in its annual "The Best of Photojournalism" contest. Some photojournalists suggest that the Web, for both still and video photography, is where the best news images will be seen. Young people entering the photojournalism profession today are wise to get training in both still and video photography.

*check*point ✓

What is photojournalism?

Who Is a Photojournalist?

That's an important question in a 21st century newsroom. Staff photographers who are assigned to cover news events and feature stories are photojournalists by job description, but all reporters generally are expected to carry cameras too and to be able to shoot competently and send files digitally. And because we live in an age where everyone has a camera in his or her pocket, it's important to be open to the idea of "citizen" photojournalism — that is, non-professionals taking photographs at the scene of important events or news stories and offering them to news organizations for publication.

TRAITS OF A PHOTOJOURNALIST

Photojournalists are reporters with cameras. They know how to use the camera and all the technical aspects of photography. But that's just the beginning. Unlike reporters who can use phones from an office or home and editors who stay at the office, photographers go out into the world, sometimes to dangerous places, including war zones and scenes of natural disasters.

Good photojournalists put aside their own views to tell other people's stories. They will jump on a plane or get into their car at a moment's notice to go to a scene that needs documenting. They are prepared for such spontaneity; like a crime scene forensic specialist, they have all their gear ready to go all the time.

Photojournalists are good communicators. They have a passion for news and human interest stories and, like their reporter counterparts, they are informed. They read newspapers and Internet sites to stay on top of current events. They are compassionate with the subjects of their photographs and they are clear with the editors and reporters with whom they work. They are good at collecting information — names, details of the event — so accurate cutlines can be written.

Dedicated photojournalists are rarely without their cameras because they want to be ready for any news or "found" situation. A **found situation** is an event or scene they come across by accident that can make a good photograph. Their cameras are the tools they need to accomplish their vision, just as painters need brushes and oil paint.

checkpoint ✓

Who is a photojournalist?

AP Stylebook Concepts

When writing stories and cutlines, you need to know how to style people's names. Follow these general AP Stylebook guidelines on when to use titles with names.

Do not use the courtesy titles Mr., Mrs., Ms. and Miss, except in quotations.

These abbreviated titles are used before full names (Dr. John Smith):

Dr. (doctor)
Gov. (governor)
Lt. Gov. (lieutenant governor)
Rep. (representative)
Sen. (senator)
the Rev. (the reverend)

Certain military titles also are abbreviated.

Other formal titles (such as the president and mayor) are capitalized before full names, such as President Barack Obama.

Do not use a comma between a name and Jr. (junior) or Sr. (senior).

Example:

Gov. John Lawrence Jr.

Photo Permissions

Photojournalists must either obtain written permission to take a person's photograph or be able to argue that the photo does not disregard a person's right of privacy. Invasion of privacy can end in a photographer — and the publisher — being taken to court. The following situations are those in which you must obtain written permission to photograph someone:

- Photographs cannot misappropriate the likeness of a living person for purposes of trade or advertising unless the person agrees in writing. For example, you cannot use a photo of the star football player as part of an advertisement for a sporting goods store without the written permission of the player.

- As a photojournalist you do not have the right to public disclosure of private facts. You cannot take photos of students, faculty or staff that depict private information about them unless you have their written permission. For example, you should not photograph the homes of faculty members for publication in the school newspaper without written permission from each person whose home you photograph.

- As a photojournalist you are not allowed to intrude upon people's privacy. For example, you cannot sit in a car across the street and take photos of all the students going into a private party, and then print the story in the school paper with a story about off-campus parties.

- Most courts will argue that photos taken on the spot for news stories do not invade a person's privacy. Those same photos published at a later date may well be an invasion of privacy. For example, there's a "Buckle Up for Safety" campaign going on at your school. On the day of a big rally, you photograph students who are not wearing seat belts as they drive off campus. Three months later, the community magazine editor wants to run a similar story and asks to reprint your photos. These photos are no longer on-the-spot news photos, so a court could argue your photos violate the subjects' right of privacy. To publish the photos, the publisher must have the subjects' written permission.

- Photographs cannot show a person under false light. For example, you cannot run a story about cheating in your school and use a photo of upstanding students who are not involved in the cheating. Doing so implies that the upstanding students have been accused of cheating. Before printing the photo of any person in an incriminating situation, make sure that person is being accused or was found guilty.

- States laws vary as to their laws and interpretations of a person's right to privacy. Err on the safe side — and get written permission if you have any doubt.

THINK *Critically*

Why do you think on-the-spot news photos do not require written permission from the people in the photos?

14.1 | Assessment

Understand Concepts

Determine the best answer for each of the following questions.

1. The visual reporting of facts and truths is called
   a. digital photography.
   b. a photo essay.
   c. a found situation.
   d. photojournalism.

2. Which is true of photojournalists?
   a. They carry camera and video equipment.
   b. They are reporters with cameras.
   c. They are always looking for a found situation.
   d. All of the above are true.

3. Cutlines, or the words beneath a photo in a newspaper, generally are written by the
   a. photo editor.
   b. photographer.
   c. designer.
   d. editor.

4. **True or False** Cutlines are written only for photos with a story behind them.

5. **True or False** Still photographs are a thing of the past.

Write Now!

Practice your writing skills with the following activities.

6. Analyze the photos on the front page of a recent edition of your local newspaper. Write a critique that answers the following questions: Why do you think the editor chose these photos? Do they explain the story? Why or why not?

7. Study three online news sources such as CBS, CNN and MSNBC. Compare and contrast the photographs each uses. What is similar about the photos? What is different? Plan, draft and write a paper that explains your findings, referring to each photo. Carefully examine your composition for clarity, engaging language and the correct use of English. Submit your paper to your teacher electronically.

Work as a Photojournalist

Goals

- Understand the structure of photo operations at a news organization.
- Understand photographic composition.
- Define "photo essay."

Key Terms

- photo editor 357
- contact sheet 361
- crop 361
- photo essay 361

FOCUS

Take a look today at the photography in your local or city newspaper. You probably will find at least one sports photo, several news photos and numerous pictures of people. If it's a day on which the newspaper runs a separate food or home section you will probably find pictures of decorated rooms or yummy ingredients for a recipe. Look at the credit lines under each photo. How many of them were taken by the same photographer? A study of your local newspaper is a peek into a day in the life of a photojournalist.

Photo Operations

Like the operations of any news outlet, the photographic operations have to be organized or nothing would get done. The demands on photography departments have grown with the advent of convergence. Photographers often get multimedia assignments. Yet, the structure of the organization still needs to accommodate assignments, new ideas and teamwork.

THE PHOTOGRAPHY STAFF

The photography staff is headed by a **photo editor**, the person in charge of the staff who also is a liaison with the news, feature, sports and any other departments necessary to producing news. Chief photo editors may have fancier titles, such as managing editor for photography, but that often depends on the size of the organization.

The photo editor is responsible for working with the editors of the other sections to know what events of the day must be covered as well as what is coming up and needs to be assigned. The photo editor makes the assignments to the photographers on staff or to freelance photographers with whom the organization has a relationship. The photo editor gives instructions to the photographer, generally based on information from the editors and/or the reporters working on the story. Instructions should be as clear as possible and include all information needed for contacts on the assignment. The photographer needs to understand the story in order to get the specific photos that work with the story. Suppose your school's girls' tennis team is on a winning streak and you want a story and photograph for the front page. A photographer needs more than instruction to "shoot the tennis team" in order to make images that go with the story.

If there is time, the sports editor, sports reporter, photo editor and photographer should meet to talk about the photographic possibilities. The reporter should alert the photographer to any star players. The photographer should ask questions. Does the star player have a routine she follows before hitting the court? Does she have a signature move, such as a two-handed backhand, that helps her win? Any such specifics help the photographer look for images that will supplement the story.

How you set up the photo staff for your student news organization probably will be depend on the number of photographers you have and their experience level. But it will be most efficient to have the photographers work independently of the section editors, reporting to a photo editor for assignments.

PREPARING TO SHOOT

When it comes to assignments, photojournalists act no differently than their word counterparts. They prepare. They get their equipment in order, including all lenses, filters, batteries, lights, film, extra film and anything else they may need. Some photographers travel with a small tape or digital recorder and ask their subjects to spell their names and say their titles into it. Others use a reporter's notebook to take names and other pertinent information.

Reporters call the contact on the assignment to make an appointment if the assignment requires setup. If reporters have an assignment to shoot an event, they arrive early so they can determine the kind of angles, action or group shots they might get, what kind of access they will have, and what lenses and lighting they will need.

© Photodisc/Jupiter Images

////// *Why should photojournalists arrive early for assignments to shoot an event?*

Getting cutline information is as much a part of a photojournalist's job as taking the picture. Think about the five W's and H that reporters use to think through their summary lead. Get the who, what, where, when, why and how of the photos you take. Get names and spell them correctly. Get phone numbers so you can contact people later if you have a question. But don't rely on getting back to people. Get the information you need at the scene whenever possible.

checkpoint ✓

Who works on the photography staff of a news organization?

Photo Composition

Learning the basics of good photojournalism isn't difficult, but it is essential if you want your photos to look better than an average snapshot. Good images begin in the minds of photographers, but it takes practice and regular shooting to translate what is in the mind into print.

COMPOSE THE PICTURE

Just as the mantra of good writers is "keep it simple," so it is for good photographs. Here are some of the elements to a good journalistic photo.

- **A strong point of interest** The most important elements are forward in the photo; get rid of clutter.

- **Balance** Photographs need not be symmetrical. Asymmetrical often works best. Place your main object off center.

- **Framing** Fill your frame so there's no wasted space.

- **The rule of thirds** Think of your frame in thirds, horizontally and vertically, like a tic-tac-toe board. Put the subject at the intersection of any two lines.

- **Contrast** It can be found in light, color, size.

////// **How does this photo show contrast?**

- **Action**   Shoot verbs, not nouns.

- **Break the patterns**   Look at lines and curves; look for marchers out of step, swimmers on the block where one moves before the starting gun.

- **Point of view**   Look at your subject from an unexpected angle. Above? Below?

What "verb" does this photo illustrate?

Analyze these two photos in terms of the elements of good journalistic photos.

DECIDE ON THE PHOTO

Selecting a photo is a collaborative effort at most publications and is a useful exercise at your student publication. When the photographer returns with pictures from the assignment, the photo editor goes over them, picking the best ones from digital images on the computer screen or a **contact sheet** — a piece of photographic paper with the negatives printed on it at film size.

The photo editor will look for pictures that have active people in them, that tell the story well and give meaning to the story. The photo editor will be in touch with designers and will look for photos that will work with the layout, though often the layout is designed after a strong picture is chosen. Photo editors advocate for the photographers, lobbying the editors to give the photographers' work prominent play. Occasionally, the photo editor may have to **crop** a picture, which means taking out unnecessary elements around the edges to improve the visual impact of the photo without removing anything meaningful.

///// *Why do you think selecting photos is a collaborative effort at most publications?*

 **check** *point* ✓

List four elements of a well-composed photograph.

The Photo Essay

A **photo essay** is a series of photographs that tell a complete story instead of focusing on a single telling moment. Because photo essays take up much space in print, they are seen only occasionally, most often in glossy magazines. The Web offers unlimited space and can be a place for photographers to show more of their work. On the Web, photographers and editors may create a slide show to tell a story or show the most compelling stories.

WHAT IS A PHOTO ESSAY?

A photo essay can be a series of photographs in print or on the Web that show the progression of a story chronologically, or it may be a variety of pictures from a single event. A photo essay may be shot by one photographer or it could contain the photographs of several. A photo essay may come from the photographer's experience or be assigned by a photo editor. On one Election Day, The New York Times assigned photographers in cities around the country to shoot voters at the polls. The result was a story in pictures of the very different ways U.S. citizens cast their ballots. In other words, there are no rules when it comes to the photo essay.

Seasoned photojournalists have told stories of strife and hardship in compelling photo essays. When photo essays are done well, they may have such emotional impact that they impel viewers to action. Yet, photo essays are allowed to be light, to show humor, joy or achievement.

Your school has plenty of photo essays waiting to be shot. You could focus on an individual — an athlete, an academic whiz, a performer — and follow him or her for a "day in the life" series of photos. It might require getting up at 5 a.m. to shoot your athlete in training or being awake at 2 a.m. to catch the academic whiz still studying. Yearbook photographers in particular may want to think about shooting assignments as photo essays when they have space and time.

checkpoint

What is a photo essay?

Digging Deeper

Roddy Scott, Freelance Photojournalist

Photojournalists often find themselves in harm's way. One such journalist was Roddy Scott, a London-based freelance photographer. He earned praise for his work in dangerous, war-torn countries such as Albania, Kosovo, Palestine, Sierra Leone, Ethiopia and Chechnya.

When Roddy's body was found among 80 Chechen fighters by Russian troops at Ingushetia, journalists were divided on how far Roddy went to get the story. Some lauded his courage, and others criticized him as being naive. Some felt his decision to join the rebels was "suicidal and crazy." Roddy was a tough, experienced traveler and journalist. He believed that journalists must see things for themselves in order to report the news accurately. Access www.cengage.com/school/langarts/journalism and click on the link to Chapter 14. Read Pat Lancaster's article "The Middle East" about Roddy Scott, and then answer the questions below.

THINK *Critically*

1. Why did Roddy insist on being in the middle of the action he was reporting on?

2. How could Roddy have gotten an accurate story and remained safe?

Source: Lancaster, Pat. "A war correspondent of 'the old school'. (The Last Word)." The Middle East Nov. 2002: 66. Global Issues In Context. Web. 28 Aug. 2011.

14.2 | Assessment

Understand Concepts

Determine the best answer for each of the following questions.

1. To take out unnecessary elements in a photograph is to
   a. make a photo essay.
   b. use a cutline.
   c. crop a photo.
   d. create a storyboard.

2. A series of photographs that tell a complete story is called a photo
   a. cutline.
   b. caption.
   c. narrative.
   d. essay.

3. A piece of photographic paper with the negatives printed on it at film size is called a
   a. contact sheet.
   b. cutline.
   c. crop.
   d. storyboard.

4. **True or False** Photo editors advocate for photographers.

5. **True or False** Photo editors choose the best photos from those submitted by the photographers.

6. **True or False** Point of view is an element of photo composition.

7. **True or False** There are strict rules that must be followed when creating a photo essay.

Write Now!

Practice your writing skills with the following activities.

8. Choose a story in your school that is of interest to you and to other students. You will need to choose a story that requires both research and interviews with people in your school and a story that would be enhanced by good photographs. Plan and write questions for your interviews and in-depth research. Locate information sources such as past interviews, Internet reports and other news stories. Evaluate and confirm the validity of your background information from a variety of sources. Plan, draft and write a news story, with a headline and photos with cutlines. Incorporate direct and indirect quotes in your story. Revise your draft using proofreading symbols.

The Role of the Photojournalist

Goals

- Identify the equipment you will need.
- Explain storyboarding.

Key Terms

- storyboard 365

FOCUS

Jonathan has been shooting still pictures since he took a photography class in summer camp during junior high. He's also been the family cameraman, shooting video at gatherings for birthdays, Thanksgiving or winter holidays since he was old enough to wield the hand-held video camera. He's not sure which type of shooting he likes better — that of the still or the moving image — but he knows that media jobs today will allow him to do both.

A Photographer's Expanding Role

As you learned earlier in this chapter, photojournalism has traditionally meant the practice of using still photography to tell stories. News outlets are redeveloping, rethinking and reinventing their organizations, so it is no surprise that photographers are taking on different types of image making and using new media to tell their stories.

CHOOSE YOUR EQUIPMENT

Photographers today have camera bags filled with more gear than they did just a decade ago. When they go out on assignment, whether it is for breaking news or features, they are likely to have their digital camera and lenses, a light handheld video camera with a handheld microphone, a laptop computer or a tablet on which they can send digital photos and video files to editors at the office, and a cellphone to keep in touch. Photojournalists have moved from film to digital cameras. They have added video cameras and computers. Their work is seen in print, on websites and on television.

How can you as a beginning photographer make the best decision about what type of camera to buy? Start by asking yourself these crucial questions:

1. What type of photos will I be taking (sports, portraits, still life or landscape)?

2. What are the lighting conditions in which I will be taking photographs (low light, outdoors or indoors)?

3. Will I be shooting mostly in the camera's automatic mode, or will I want to learn the finer points of shooting in all-manual mode?

4. How important are the camera's size and portability to me?

5. How much money do I have available to spend?

Once you've answered these questions, you need to do some research. Many websites offer competent reviews, user forums for users and examples of photographs taken with various cameras.

A beginning high school photographer should consider starting with an automatic "point-and-shoot" camera. However, if photography continues to interest you, then you should consider investing in an SLR camera and enrolling in a photography class. An SLR camera has changeable lenses and will give you more creative control over your photos. It also will allow you to shoot in formats such as TIFF and RAW.

STORYBOARD TO INCLUDE ALL ASPECTS

If the story they are covering is not breaking news, photographers can plan the still and moving pictures they would like to get. Of course, they can't know for sure what they will get until they are on the scene, but there is always value in thinking an assignment through before taking off for the scene. They may work with the photo editor and story editor to storyboard the elements they want in each medium. A **storyboard** is a visual outline of the vision you have for print, Web and other media.

checkpoint ✓

What equipment do photojournalists carry?

14.3 | Assessment

Understand Concepts

Determine the best answer for each of the following questions.

1. **True or False** Storyboarding is a print outline of the story.

2. **True or False** Modern photographers must be ready to shoot both still photos and videos.

Write Now!

Practice your writing skills with the following activities.

3. Choose a story from your local or school newspaper that does not have a photo. Make a list of three photo ideas for the story.

Review Journalism Concepts

14.1   What Is Photojournalism?

Photojournalism is visual reporting of facts and truths. It is telling news and feature stories through photography and telling them with the same objectivity, accuracy and fairness required of all journalists. Photojournalism uses pictures to document stories. Photographs have cutlines, the text that explains the images.

Traditionally photojournalism referred to still photographs, one-frame images taken on film or digitally. Today photographers also work with multimedia tools to create video journalism, or using video to tell the story. Reporters who tell stories with their cameras are called photojournalists. These reporters know how to use their cameras and all the technical aspects of photography; plus, they must go to where the story is. Often the story is in a dangerous place. Photojournalists are always in search of a found situation, an event or scene they come across by accident that can make a good photograph.

14.2   Working as a Photojournalist

The structure of photo operations in a news organization must accommodate multimedia assignments and teamwork. The photo staff is headed by a photo editor. Staff photographers are the shooters, the ones who take the pictures, get information needed for the cutlines, and process the prints or upload the photos. Photo assignments are instructions to the photographers. Good journalistic photography begins with good photographic composition; however, photo editors may crop photos to remove unnecessary elements.

A photo essay is a series of photographs that tell a complete story. The story can be told in photographs that show the progression of a story chronologically, or a variety of pictures from a single event.

14.3   The Role of the Photojournalist

Photojournalists have camera bags filled with gear that may include a digital camera with lenses, a video camera and microphone, and a laptop computer. Their work is seen in print, on websites and on television. Unless the story is breaking news, photojournalists may storyboard their work. Storyboarding is a visual outline of the vision the photographer has for the photo story.

Develop Your Journalism Language

Write the letter of the term that matches each definition.

_____ 1. A visual outline of the vision the photojournalist has for the story

_____ 2. A series of photographs that tell a complete story, not just a telling moment

_____ 3. A piece of photographic paper with the negative printed on it at file size

_____ 4. A photo opportunity that photojournalists come across by accident

_____ 5. A photojournalist who takes video

_____ 6. A one-frame image taken on film or digitally

_____ 7. Head of the photography staff

_____ 8. Take out unnecessary elements to improve the composition of the photo

_____ 9. Words under the photo

_____ 10. Reporter with a camera

_____ 11. Visual reporting of facts and truths

_____ 12. The art of telling the story with video

a. contact sheet
b. crop
c. cutline
d. found situation
e. photo editor
f. photo essay
g. photojournalism
h. photojournalist
i. still photograph
j. storyboard
k. video journalism
l. videographer

13. The photojournalism profession is changing and embracing new technologies, but this traditional type of photography continues to play an important role in journalism.
   a. storyboarding
   b. still photography
   c. video journalism
   d. photo essays

14. When a photojournalist comes across an event or scene that makes for a good photo, it's called a
   a. cutline
   b. photo assignment
   c. crop
   d. found situation

15. Which is the photography staff's liaison with the news, feature, sports, and any other departments necessary to producing news?
   a. photo editor
   b. staff photographer
   c. photo assigner
   d. photo essayists

16. To __?__ a photo means to remove all unnecessary elements.
   a. videograph
   b. cutline
   c. crop
   d. storyboard

Think Critically

17. How do photos make news stories more powerful for readers?

18. Why is photojournalism called the visual documentation of history?

19. Why is it important for photojournalism to change with the times and use multimedia?

20. Why do photo editors look for compelling photos for the front page of their newspapers?

21. Why are cutlines added under a photo in a story?

22. How is photojournalism different from other types of photography, such as fine art or documentary photography?

23. How is video journalism different from traditional photojournalism?

24. Why must photojournalists know how to use both still and video cameras?

25. Why are photojournalists called reporters with cameras?

26. Why do photojournalists sometimes need to go to dangerous places?

27. Why must photojournalists have their camera gear ready at all times?

28. Why do staff and freelance photographers need photo editors?

29. Why are photojournalists concerned about obtaining the five W's and H?

30. What does "show verbs, not nouns" mean?

31. How does a contact sheet help photo editors?

32. Why should photographers make sure their equipment is always in good working condition?

33. How does storyboarding help photographers and photo editors plan the photos?

Make Academic Connections

34. **PHOTOGRAPHY** Choose three photo subjects of your choice and shoot a series of photos of each subject. Each photo series should be different. For example, you might take photos of a person, of nature and of an animal. Choose one photo from each series. Write a headline and a feature story that shares the story behind each photo. Write a a cutline for the photos. Send each story with a headline, photos and cutlines to your teacher electronically.

35. **HISTORY** Use your research skills to research and identify the development of American photojournalism through people and events. Plan, draft and write a paper that describes your findings. Carefully examine and edit your paper for clarity, engaging language, and the correct use of the conventions and mechanics of written English.

36. **ECONOMICS**   Use your research skills to obtain the starting salaries of three photojournalists in major news organizations and in the news organizations in your community. Make a chart of starting salaries.

37. **CAREERS**   Choose something that interests you, such as sports or theater. Research the careers of photojournalists who specialize in that subject. Create a fact sheet that includes information about the publications they shoot photos for and the education, or knowledge, they need in addition to photojournalism. For example, if you want to write about sports, it would be helpful to know about all sports, the top players and the rules of the sports. For theater, you need to know about actors, directors, playwrights and other people associated with the theater.

38. **SOCIAL STUDIES**   Test how well you can understand a story just by the photographs. Use the Internet to look at a story with photos. Do not read the story. Using only the photos, write a short summary of what you think the story is about. After you have completed your summary, read the story to see how close you came.

39. **ART**   Using computer graphics and other art supplies, create a bulletin board that identifies and describes the elements of composing a photo. Include "keep it simple" as the first element.

40. **WRITING**   Write a journal entry that describes how you feel about a possible career as a photojournalist. Is this something you would enjoy? Why or why not? What most excites you about photojournalism? What least excites you? If you chose to be a photojournalist, which type would you be? A sports photographer? A news photographer? A foreign war photographer?

Writing Portfolio Activity

41. Give yourself a photo assignment for a photo essay, such as of how young people spend a typical day. Spend a day taking photos for the photo essay. Choose the ones you think best tell the story. Write cutlines. Add your photo essay to your portfolio.

AP Stylebook Workshop

Following AP style guidelines, use the correct punctuation and abbreviations of titles with names.

42. The Reverend Maurice Mueller gave the keynote speech at the conference.

43. Doctor Smith wrote a prescription for her patient, Mrs. Yolanda Terry.

44. Martin A. Sanders, senior, won the award for the best photograph of the year.

45. Governor John Lawrence junior was a photographer before entering politics.

CREATIVITY AND INNOVATION: Think and Work Together Creatively

Award-winning photojournalists know the secrets of producing well-received photos. They have learned to use creativity and innovation in their work, and how to successfully work with others. These attributes, to

- Think creatively
- Work creatively with others

will help you as a high school student as well as in your future career. Let's look at each in more depth to see how it will help you succeed.

THINK CREATIVELY

Creative thinkers use different techniques to help them come up with different ideas. For example, they may brainstorm ideas for photos for a story. Or, they may daydream what shots would be worthwhile taking. They study the photos of a wide variety of newspapers, news magazines and online news sources. And, they keep their eyes always on the alert for those found situations.

Don't be afraid of suggesting new story ideas, even ones that may seem a bit radical. A story that may not work for the high school paper might fit perfectly into the high school magazine format.

Don't be afraid to change your mind. Constantly analyze, evaluate, elaborate and refine your ideas. Always strive to improve on your ideas.

Trust yourself and your own instincts and intuition. If you see a photo you think is good, shoot it. If you have an idea for a story or for a photo essay, pitch it. Your ideas may not always be approved, but don't let that stop you. People who think creatively know that the next story or photo essay idea may be the one that is picked up for development and publication.

WORK CREATIVELY WITH OTHERS

News organizations, including the one in your high school, have editors. To be successful, you must be able to work with editors, reporters, photographers, copy editors and everyone else who handles your story. Photojournalists do not work alone to produce a story.

To successfully work with your journalistic team, you must be able to develop, implement and communicate your ideas effectively to the team members. Your idea may be yours and you want to run with it, but it's not quite right for the news organization, so changes are suggested. You must be open and responsive to the new perspective and be able to incorporate the team's feedback into your work. It's important that you are able to demonstrate creativity and your inventiveness in your work while, at the same time, also understanding the limits of the news organization.

Not every photo and not every story you pitch will be accepted for publication. To be successful, you need to view failure as an opportunity to learn. In your career, you will most likely have times of success and times of failure. Creative thinkers are able to step back and take a longer view to see that success is a process of many smaller steps, and many of the smaller steps are failures from which they were able to learn.

THINK *Critically*

How creative are you? How well do you work creatively with others? Spend time thinking about these two questions, and then write the answers on a sheet of paper. On another sheet, write the ways in which you could become more creative and innovative and ways you could work more creatively with others.

REAL PEOPLE REAL CAREERS

Robert Hanashiro | Photojournalist

Photographers working for modern news organizations often are called by other names — visual storytellers, visual journalists and content producers, among them. Robert Hanashiro hates those names. "We are still photojournalists," says Hanashiro, a USA Today photographer based in Los Angeles.

He acknowledges that "the Internet has opened up a lot of different ways of telling our readers stories, and I really think that's great." He has captured audio to go with slide shows and shoots video too. "I enjoy and appreciate both," he says. "My biggest concern . . . is that added responsibilities like capturing audio can hurt the photography. Photography can be a powerful way to tell a story and I hate to see juggling audio and video take away from that."

Hanashiro knows a thing or two about powerful pictures. He shoots a wide variety of them. "Spending a morning shooting one of USA Today's teachers of the year on Tuesday, a portrait of actor Ben Stiller on Wednesday, and then an NBA game on Thursday keeps me on my toes," he says. Without a doubt, Hanashiro says, sports photography is his favorite. "The athleticism, emotion and excitement of sports, whether it's the Olympics or a Friday night high school football game, still give me goose bumps." His love of sports goes back to high school in Fresno, Calif., where he was editor of the school newspaper and worked on the yearbook. He wanted to be a sports writer and went to California State University, Fresno. "Photography was always a hobby and I sort of drifted into that in college and settled on making that my career when I was able to get onto the campus daily newspaper staff as a photographer when I was a sophomore."

He started down the path to journalism long before that, however. "My father owned a small weekly newspaper just outside of Fresno, so I guess I've always had printer's ink in my veins," Hanashiro says. "My earliest memories of my dad, Seico, are of him sitting at a Linotype machine banging out copy for the paper."

TAKING A PICTURE VS. TELLING A STORY

Hanashiro defines a photojournalist as "a journalist who utilizes photography to tell stories." He says a great photograph "makes you look at it a long time. It makes you think. It makes you emotional, whether it's a laugh, a tear, or it makes you angry." To get those great pictures photojournalists have an instinctive great "eye," Hanashiro says, and also have traits such as "curiosity, fortitude, quick thinking, getting along with all people, knowing when and when not to cross the line and being a bit of a risk taker."

Anyone can learn to use a camera, and technology has made it easier to take pictures, Hanashiro says. However, "there is a big difference between 'taking a picture' and telling a story with a picture. I see way too many button-pushers out there these days, people who can utilize the technology like auto-focus, auto-exposure, 10-frames-per-second motor drives and zoom lenses. But as far as I know there isn't a 'decisive moment' button on these new high-tech cameras."

Source: Personal interview with Robert Hanashiro.

THINK *Critically*

1. Why do you think Hanashiro dislikes names such as visual storyteller and content producer?

2. What is Hanashiro's description of a great photo? What is yours?

15 Design

USA Today: Designed for Readers

USA Today may not be every journalist's or reader's cup of tea. However, no one will argue that it was the first newspaper to be edited and designed for readers and that it has had lasting impact on newspaper design.

In its first edition on Sept. 15, 1982, USA Today used bold design and rich color to announce that it would indeed be a different product from anything readers or other journalists had ever before seen. It had short stories and a variety of graphics and a full-page color map of the U.S. with weather from all over the country. It was designed for a generation that had grown up with television news. Even the newspaper boxes on the street looked more like TV sets than newspaper racks.

In the more than 25 years since its creation, USA Today has tweaked its design and editing strategy to keep up with modern thinking and created complementary designs for its website and mobile applications. In a challenging time for news organizations, USA Today has continued to use design to build recognition of its brand and take readers from print to other platforms.

THINK *Critically*

1. How was USA Today different from other newspapers when it appeared in 1982?

2. Why do you think USA Today designers created similar looks on the website?

Get Readers Into the Story

Goals

- Identify points of entry.
- Explain how points of entry help get readers into the news story.

Key Terms

- visual journalism 373
- design 373
- points of entry 373
- breakout box 374
- sidebar 375
- chart 375
- locator map 376
- informational graphics 376
- cutline 377
- primary headline 378
- secondary headline 378

FOCUS

If you look at newspapers and magazines from the early part of the 20th century you will notice that the publications are black and white and very gray. Big, bold, black headlines were the only way newspaper editors had to grab readers' attention and direct it to the most important story. Contemporary design — for newspapers, news magazines and the Web — is much more colorful and creative. Now, editors and designers work together to package stories in appealing ways, and they have many more tools and options than they had 25 years ago.

Design With Points of Entry

The design of a newspaper page often is called **visual journalism** because it involves all the elements of journalism — the stories, graphics, photographs, cutlines and headlines. **Design**, also called the layout when referring to a print product, refers to the plan of how the elements are presented on the page. Designers use all the elements to present a compelling package with lots of places for readers to get into the page.

Points of entry are the elements on a page through which readers enter. Think of points of entry as portals to the page you want your readers to read. Points of entry include stories, photos and graphics, as well as headlines, charts, breakout boxes, pullout quotes and more.

If you are designing a full-display page with more than one story on it, such as the front page of your school newspaper, you will be thinking about the points of entry. Imagine your editors have picked these four stories to display on the front page:

- Retirement of the science department head, a favorite teacher

- Profile on a foreign exchange student from France

- News story on the girls' basketball team, which has made it to the local championships

- Feature on students' spring break plans

Once you know the stories you want for the page, you will list the photos, illustrations, informational graphics and other elements that could become points of entry. In this case,

- A compelling photo of the science teacher conducting an experiment in class

- A snapshot-like photo of the foreign exchange student in front of a local landmark

- An action photo of the leading scorer on the girls' basketball team

- An illustrated list of the top 10 spring break destinations.

Next, designers and editors talk about story and art placement with an eye toward what points of entry they have and where each should go. Everyone agrees that the action sports photo is the best element for the page and it should be the dominant image. The story of the team's success is newsworthy and will go at the top of the page. As one more point of entry, the designer suggests a **breakout box** — a black-outlined box that is separate from the story — containing a schedule of the next games.

The spring break story may not be the "newsiest" of those on the story list, but it is fun to read. You and the editors want to put it at the top of the page. It has lots of students' names in it, is written in a humorous way and will surely get students talking. The graphic to go with it — an illustrated list of the top 10 spring break spots — helps the story, but you suggest that the photographer get head shots of two or three of the people quoted. A couple of small photos of classmates will draw readers into that story.

The story about the favorite science teacher retiring is what editors like to call "a good read." It is an interview with him about all his years of teaching, and it recounts some of the experiments for which he became well-known. To keep the story from getting bogged down in important but boring facts, the editors create another breakout box, this one with biographical information such as where the teacher went to college, how many children and grandchildren he has, and what his hobbies are.

Last is the feature on the foreign exchange student. Because the picture of her in front of the

© Digital Vision/GettyImages

///// **Why do you think the designers and editors agreed to place this action sports photo as the dominant image on the page?**

local landmark isn't as compelling as the other art, you all decide the story will go lower on the page and the photo will be the smallest of all the photos used. The designer has a good idea for making the photo a better design element. She adds a thin white border around the photo to make it look like a postcard instead of a routine snapshot. A headline mimicking postcard language, something like "Wish you were here," will make the story more attractive.

check *point* ✓

Name the points of entry you are likely to see on every newspaper page.

Present Information

You have heard the saying "think outside the box." Newspapers and magazine designers take it seriously — and sometimes literally. The object of good news design is to get readers to read the articles. Design is the presentation of information on the page. These days, when designers face a blank page on their computer screen they can choose from many elements to help them present information well.

GRAPHIC ELEMENTS

Graphic elements used in the design to present information include breakout boxes, sidebars, bar charts, locator maps and informational graphics. Used effectively, these elements help editors, reporters, photographers and designers present pages that will wow their readership.

Breakout boxes are used to relieve the overall grayness of the type and to complement the other elements on the page. Boxed information should be short. It may be bulleted or otherwise set apart with a typeface that is different from the usual body copy typeface. Readers scanning the page may land on the box before they get to the accompanying story, so the information in the box should complement the story. Boxed information can go with long or short stories. The information in the box shouldn't be repeated in the story. Breakout boxes include sidebars, charts, locator maps and informational graphics.

Sidebars are stories related to a main story. Sidebar information can be presented in a box to make it easier to read, but it does not have to be. Biographical information often is treated this way. So are statistics for athletes, or credits for actors.

Charts are a good way to present comparative or statistical information. A **chart** is a graphic used to compare data such as amounts and percentages. Imagine you have a story on the number of students who graduated with honors, and you want to show how much the number has increased in five years. A bar chart, using vertical or horizontal bars to show the increase from one year to the next, gives readers a quick picture of the situation. Charts can be used in all types of stories, but stories with numbers to compare benefit the most from charts.

Locator maps, which help the reader place the geographic area you are talking about, also help readers get the picture quickly. Locator maps can be global or as local as a neighborhood.

Informational graphics are the visual display of information. They are the visual elements that tell all or some of a story. A locator map can be an informational graphic because it helps tell where the story is set. Charts are informational graphics that may help the reader understand the story more quickly. But informational graphics have become more sophisticated in the changing technological world that newspapers inhabit. Some in the newspaper industry believe graphics should be recognized, like photography, for Pulitzer Prizes, the highest award in journalism.

Informational graphics can illustrate a concept, as USA Today does frequently on the weather page. It has explained many a weather phenomenon, from waterspouts to hurricanes, with colorful illustrations and researched information. Websites now allow for interactive graphics. With software programs such as Adobe Flash, an illustration can become animated. Web users can run a mouse over specific elements and watch illustrations turn, or unveil a box with even more information.

Long stories may benefit from more than one graphic element. For example, you might see a way to use a box for information but also use a map to show the location of a story. You also might see a way to use a list and a map in a story.

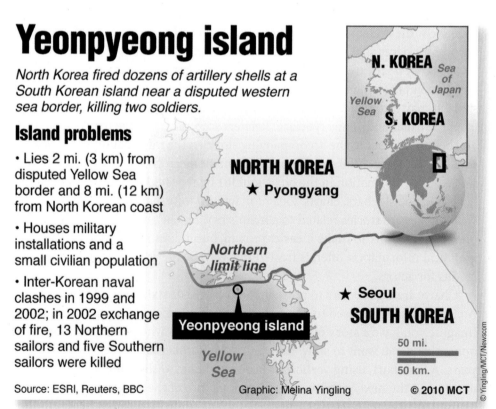

Yeonpyeong island

North Korea fired dozens of artillery shells at a South Korean island near a disputed western sea border, killing two soldiers.

Island problems

- Lies 2 mi. (3 km) from disputed Yellow Sea border and 8 mi. (12 km) from North Korean coast

- Houses military installations and a small civilian population

- Inter-Korean naval clashes in 1999 and 2002; in 2002 exchange of fire, 13 Northern sailors and five Southern sailors were killed

Source: ESRI, Reuters, BBC

Graphic: Melina Yingling

© 2010 MCT

Explain how the use of a combination locator map–informational graphic can enhance a news story.

Bee decline

Scientists now say one of the causes of colony collapse disorder (CCD), killing honey bees across the U.S., may be parasite-carrying honey bees from Australia.

Who's in the colony

Queen
• Fertile female, one in each colony; only lays eggs

Drone
• Male; task is to mate with queen, die shortly thereafter

Worker
• Infertile female; thousands in colony, collect pollen, nectar

Symptoms of CCD

• Failure to return to hive; no evidence of dead bodies

• Queen bee and adequate food supplies are left behind

• Other insects, predators don't immediately invade abandoned hive

Mix of causes may sicken bees

Pesticides	Stress	Parasites	Nutrition
• Variety of pesticides used in the different areas reporting CCD	• Strain from being moved long distances by beekeepers to pollinate crops	• Varroa mite, a bloodsucking parasite	• Fed corn syrup diet in winter
• Difficult to test for all possible pesticides simultaneously	• Sudden changes in time zone, climate	• Pathogen, Israeli acute paralysis virus	• Nutritionally inferior nectar and pollen of modified crops
		• Not all CCD colonies contain parasites	• Little variety in diet; colonies pollinate one crop

Source: Mid-Atlantic Apiculture Research and Extension Consortium
Graphic: Melina Yingling

© 2010 MCT

© Yingling/MCT/Newscom

///// *How would this informational graphic on bee decline enhance a story about this phenomena?*

PHOTOGRAPHS AND CUTLINES

Photographs are usually the most compelling point of entry on any page. They are dominant and strong, and for that reason get the most prominent place on the page. If you are designing a news front page, you probably will have several photographs to place as points of entry into the news package, but one will be more important than the others.

Cutlines, also called captions — the words under photos that explain who or what is pictured — work with the photographs but also work alone. Readers who are scanning may land on the cutline before they look at the picture. Cutlines are separate points of entry on which designers and editors need to work together. The words may be as cleverly written or as information-laden as the headline is. Remember, the words under the picture may be the words that help the reader make the leap from cutline and photo into the story.

HEADLINES AND TYPE

Primary and secondary headlines are points of entry almost as compelling as photographs. The **primary headlines** are the large, active, boldface headlines that state the story clearly and demand immediate attention. **Secondary headlines** are those on less important stories. They will be about half the size of your primary headlines and generally in a lighter typeface. Some feature sections and certain news stories might call for a fancy or unusual typeface, but for the most part designers recommend staying consistent with fonts and typefaces.

checkpoint

How do breakout boxes, charts, photographs and other points of entry help readers get into the story?

AP Stylebook Concepts

AP style tells us how to treat academic degrees. The preferred form is to avoid an abbreviation and use a phrase to explain.

Example My algebra teacher has a doctorate in mathematics.

Note that the abbreviation for "doctorate" is "Ph.D."

Use an apostrophe in bachelor's degree, master's degree, etc., but no possessive when using formal terms such as Bachelor of Arts and Master of Science.

Examples

I plan to pursue a master's degree in science after graduating from Harvard.

I plan to pursue a Master of Science degree after graduating from Harvard.

Use abbreviations such as B.A., M.A. and Ph.D. only when the need to identify many people by degree would make the preferred form cumbersome. Use these abbreviations only after a full name, and set them off by commas.

Example The presenters at the conference were Johann Smith, Ph.D., Theresa Mendez, M.D., and Irene Paris, Ph.D.

Editorial Ethics

The Photojournalism Code of Ethics

In the age of digital cameras and Adobe Photoshop, editing, manipulating and retouching photographs is easier than ever before. The possibilities raise legal and ethical issues for news organizations and credibility issues for individual visual journalists as well as the profession as a whole.

The National Press Photographers Association developed a code of ethics to promote high quality in all forms of visual journalism. The code says visual journalists and those who manage visual news production must uphold the following standards in their daily work.

1. Be accurate and comprehensive in the representation of subjects.
2. Resist being manipulated by staged photo opportunities.
3. Be complete and provide context when photographing or recording subjects.
4. Treat all subjects with respect and dignity. Give special consideration to vulnerable subjects and compassion to victims.
5. Do not intentionally contribute to, alter, or seek to alter or influence events.
6. Editing should maintain the integrity of the photographic images' content and context.
7. Do not pay sources or subjects or reward them materially for information or participation.
8. Do not accept gifts, favors or compensation from those who might seek to influence coverage.
9. Do not intentionally sabotage the efforts of other journalists.

THINK *Critically*

1. Why do news organizations need ethical standards for photographs?
2. Choose one of the standards and think of a specific example that relates to the standard.

15.1 | Assessment

Understand Concepts

Determine the best answer for each of the following questions.

1. The design of a newspaper often is called
   a. artistic news.
   b. journalistic style.
   c. the entry point.
   d. visual journalism.

2. The way that a reader enters a page is a
   a. point of entry.
   b. point of view.
   c. reference point.
   d. turning point.

3. Which of the following is NOT likely to be presented in a breakout box?
   a. contact information for an agency described in a story
   b. location and time of an upcoming event
   c. names of the people in a photograph
   d. other titles by the author featured in a book review

4. **True or False** Design and layout are synonymous.

5. **True or False** Once you know how you want the page to look, you can choose the stories that will work best with the design.

Write Now!

Practice your writing skills with the following activities.

6. Choose a feature story in your school or local newspaper. Think of a topic for a sidebar to accompany the story. Research the topic and write a sidebar related to the story.

7. Using your computer and desktop publishing software, prepare a page layout for a high school newspaper. Include the headlines and any subheads for the stories. Write the first paragraph of each story. Include the five W's and H in this paragraph or include this information in the photo or illustration captions. For each photo or illustration, create a storyboard that demonstrates how they have been cropped to communicate and emphasize the topic. In your newspaper page, include breakout boxes, with headlines; subheads, if appropriate; and cutlines. Send your newspaper page to your teacher electronically.

8. Write an article for your school's website about the weather in your area of the country. Use the Internet to obtain an appropriate weather map to include in your article. Write a headline for your article and cutline for your map. Send your article to your teacher electronically.

Collaborate on Design

Goals

- Describe who in the newsroom works together on story presentation.
- Explain the elements that make reader-friendly packages.

Key Terms

- package 381
- layout 383
- anchored 384
- banner 384
- ears 384

FOCUS

People who sell cereal, Barbie dolls and cars know how to make their products look inviting, pretty or classy so consumers will want to buy what they are selling. Newspaper design is about selling too. It is putting all the elements together into a single page, or package, that will make readers want to read it now and not miss a word.

Work Together

Journalism could be considered the ultimate group project. In today's busy newsrooms, editors, reporters, designers and photographers are encouraged to work together on story presentation from the time the story is conceived. That sounds easier than it is. Everyone in the newsroom is pressed for time with regular daily tasks, and many of those tasks are done alone — reporting and writing, for example, or copy editing. Working together on the presentation is in everyone's best interest because different people are responsible for the various elements needed to make pages pop. Those elements, when put together, are referred to as the **package**. Elements of the package include headlines, graphic elements such as bar charts and sidebars, photographs and cutlines and the story itself.

Here's how a collaborative effort might work at your school newspaper.

- A content editor assigns a reporter a story on the after-school job market in your community. The reporter begins researching and finds that the part-time, after-school job market is hot. A dozen kinds of businesses are in need of high school-aged employees and they offer after-school and weekend hours. The content editor envisions the story for the feature section front, so it's time to get a designer and a photo editor involved.

With computer spell check and grammar check programs, it's easy to get sloppy with usage, but good journalists also must be good writers. Even photo-journalists need to be able to write good cutlines. One major usage problem is confusing the words their, there and they're.

"Their" is a possessive adjective that modifies a noun. For example, "The reporters boarded their bus, which followed the presidential bus."

"There" often begins a sentence or it may be used as an adverb. For example, "There are two buses for the reporters, one here and one over there."

"They're" is the contraction of "they are." For example, "They're supposed to ride on the reporter's bus unless they have an interview with the president."

///// *Why do you think working together on the layout for a story is in the best interest of all the journalists involved in developing it?*

- The editors, designer and reporter meet to discuss the elements they can pull together to display this story effectively on a feature section front. The reporter has interviewed some students who work at after-school jobs, and the photo editor suggests several ideas for photos. With the reporter's help, the photo editor contacts the stores and the students who work there to get permissions and set a time and date to take photos. Then the photo editor assigns a photographer to take the photos.

- The designer, after listening to the reporter and the photo editor, begins sketching some basic ideas for a section front design. It's just boxes and squiggles drawn by hand, but it's a quick way of showing the reporter, editor and photo editor how things might work. They give the designer some immediate feedback and more quick drawing ensues.

- The designer asks the reporter if there is enough material to do a chart of the businesses by category most likely to employ students, such as retail, food service, child care, and home and garden help. They decide that can be done and they get busy working on a bar chart.

- Once all elements are ready, the editor, designer and photo editor talk again about the central point of the story and how they can best make it clear for the reader.

© Cultura/Jupiter Images

- The designer starts putting the package together, now on the computer screen. The elements include one dominant color photo of a student waiter, a secondary photo of a student helping a customer at a local bookstore, two cutlines, a chart showing where students can expect to find the most jobs, and, of course, the story, over which a primary bold headline asks the question "Want to work?" Then a secondary headline tells readers "Local businesses need high school students."

check *point* ✓

Who in the newsroom works together on story presentation?

Reader-Friendly Packages

Modern-day design, whether for the Internet or print, is all about making news easy and quick to read. Just as carmakers have come up with bells and whistles — such as in-car GPS systems and Bluetooth capability — to make consumers want their product, newspaper editors and designers also look for ways to stand out and make readers buy theirs.

DESIGN FOR READERS

Most newspaper editors would probably say they design their pages with their readers in mind. No doubt they want readers to feel comfortable with the newspaper, to recognize easily where their favorite features are located, and to find it interesting to read as well as to look at. You want that for your school publication, too. Yet most newspapers do little to make their product reader friendly.

What is reader friendly? Richard Curtis, the designer behind USA Today, had to figure that out more than 25 years ago. He said, "You can't have a well-designed newspaper without good stories." The newspaper might look flashy and interesting, but if it doesn't have substance it won't be a product readers will buy.

WHAT READERS WANT

In 25 years USA Today's circulation grew from zero to 2 million. It grew steadily when other newspapers around the country were losing circulation or shutting down, and while many in the profession of journalism were lamenting USA Today's supposedly terrible influence on the newspaper business as a whole. There are many reasons USA Today succeeded, but chief among them is that it was designed for readers.

Many newspapers have been incorporating reader-friendly ideas to try to reduce circulation decline. Among elements that work for readers are

- The **layout** or design — how pages are presented — is predictable and consistent. Give readers a familiar and easy-to-decipher look.

- Give your readers regular features — elements they can look for every day. USA Today has a cover story on each section front and a two-column news digest on the left of each section. Your publication can have regular features too.

- Regular features are **anchored**, or put in the same place, so they are easily found each day. Once you establish regular features, make sure your readers can find them.

- Stories are short or broken into multiple elements. Most stories should be short enough to require no jump, or spillover, to another page.

- Graphics — maps, charts, informational graphics and illustrations — are simple.

- The **banner**, the long space across the top of a page, and **ears**, space on each side of the masthead at the top of each section, effectively promote what's inside the paper.

As you look at the front page of your local newspaper or USA Today, think about what makes you want to read more about each story. Ask yourself the following questions: What are the points of entry? How do the primary headlines entice you to read the story? How do the secondary headlines? What information is in the banner and in the ears to make you want to know more? How do the photos and cutlines pull you into the stories? As you analyze the front pages of other successful newspapers and online news sites, you learn more about what works and does not work for your high school newspaper.

Following are some ideas you can use to improve the design of your school newspaper:

- More color
- More lists
- Fewer display stories on section fronts (and fewer jumps to another page)
- Shorter stories
- Smaller photos and more of them
- More digests, or compilations, of short stories
- Better headlines

checkpoint ✓

What elements of design do readers say they like?

15.2 | Assessment

Understand Concepts

Determine the best answer for each of the following questions.

1. Who assigns a photographer to take the photos for a story?
   - **a.** content editor
   - **b.** designer
   - **c.** photo editor
   - **d.** reporter

2. Who puts the package together on the computer screen?
   - **a.** designer
   - **b.** editor
   - **c.** photographer
   - **d.** reporter

3. An advice column that routinely appears at the top of the second page of the lifestyle section of a newspaper is an example of a feature that is
   - **a.** anchored.
   - **b.** balanced.
   - **c.** constant.
   - **d.** designated.

4. **True or False** Front page stories must be long enough to require a jump.

5. **True or False** Readers respond positively to the use of elaborate graphics in a newspaper.

6. **True or False** The designer listens to ideas from the reporter and photo editor before sketching ideas for a section front design.

Write Now!

Practice your writing skills with the following activities.

7. Use the information about reader preferences presented in this lesson to evaluate your school or local newspaper. Write a story about changes your school or local newspaper should make to address the preferences presented.

8. Choose a national newspaper such as USA Today or The Wall Street Journal and a news magazine such as Newsweek or Time. Plan, draft and write a paper that compares and contrasts the design of the newspaper and the news magazine. Cite the similarities and differences of the entire package, including the front page of the newspaper with the cover of the news magazine, the banners, photos and captions, breakout boxes, the length of the stories and so on. Edit your draft, using proofreading symbols, for clarity, engaging language and the correct use of English. Turn in your draft along with your final paper.

9. Use a digital camera to shoot a photo story appropriate for a high school publication. Crop the photos to communicate and emphasize your topic. Write cutlines that answer the five Ws and H for the photos. Use a computer grid to arrange the photos into an acceptable layout. Send your layout to your teacher electronically.

15.3

Design News Pages

Goals

- Identify principles of design.
- Apply principles of design.

Key Terms

- navigate 386
- hierarchy 386
- dominance 386
- rhythm 387
- grid 389
- digest 389

FOCUS

News organizations are made up of people who got into the business for different reasons and with different skills. Writers and editors may have entered the profession because they love putting words together. Reporters may have joined a paper because they are curious and love to dig up information. Photojournalists may have come to the organization because they see the world through pictures. For them taking photographs of news events is a way to show others those events. Artists and designers see news organizations as a place to practice their craft. Because creative design is encouraged by bosses and appreciated by readers, designing newspaper pages can be a satisfying career.

Basic Design Principles

Newspapers do not all look alike. That's because each news organization pays attention to the desires of the readers in the city or town it serves. There are, however, overall guidelines for designing newspapers drawn from years of trial and error, readership surveys and community feedback. Also, the overall look of newspapers has changed with technology and the competition that newspapers now have from television and the Internet.

Newspaper designers want to make their pages easy to read and **navigate**, or get around. To do that they follow these basic design principles:

- **Hierarchy** Establish **hierarchy**, which refers to the order of things, with the most important being at the top. Designers make clear to readers which story is most important. Don't give all stories equal weight or readers won't know where to start. Place the story in the spot in which readers will see it first, usually the top of the page, with a large, clearly written headline.

- **Dominance** Create **dominance**, or visual impact. Every page should have one dominant element, the most prominent point of entry for the reader. On most newspaper pages it will be a standout photograph, but it also could be a graphic, or a combination of a photograph and graphic. When deciding on a dominant image you are setting the tone for the page. If you choose a news-related photograph, you are telling the reader "this is a news page."

- **Contrast** Use vertical and horizontal elements, use primary and secondary headlines and vary color and tone. You might have a large dominant photo but you will contrast it with smaller photos for other stories.

- **Balance** Place elements so they don't appear bunched together or weighted on one side or the other. Some designers like the top half of the page to mirror the bottom half. Most important is not to make it look too heavy or light on top or bottom, or side to side.

///// **Why is this a good story to use at the top of the front page?**

- **Rhythm** In language, it means the irregular alteration of stress or pitch. In design, **rhythm** means irregular alteration of the design elements. Stagger pictures, headlines and subheads and you will help your reader move from one piece to another.

- **Unity** Use design to tie elements together. For example, cross column gutters with headlines or photos. Use similar colors or the same typefaces on stories that go together.

- **Consistency** Keep features that run every day in the same place. Byline type, headline fonts, section-front banners and mastheads should not change.

What are the basic design principles?

Apply Design Principles

In the whiz-bang world of new technology, it may seem that everything can be done by computer. What sometimes is forgotten is that vision begins in the human mind.

SKETCHES

When designers first hear editors and reporters talk about their stories and the extra elements that will go with them, they begin to see in their mind how they might present the package on a page. Many designers like to sketch their ideas by hand, often when they are still in meetings about the stories. They quickly put down on paper a couple of possibilities for their colleagues to see.

Richard Curtis, retired managing editor for graphics and photography at USA Today, says using sketches invites collaboration. He has sketched design ideas on tracing paper, memo pads, even paper napkins. He finds the editors and reporters are more likely to suggest changes, or even draw on the sketch themselves, if it is perceived as a work in progress.

Leon Lawrence III, design director for USA Weekend magazine, encourages editors with whom he works on regular features — such as the multiple-item Who's News page or larger pieces, such as the two-page cover story spreads — to sketch their ideas for him. Seeing the editors' sketches helps him understand how they conceived and assigned the story.

© Photodisc./Jupiter Images

///// *Why do you think it is useful for editors and designers to sketch their ideas for story layouts?*

COMPUTER LAYOUT

Eventually, designers translate their vision to a computer screen. The layout and design software provides a **grid** — a framework of lines dividing a page into standardized columns — on which to place the page elements. They will probably begin with the dominant image, placing it on the grid in the position that will best show it off. If designing a front page, designers will place the dominant image and story toward the top. They will make the headline on that lead story the biggest and boldest on the page. Once these are in place, designers will decide placement of other stories, photos and graphic elements.

Computers have helped standardize newspaper design. The technology makes it easier for reporters and editors to send to the designer all the elements they need. Templates can be established for regular features. Style sheets make it possible to standardize headlines and body type.

Your body copy is likely to be 9-, 10- or 11-point type in a Roman typeface with appropriate leading to make it readable. Your news headlines will be in type styles you have chosen for consistency. They won't change from one issue to another. On feature second fronts, or other stories with a feature bent, you might want to mix up type styles for contrast or just to be creative.

Graphics are good points of entry and helpful to layout. However, they should be used for a reason, usually to break longer stories into separate elements or to supply information pertinent to the story.

DESIGN TIPS

- Keep it simple. Readers consistently say they don't want to look at cluttered or overly designed pages. Suppose you have six short stories about club meetings and other after-school activities that you plan to put on an inside page of your school newspaper. Designing them as separate pieces with individual headlines will make the page look cluttered. Readers won't know where to begin. Instead, you decide to organize the information. You design the six single pieces into one **digest**, or collection of stories. You put them in a box under the heading "After-School Activities," and use subheads to identify each group. Now readers can easily tell what is in the box and pick out activities of interest to them.

- Use consistent typography. The more typefaces you use, the more confused your readers will be, so decide what fonts and typefaces you will use and stay with them. You will serve your readers better if you spend more time on what your headlines say than on what font they are in.

- Surprise your readers occasionally. Give them a photograph that's humorous, a headline that is truly clever, a graphic that explains a story simply. Suppose your best news photographer shows you an artistic nature photograph, an autumn scene taken in a nearby park for a photography class in the art department. Though it isn't "newsy" it will invite readers into a story you have on fall happenings around town. You might decide to make it the dominant image on the page.

- Make friends with reporters, editors, photographers and graphic artists on the staff so that collaboration is natural. You'll benefit from the ideas they bring, and they can help you get the elements you need — particularly graphics and photography.

checkpoint

Why should designers keep the newspaper design simple?

Digging Deeper

Visual Journalism

To be tops in newspaper design, a paper must find the perfect balance of words and visual elements on the page. As newspapers publish the news, trying to capture the attention of readers and engage them in the stories, they also know the Society for News Design (SND) is watching closely.

The SND is an international organization for news media and visual communication professionals who create print/web/mobile publications and products. The SND keeps a sharp eye on these media around the world, and once a year they host the Best of News Design Competition. Access www. cengage.com/school/langarts/journalism and click on the link to Chapter 15. Read the Gulf News article about awards in visual journalism, and then answer the questions below.

THINK *Critically*

1. What does Gulf News Design Director Miguel Angel Gomez describe as "efficient design"?

2. According to the article, what are the trends in newspaper design?

Source: "Thumbs up for visual journalism." Gulf News 16 Mar. 2010. Global Issues In Context. Web. 12 Sep. 2011.

15.3 | Assessment

Understand Concepts

Determine the best answer for each of the following questions.

1. A newspaper designer can create dominance by using
   a. mirror images on the page.
   b. staggered headlines.
   c. a standout photograph.
   d. a variety of typefaces.

2. Which refers to the irregular alteration of the design elements?
   a. grid
   b. unity
   c. rhythm
   d. package

3. **True or False** The development of basic design principles has resulted in a standardized look for most newspapers.

4. **True or False** Making friends with colleagues will help you collaborate on newspaper design.

Write Now!

Practice your writing skills with the following activities.

5. Choose a front page of a section of your school or local newspaper and draw a sketch for an alternative version of the page. Use the basic design principles and keep the design tips in mind as you create your page. Choose one story and add a standout element. Next, use a computer and software package that provides a grid to turn your sketch into a front page layout suitable for publication in a mainstream newspaper. Give your paper sketch to your teacher, but send your layout, with stories and other elements in place, to your teacher electronically.

6. Research a foreign online news source. If English is your second language, choose a news source in your first language. If English is your first language, choose a news source written in English, such as a source from Australia, Ireland, England, Scotland or Wales. Study the design of the home screen of the website. Plan, draft and write a paper that compares and contrasts the design of the foreign news site's home screen with an American news site's home screen. Using proofreading symbols, edit your paper for clarity, engaging language and correct English. Turn in your draft with your final paper.

Review Journalism Concepts

15.1 Get Readers Into the Story

Design, also called the layout, refers to the plan of how various elements will get placed on the page. Designers use a variety of elements to present a compelling package with many ways for readers to get into the page. These points of entry include words, graphics, photographs, cutlines and headlines. Graphic elements used in the design to present information include breakout boxes, sidebars, bar charts and locator maps. Used effectively, these elements help editors, reporters, photographers and designers present pages that will entice readers and hold their attention.

15.2 Collaborate on Design

It is important to know how to work together on design. Although many tasks such as writing and editing are done alone, editors, reporters, designers and photographers work together to create a reader-friendly package. Working together is important because different people are responsible for the various elements needed to make pages pop for readers. Understanding what elements make reader-friendly packages helps everyone do his or her own job. Elements of the package include headlines, graphic elements such as bar charts and sidebars, photographs and cutlines, and the story itself.

15.3 Design News Pages

Newspapers do not all look alike, but there are basic design principles that can be applied when designing pages. Newspaper designers want to make their pages easy to read and navigate. The basic principles of design include hierarchy, dominance, contrast, balance, rhythm, unity and consistency. In addition, there are simple design tips that can be used to help produce reader-friendly pages.

Sketches are often used as a first step when applying design principles. Designers sketch ideas as they talk with editors and reporters about their stories and the extra elements that will go with them. Using sketches invites collaboration as editors and reporters suggest changes or even draw on the sketch themselves. After the preliminary work, designers translate their vision to a computer screen. The layout and design software provides a grid with standard columns to guide the placement of the page elements. Templates can be established for regular features, and style sheets help standardize headlines and body type.

Develop Your Journalism Language

Write the letter of the term that matches each definition. Some terms will not be used.

_____ 1. Active, boldface headline that demands immediate attention

_____ 2. Collection of stories

_____ 3. Get around

_____ 4. Headlines on less important stories

_____ 5. Irregular alteration of the design elements

_____ 6. Long space across the top of a page

_____ 7. Elements on a page through which readers enter

_____ 8. Order of things

_____ 9. Put in the same place

_____ 10. Space on each side of the masthead at the top of each section

_____ 11. A framework provided by design software for building a page

_____ 12. The design of a newspaper page

_____ 13. The presentation of elements of journalism on the page

_____ 14. Visual impact

_____ 15. Words under a photo that explain who or what it shows

a. anchored
b. banner
c. breakout box
d. cutline
e. chart
f. design
g. digest
h. dominance
i. ears
j. grid
k. hierarchy
l. informational graphics
m. layout
n. locator map
o. navigate
p. package
q. points of entry
r. primary headline
s. rhythm
t. secondary headlines
u. sidebar
v. visual journalism

16. A design where the top half of the page mirrors the bottom half is an example of
    a. balance. b. contrast.
    c. dominance. d. rhythm.

17. A graphic comparing data such as amounts and percentages is a
    a. callout. b. chart.
    c. data grid. d. pullout.

18. Which might a designer suggest as a point of entry that is separate from the story?
    a. banner b. breakout box
    c. ears d. grid

19. Which is also called a layout when referring to a print product?
    a. digest b. visual journalism
    c. design d. breakout box

20. Which refers to a visual element that tells all or some of a story?
    a. locator map b. sidebar
    c. chart d. informational graphic

Think Critically

21. Explain the difference between a breakout box and a sidebar.

22. How are the layout and the package related?

23. What type of informational graphic would you use to illustrate the path of a new bike trail that will connect a neighborhood park, a nearby lake and a community parking lot? Create a sketch of your illustration.

24. Why are there multiple points of entry on a page?

25. What is the purpose of a breakout box? Give an example of the type of information that is likely to appear in a breakout box.

26. What type of content might appear in a sidebar about the election of a new mayor?

27. What type of graphic element would you use to show the relationship between the number of people eligible to vote, the number of people registered to vote and the number of people who actually voted in an election?

28. Why would a newspaper include a locator map in a story about a chemical leak in a neighboring county?

29. What is the purpose of a cutline that accompanies a photograph? How do the five W's relate to cutlines?

30. Describe a situation when a fancy or unusual typeface might be appropriate for a newspaper headline.

31. Describe the relationship among editors, photographers, designers and reporters when working on a story presentation.

32. Explain why readers want regular features anchored. Give some examples of features that often are anchored.

33. Describe the ears of a page and give three specific examples of how they might be used.

34. What is a digest and why is it used? How might a digest be used in the business section?

Make Academic Connections

35. **HISTORY** Use your Internet research skills to find sources of information on the history of newspaper design. Plan, draft and write a paper that identifies the history and development of American newspaper design through people and events. Include information on how technology has affected newspaper design. As you gather background information, evaluate and confirm the validity of the information from a variety of sources. Be sure to edit your draft for clarity, engaging language and correct English. Use the review tool on your computer to make the corrections. Send the draft and final paper to your teacher electronically.

36. **CAREERS** Research the educational requirements for careers in design of newspapers and online news sites. Write a story suitable for your high school newspaper about your findings. In your story, include information on the different jobs in design of newspapers and online news sites, the educational requirements and the salary range. Include photos, with cutlines, and at least one breakout box.

37. **READING** Choose a traditional newspaper that also has an online version. Read the lead story in the print version and then online. Describe any differences between the stories and the informational graphics in print and online. Create a presentation of your findings. Illustrate your work with the printed newspaper page, or a photocopy, and a printout of the Web page screen.

38. **ART** Create a poster that illustrates the effective use of basic design principles.

39. **WRITING** Write a paragraph that describes how you feel about the need to collaborate with others in developing a story presentation.

Writing Portfolio Activity

40. Occasionally, newspapers publish special sections devoted to a specific topic. Some special sections, such as back-to-school sections, are published each year. Others are devoted to special events such as a community's bicentennial or the opening of a skateboard park. Special topics such as home remodeling, outdoor grilling or volunteering also are featured in special sections. Choose a topic for a special section and create a sketch of the front page of the section. Create a bulleted list of the items you would include in the package. Add the sketch and package list to your portfolio.

AP Stylebook Workshop

Correct the following according to AP style.

41. Our newspaper adviser is studying for a Master's of Science degree in journalism.

42. Ninth-grade teacher Jeanne Jones, chemistry Ph.D., has resigned to become a pharmacist.

43. Eight students said they intend to pursue bachelors degrees at State University.

COMMUNICATION AND COLLABORATION: Work on a Team

As you have read in this chapter, to be a successful designer — or other type of journalist — you must work as a team member. Good team members are able to

- Communicate clearly
- Collaborate with others

COMMUNICATE CLEARLY

To communicate clearly, you need to articulate your thoughts and ideas effectively when you speak to others. Also, you must be able to communicate clearly when writing emails and other correspondence. And you must have good nonverbal communication.

When speaking, think first. Speak with confidence and succinctly. Speak in a clear voice and loudly enough that everyone can hear you. When writing, carefully check what you've written. Reading what you've written aloud will help you hear errors. Be aware of your nonverbal communication — your gestures and facial expressions — when speaking or listening.

Communicating clearly also means that you practice good listening skills and are able to hear and understand what others say. Do not form an opinion until you hear what the speaker has to say.

You live in a global and technological world. To communicate effectively with other journalists and to provide the public with information, you need to be up to date on all the technologies available to you, and you need to be able to communicate with a diverse population in diverse environments. Being multilingual is an asset in journalism.

As a good communicator you will be able to use your skills for a range of purposes, including to inform, instruct, motivate and persuade.

COLLABORATE WITH OTHERS

Skills that will help you collaborate with others also help you as a student when working on group projects, as well as when working on a team as a student journalist. Collaborating means remembering that everyone is different and everyone on the team must respect each other's differences. It begins with the desire to get along with other team members, whether that team consists of other students or colleagues at a news organization.

Respect for other people and a willingness to take your ideas and allow them to be changed and molded by the group will serve you well when collaborating with others. Collaboration requires valuing the contribution of all members of the group and making compromises to achieve the common goal. For example, let's imagine you are the designer for the website of your high school newspaper. In the editorial meeting, you sketch a front page that includes breakout boxes, photos and six stories. The editor suggests that only five stories are worthy of being on the front page, which requires that you change your design. The reporter whose story is being cut disagrees and suggests that if you give the story a different placement on the page, the story will work. What should you do?

Good collaborators talk over decisions and find the solution that works best for the website, not for one individual. Collaborating also requires you to take responsibility for your part of the project.

THINK *Critically*
Write an article for a website about ways to communicate clearly and to collaborate with others as a student and as a student journalist.

REAL PEOPLE REAL CAREERS

Kat Downs | Information Designer

© Photo courtesy of Kat Downs

Kat Downs is an information designer and the editor for innovations in graphics at The Washington Post. As she puts it on her blog: "That means I try to come up with creative ways of using technology, multimedia and information graphics to tell stories." It also means she gets involved in some of the most important stories the Post has to tell.

Among her favorites is one called "The Cost of War: Coming home a different person," which was about soldiers returning from war with traumatic brain injuries. "It had interactive graphics as well as several videos and a photo gallery," explains Downs. "I worked on the project through the conception, storyboarding, design and build phases and I thought it turned out to be a very strong story that people really connected with. It's the kind of story that makes you feel like you are doing a service and that you're helping people understand the news in a new way."

Downs says being a visual journalist means she's working in a vibrant, fast-paced environment. "Traditionally, people have thought of journalists as writers. Now, we have dozens of different specialties to choose from: photography, development, design, production, mobile products, social media and more. We are all telling stories in different ways and finding an audience for it. Journalism isn't writing; it's storytelling. I'm really excited about all the new tools we have at our disposal and about figuring out how we will use them moving forward."

LESSONS LEARNED AT HOME

Downs first got interested in journalism as a teenager when she worked on her high school newspaper in Franklin, N.C. "I was a photographer, reporter and, eventually, a section editor. I loved every aspect of the newspaper production process and so when I went to college, I thought journalism would be the right major for me. I went to the University of North Carolina at Chapel Hill, where the visual journalism program is really strong."

But before she discovered journalism, she says, she was encouraged to be creative. "My mom is an amazing seamstress and she designed a lot of my clothes growing up. I ended up using that creativity in a different way by designing graphics and web presentations, but the essence is the same: building beautiful, functional things that people can enjoy."

As one of seven children — she has six sisters — Downs appreciated other lessons learned at home. "I'm the youngest in a big family," she says, "and so I always learned by watching and figured out how to get along with people and work together from an early age."

Source: Personal interview with Kat Downs.

THINK *Critically*

1. Why do you think that working together in a team results in better storytelling, particularly on the Web?
2. How is design different for a website than for a print publication?

16

Public Relations and Advertising

16.1 Write for Public Relations

16.2 Write Advertising Copy

Gulf Oil Spill: A PR Disaster for BP

On April 20, 2010, when the Deepwater Horizon oil rig owned by British Petroleum (BP) exploded in the Gulf of Mexico off the Louisiana coast, it was clear the global oil and gas company, headquartered in London, had a disaster on its hands beyond the physical one that would affect lives and livelihoods for months to come. The Gulf oil spill, which killed 11 workers and injured 17 more, was a tragedy for families who lost loved ones on the exploding rig. It also created a crisis for the tourism industry and other businesses in affected areas. But it was a crisis of image for BP, demanding a public relations operation that was ready to handle and control the damage. Unfortunately, even on the first day, as charges of wrongdoing began flying, the company's public relations (PR) department was slow to react. PR professionals, the people who create and protect a company's reputation, know that being prepared for such crises is critical and communicating truthfully is the best practice. They know that when a crisis does come, responding quickly to public concerns is one way to salvage a reputation. BP's team was not ready, and it may take a very long time for the company to recover consumer trust.

> **THINK** *Critically*
> 1. Why should a public relations department be ready to handle a crisis?
> 2. Why might it take BP a long time to regain consumer trust?

Write for Public Relations

Goals

- Define "public relations."
- Explain the elements of a press release.

Key Terms

- public relations 399
- publicist 399
- press release 400
- media kit 402

FOCUS

As you read through your Facebook feed on your smartphone one morning, you notice that lots of your friends are talking about a new restaurant next to school. Some say they read about it on the local newspaper's website; others say they heard about it on the radio. Everyone is excited because the restaurant is offering half-price sandwiches on opening day. You link to the restaurant's website to review the menu and begin making plans for lunch without a thought as to how the word got out so fast. How did it? You're about to learn all about how the word got out in this chapter.

What Is Public Relations?

Public relations, often referred to simply as PR, is the practice of presenting image and information. Individuals, businesses, government agencies and nonprofits are among those that might use PR specialists to advance or protect their reputations or seek advantageous media light.

People who work in public relations — **publicists** — are hired by businesses, colleges and universities, medical centers, individuals such as celebrities, governments and government agencies and other types of organizations to manage their clients' relationship with the media. Many large organizations have their own public relations departments. They employ a number of publicists to present and enhance their reputation and to build awareness about the company and products. Public relations agencies are usually independent of any one business or individual but may serve a variety of clients. In Hollywood, for example, there are agencies where dozens of publicists are employed to work with a variety of clients — actors, musicians, moviemakers and others with entertainment interests.

Public relations isn't journalism, exactly. But it is taught in college and university journalism departments and requires some of the same skills as those needed by journalists. It is a publicist's job to get information out to the public, just as it is a journalist's job to inform. To do that, publicists plan media campaigns, write press releases and scripts for video or audio releases, organize news conferences and often act as the spokesperson for the person, organization or business.

Publicists write press releases for a variety of reasons, including to announce the opening of a new business. In what other situations would a press release be needed?

THE PRESS RELEASE

One of the most important tools used by PR people is the **press release**. A press release is a story written by the publicist to announce to the press something newsworthy, such as a restaurant opening.

Press releases are written to get the attention of reporters, editors and producers working in news organizations. Publicists write press releases to

- Announce new products, such as a new music player or laptop computer, or the opening of a new business

- Announce a new service, such as home grocery delivery

- Announce an event, such as a rock concert in a local park

- Announce a promotion of an important business person

- Introduce an important person to the community, such as a new university president or high school principal

- Manage a crisis, such as a product recall or industry accident

- Inform the community of a new campaign or program, such as a bike-sharing or anti-litter effort

- Tell reporters about plans for a news conference

checkpoint ✓

What is public relations?

Write a Press Release

Writing a press release is similar to writing a news story in a number of ways. These include:

MAKE SURE THE LEAD HAS A CENTRAL POINT   Remember that your press release will land on the desk or in the email box of busy reporters and editors. They may not get past the first paragraph if you don't grab their interest immediately. Get to the point quickly.

USE FACTS TO TELL THE STORY   Good publicists use well-chosen facts to tell the story. Do not embellish or exaggerate the facts or you risk your own reputation for reliability. In a news release, as in a news story, you will use facts to make your point.

USE THE INVERTED PYRAMID FORMAT   A well-done press release mimics the news story format — put the most important information at the top, that of lesser importance in descending order.

USE AP STYLE   If you would like news organizations to use your press release almost as it is written, then show them you write like a professional journalist, in AP style.

AVOID JARGON   Write your press release as if it were going directly to a mainstream audience even if it is going to a beat reporter who understands your industry. The easier it is to understand, the more likely reporters will want to use it.

Press release writing is different from newswriting in these ways:

- When writing a press release, you tell one side of a story, yours. There is no expectation of objectivity or balancing another side.

- You may "spin" or present the information in a biased way that benefits your client as long as you use facts without exaggerating or embellishing.

AP Stylebook Concepts

The 2011 edition of the stylebook included a new section on food terminology. With the increase in food journalism and journalists writing in both new and traditional media, it was time for AP to set style on many terms.
Among the new foods included:

- sloppy Joes
- s'mores

Most food names are lowercase.

Example   apples, cheese, peanut butter

Brand names and trademarks are capitalized, but the food is not.

Examples   Tabasco sauce, Rice Chex cereal

Proper names or adjectives are capitalized, but the food is not.

Examples   Russian dressing, Swiss cheese.

Use lowercase, however, when the food does not depend on the proper noun or adjective for its meaning. For example, both words in "french fry" are lowercase because "french" refers to a style of cutting, not to France.

Readers of press releases expect the information to be slanted in favor of the organization or person. The purpose of a press release is to show the organization or person in the best light possible.

EXAMPLE OF A PRESS RELEASE

A press release is written from facts, and those following are about a local business that is opening a new store. Suppose you are a publicist for the business and must write a press release for the local media from these facts.

FACTS The company you represent, Super Sprinkles, is a locally owned cupcake business. It has been doing business in the suburbs of Springfield for five years. Super Sprinkles is opening a new cupcake store — its third — on Main Street in downtown Springfield. Its two existing stores are crowded all day every day. Super Sprinkles' most popular cupcake is the "Chocolate Explosion." It is chocolate cake and icing with chocolate pudding in the center. The grand opening of the new store is Nov. 15. Customers will get free samples and discounted prices on cupcakes. The owner, Barbara Johnson, says: "We are proud to be opening in downtown Springfield. We feel certain that a city store will do as well as the two locations in the suburbs. The cupcake boom isn't going away." Johnson, who is 35, grew up in Springfield.

Once you have the facts you will want to establish the goal of the press release — in this case, to inform the public that Super Sprinkles will have a new downtown store. The message that must come across loud and clear in your press release is that the popular cupcake store soon will be downtown. See the Press Release for Super Sprinkles on page 403.

////// *Why should you include a photograph of cupcakes — or even a cupcake itself — in the media kit for Super Sprinkles?*

WHAT IS A MEDIA KIT?

A **media kit** provides elements beyond the press release. It will include a press release and may also include still photography that could be used with a print or Web story, a video interview with a pertinent person, and a video that shows the product. The media kit might also include a sample of the product or a means to get a sample of the product, such as a coupon or ticket.

A media kit for Super Sprinkles might include:

- Still photography of cupcakes — including the signature Chocolate Explosion

- A photo of owner Barbara Johnson and a photo of the new location

- A video interview with Johnson and a video showing how a cupcake is make, from batter to bakery box. Videos can be used by broadcast and online outlets.

Press Release for Super Sprinkles
April 23, 2012

Contact: Barbara Johnson
Super Sprinkles
121 Main Street
Springfield, OH 45502
937-555-5555

Super Sprinkles Is Coming to Main Street

Super Sprinkles, the locally owned cupcake store with two successful

shops in suburban Springfield, will open a third store Nov. 15. This one

is at 121 Main Street in the center of downtown.

Customers will get free samples of cupcakes like the Super Sprinkles

signature "Chocolate Explosion" during the grand opening week,

Nov. 15-22.

Owner Barbara Johnson, who grew up in Springfield and opened her

first store five years ago, said, "We are proud to be opening in downtown

Springfield. We feel certain that a city store will do as well as the two lo-

cations in the suburbs. The cupcake boom isn't going away."

Your media kit also should include coupons for a free cupcake at one of
the existing stores so reporters will have an incentive to try the product before
opening. An ambitious publicist might have cupcakes, including the Chocolate Explosion, sent to the appropriate editor or reporter.

check *point* ✓

What is the difference between a press release and a media kit?

Truth in Advertising Is Required by Law

Do you believe everything you see in a newspaper or online advertisement? What about a television commercial? Advertising in the U.S. is required by law to be truthful under the Federal Trade Commission Act. It cannot be deceptive or unfair, and advertisers must be able to back up their claims.

The interpretation of whether advertising is deceptive and unfair is left up to the FTC. It says an ad is deceptive if:

(a) it is likely to mislead consumers acting reasonably under the circumstances, and

(b) the claim is important to a consumer's decision to buy the product.

For example, if an advertiser claims that his product is good for the environment and the idea that it's good for the environment is important to consumers buying the product — but there's no evidence that it is good for the environment — the ad could be seen as deceptive by the FTC (not to mention consumers).

The FTC says an advertisement can be seen as unfair if it causes, or is likely to cause, substantial injury to the consumer that the consumer could not reasonably avoid. Ads judged to be unfair often are thought to harm consumer health or safety, or even someone's bank account.

What penalties can be imposed against a company that runs a false or deceptive ad? That depends on the violation. The FTC or the courts have imposed such remedies as:

- **Cease and desist orders**   Companies have been told to stop running the ads, to substantiate claims in future ads and to pay a fine.

- **Monetary remedies**   Civil penalties range from thousands to millions of dollars. Sometimes advertisers have been ordered to give full or partial refunds to all consumers who bought the product.

- **Corrective advertising, disclosures and other informational remedies**   Advertisers have been required to take out new ads to correct the misinformation in the original ad, notify purchasers about deceptive claims in ads and include specific disclosures in future ads.

THINK *Critically*

1. Why do you think the government requires truth in advertising?

2. What are some ways advertisers may be penalized if they mislead consumers?

16.1 | Assessment

Understand Concepts

Determine the best answer for each of the following questions.

1. Which refers to the person hired by organizations and individuals to manage their clients' relationship with the media?
   a. public relations correspondent
   b. media consultant
   c. publicist
   d. public relations reporter

2. Which do you always want to do in a press release?
   a. Avoid jargon.
   b. Include photos, a video and sample.
   c. Exaggerate the facts.
   d. Open with a quotation that leads into the story.

3. **True or False** Although public relations isn't journalism exactly, it is taught in college journalism departments and requires journalistic skills.

4. **True or False** It is never a good idea to include a product sample in a media kit.

Write Now!

Practice your writing skills with the following activities.

5. Think of a celebrity whose publicist you'd like to be. Use the Internet to research the celebrity. Evaluate and confirm the validity of the background information in your research from a variety of sources. Write a press release about the celebrity on something he or she will soon participate in, such as a charity event, a new show or the release of a new song. Incorporate at least one direct quote. Revise and edit your press release using proofreading symbols. Attach your draft to your final edited press release for your teacher.

6. Write a paragraph that explains which you would rather be — a reporter or a publicist. Explain why.

7. Plan, draft and write a paper that discusses whether you think it is responsible or irresponsible media action to use press releases from publicists as sources for news stories. Provide specific examples where you think it is responsible for news organizations to use press releases and specific examples when you think it is irresponsible. For example you might say that it is responsible to report the opening of a new store, but irresponsible to promote a company's image. Edit your paper for clarity, engaging language and correct English.

16.2

Write for Advertising

Goals

- Define what advertising is.
- Explain how to write advertising copy.

Key Terms

- advertising 406
- copywriter 406
- logo 407
- tagline 407

FOCUS

Open your favorite magazine and you will find advertising throughout it. Some of the ads are as interesting as the articles. Advertisers want to be seen in publications that reach the audience most likely to buy their products. That's why women's magazines, for example, are filled with ads for beauty products and designer fashions. Teen magazines are filled with ads for clothes and hair products. Sports magazines are filled with ads for sports products. It takes clever, creative people to put together an ad that will make the audience want to buy the product.

What Is Advertising?

Some people confuse advertising and public relations. Both are about image and getting information to the public. But **advertising** is a paid medium whose goal is to move the audience to buy or do something. The ad's target is the audience that will buy the product, while a publicist's target is the media. The person who writes the ad copy is called a **copywriter**.

ELEMENTS OF AN ADVERTISEMENT

You want your ad copy to be powerful and persuasive. Each word has to work hard to get the message across. Most advertising will include

- A headline — the first line of copy the reader will see.
- A subhead — if needed.
- A photograph, graphic or illustration.
- Text (written copy), with a lead paragraph that gets the point across quickly.
- Request for action — asking the audience to buy, do, try or attend.

- The company **logo**, or symbol.
- The company **tagline**, a motto or slogan for which the company is known.

 checkpoint

> What is advertising?

Write Advertising Copy

Advertising copywriters think like journalists in at least one way — they want their message to be clear. Some years ago Nike, the sportswear company, developed a campaign around three words, "Just do it." The rental car company Avis, which was second to Hertz, developed a campaign around the motto "We try harder." The fast-food restaurant Wendy's suggested its burgers were bigger than the competition's with a question: "Where's the beef?" These are all clear — and memorable — messages.

Copywriters follow a few guidelines as they develop creative copy.

- **Hook the reader with a headline.** It's the first thing the reader will see. If you were writing an ad for Super Sprinkles you might write a headline such as "Super Sprinkles Cupcakes. Now Downtown."

- **Be free with adjectives and adverbs.** Super Sprinkles doesn't have just cupcakes — it has delicious cupcakes.

- **Every word counts, so choose your words carefully.** Advertising copywriters keep a dictionary and thesaurus close at hand. Maybe you want Super Sprinkles cupcakes to be more than delicious. How about scrumptious, tasty, yummy or even divine?

- **Show the benefits of what you are advertising.** Tell the audience why they need your product or company. Super Sprinkles cupcakes are a deserved treat and they are now even easier to find because there's a third location, in the midst of the city's workforce.

checkpoint

> In what way do copywriters think like journalists?

grammar tip

Capital letters are important to help readers understand the meaning of your words. Capitals are used for several reasons. They are used to begin a sentence. They also indicate the personal pronoun "I." For example,

> The copywriter and I worked together on the ad.

Capital letters also indicate proper nouns, names and titles. For example,

> The ad is for the Springfield Music Fest starring Mary Max, who will sing her hit single "Romance."

Digging Deeper

Truth in Advertising

How much leeway should advertisers have in presenting the human form? Off Our Chests, the online women's magazine and apparel brand, is lobbying to make sure that all photos of the human form that advertisers have modified in any way carry a label that discloses this fact. Access www.cengage.com/school/langarts/journalism and click on the link to Chapter 16. Read the Business and Finance Week article, "'Off Our Chests' Online Women's Magazine & Apparel Brand Begins Lobbying for Passage of the Self Esteem Act," and then answer the questions below.

THINK *Critically*

1. Do you agree with the Off Our Chest publishers that modified photos of the human form in advertisements should carry labels? Why or why not?

2. How great an influence do you think advertising has on our culture? In your opinion, is advertising a good thing or a bad thing for society? Explain your answer.

Source: "'Off Our Chests' Online Women's Magazine & Apparel Brand Begins Lobbying for Passage of the Self Esteem Act." Business & Finance Week 10 Sept. 2011: 17. Global Issues In Context. Web. 12 Sep. 2011

16.2 | Assessment

Understand Concepts

Determine the best answer for each of the following questions.

1. Which refers to the first line of copy the reader will see in an ad?
   a. subhead
   b. headline
   c. logo
   d. tagline

2. **True or False**   Advertisements always include a request for action — asking the audience to buy, do, try or attend.

3. **True or False**   In advertising writing, you have more space for words than you do in news writing.

4. Unlike reporting the news, in advertising writing, you can be free with
   a. nouns.
   b. verbs.
   c. adjectives and adverbs.
   d. pronouns.

Write Now!

Practice your writing skills with the following activities.

5. Study the ads in your high school newspaper and community paper. Notice that there are three types of ads — classified, display and public service. Classified ads are small ads in the back of the paper and used by individuals to sell items such as a computer and by companies looking for employees to fill job openings. Display ads are larger than classified ads and used to sell products for a company such as a retail store or car dealership. Public service ads (PSA) provide information to the community. These ads usually mention they are a public service ad. Write a classified ad for something you want to sell. Write a display ad for something the school could sell. Write a public service ad for an upcoming public event at your school.

Review Journalism Concepts

16.1 Write for Public Relations

Public relations, often referred to simply as PR, is the practice of presenting image and information. Individuals, businesses, government agencies and nonprofits are among those who might use PR specialists to advance or protect their reputations or seek advantageous media light.

People who work in public relations — publicists — are hired by businesses, colleges and universities, medical centers, individuals such as celebrities, governments and government agencies, and other types of organizations to manage their clients' relationship with the media. Public relations isn't journalism, but it is taught with journalism classes because it requires some of the same skills. One of the most important tools used by PR people is the press release, a story written by the publicist to announce to the press something newsworthy, such as a restaurant opening.

Writing a press release is similar to writing a news story in that there is a central point in the lead, there are facts that tell the story and the inverted pyramid format is used, as is AP style. You also need to avoid jargon. Press releases are different from news stories in that releases are slanted in favor of the organization or person about whom the release is written. A media kit provides elements beyond the press release. It may include still photographs, a video, and the product or a means to get the product.

16.2 Write for Advertising

Some people confuse advertising and public relations. Both are about image and getting information to the public. But advertising is paid messages and is concerned with sales — moving the audience to buy or do something. The ad's target is the audience that will buy the product, while the target of public relations is the media. A copywriter, who writes the ad copy, is advertising's publicist. The elements of an advertisement include a headline; a subhead, if needed; a photograph; text; a request for action; and the company logo and tagline.

Like news reporters, copywriters want their ads to be clear. Copywriters want to hook the reader with a head, be free with adjectives and adverbs, make every word count, and show the benefits of what they are advertising.

Develop Your Journalism Language

Write the letter of the term that matches each definition.

_____ **1.** A company's symbol

_____ **2.** A story written by a publicist to announce to the press something newsworthy, such as a new product hitting the market

_____ **3.** A motto or slogan for which the company is known

_____ **4.** Paid medium whose goal is to move the audience to buy or do something

_____ **5.** A writer of ad copy

_____ **6.** A person hired by organizations and individuals to manage their clients' relationship with the media

_____ **7.** Includes a press release and more, such as still photographs, video and a sample of the product

_____ **8.** The practice of presenting image and information

a. advertising
b. copywriter
c. logo
d. media kit
e. press release
f. public relations
g. publicist
h. tagline

9. Whom would you hire to write an ad to sell an online course?
a. copywriter
b. editor
c. publicist
d. reporter

10. Whom would you hire to write a press release about a new cafe opening across the street from your school?
a. copywriter
b. editor
c. publicist
d. reporter

11. News reporters and advertising copywriters are alike in that they
a. work exclusively in print.
b. mostly work as freelancers.
c. use a lot of adjectives and adverbs.
d. want their message to be clear.

12. News stories and ads both include a
a. logo.
b. tagline.
c. request for action.
d. headline.

13. Unlike a press release, a media kit
a. includes additional items such as photos, video and a product sample
b. is written by a copywriter.
c. is written in AP style.
d. contains information on a celebrity.

Think Critically

14. What might you include in a media kit announcing a new clothing store geared toward young people between ages 13 and 18?

15. Why might a government hire a publicist?

16. Why do you want to avoid jargon when writing a press release?

17. Why do you think press releases are written in AP style?

18. When would a company hire a copywriter and when would a company hire a publicist?

19. Why are public relations and advertising courses taught in college journalism departments?

20. Why should you put your central point in the lead of a press release?

Make Academic Connections

21. **ETHICS**   Advertorials are advertisements that read like a story. They mainly are found in magazines and online. Collect at least three advertorials from magazines and three from online sites. As you study the advertorials, ask yourself if you think most readers would be able to distinguish between a paid advertorial and a review written by a journalist. Plan, draft and write an opinion piece about your thoughts on advertorials. Back up your opinion with facts and distinguish between responsible and irresponsible action on the part of the news organization in printing advertorials.

22. **CAREERS**   Research the careers of copywriters and publicists. Create a fact sheet that includes information about education and skills required, salary and the outlook for job availability.

23. **WRITING**   Record a popular television commercial, and then rewrite it in your own words for a high school viewing audience. Next, rewrite the ad for your high school newspaper, and finally for a high school news website.

24. **DESIGN**   Use a computer grid to design a display ad for a product you use, listen to, eat or wear. Include at least one photograph and one illustration that have been cropped to communicate and emphasize your product. Prepare the complete layout of your ad for a high school audience.

25. **MARKETING**   Use your reporting skills to interview four business people in your community about their advertising. Ask questions such as how often they run ads, in which media they advertise, how they decide where to advertise and what type of return on their money they believe they receive for their ads. Collect copies of their ads or recordings of their broadcast commercials. Create a multimedia presentation about your findings and the conclusions you reached about advertising from your small sampling. Deliver your presentation to your classmates.

26. **ECONOMICS** Obtain information about the costs of printing your school newspaper, news magazine and any other school publication. Also obtain a copy of price list for the ads these publications contain. Include the cost of display and classified ads. Calculate the number of ads that need to be sold to reach the break-even point for each publication.

27. **POLITICS** Interview three adults in your community about how they think people's votes are influenced by political commercials on television. Compare and contrast their ideas along with your conclusions in a paper. Before you begin your interviews, plan and write relevant questions. Plan and draft your paper, and then revise and edit it for clarity, engaging language and correct English.

28. **SOCIAL STUDIES** Select a website from a foreign country that carries ads for a product that is also sold in the United States. If English is your second language, choose a site in your native language. If English is not your second language, choose a website in English. Find an ad for the same or a similar product on an English-language website. Write a feature article that compares and contrasts the two ads

Writing Portfolio Activity

29. Create a media kit for your high school that announces an annual event that celebrates your school, such as homecoming. In your media kit, include the following:

- A press release about the upcoming celebration and the highlights of the school. Include a headline and subhead.
- At least one photo that you took of the school buildings.
- A history of the school.
- A display ad for your school and the celebration that can be used in print and online.
- A 30-second video ad about the celebration that names the highlights of your school.

AP Stylebook Workshop

Capitalize, or do not capitalize, the following according to AP style.

30. The publicist had a sandwich and a pepsi for lunch.

31. She shared her french fries with the whole team.

32. The copywriters added swiss cheese to their salads.

33. The publicist sent sloppy Joes to everyone for lunch.

34. The publicist sent coupons for s'mores to everyone in the local media.

35. The copywriter wrote ads for tabasco sauce and russian dressing.

PRODUCTIVITY AND ACCOUNTABILITY: Manage Projects That Produce Results

Public relations and advertising are fast-paced, competitive businesses. To be a successful publicist or copywriter, you need to develop skills that will serve you well throughout your life. You need to be able to

- Manage projects
- Produce results

MANAGE PROJECTS

Whether working on a class assignment or a professional media kit, you need to set and meet goals for the project. For example, imagine you are assigned to write a feature for the high school newspaper, and your deadline is one week away.

You begin by planning your time — the time you need for research and the time you need for planning, drafting and writing the feature. You feel confident that you can easily make the deadline. And then your life turns upside down.

Your best friend has a crisis with her boyfriend and keeps texting you. The big game is coming up and you want to be at your best, so you step up your practice. Your mom is after you to clean your room. Your little brother fell and broke his arm and you have to watch over him. Suddenly the deadline that seemed so far away is upon you.

Good project managers prioritize, plan and manage work to achieve the intended results by deadline. They know that life hands you curves when you least expect them, so they plan on obstacles and competing pressures getting in the way. They always think of deadlines as being close and they get started, doing today what could be put off until tomorrow.

PRODUCE RESULTS

Consider the following guidelines as you manage public relations and advertising projects:

- Work positively and ethically
- Manage time and projects effectively
- Multitask
- Participate actively and be reliable and punctual
- Collaborate and cooperate effectively with teams
- Respect and appreciate team diversity
- Be accountable for results

When you work positively and ethically, you focus on how the project will work instead of how it might fail. You use good time management skills and are able to work on different areas of the project at the same time. For example, you can think about headlines and captions as you plan and take the photos.

When working on a team, you show up on time and let your team know they can count on you. You are reliable because you always produce your part of the project. You take pride in your work and in your participation in the team. You are kind to everyone on your team, and you show respect for all team members regardless of your differences. People want you on their team because they know you will present your ideas, while at the same time respecting and appreciating the ideas of your team members.

THINK *Critically*

Make a list of the attributes and skills you possess that will help you manage projects that produce good results. At the end of your list, note the areas in which you want to improve.

REAL PEOPLE REAL CAREERS

David Allen | Senior Manager of Media Relations for AARP

David Allen, senior manager of media relations for AARP, says he fell into his public relations career. "A colleague mentioned a job opening at an agency, I applied, and that was the beginning," Allen says. He may make it sound easy, but Allen was well prepared when that tip about a job opening came along.

© Photo courtesy of David Allen

He was an intern at a public relations agency for two summers during his years studying at James Madison University in Harrisonburg, Va. Among his responsibilities: preparing news briefings, which meant scanning top news sites and newspapers each day for clips related to the agency's clients and preparing a set of clips for team members. "Reading newspapers and news sites every morning definitely helped me become more familiar with reporters and how they wrote their stories, giving me a better sense of how to prepare pitches a bit later in my career," Allen says.

But Allen went to JMU for a degree in political science, a subject that had interested him since he was a child. "I was fascinated by President Carter, as he was from my home state of Georgia," Allen says. "That interest grew as I experienced the end of the Cold War, the fall of the Berlin Wall and the dissolving of the USSR."

Allen grew up in Atlanta, the third of four children in a multiracial family. As he explains it: "Three of the four children were adopted. My parents are Caucasian, my brother is their biological child, my older sister is biracial, I'm African American and my younger sister is Japanese." His untraditional family life presented an uncommon set of challenges and rewards, Allen says, "and I think it helped better prepare me for today's global society."

THE CHALLENGES OF PUBLIC RELATIONS

Today, Allen helps position AARP as the leading voice for Americans who are 50 and older. He works on health-related issues, "many of which are complex and not easy for anyone to understand," he says. But he's up to the challenge. In fact, he says he enjoys the "many facets of public relations — the challenge of pushing through the clutter to reach a reporter, the opportunity to learn about a number of different subjects, the interaction with people — all resting on top of the foundation of excellent writing skills."

Source: Personal interview with David Allen.

THINK *Critically*

1. How did Allen's childhood help him in his career?
2. How did reading newspapers prepare Allen for a career in public relations?

17

Yearbooks

17.1	**Plan and Organize the Yearbook**
17.2	**Report and Write Yearbook Features**
17.3	**Design and Photograph Images for Memorable Pages**
17.4	**Get Down to Business**

Using Facebook Photos in a Yearbook

Sometimes it all comes down to a deadline. That's the reason students at a Maryland high school cited to explain why they had published pictures downloaded from Facebook in their high school yearbook.

As publication deadlines approached, the yearbook staff did not have pages ready. They decided to use students' pictures from Facebook. But the staff didn't ask permission of the students whose pictures they used. The staff also neglected to credit the photos.

Some legal experts say images posted on the Web are not private, at least if judged by legal standards, because there can be no expectation of privacy on the Internet. Other legal experts say the images belong to the person who posts them and to the site on which they are posted, and taking them without permission is not legal.

THINK *Critically*

1. Do you think the yearbook staff had a right to use the photos? Why or why not?

2. Why do you think the law is hazy on who owns the rights to photos on sites such as Facebook?

Plan and Organize the Yearbook

Goals

- Draft a strategic plan and time the delivery of the book.
- Discuss effective methods for managing the yearbook staff.
- Use themes and ladders to help plan the book.

Key Terms

- strategic plan 417
- sections 418
- theme or concept 421
- ladder 422

FOCUS

Even as the world gets increasingly digital, the printed high school yearbook you get at the end of each year remains popular. It is a link to your past or, as one yearbook adviser calls it, a permanent record of your communal experience. Your yearbook may not cover all of your high school experiences, but it will showcase the highlights, such as the annual crosstown football rivalry, the annual musical and the debate team's big win. A yearbook is a history and reference book that requires a combination of news and feature reporting, photography and design. It is a record of the big moments, a directory of who was there and a peek at what your school culture was like during the year.

Draft a Strategic Plan

Organizations of all shapes and sizes usually begin a new project by drafting a **strategic plan**, a road map to achieving specific goals. A high school yearbook needs a strategic plan. For a yearbook staff, strategic planning involves deciding on a theme or concept, defining areas of coverage, scheduling deadlines, listing priorities, storyboarding and outlining the book, and deciding on staff members' responsibilities. A strategic plan is as an investment that will pay off in the team's unity and focus and, ultimately, a more successful yearbook.

Drafting the strategic plan may take several weeks as the whole staff gets involved. It takes organization and management to make sure the staff follows the plan and, of course, submits their assigned pages on deadline, but it will help if everyone is involved from the beginning.

ORGANIZE THE STAFF

The first step is to organize your staff, so you all know your roles and responsibilities. Knowing exactly what you are responsible for helps you focus. In your strategic plan you will have defined **sections**, or areas of coverage you want in the yearbook. Assign editors to be in charge of specific sections.

Recognize the strengths and interests of each staff member. Hold a staff discussion of members' interests and involvement in extracurricular activities before making section assignments. Also consider staff members' strengths and weaknesses as they apply to specific yearbook jobs. For example, assess who writes well and who is better at design.

Also recognize lines of authority, or who reports to whom. If people overstep their authority, disorganization may result. For example, a student life editor should not direct a sports staffer's story, because the sports editor's vision may be compromised and the staffer may become confused. Assigning authority to particular editors also helps keep a teacher-adviser from getting overloaded or making decisions students should make.

There are many ways to organize a staff, and your group will have to determine what is workable considering how many people you have and what your goals for the yearbook are. Here is a basic yearbook staff organization with some outlined responsibilities.

YEARBOOK ADVISER   Advisers usually are teachers who advise students in making decisions involving the content and financing of the publication. The yearbook adviser is in charge of instructing staffers on the basics of planning, writing, editing, design and photography. After helping students learn these skills, the adviser helps with problems that arise.

EDITOR-IN-CHIEF   Yearbook editors-in-chief are students who have ultimate responsibility for the development and content of the book as well as overseeing the total operation of production, finances and editorial policy. Sometimes they are chosen by a student publications board after an application and interview process. Sometimes a teacher or adviser makes the assignment. In some schools they are elected by their peers. However they get the job, editors-in-chief — and there may be more than one — generally work closely with advisers, who may guide them in decision making. Good editors-in-chief have the creative vision and management ability to keep people moving forward and the book on schedule.

BUSINESS MANAGER   The business manager oversees the finances of the yearbook. Publishing the yearbook costs

///// *Example of a Yearbook Staff Organization*

money, and the business manager helps find and organize ways to finance the production. Business managers organize, oversee and maintain accurate records for advertising and book sales plus any fundraisers.

SECTION EDITORS   Section editors oversee writers and photographers in developing the various sections of the book. They, along with other editors, make decisions about the section design and specific content. They are in continuing discussions with writers and photographers to be sure the vision of each assignment is clear. Once assignments are written, editors then edit assignments for content as well as style, grammar, punctuation and spelling.

PHOTO EDITOR   Photo editors are responsible for assigning photographers. They work with section editors to understand the assignment's requirements and with photographers to help them produce the best pictures possible.

PHOTOGRAPHERS   Photographers work with editors and staffers to plan coverage of the assigned event. They should carry cameras constantly so they are ready for candid pictures of student life and academics. In addition to taking photographs, photographers gather information for captions, including names that are correctly spelled, and a description of action in the photos.

GENERAL STAFFERS   Editors usually assign yearbook staffers to particular spreads. They communicate with their section editors about possible story angles. They also suggest information to include on the spread. They think more like magazine writers than news reporters because they cannot write a timely story. Still, they cover events in their entirety and apply journalistic principles — accuracy, fairness, honesty — to their reporting.

TIME THE DELIVERY

Yearbooks generally are delivered in either spring or summer/fall. A yearbook covers an entire year, so the delivery date is important.

SPRING DELIVERY   These books are delivered before the school year ends. The final deadline for content is usually sometime in March. For spring-delivery books, the staff needs to determine how to cover spring activities. Some yearbook companies now offer digital enhancements of the book that allow for coverage of post-deadline activities. Some books include a supplement that covers such events as prom, graduation and spring sports. Other books choose to make the year run March to March.

SUMMER/FALL DELIVERY   These books are usually delivered in August or September. Their final deadline usually is sometime in June, so they can include the entire year from June to June. Their biggest challenge is how to deliver the book to seniors who have graduated.

check point ✓

What are the elements involved in the strategic plan for a yearbook?

Manage the Staff

Managing a yearbook staff is easier if the staff is organized into areas of responsibility. These follow the sections defined in your strategic plan. Possible areas include student life, academics, sports, organizations and people.

Student life focuses on students and what they do outside the classroom. It covers extracurricular activities such as band or theater; off-campus hangouts such as the local coffee shop or smoothie spot; individual pursuits such as music lessons and recitals, or riding lessons and shows; big events such as homecoming and prom; and cultural topics like fashion, music and locker decoration.

Academics focuses on what students do in the classroom and includes the various academic departments and class presentations, field trips, study habits and perhaps clubs affiliated with curricula.

Sports includes all varsity, junior varsity and freshman teams, both guys' and girls'; intramurals; and sports-related clubs such as athletic boosters and cheerleaders.

Organizations includes all the groups that are active in the school, such as the chess club, National Honor Society and film club — in other words, all clubs both big and small.

People includes seniors, underclassmen and faculty/staff. This is a reference section that contains the portraits and usually has mini-features or other information to draw in readers.

Managing the staff takes meetings and communication. Yearbook editors and advisers may want to set up weekly meetings where they will discuss their

///// *Why do you think it would be a good idea for members of a yearbook staff to attend weekly meetings?*

© Photodisc/Jupiter Images

progress, problems and any adjustments that should be made in the schedule or the book's content.

To keep things running smoothly the staff may want to make a deadline chart and hang it prominently in the work space. As elements come in on deadline, check them off. It will be a visual cue that deadlines are important and that the book is progressing. It also can serve as a reminder of upcoming deadlines to staffers and as a visual nudge to procrastinators.

check *point* ✓

What are some effective methods for managing a yearbook staff?

Plan the Yearbook

Once you have developed a good strategic plan for the yearbook you are on your way to putting it together. A plan may not address every issue, but if something goes wrong, a solid plan will help the staff keep on track.

THEME OR CONCEPT

One of the first decisions editors and staff must make about the yearbook is a theme or concept. A **theme** or **concept** is the prism through which the staff may look at all the other coverage. A yearbook tells the story of the year through pictures and words. The theme or concept is what gives that story unity and coherence. Establishing a theme or concept works together with organizing the book into sections. You use the theme or concept to plan each section.

For example, one high school yearbook staff came up with the theme "Redefine" and, within each section, looked for ways to explore it. Was there a way in which homecoming was being redefined? Were students and teachers redefining themselves with new challenges in classroom and extracurricular activities?

Themes or concepts can be words or catchphrases (Elements, Transitions, Enough Said, Tell It Like It Is). They might be based on an anniversary (The Gold Standard), school colors (True Blue), school pride (Second to None), changes in the school (A Work in Progress) or just fun (Get Over It, Takes One to Know One).

Whatever the theme or concept, it serves as the glue that holds the story of the year together. The editors and staff need to keep it in mind as they plan the cover, end sheet, opening, dividers, closing, section designs and all of the coverage. Before settling on a theme or concept, the editors and staff need to make sure it fits their school and year. For example, a school pride theme will not work if the student body is apathetic.

LADDER

The next step is to decide on the sections you want in the final copy and how to order those sections. The staff prepares a **ladder** of the yearbook's contents, a page-by-page plan of what will be included in the book.

Although the ladder can be flexible, you need to plan the content of every double-page spread. If an unexpected event needs coverage or if stories conceived at the beginning of the year do not work out as expected, you can alter the ladder. The ladder will help all members of the yearbook staff understand what they are expected to do and what their assignments are.

Before deciding what goes on every spread, make a list of all the events, sports, clubs and classes that must be covered. Then brainstorm other features that will record and mark the year, such as fashion and students' use of technology. Your list might look something like this:

Title Page: Springfield High School Spirit

Student Life: A look at the way students live at school

- Locker decoration
- Lunching in the lounge
- Using cellphones the minute the bell rings at 3 p.m.
- Decorating seniors' cars the first day of senior year
- Runs to the local coffee shop
- School fashions

Academics: What we study

- Cool chemistry experiments — things we blow up
- A French class trip to Paris at spring break
- Student art exhibits around school
- Students who take private music lessons
- Studying for midterms

Sports: The way we play

- Football rivalry, the year's big game
- First-game jitters
- Athletes' superstitions
- Profiles of MVPs, male and female
- The freshman on the varsity team

People: Faces of Springfield High

- A variety of mini-features that tie spreads together, like getting a driver's license, turning 18, being left-handed, or individual student profiles or favorites lists

Left page	#	#	Right page	Signature
		1	title page	1 mc & ec
opening	2	3	opening	1 mc & ec
opening	4	5	opening	1 mc & ec
opening	6	7	opening	1 mc & ec
opening	8	9	opening	1 mc & ec
opening	10	11	opening	1 mc & ec
STUDENT LIFE DIVIDER	12	13	STUDENT LIFE DIVIDER	1 bb & hc
STUDENT LIFE MAGAZINE	14	15	STUDENT LIFE MAGAZINE	1 bb & hc
STUDENT LIFE MAGAZINE	16	17	STUDENT LIFE MAGAZINE	1 bb & hc
spring activities	18	19	spring activities	1 bc & cf
summer	20	21	summer	1/zb
homecoming	22	23	homecoming	1/cu
homecoming	24	25	homecoming	1/ml
living in college town	26	27	living in college town	1/zl
jobs	28	29	jobs	4/bb
idiosyncrasies/addictions	30	31	idiosyncrasies/addictions	2/bb
fashion	32	33	fashion	2/zb

Deadlines

- DEADLINE 1 — NOV. 5 — 48 pages
- DEADLINE 2 — NOV. 26 — 56 pages
- DEADLINE 3 — DEC. 24 — 48 pages
- DEADLINE 4 — JAN. 28 — 52 pages
- DEADLINE 5 — FEB. 18 — 54 pages
- DEADLINE 6 — MAR. 3 — 46 pages

Clubs/Organizations: How we help

- Budgeting time among classes, studying and clubs

- Why students do or don't join clubs

- The literary magazine — students at work looking at submissions, designing pages

Your final ladder will be even more detailed. This gives you an idea of how you can brainstorm to begin your ladder so you can be sure to cover all the important events and aspects of school life during the year. Once the staff has a ladder, it is time to assign responsibility for each of the spreads.

MAKE ASSIGNMENTS

Once you organize your coverage into sections, you will want to assign staff members to each spread. If your staff is small, assign one editor to oversee each section and have staffers take assignments for all sections. If your staff is large enough, you may be able to assign an editor to oversee each section as well as staffers who will work only for that section.

Once assigned to sections, the staff can begin brainstorming specific coverage and story ideas and reasonable deadlines for each. Advisers work with editors to be sure the deadlines meet the criteria the printer will have for keeping the book on schedule.

After areas of coverage are defined and story ideas proposed and accepted, it will be time to make spread assignments. With the help of the editor-in-chief, each section editor should make spread assignments and attach a specific deadline to each. Knowing that you have deadlines months in advance

© Photodisc/Jupiter Images

////// *Which yearbook section would you be most interested in working on?*

may create a false impression that you have lots of time and that things don't have to be done immediately. They do. Don't procrastinate.

The section editor and staffer also should discuss the specifics of the assignment. Who would be the best people to interview and quote? Will there be obstacles to getting access? Raise any questions up front. If you encounter surprises while reporting, call your editor to discuss how to handle them.

Of course, pictures are the most important part of the yearbook, so the section editor who makes a spread assignment will also bring the yearbook photo editor into the process. With the reporter, the editors discuss picture possibilities, and then the photo editor assigns a photographer to shoot the story.

Although each section of the yearbook will work on its own, reporting to the editor-in-chief periodically, there will be times when collaboration is necessary. For example, a big school event such as homecoming could be included in two sections of the yearbook — Student Life and Sports. In reporting this type of event, a meeting of the staffers involved is vital to discuss who will do what to make sure everything is covered. Determining the dominant stories and their design is helpful so editors will not assign staffers to write a 1,000-word story on one aspect of an event when only 200 words will fit. Having a solid coverage and design plan ahead of time is vital to a smooth-running, all-inclusive publication.

check *point* ✓

How does preparing a ladder help in planning a yearbook?

AP Stylebook Concepts

Follow these guidelines when citing addresses and street names in your stories. Use the abbreviations Ave., Blvd. and St. only with a numbered address: 2500 Main St.

Spell out Avenue, Boulevard and Street and capitalize them when used in a formal street name without a street number: Main Street

Other words used with street names — such as Drive, Road and Place — are always spelled out and capitalized.

Use figures for address numbers: 20 Michigan Ave.

For additional information, see the AP Stylebook appendix at the back of this textbook.

Like That Song? Check the Copyright

The lyrics to Bob Dylan's song "Forever Young" would make the perfect accompaniment to a photo collage of the senior class on the last page of the yearbook. Unfortunately, you cannot use the lyrics without permission and to do so is unethical as well as illegal.

Song lyrics, poems, cartoon characters, magazine clippings, album covers, sound recordings and much more are protected by copyright and can't be used without permission from the copyright owner. Copyright laws protect the authors and artists of original works. A work is automatically copyrighted when it is put into fixed form.

Slogans, titles, names, short phrases, instructions and recipes are not protected by copyright because they lack the originality and creativity necessary to distinguish them from the ideas they represent. For example, the words of a slogan such as Nike's "Just Do It" cannot be copyrighted. Student editors could use "Just Do It" as a headline on a page of pictures of athletes. However, the words "Just Do It" together with the Nike "swoosh" can be copyrighted because together they create something original.

Copyright law makes a distinction between ideas and expression. You cannot copyright an idea. For example, you cannot copyright the idea of a story on school spirit. Any school newspaper can do a story on school spirit even if they got the idea from your newspaper. You can, however, copyright the story in its fixed form, meaning when it is done and printed.

Copyrights can run out and the work becomes part of the public domain. That's why works by long-dead novelists or songwriters can be used without permission and why moviemakers can freely make movies from classics like Jane Austen novels. Generally, for works created on or after January 1978, the copyright lasts for the life of the originator plus 70 years.

An exception to the copyright law called fair use allows for use of limited amounts of copyrighted work for purposes of news reporting or education. Because the requirements to judge fair use are vague, students need to consider carefully whether fair use applies. Consult with your adviser and, perhaps, the Student Press Law Center if you have questions about fair use.

If you think you really must have the lyrics from a particular song or poem, then you can seek permission from the copyright holder. Just giving credit is not enough. If you think you can use the lyrics without getting caught, you are being unethical.

THINK *Critically*

1. Why is doing something illegal also unethical?
2. What do you think would happen if there were no copyright laws?

17.1 | Assessment

Understand Concepts

Determine the best answer for each of the following questions.

1. Like most organizations, a high school yearbook needs a __?__, or a road map to achieving specific goals.
   a. theme
   b. multiplatform
   c. strategic plan
   d. storyboard

2. The __?__, usually a teacher, is responsible for teaching the staff the basic skills needed so they can complete the yearbook.
   a. section editor
   b. reporter
   c. editor-in-chief
   d. yearbook adviser

3. Before making assignments, the yearbook __?__ should be defined.
   a. sections
   b. photographs
   c. king and queen
   d. title

4. **True or False** A ladder will help solidify the coverage for each section you want to use in the yearbook.

Write Now!

Practice your writing skills with the following activities.

5. Using last year's yearbook, or a yearbook from another school, make a ladder for that yearbook. Then write a report stating your opinion of the yearbook. Include what you think may be missing and what is exceptional.

6. On the ASNE High School Journalism website, you can learn what students in other parts of the country are writing about in their yearbooks. You can also test your skills, learn about scholastic journalism resources and even find information on scholarships to study journalism in college. Plus, you can follow links for information on subjects such as how to get your first job, how to get clips and what is rewarding about a job in journalism. Spend time on this ASNE High School Journalism website, and then plan, draft and write a paper that discusses ideas from other schools that you might use in your high school yearbook. Include information on as many of the following as possible: a strategic plan, sections, planning delivery time, the staff, theme or concept, the ladder, and assignments. Using proofreading symbols, edit your paper for clarity, engaging language and correct English. Turn in your edited version along with your final paper.

17.2

Report and Write Yearbook Features

Goals

- Understand the obligations of yearbook reporting.
- Write memorable yearbook stories.

Key Terms

- active voice 429

FOCUS

Ask your grandparents if you can look at their high school yearbooks. Do the hairstyles look funny? Look at the glasses and other fashions on your grandparents and the other students. What was trendy then? Are there computers in classrooms? In what clubs and sports could your grandparents participate? What were the big events at their schools? Books from years past are a window to other eras. Yours will be, too, but you must tell the complete story so the book stands the test of time.

Report for the Yearbook

As a yearbook staffer, you should approach reporting yearbook stories the same as you would approach newspaper or magazine journalism. You must be accurate, above all else. You must get all the facts. You must be honest about how you got them and fair to the sources involved.

The first step to covering any story is preparation. Yearbook reporting is no different. You must do your homework to do the assignment well and to put the story into a historical context. For example, a yearbook reporter is assigned to cover the girls' basketball team in the state finals. To prepare for this assignment the reporter researches the stats and surprises of the season's games. She also researches the history of the girls' basketball team and discovers that the team last played for the state title 30 years ago, soon after Title IX (of the Education Amendments of 1972 to the Civil Rights Act of 1964) required that women be given the same opportunity as men to play sports. This information makes this game significant and the story powerful.

Some stories have more elements to consider than others, particularly when you are trying to put them into historical context. Regardless of how straightforward a story may seem, students should discuss the possible angles of the story with their editors. Outline and plan your stories before plunging into the assignment. Photos are important to the yearbook, but the story puts the photos in context. To write effective yearbook stories:

- Be familiar with the event you are covering. For example, if the assignment is to cover some aspect of homecoming, look at other strong yearbooks to see various ways in which homecoming might be covered. Determine what worked and what could have been included or deleted to improve the story.

- Brainstorm ideas to make your story unique. Look for details or amusing anecdotal mishaps that may set this year's homecoming apart from every other year's.

- Use sidebars. Using a sidebar — a supplement to your main story — could be a good way to get student opinion and quotes into the yearbook. For example, if your main story highlights an annual fundraiser that raised more money than ever before for a local charity, you might do a sidebar to give students an opportunity to say why it was meaningful this year.

In addition to different story angles, you should consider whom you are going to interview. You will want the most important figures of the story — the homecoming queen, the captain of the basketball team, the class president — but do not stop there. Yearbook writers need to interview a wide range of people — guys and girls; freshmen, sophomores, juniors and seniors; highly involved students and no-shows. You'll want as many names and voices in your story as possible, because people read yearbooks to see themselves and their friends. That makes it all the more necessary to get the facts straight and the names spelled correctly. Ask sources to spell their first and last name for you. The same goes for photographers and the people they photograph. Get contact information for the people with whom you talk so you or your editors can contact them to verify facts.

 checkpoint

How is reporting for a yearbook similar to other forms of journalism?

Write Yearbook Features

A yearbook records the stories and experiences that take place at a high school over one year. Staffers should write stories using the feature-writing style. Features allow the writer to present the characters and emotions that make for a more engaging story.

WRITE IN THE ACTIVE VOICE

Even though you are writing a story for a history book, write in the present tense and the **active voice**, in which the subject performs the action expressed

grammar tip

To make your writing more interesting, vary the length of your sentences. Within the same paragrah, have both long and short sentences. Sentence length gives readers signals to the meaning of the emotion behind the words. Longer sentences allow the reader to slow down and ponder the words. Short sentences cause the reader to read more rapidly and signal intensity. Varying sentence lengths will help your readers think of you as a good writer.

Another way to add interest to your copy is to vary the way you start sentences. This will also help you vary your sentence length. You could start some sentences with an introductory phrase or word. You could begin other sentences with the article "the," others with a quotation, and so on.

in the verb. For example, instead of writing "The touchdown was scored by John" (past tense, passive voice), write "John scores the touchdown" (present tense, active voice). You want your readers to feel as if they are there with you experiencing the event, seeing what you see. Start with a compelling lead, avoid long sentences and paragraphs, and use colorful and descriptive quotes.

Space for words in yearbooks is limited, so writers need to keep the main story as short as possible. However, yearbooks are good places to use other points of entry into a story or a page. Think about using captions and elements such as lists, fast-fact boxes or charts to help tell the story.

In history, people — not places or things — create and cause most events worth recording. Yearbooks are history books, so write about the people who make things happen. Readers also want to read about their peers, so focus on people because they make the stories relevant, memorable and unique.

As you write, include strong, meaningful quotes to put reactions and emotions into words. Let the students tell the story and avoid editorializing, or inserting your opinion. Remember that your audience is your peers, not a group of academics. Have fun with your writing without sacrificing quality and legitimacy. Good writers also are good readers. As a yearbook reporter, you should read a variety of publications to expose yourself to different ideas and possibilities in writing.

ETHICAL CONSIDERATIONS

Ethical considerations are as much a part of the reporting process for yearbooks as they are for any other kind of journalism. Even though you are interviewing your peers and the yearbook is a school publication, you still must adhere to ethical principles. Sources are still sources and should not be treated with less respect just because you sit next to them in chemistry class.

Explain to your sources what you are writing about and why. Quote sources accurately and in context.

Never use pictures you don't have permission to use. Respect copyrights. If you are taking pictures of a school activity, ask permission from the appropriate people. Do not manipulate images in the darkroom or with digital software programs such as Photoshop unless you label them as photo illustrations.

checkpoint ✓

Why should reporters use feature-writing style when writing for yearbooks?

17.2 | Assessment

Understand Concepts

Determine the best answer for each of the following questions.

1. Which statement is not true?
   a. Effective yearbook reporters put stories into a historical context.
   b. Effective yearbook reporters outline and plan stories before carrying out their assignments.
   c. Effective yearbook reporters rely on photographs to put the story into context.
   d. Effective yearbook reporters ask sources to spell their first and last names and ask for contact information.

2. Which of the following uses active voice?
   a. Stories are usually written by journalists.
   b. The story was written by the journalists.
   c. The journalist wrote the story.
   d. How many stories has the journalist written?

3. **True or False** A sidebar is a good way to get student opinion and quotes into your main story.

4. **True or False** Ethical considerations are not important to yearbook reporting because the sources are your peers and the yearbook is a school publication.

Write Now!

Practice your writing skills with the following activities.

5. Write a short feature for your high school yearbook that illustrates an event the seniors held, such as a day of volunteering. Write a headline for your feature.

6. Select an event at your school for a photo page that tells a story. After you take the photographs, use a computer program to crop the photos to communicate and emphasize your topic. Design and prepare a layout suitable for publication in your high school's yearbook. Include captions for the photographs and a headline for the photo layout.

7. You are the editor of your high school yearbook. A terrible accident involved four seniors from your school, and none of the students survived. Your staff is looking to you to guide them in a responsible and ethical way to deal with the deaths of the seniors in the yearbook. Write a speech to the yearbook staff that describes how you plan to handle the tragedy in the yearbook. Some questions you might want to ponder include the following: Should you ignore the deaths? Should you include the students' photos with the senior class even though they will not graduate? Should you show a photo of the vehicle? Should you write a memorial and include their photos in the memorial? If so, where in the yearbook should you place the memorial? Carefully write out your thoughts before you write the speech.

17.3

Design and Photograph Images for Memorable Pages

Goals

- Explain the elements of yearbook design.
- Describe how photographers can shoot memorable photos.

Key Terms

- photo request form 434
- depth of field 435

FOCUS

Watch the students at any high school on the day yearbooks are delivered. No one is concentrating on classes. Everyone is too busy flipping through the pages of the yearbook, looking for photographs of themselves, their friends and the events that took place over the year. The yearbook is the school's memory book, and it will stay on shelves for years to come.

Yearbook Design

In the design stage, all the elements are brought together to create spreads that pop with color and life. Editors and designers sort through photos, edit copy and package the work to attract the eye. An important thing for young designers to remember is to strive for consistency among the spreads of the yearbook.

DESIGN AS GUIDE

The yearbook's design guides readers through the pages and tells them what to look at first. In designing a spread, the first step is to determine the dominant element. For example, if you are designing a spread with a bold headline about the homecoming coronation, then the largest photo should be of the homecoming queen as she is crowned. Readers naturally assume the largest headline and the largest photo are paired together.

When designing the spread it's important to pay collective attention to the subjects in the photos. For example, if you are laying out a spread for the student life section, make sure your photos show a representative mix of students. The photos on the spread should show a variety of students engaged in a range of activities. There also should be variety in the number of students in each picture. If one person dominates the main photo, look to add photos with two, three and four people in them.

Yearbooks are a good place to use classic, straightforward design. Remember, readers will look at this design for years to come. Crisp and clean design can transcend time and keep the yearbook looking good no matter when someone looks at it.

Establish style guides for each section of the book. What column or grid plan will be used? What will the headline look like? What size will the copy and captions be? Answering these major questions as well as deciding on smaller details, like how much leading will be used in copy, will help each section have a consistent look within the larger context of the theme or concept.

Keep the fonts simple and straightforward. Too many fonts and colors on one page make it look cluttered and distract from the photos and copy. Remember, the point of the design is to enhance the photos and the copy, not distract from them. If, as a staff, you plan a theme, color scheme and visual style early on, your designers will have an easier time.

Each section of your yearbook is like a chapter and some variations in design will help distinguish them. For example, your student life section might use cut-out photos — those with backgrounds dropped out — and muted shades of the yearbook colors, while the sports section includes big action shots on each page and uses bolder shades of the colors.

CHECKLIST FOR DESIGNERS

- Designing a page begins with a dominant element.

- If your yearbook uses color, decide on a few colors at the start that will thread the pages of the entire yearbook together and give it consistency. The same thing applies to fonts.

- Pay attention to the size of images and fonts.

- Determine how to use white space between photos or copy as well as to isolate secondary coverage.

- Crop photos carefully. Don't crop them at awkward points, such as a subject's knees. You will learn more about using photography in the yearbook in the next section.

check *point* ✓

What does the yearbook design guide readers to do?

Photograph Memories

Because photographs are so important to the yearbook design, the staff must plan and choose them carefully. There is a lot more to taking photographs than the photographer showing up at an event and snapping pictures. Like reporters, good photographers must prepare for their assignments.

PHOTOGRAPHY ASSIGNMENTS

Photographers usually receive assignments from a staffer or section editor via the photo editor. An organized photo request system helps photographers understand their assignments. You can set up a photo request system either in the computer program you use or on paper.

Staffers or editors fill out a **photo request form** that details the who, what, when, where, why and how of the event or story. The form should include space to write details such as the focus or angle of the story, how many photos may be needed, and anything else that will help the photographer take the desired pictures. Staffers also should include contact information for themselves as well as the contacts for the story. If photographers don't understand some part of the assignment, they can call the staffer or story contacts for additional information so they will take the desired photos.

PLAN AHEAD

Photographers need to plan their time to arrive early or on time for any event or person they are assigned to photograph. They also should be familiar with the venue in which the photos will be shot. Many professional photographers scout out locations the day before and arrive early to stake their position. Location is important to help get close-up shots or, in the case of sports, action shots. A yearbook captures moments and expressions, so some close-up work should be expected. Photographers also need to check equipment beforehand to make sure it works.

Photographers and staffers sometimes may work together, which can work out well for both. The staffer can be sure to write copy to go with some of the photographer's best shots. The staffer also can help ensure that a wide variety of students are photographed in a range of situations.

Sports photography creates another challenge. Photographers need to know something about the sport so they can position themselves effectively and anticipate the action.

TAKE MEMORABLE PICTURES

Wise photographers always establish a good rapport with the person or people running an event. They are the folks who can give a photographer access to the people and places they need to get the best shots. Suppose a famous band is playing at your high school and you, a staff photographer, want to get backstage. Contacting the proper public relations people before the show will help you get the access you want.

With digital cameras, you have no reason to limit the number of photos you take. Take more photos than you know you'll need to give the editors and designers several options. Digital cameras allow you to see the images before you leave the event, making it more likely you'll have taken a useable image.

Almost everyone owns some kind of camera. Ask students and their parents to submit their own photos of school events for consideration. Remember, though, that these pictures often are posed rather than candid, so you may not be able to use them. They also may not be at high enough resolution for printing purposes.

Avoid repetitious photos that feature the same groups of people. There are plenty of students in your school to feature, so mix it up. Make sure you include students from every class and every clique. Develop a system to keep track of who's been pictured so the same people don't make it into the book over and over while others are neglected.

Shoot non-traditional angles. Instead of photographing the subject straight on, experiment with shooting from above or below. Play around with the **depth of field,** or the amount of space that is in focus in your photograph. Reducing the depth of field increases the interest of the subject at hand.

Get close. Show the emotions and reactions to events by focusing on faces. If you're shooting action, crop out the extraneous background and people. Zoom in on what's happening.

*check*point ✓

Name three ways photographers can take memorable photos.

////// *Why is it important to include photos of students from every class, social group and activity for the yearbook?*

17.3 | Assessment

Understand Concepts

Determine the best answer for each of the following questions.

1. Which refers to the amount of space that is in focus in your photograph?
   a. depth of field
   b. field of range
   c. space field
   d. focus range

2. Which refers to a basic form that staffers or editors fill out detailing the five W's and H of an event or story to be photographed?
   a. IRS form
   b. adviser's form
   c. photographer's form
   d. photo request form

3. **True or False** Photographers can arrive late to an event they are shooting as long as they are sure they will get the right photos.

4. **True or False** Each section of your yearbook is like a chapter, and some variations in design should help distinguish one from another.

Write Now!

Practice your writing skills with the following activities.

5. Design a photo request form that could be used by staff members of your school newspaper.

6. Use a computer program and the checklist for designers in this section to redesign a page from last year's yearbook. If your yearbook has color, decide on a few colors at the start. Pay attention to the size and type of fonts you want to use. Determine how to use white space between photos. Leave room for photos and identify the type of photos you want to use. Make sure your design has a dominant element. Once you have completed your page, send it to your teacher electronically.

7. Use the Internet to research the history of yearbooks, including information on design and yearbook photography. Plan and write relevant questions for in-depth research. Find information sources for background information. Evaluate and confirm the validity of the background information from a variety of sources. Draft a paper that discusses and identifies the history and development of American yearbooks through the people and events of the yearbooks you study. Cite your sources. Once you have completed your draft, edit it for clarity, engaging language and correct English.

Get Down to Business

Goals

- Develop a budget for your yearbook.
- Understand ad sales and other financing options.

Key Terms

- business manager 437
- budget 437
- expenses 437
- income 438
- sales pitch 438
- advertising manager 439

FOCUS

John always wanted to work on his high school's yearbook. Now in his senior year, he knew this was his last chance. He was intimidated by all the creative people on the staff — photographers and artists whose work he admired, terrific writers and editors with vision. He wasn't sure how he could contribute until the day he read an ad in the school newspaper seeking people interested in yearbook work. The ad included a position John, a math whiz, thought he could do well. The job was business manager. He applied, and the yearbook adviser agreed that John had a head for the financial side of a yearbook and a personality that would allow him to motivate others. John got the job.

Develop a Budget

In many ways the financial side of the school yearbook parallels the editorial side. It, too, requires organization, management and a strategic plan. The first part of this chapter dealt with creating a strategic plan. Why? To reach a creative destination you must strategically map out how to get there. The same is true for the business side. The business manager must set financial goals and develop a strategic plan for how to meet them.

Your yearbook staff should have a finance component that will operate separately, ideally under a business manager. The **business manager** is in charge of the money side of the publication. He or she begins by asking two questions: How much money is the staff expected to raise, and how will the staff raise it?

The first step to managing the business side of the yearbook is planning a **budget**, a document that sets out the expected expenses and income for the year. To develop a budget, the business manager asks the editorial staff to list its **expenses** — all the things that will cost money. These may include cameras, computer equipment, paper, office supplies and promotional materials. Also included are big costs such as those involved in printing. Your yearbook publishing company representative can help determine the cost of printing plus any extras the staff wants to include. Your business staff also will look at where it will get its **income**, the money to pay the expenses.

checkpoint ✓

What are the two components of a yearbook's budget?

Finance the Yearbook

Selling advertising space is likely to be your chief source of income, with book sales, fundraising and a grant from the school all possible additional sources. Advertising, book sales and fundraising are the most popular methods of raising money.

ADVERTISING

When selling advertising space, remember that the audience for the yearbook is teenagers. Your best potential customers are teen-oriented businesses. Think about where your schoolmates spend their money: clothing stores, fast-food restaurants, movie theaters, coffee shops, tanning salons, hair salons, car dealerships, gas stations and more. All are good places to make contacts and to try to sell an ad. Approach all the vendors who have contracts with your school and colleges that come to recruit on campus. In addition to business ads, senior-parent ads can increase your income. Parents and friends of seniors purchase these ads that include a message and usually a picture.

Good salespeople not only go after new customers, but they also keep the customers they have. They first should call on the advertisers in the previous year's book and try to renew their business or, better yet, persuade them to buy a bigger ad.

To sell ad space, you must come up with a good **sales pitch** — a presentation that briefly explains why your publication is a good place to advertise. You want to convince potential customers that they will benefit from advertising in your school's yearbook. Use facts to make your pitch: Students are customers; the ad will bring community support to the business because local people like local businesses that support their schools; the ad has a lasting effect because it is in a book that is treasured, not a newspaper that is thrown away. Consider surveying students about their spending habits. The information gathered can be used to show potential advertisers how much the teen market spends. Your yearbook publishing company may have marketing and sales guides your team can use.

ORGANIZE THE AD SALES STAFF   Like the yearbook staff, the ad staff, if large enough, should have a chain of command to keep things organized. Most likely, the yearbook adviser will work closely with the head of the advertising staff, or **advertising manager**. The advertising manager should report to the business manager, who keeps track of all the financial aspects of the yearbook.

All members of the ad staff should be given responsibility for specific potential customers. The salespeople develop presentations and make appointments to see their clients as soon as possible because it may take more than one meeting to get them to say yes. On smaller staffs the editors and staffers become the sales staff.

To be efficient, the ad staff might divide the list of potential customers by category. For example, one sales representative might be assigned all clothing retailers, while another handles fast-food restaurants. Selling by category, or specializing, helps sales representatives because they get to know their category. They know their potential customers and the customers' competition and should understand the potential customers' advertising needs and concerns.

Another way to organize the staff, especially if the entire staff is selling, is by territory. Divide your sales area into several territories. Each territory can be assigned to a team. Friendly competition among teams can be a good motivator. Teams can compete for prizes, free yearbooks, or whatever the budget allows.

PREPARE THE AD SALES STAFF   Good salespeople take a portfolio of examples with them when they go to meet a possible advertiser. They may have some proposed new ads to show, or examples of the previous year's ad with suggested changes to update it.

All ad staff members need to know the cost of advertising space in the yearbook, how to fill out a contract with a potential customer and what kind of deals, if any, they are allowed to offer. Ad staff members may do some role-playing exercises before embarking on a sales pitch, which should be done in person. In role-playing, you come up with possible scenarios and ways to handle them. For example, say you are dealing with a potential customer who has never advertised in a yearbook and therefore isn't sure about its effectiveness. You will want to have some prepared data on how other businesses experienced a jump in sales as a result of yearbook advertising. Know your situation and anticipate all possible scenarios. A stumbling salesperson doesn't instill confidence in a potential client.

SENIOR ADS

Senior ads are advertising space sold to parents, relatives and friends of graduating seniors in which they congratulate their seniors, reminisce about their growing up and wish them well. Some ads show pictures of the senior and his or her family. These ads, sold in various sizes, increasingly make up a large chunk of income for yearbooks. The ad sections often are produced in color, and families are encouraged to purchase their ads early in the year, with price breaks sometimes given as incentives to get the ads coming in. Full-page ads may cost hundreds of dollars, and yearbook staffs often offer to design the ads for parents or produce them as the buyers design them. However you choose to provide them, senior ads are a smart business move.

BOOK SALES

The next largest source of income is actual book sales. If you are lucky enough to have the cost of the yearbooks included in tuition or an activity fee, this will not be a consideration. If you need to market your product, however, brainstorm opportunities and incentives to increase sales. Generally, the more books you order, the lower the per-unit price.

Look for creative ways to reach your readers. Set up a table at open houses and parent-teacher conferences. Advertise in monthly school mailers that go home to parents. Hang posters and make announcements about when and where students can purchase books and how much they cost. Consider gradually raising the cost as the year progresses to encourage students to order early.

FUNDRAISING

Organized fundraisers are another way to produce income for your yearbook. There are opportunities such as joining with a local business to sell coupons or deliver fliers. Some restaurants offer fundraising deals through which the restaurant gets a big crowd and the school gets a percentage of the profits. More traditional fundraisers, such as car washes, bake sales and pancake breakfasts, can bring in some income. Selling candy, wrapping paper or others items to get a percentage of the profit could be investigated. However, remember that all these activities take time and energy away from production. If you must use a fundraiser, look for one that gives you the greatest return for the smallest investment of time. Remember to include the projected costs of organizing a fundraiser in the yearbook's budget when it is drafted at the beginning of the year.

////// *A car wash is a popular way to raise money to pay the expenses involved in publishing a yearbook. Think of other ideas for fundraisers your school could hold to benefit the yearbook.*

© gchutka/iStockphoto.com

The key to a good fundraiser is good organization. Your business manager may want to pull together a small group of students who have an interest in marketing or event planning to plan and execute fundraisers. The execution of any plan usually is made easier with more people, so enlist as many volunteers as possible. All editorial and business staff members also should get their parents, friends, teachers and siblings to advertise to their friends and co-workers by word of mouth.

Name the ways in which yearbooks raise the money they need to publish.

17.4 | Assessment

Understand Concepts

Determine the best answer for each of the following questions.

1. Which person is in charge of the money side of the yearbook?
   a. adviser
   b. advertising manager
   c. business manager
   d. assignment editor

2. This document sets out the expected expenses and income for the yearbook.
   a. database
   b. spreadsheet
   c. nut graph
   d. budget

3. **True or False**   Sales of the book itself is the largest source of income for the yearbook.

4. **True or False**   Fundraising is one way to increase income for the yearbook.

Write Now!

Practice your writing skills with the following activities.

5. Use a computer to create a display ad for your yearbook that could appear in the school newspaper and on the newspaper's website. You may have to make changes to the ad for the newspaper or the website. For example, if the newspaper is printed only in black and white, you can add color for the website ad. Use the design and photographic information you learned in this section to help you design your ad. Use truthful information and strong advertising appeals to sell the yearbook. Send your ad to your teacher electronically.

Sayonara, Sycamore High — The Final Entry in One Senior's News Blog

By Brandon Sosna, Sycamore High School, Cincinnati, Ohio, "Take a Hike: Choking on My Own Words" [Excerpted]

Two years ago, I came up with the column idea that every week I would tell a different individual to "take a hike."

Now it's my turn. I'm choking on my own words.

Writing this final piece is more difficult than I thought it would be. I'm going to miss this place — the tears on my keyboard are evidence of that.

I don't know what it is about SHS that makes me not want to leave. It could be a fear of the future, of the challenges to come.

But really, deep down, I think it's that I'm truly going to feel a void in my life without 7400 Cornell Road. I don't know that I will ever be as welcome anywhere as I am here, excluding my own home. I love SHS. And SHS loves me.

And now as I prepare to graduate, I can confidently look in the mirror and know that the man staring back in the glass is me, truly me, and that this proverbial man is satisfied with what he sees.

I would not be that way without SHS. As cliche as it is, you can take me out of SHS, but you can never take SHS out of me. I know that come my last day of class on Friday, May 20, I will walk out of my final bell and take multiple laps around the building. If it were up to me, I would never leave.

I leave with the hope that one day we will cross paths once again. Until then, this is goodbye. I wish only the best for all of you and that you all accomplish the goals you set for yourself.

Always remember: head in the sky, feet on the ground. Be great today. And tomorrow. And the next day.

Ending this without a special, special thanks to Mrs. Cheralyn Jardine, my journalism adviser, would be an unquantifiable travesty. Mrs. Jardine — I will never lose sight of all that you did for me and I know I would not be going to Penn without you. Thank you.

So this is it: time to say goodbye for real. I've learned how to write many things in the last four years, but forming the proper sayonara sentence is something I could never prepare for. A simple goodbye will have to do.

THINK *Critically*

Assume you have been writing a daily or weekly blog for your school's on-line publication. Write the final entry for your blog.

CHAPTER 17 | Assessment

Review Journalism Concepts

17.1 Plan and Organize the Yearbook

Planning your yearbook begins with drafting a strategic plan, which is a road map to achieving goals. A successful yearbook staff is organized, so all members know their roles and responsibilities. In your strategic plan, you need to define sections, or areas of coverage you want in the yearbook. A plan for the book is necessary. A theme or concept — the prism through which the staff may look at all the other features — is one way to organize your yearbook. Once the staff formalizes the theme or concept, it needs to plan a ladder, a page-by-page plan for the entire book.

17.2 Report and Write Yearbook Features

Yearbook reporting requires the same mindset as that of any newspaper or magazine journalist. The obligations to be accurate and get the facts are the same. Use a feature-writing style, which allows you to present characters and emotion for a more engaging story. Write stories in the active voice, in which the subject performs the action expressed in the verb. Staffers must remember ethics when dealing with sources and attribution of photos.

17.3 Design and Photograph Images for Memorable Pages

Photographs are important to your yearbook, so the photographers need to understand their assignments. Editors use a photo request form to explain the assignment to photographers. The form details the 5 W's and H. Photographers must plan ahead to shoot memorable pictures for the yearbook. Changing the depth of field, the amount of space that is in focus, helps create memorable photos. The design of the yearbook guides readers through the pages and tells them what to look at first.

17.4 Get Down to Business

The yearbook staff includes a business manager, who is in charge of the finances. The business manager plans a budget that sets out the expected expenses and income for the year. Expenses are all the things that cost money. The business manager also looks at the income, the money to pay for the expenses. Most yearbooks are financed by advertising sales, book sales, fundraisers and school grants. Advertising sales require a good sales pitch, a presentation that briefly explains why your publication is a good place for the advertiser. The advertising manager, who is in charge of ad sales, works closely with the business manager.

Develop Your Journalism Language

Write the letter of the term that matches each definition.

_____ 1. Manager who keeps track of all the financial aspects of the yearbook

_____ 2. Presentation that briefly explains why your publication is a good place for an advertiser to be seen

_____ 3. A form that details the who, what, when, where, why and how of the event or story to be photographed

_____ 4. A road map for achieving specific goals

_____ 5. The amount of space that is in focus in your photograph

_____ 6. Money to pay for expenses

_____ 7. The subject performs the action of the verb

_____ 8. An idea that ties together all the elements of the yearbook

_____ 9. A document that sets out the expected expenses and income for the year

_____ 10. Areas of coverage you want in the yearbook

_____ 11. Head of the staff that sells ad space in the yearbook

_____ 12. Things on which the yearbook staff will need to spend money

_____ 13. Page-by-page plan of what will be included in the yearbook

a. active voice
b. advertising manager
c. budget
d. business manager
e. depth of field
f. expenses
g. income
h. ladder
i. photo request form
j. sales pitch
k. sections
l. strategic plan
m. theme or concept

14. A (n) __?__ is a way to plan the costs and profits of the yearbook.
    a. income statement
    b. budget
    c. strategic plan
    d. expenses

15. With which should the yearbook staff begin?
    a. strategic plan
    b. sections
    c. budget
    d. selection of printer

16. With which should a photographer be familiar?
    a. sales pitch
    b. depth of field
    c. active voice
    d. budget

17. Who is directly in charge of the advertising sales staff for a high school yearbook?
    a. business manager
    b. advertising manager
    c. adviser
    d. editor-in-chief

18. With which should students selling advertising be familiar?
    a. cost of ad space
    b. teen spending habits
    c. sales pitch
    d. all of the above

Think Critically

19. Why do yearbook staffs and organizations of all shapes and sizes usually begin a new project with a strategic plan?

20. Why does a yearbook staff need an adviser?

21. What is the difference between the role of a yearbook's business manager and the role of its advertising manager?

22. Why should the yearbook staff define the sections in the strategic plan?

23. What advantages might a large staff have over a small staff? What advantages might a small staff have over a large staff?

24. Why is a theme a good idea for a yearbook?

25. Why is it a good idea for the yearbook staff to have a style guide?

26. Why do you want to use feature-style writing for yearbook stories?

27. Are ethics as important in yearbook writing as in other types of journalism? Why or why not?

28. Why should staffers or editors fill out photo request forms for photographers?

29. How can a ladder help a yearbook staff?

30. Why are photos important to a yearbook?

31. Why is design important to a yearbook?

32. Why does a yearbook staff need a budget?

33. Why is a business manager important to a yearbook?

Make Academic Connections

34. **HISTORY**   Use your interviewing skills to interview an adult about his or her high school yearbook. Write a summary including how that yearbook is different from yours today.

35. **CAREERS**   List all types of careers you can think of that connect to yearbooks. Be creative. Post your list on the bulletin board and compare it with those of other students.

36. **SOCIAL STUDIES**   Choose three foreign countries. Use the Internet to research whether schools in those countries have yearbooks. Write a one-page fact sheet about your findings.

37. **ART**   Use computer graphics or other art supplies to create a cover for your yearbook. Post your cover on the bulletin board.

38. **ECONOMICS**   Use computer software to create a realistic budget for a yearbook. Include types of expenses and sources of income.

39. **WRITING**   Write an article that describes how you feel about being on the yearbook staff. Why do you want to/not want to be on the staff? If you want

to work on the yearbook, what position do you want? Why do you want this position? What are your qualifications for this position?

40. **LANGUAGE ARTS**   List three themes or concepts your yearbook staff could use this year. Write a short paragraph explaining each.

41. **PHOTOGRAPHY**   Take photographs for a two-page spread that shows a normal day at your school. You should have between four and eight photos. Write a two-paragraph feature that goes with your spread. Add a headline for the feature and a caption for each photo.

42. **MARKETING**   Conduct a marketing survey among the first-, second- and third-year students in your school to gain their suggestions about how to improve this year's yearbook. Write a list of questions that allow the students to rate last year's book. Include questions on the sections chosen, photographs, features, design and other elements. Some questions you might ask are: Did you buy a yearbook this year? Why or why not? What is your favorite story, photograph, section? What would you like to see in the yearbook that is missing this year? Distribute your list to students. Give students a deadline. Compile and analyze the responses in a computer database, then write a summary of the findings.

Writing Portfolio Activity

43. Use computer software to design a two-page spread for a yearbook that includes photos and a feature story about an event or club at your school. Use photos that you have cropped to communicate and emphasize your topic. Add a headline for the feature and a caption for each photo. Add your design to your portfolio.

AP Stylebook Workshop

Correct the following, if necessary, according to AP style.

44. 2717 Observatory Avenue

45. Erie Ave.

46. 85 Edwards Dr.

47. Sixteen Morningside Boulevard

48. Stetson Place

49. 2500 Main Street

50. Pleasant Rd.

INITIATIVE AND SELF-DIRECTION: Plan Your Future

Soon you will graduate from high school and enter college. You will need initiative and self-direction because your time will be less structured than in high school. Having initiative and self-direction means you know how to

- Manage goals and time
- Work independently
- Be a self-directed learner

MANAGE GOALS AND TIME

Set reasonable goals and ones that you can manage. For example, if you set a goal to complete an assignment by a certain date, you will feel good about completing the assignment and about accomplishing your goal.

You also need to balance short-term and long-term goals. For example, when planning a paper, you need to set a goal to accomplish a specific amount of research; a goal to draft the paper; a goal to edit, proofread and copy edit the paper; and a goal to complete the final paper by the deadline.

To accomplish each short-term goal that leads to the long-term goal of completing the paper, set deadlines for each goal so you can use your time and manage your workload efficiently.

WORK INDEPENDENTLY

In college, and on the job, you will be the only one to monitor how you spend your time. To succeed in college and become a successful journalist, you will need to define, prioritize and complete tasks without anyone looking over your shoulder. You will need to break down the steps needed to complete a photo assignment, for example. And you will need to be able to look at which steps are the most important and which must come first.

BE A SELF-DIRECTED LEARNER

Successful students — both in high school and college — go beyond the curriculum to explore the subject. For example, if you are a sports photographer who specializes in contact sports, such as football, do not turn down an assignment for taking photos of the president visiting the community. A professional journalist would jump at the chance for the additional assignment. This allows you to expand your learning to gain expertise in other areas.

Self-directed learners take the initiative to improve their skills. While in school, aim toward a professional level by constantly improving your skills. Reflect critically on your experiences to figure out how you can do better in the future.

Self-directed learners commit themselves to learning as a lifelong process. As you leave high school, your learning will continue in college or on the job. As you grow and mature, so will the world. As you have learned in this course, the world of journalism has changed radically with the onset of the Internet and other technology. As a self-directed lifelong learner, you keep up with the changes in your profession — and in the world. Being well-informed will help you be successful and in demand in the highly competitive and ever-changing business of journalism.

THINK *Critically*
Are you self-directed? Do you take the initiative and successfully manage your life? Write down a list of your long-term goals. For example, do you hope to have a successful career in journalism? To get married? To live in Europe? To write a novel? After each long-term goal, make a list of short-term goals you will need to complete to achieve your long-term goals. For example, to have a successful journalistic career, you need to write and to attend college.

Robert Penuela | Yearbook Adviser

© Photo courtesy of David Allen

Robert Penuela, yearbook adviser at Roosevelt High School in Los Angeles, used to worry about the future of the hardcover keepsake book, as any adviser would with the advent of digital publishing and the increasing popularity of e-books. But no more. "I honestly believe that yearbooks will continue, but like literature canons, they will expand," says Penuela, who has been a yearbook adviser since 2003. "The books will continue, but I believe that they will also expand into offering a free e-book edition so it can be carried with you online, on an e-book reader and more."

In fact, such digital enhancements to the 21st century yearbook are already available. But what makes Penuela worry less about the future of the book itself is he sees the value in a keepsake book and he's convinced that "having a book for friends and staff to sign, that's the gold." After all, a written message in the front of yearbook lasts a whole lot longer than a Facebook wall message.

That doesn't mean, however, that the digital revolution hasn't touched the production of keepsake books, Penuela says, "The first year or two that I was adviser, yearbooks were in that in-between stage — some things were digital and some were old school. We actually used film and had to wait for the film to be developed and returned. Now, it can all be done online. We use digital cameras, upload the photos and use online software to design the yearbook. Students can even work on the yearbook from home. It's changed a lot."

HOW HE BECAME A YEARBOOK ADVISER

Penuela says he fell in love with photography when he was 6 years old and has always taken pictures and been a writer. But as far as preparing to become a high school yearbook adviser goes, "The love of photography, design and writing is what helped — and the fact that I loved working with students beyond the usual English classroom hierarchy and borders."

Source: Personal interview with Robert Penuela.

THINK *Critically*

1. Do you think of yearbooks as the record of your years in high school? Why or why not?

2. Do you think a digital edition of the yearbook could become more popular than the print edition? Why or why not?

THE ASSOCIATED PRESS STYLEBOOK

An abridged version of the Associated Press Stylebook is provided for your reference so you can become familiar with the style used by professional journalists. This reference guide covers the AP Stylebook features found within this textbook plus thousands more entries. You can order the complete version of the AP Stylebook in three formats, with more information on each at apstylebook.com.

THE SPIRAL-BOUND AP STYLEBOOK

The AP Stylebook and Briefing on Media Law, a spiral-bound style manual produced by the world's leading news agency, is an essential handbook for all writers, editors, students and public relations specialists.

- We update our Stylebook every year, adding new listings and updating existing ones.

- The Stylebook includes thousands of A-Z listings and has separate chapters for sports, photo captions, social media and food terms. It also includes a briefing on media law, as well as a quick reference guide to point out some of the most commonly used listings.

AP STYLEBOOK ONLINE

AP Stylebook Online is a Web-based, searchable version of the AP Stylebook with online-only bonus features.

- As AP updates its style throughout the year, users can get email updates and check the new entries and recent changes section online.

- Subscribers can submit questions via "Ask the Editor" and search thousands of previously answered questions in the archive. "Ask the Editor" has more listings than the Stylebook itself.

- Pronouncers include phonetic spelling of hundreds of words as well as audio files so you can hear the right way to say names in the news.

- Capital IQ provides detailed profiles of publicly traded companies, updated throughout the year.

- Add your own listings and include your own notes on AP's entries.

AP STYLEBOOK MOBILE

Stylebook Mobile applications feature searchable listings for the main, sports, punctuation, social media and food sections, along with the ability to add your own custom entries as well as notes on AP listings.

- Star your favorite entries to easily find the listings you go to over and over again.

- With Stylebook Mobile, you can take the AP Stylebook with you anywhere.

- Stylebook Mobile is available for iPhone, also compatible with iPod touch and iPad, as well as for BlackBerry.

Visit us online

Visit our website, www.apstylebook.com, to learn more about the AP Stylebook in all formats. You can take a virtual tour of AP Stylebook Online or to look inside the Stylebook Mobile applications, and check out the Ask the Editor FAQs.

Follow us on Twitter at http://twitter.com/APStylebook

Check out our Facebook page at http://www.facebook.com/apstylebook

AP Stylebook (abridged)

A

a- The rules of prefixes apply, but in general no hyphen. Some examples: achromatic atonal

AAA Formerly the American Automobile Association. Headquarters is in Heathrow, Fla.

a, an Use the article *a* before consonant sounds: *a historic event, a one-year term* (sounds as if it begins with a *w*) *a united stand* (sounds like *you*).

Use the article *an* before vowel sounds: *an energy crisis, an honorable man* (the *h* is silent), *an NBA record* (sounds like it begins with the letter *e*), *an 1890s celebration.*

abbreviations and acronyms A few universally recognized abbreviations are required in some circumstances. Some others are acceptable depending on the context. But in general, avoid alphabet soup. Do not use abbreviations or acronyms that the reader would not quickly recognize.

Guidance on how to use a particular abbreviation or acronym is provided in entries alphabetized according to the sequence of letters in the word or phrase.

An *acronym* is a word formed from the first letter or letters of a series of words: *laser* (light amplification by stimulated emission of radiation). An *abbreviation* is not an *acronym*.

Some general principles:

BEFORE A NAME: Abbreviate titles when used before a full name: *Dr., Gov., Lt. Gov., Mr., Mrs., Rep., the Rev., Sen.* and certain military designations.

AFTER A NAME: Abbreviate *junior* or *senior* after an individual's name. Abbreviate *company, corporation, incorporated* and *limited* when used after the name of a corporate entity.

In some cases, an academic degree may be abbreviated after an individual's name.

WITH DATES OR NUMERALS: Use the abbreviations *A.D., B.C., a.m., p.m., No.,* and abbreviate certain months when used with the day of the month.

Right: *In 450 B.C.; at 9:30 a.m.; in room No. 6; on Sept. 16.*

Wrong: *Early this a.m. he asked for the No. of your room.* The abbreviations are correct only with figures.

Right: *Early this morning he asked for the number of your room.*

IN NUMBERED ADDRESSES: Abbreviate *avenue, boulevard* and *street* in numbered addresses: *He lives on Pennsylvania Avenue. He lives at 1600 Pennsylvania Ave.*

STATES: The names of certain states and the *United States* are abbreviated with periods in some circumstances.

ACCEPTABLE BUT NOT REQUIRED: Some organizations and government agencies are widely recognized by their initials: *CIA, FBI, GOP.*

If the entry for such an organization notes that an abbreviation is acceptable in all references or on second reference, that does not mean that its use should be automatic. Let the context determine, for example, whether to use *Federal Bureau of Investigation* or *FBI.*

AVOID AWKWARD CONSTRUCTIONS: Do not follow an organization's full name with an abbreviation or acronym in parentheses or set off by dashes. If an abbreviation or acronym would not be clear on second reference without this arrangement, do not use it.

Names not commonly before the public should not be reduced to acronyms solely to save a few words.

SPECIAL CASES: Many abbreviations are desirable in tabulations and certain types of technical writing.

CAPS, PERIODS: Use capital letters and periods according to the listings in this book. For words not in this book, use the first-listed abbreviation in Webster's New World College Dictionary. Generally, omit periods in acronyms unless the result would spell an unrelated word. But use periods in two-letter abbreviations: *U.S., U.N., U.K., B.A., B.C.* (*AP*, a trademark, is an exception. Also, no periods in *GI* and *EU*). In headlines, do not use periods in abbreviations unless required for clarity.

Use all caps, but no periods, in longer abbreviations when the individual letters are pronounced: *ABC, CIA, FBI.*

Use only an initial cap and then lowercase for acronyms of more than six letters, unless listed otherwise in this Stylebook or Webster's New World College Dictionary.

addresses Use the abbreviations *Ave., Blvd.* and *St.* only with a numbered address: *7600 Pennsylvania Ave.* Spell them out and capitalize when part of a formal street name without a number: *Pennsylvania Avenue.* Lowercase and spell out when used alone or with more than one street name: *Massachusetts and Pennsylvania avenues.*

All similar words (*alley, drive, road, terrace,* etc.) are always spelled out. Capitalize them when part of a formal name without a number; lowercase when used alone or with two or more names.

Always use figures for an address number: *9 Morningside Circle.*

Spell out and capitalize *First* through *Ninth* when used as street names; use figures with two letters for *10th* and above: *7 Fifth Ave., 100 21st St.*

Abbreviate compass points used to indicate directional ends of a street or quadrants of a city in a numbered address: *222 E. 42nd St., 562 W. 43rd St., 600 K St. N.W.* Do not abbreviate if the number is omitted: *East 42nd Street, West 43rd Street, K Street Northwest.* No periods in quadrant abbreviations — NW, SE — unless customary locally.

Use periods in the abbreviation *P.O.* for P.O. Box numbers.

a.m., p.m. Lowercase, with periods. Avoid the redundant *10 a.m. this morning.*

B

Baby Bells A collective description of the regional telephone companies formed out of the breakup of the Bell System of AT&T. Avoid except in quotes.

baby boomer Lowercase, no hyphen.

baby-sit, baby-sitting, baby-sat, baby sitter

baccalaureate

Bachelor of Arts, Bachelor of Science *A bachelor's degree* or *bachelor's* is acceptable in any reference.

baseball The spellings for some frequently used words and phrases, some of which are exceptions to Webster's New World:

left-hander	put out (v.)
line up (v.)	putout (n.)
lineup (n.)	RBI (s.)
play off (v.)	RBIs (pl.)
playoff (n., adj.)	

NUMBERS: Some sample uses of numbers: *first inning, seventh-inning stretch, 10th inning; first base, second base, third base; first home run, 10th home run; first place; one RBI, 10 RBIs. The pitcher's record is now 6-5. The final score was 1-0.*

C

cabinet Capitalize references to a specific body of advisers heading executive departments for a president, king, governor, etc.: *The president-elect said he has not made his Cabinet selections.*

call letters Use all caps. Use hyphens to separate the type of station from the base call letters: *WBZ-AM, WBZ-FM, WBZ-TV.*

Citizens band operators, since 1983, are not required to be licensed by the Federal Communications Commission. Identification of such stations, either by the call sign previously assigned or made up by the operator, including the letter *K*, the operator's initials and the operator's ZIP code, is optional.

Amateur radio stations, which operate with greater power than citizens band stations and on different frequencies, typically mix letters and figures: *K2LRX.*

capitalization In general, avoid unnecessary capitals. Use a capital letter only if you can justify it by one of the principles listed here.

Some basic principles:

PROPER NOUNS: Capitalize nouns that constitute the unique identification for a specific person, place or thing: *John, Mary, America, Boston, England.*

Some words, such as the examples just given, are always proper nouns. Some common nouns receive proper noun status when they are used as the name of a particular entity: *General Electric, Gulf Oil.*

PROPER NAMES: Capitalize common nouns such as *party, river, street,* and *west* when they are an integral part of the full name for a person, place or thing: *Democratic Party, Mississippi River, Fleet Street, West Virginia.*

Lowercase these common nouns when they stand alone in subsequent references: *the party, the river, the street.*

Lowercase the common noun elements of names in all plural uses: *the Democratic and Republican parties, Main and State streets, lakes Erie and Ontario.* Exception: plurals of formal titles with full names are capitalized: *Presidents Jimmy Carter and Gerald R. Ford.*

cellphone

cents Spell out the word *cents* and lowercase, using numerals for amounts less than a dollar: *5 cents, 12 cents.* Use the $ sign and decimal system for larger amounts: *$1.01, $2.50.*

comma (,) The following guidelines treat some of the most frequent questions about the use of commas. For detailed guidance, consult the punctuation section in the back of Webster's New World College Dictionary.

IN A SERIES: Use commas to separate elements in a series, but do not put a comma before the conjunction in a simple series: *The flag is red, white and blue. He would nominate Tom, Dick or Harry.*

Put a comma before the concluding conjunction in a series, however, if an integral element of the series requires a conjunction: *I had orange juice, toast, and ham and eggs for breakfast.*

Use a comma also before the concluding conjunction in a complex series of phrases: *The main points to consider are whether the athletes are skillful enough to compete, whether they have the stamina to endure the training, and whether they have the proper mental attitude.*

WITH EQUAL ADJECTIVES: Use commas to separate a series of adjectives equal in rank. If the commas could be replaced by the word *and* without changing the sense, the adjectives are equal: *a thoughtful, precise manner; a dark, dangerous street.*

Use no comma when the last adjective before a noun outranks its predecessors because it is an integral element of a noun phrase, which is the equivalent of a single noun: *a cheap fur coat* (the noun phrase is *fur coat; the old oaken bucket; a new, blue spring bonnet.*

WITH NONESSENTIAL CLAUSES: A nonessential clause must be set off by commas. An essential clause must not be set off from the rest of a sentence by commas.

WITH NONESSENTIAL PHRASES: A nonessential phrase must be set off by commas. An essential phrase must not be set off from the rest of a sentence by commas.

WITH INTRODUCTORY CLAUSES AND PHRASES: A comma is used to separate an introductory clause or phrase from the main clause: *When he had tired of the mad pace of New York, he moved to Dubuque.*

The comma may be omitted after short introductory phrases if no ambiguity would result: *During the night he heard many noises.*

But use the comma if its omission would slow comprehension: *On the street below, the curious gathered.*

WITH CONJUNCTIONS: When a conjunction such as *and, but* or *for* links two clauses that could stand alone as separate sentences, use a comma before the conjunction in most cases: *She was glad she had looked, for a man was approaching the house.*

As a rule of thumb, use a comma if the subject of each clause is expressly stated: *We are visiting Washington, and we also plan a side trip to Williamsburg. We visited Washington, and our senator greeted us personally.* But no comma when the subject of the two clauses is the same and is not repeated in the second: *We are visiting Washington and plan to see the White House.*

The comma may be dropped if two clauses with expressly stated subjects are short. In general, however, favor use of a comma unless a particular literary effect is a desired or if it would distort the sense of a sentence.

INTRODUCING DIRECT QUOTES: Use a comma to introduce a complete one-sentence quotation within a paragraph: *Wallace said, "She spent six months in Argentina and came back speaking English with a Spanish accent."* But use a colon to introduce quotations of more than one sentence.

Do not use a comma at the start of an indirect or partial quotation: *He said the victory put him "firmly on the road to a first-ballot nomination."*

BEFORE ATTRIBUTION: Use a comma instead of a period at the end of a quote that is followed by an attribution: *"Rub my shoulders," Miss Cawley suggested.*

Do not use a comma, however, if the quoted statement ends with a question mark or exclamation point: *"Why should I?" he asked.*

WITH HOMETOWNS AND AGES: Use a comma to set off an individual's hometown when it is placed in apposition to a name (whether *of* is used or not): *Mary Richards, Minneapolis, and Maude Findlay, Tuckahoe, N.Y., were there.*

If an individual's age is used, set it off by commas: *Maude Findlay, 48, Tuckahoe N.Y., was present.*

NAMES OF STATES AND NATIONS USED WITH CITY NAMES: *His journey will take him from Dublin, Ireland, to Fargo, N.D., and back. The Selma, Ala., group saw the governor.*

Use parentheses, however, if a state name is inserted within a proper name: *The Huntsville (Ala.) Times.*

WITH YES AND NO: *Yes, I will be there.*

IN DIRECT ADDRESS: *Mother, I will be home late. No, sir, I did not take it.*

SEPARATING SIMILAR WORDS: Use a comma to separate duplicated words that otherwise would be confusing: *What the problem is, is not clear.*

IN LARGE FIGURES: Use a comma for most figures greater than 999. The major exceptions are: street addresses (*1234 Main St.*), broadcast frequencies (*1460 kilohertz*), room numbers, serial numbers, telephone numbers and years (*1876*).

PLACEMENT WITH QUOTES: Commas always go inside quotation marks.

WITH FULL DATES: When a phrase refers to a month, day and year, set off the year with a comma: *Feb. 14, 1987, is the target date.*

composition titles Apply the guidelines listed here to book titles, computer game titles, movie titles, opera titles, play titles, poem titles, album and song titles, radio and television program titles, and the titles of lectures, speeches and works of art.

The guidelines, followed by a block of examples:
—Capitalize the principal words, including prepositions and conjunctions of four or more letters.
—Capitalize an article — *the, a, an* — or words of fewer than four letters if it is the first or last word in a title.
—Put quotation marks around the names of all such works except the Bible and books that are primarily catalogs or reference material. In addition to catalogs, this category includes almanacs, directories, dictionaries, encyclopedias, gazetteers, handbooks and similar publications. Do not use quotation marks around such software titles as WordPerfect or Windows.
—Translate a foreign title into English unless a work is generally known by its foreign name. An exception to this is reviews of musical performances. In those instances, generally refer to the work in the language it was sung in, so as to differentiate for the reader. However, musical compositions in Slavic languages are always referred to in their English translations.

EXAMPLES: *"The Star Spangled Banner," "The Rise and Fall of the Third Reich," "Gone With the Wind," "Of Mice and Men," "For Whom the Bell Tolls," "Time After Time,"* the NBC-TV *"Today"* program, the *"CBS Evening News," "The Mary Tyler Moore Show."*

Reference works: *Jane's All the World's Aircraft, Encyclopaedia Britannica, Webster's New World Dictionary of the American Language, Second Edition.*

Names of most websites and apps are capitalized without quotes: *Facebook, Foursquare.*

Exception: "FarmVille" and similar computer game apps are in quotes.

Foreign works: *Rousseau's "War,"* not *Rousseau's "La Guerre."* But Leonardo da Vinci's *"Mona Lisa,"* Mozart's *"The Marriage of Figaro"* if sung in English but *"Le Nozze di Figaro"* if sung in Italian. Mozart's *"The Magic Flute"* if sung in English but *"Die Zauberfloete"* if sung in German. *"Die Walkuere"* and *"Gotterdammerung"* from Wagner's *"Der Ring des Nibelungen"* if sung in German but *"The Valkyrie"* and *"The Twilight of the Gods"* from *"The Ring of Nibelungen"* if sung in English. Janacek's *"From the House of the Dead,"* not Janacek's *"Z Mrtveho Domu."*

— For other classical music titles, use quotation marks around the composition's nicknames but not compositions identified by its sequence.

EXAMPLES: *Dvorak's "New World Symphony." Dvorak's Symphony No. 9.*

D

Dacron A trademark for a brand of polyester fiber.

dad Uppercase only when the noun substitutes for a name as a term of address: *Hi, Dad!*

dalai lama The traditional high priest of Lamaism, a form of Buddhism practiced in Tibet and Mongolia. *Dalai lama* is a title rather than a name, but it is all that is used when referring to the man. Capitalize *Dalai Lama* in reference to the holder of the title, in keeping with the nobility entry.

datelines Datelines on stories should contain a city name, entirely in capital letters, followed in most cases by the name of the state, county or territory where the city is located.

DOMESTIC DATELINES: A list of domestic cities that stand alone in datelines follows. The norms that influenced the selection were the population of the city, the population of its metropolitan region, the frequency of the city's appearance in the news, the uniqueness of its name, and experience that has shown the name to be almost synonymous with the state or nation where it is located.

No state with the following:

ATLANTA	HOUSTON
BALTIMORE	INDIANAPOLIS
BOSTON	LAS VEGAS
CHICAGO	LOS ANGELES
CINCINNATI	MIAMI
CLEVELAND	MILWAUKEE
DALLAS	MINNEAPOLIS
DENVER	NEW ORLEANS
DETROIT	NEW YORK
HONOLULU	OKLAHOMA CITY
PHILADELPHIA	SAN ANTONIO
PHOENIX	SAN DIEGO
PITTSBURGH	SAN FRANCISCO
ST. LOUIS	SEATTLE
SALT LAKE CITY	WASHINGTON

Stories from all other U.S. cities should have both the city and state name in the dateline, including *KANSAS CITY, Mo.,* and *KANSAS CITY, Kan.*

Spell out *Alaska, Hawaii, Idaho, Iowa, Maine, Ohio, Texas* and *Utah.* Abbreviate others as listed under the full name of each state.

Use *Hawaii* on all cities outside Honolulu. Specify the island in the text if needed.

Follow the same practice for communities on islands within boundaries of other states: *EDGARTOWN, Mass.,* for example, not *EDGARTOWN, Martha's Vineyard.*

WITHIN STORIES: In citing other cities within the body of a story:

— No further information is necessary if a city is in the same state as the datelined city. Make an exception only if confusion would result.

— Follow the city name with further identification in most cases where it is not in the same state or nation as the dateline city. The additional identification may be omitted, however, if no confusion would result. There is no need, for example, to refer to *Boston, Mass.,* in a story datelined *NEW YORK.*

— Provide a state or nation identification for the city if the story is undated. However, cities that stand alone in datelines may be used alone in undated stories if no confusion would result.

daylight saving time Not *savings.* No hyphen.

When linking the term with the name of a time zone, use only the word *daylight: Eastern Daylight Time, Pacific Daylight Time,* etc.

Lowercase *daylight saving time* in all uses and *daylight time* whenever it stands alone.

A federal law specifies that daylight time applies from 2 a.m. on the second Sunday of March until 2 a.m. on the first Sunday of November in areas that do not specifically exempt themselves.

dollars Always lowercase. Use figures and the $ sign in all except casual references or amounts without a figure: *The book cost $4. Dad, please give me a dollar. Dollars are flowing overseas.*

For specified amounts, the word takes a singular verb: *He said $500,000 is what they want.*

For amounts of more than $1 million, use up to two decimal places. Do not link the numerals and the word by a hyphen: *It is worth $4.35 million. He is worth exactly $4,351,242. He proposed a $300 billion budget.*

The form for amounts less than $1 million: *$4, $25, $500, $1,000, $650,000.*

E

each Takes a singular verb.

each other, one another Two people look at *each other*. More than two look at *one another*.

Either phrase may be used when the number is indefinite: *We help each other. We help one another.*

earl, countess

earmark

earth Generally lowercase; capitalize when used as the proper name of the planet. *She is down-to-earth. How does the pattern apply to Mars, Jupiter, Earth, the sun and the moon? The astronauts returned to Earth. He hopes to move heaven and earth.*

earthquakes Hundreds of earthquakes occur each year. Most are so small they cannot be felt.

The best source for information on major earthquakes is the National Earthquake Information Service operated by the U.S. Geological Survey in Golden, Colo.

Online: http://www.usgs.gov

Earthquake magnitudes are measures of earthquake size calculated from ground motion recorded on seismographs. The Richter scale, named for Dr. Charles F. Richter, is no longer widely used.

Magnitudes are usually reported simply as *magnitude 6.7,* for example. Hyphenate as a compound modifier: *magnitude-6.7 quake.*

In the first hours after a quake, earthquake size should be reported as a *preliminary magnitude of 6.7.* Early estimates are often revised, and it can be several days before seismologists calculate a final figure.

The most commonly used measure is the *moment magnitude,* related to the area of the fault on which an earthquake occurs, and the amount the ground slips.

The magnitude scale being used should be specified only when necessary. An example would be when two centers are reporting different magnitudes because they are using different scales. The various scales usually differ only slightly.

With each scale, every increase of one number, say from *5.5* to *6.5,* means that the quake's magnitude is 10 times as great. Theoretically, there is no upper limit to the scales.

A quake of magnitude 2.5 to 3 is the smallest generally felt by people.

—Magnitude 4: The quake can cause moderate damage.

—Magnitude 5: The quake can cause considerable damage.

—Magnitude 6: The quake can cause severe damage.

—Magnitude 7: A major earthquake, capable of widespread, heavy damage.

OTHER TERMS: The word *temblor* (not *tremblor*) is a synonym for earthquake.

The word *epicenter* refers to the point on Earth's surface above the underground center, or focus, of an earthquake.

email Acceptable in all references for *electronic mail.* Many *email* or Internet addresses use symbols such as the at symbol (@), or the *tilde* (∼) that cannot be transmitted correctly by some computers. When needed, spell them out and provide an explanatory editor's note. Use a hyphen with other *e-* terms; *e-book, e-business, e-commerce.*

F

face to face When a story says two people meet for discussions, talks or debate, it is unnecessary to say they met *face to face.*

fact-finding (adj.)

factor A financial organization whose primary business is purchasing the accounts receivable of other firms, at a discount, and taking the risk and responsibilities of making collection.

Faeroe Islands Use in datelines after a community name in stories from this group of Danish islands in the northern Atlantic Ocean between Iceland and the Shetland Islands.

Fahrenheit The temperature scale commonly used in the United States.

The scale is named for Gabriel Daniel Fahrenheit, a German physicist who designed it. In it, the freezing point of water is 32 degrees and the boiling point is 212 degrees.

To convert to Celsius, subtract 32 from Fahrenheit figure, multiply by 5 and divide by 9 ($77 - 32 = 45$, times $5 = 225$, divided by $9 = 25$ degrees Celsius).

In cases that require mention of the scale, use these forms: *86 degrees Fahrenheit* or *86 F* (note the space and no period after the *F*) if degrees and Fahrenheit are clear from the context.

fallout (n.)

food A list of food guidelines appears in the current edition of the Associated Press Stylebook.

G

GAAP The acronym stands for *generally accepted accounting principles.* Spell out on first reference.

gage, gauge A *gage* is a security or a pledge.

A *gauge* is a measuring device.

Gauge is also a term used to designate the size of shotguns.

gaiety

gale

gallon Equal to 128 fluid ounces. The metric equivalent is approximately 3.8 liters. There are 42 gallons in a barrel of oil.

To convert to liters, multiply by 3.8 (3 gallons × 3.8 – 11.4 liters)

Gallup Poll Prepared by the Gallup Organization, Princeton, NJ.

H

habeas corpus A writ ordering a person in custody to be brought before a court. It places the burden of proof on those detaining the person to justify the detention.

When *habeas corpus* is used in a story, define it.

hacker The term has evolved to mean one who uses computer skills to unlawfully penetrate proprietary computer systems.

Hades But lowercase *hell.*

Hague, The In datelines: *THE HAGUE, Netherlands (AP)*
In text: *The Hague.*

half It is not necessary to use the preposition *of*: *half the time* is correct, but *half of the time* is not wrong.

half- Follow Webster's New World College Dictionary. Hyphenate if not listed there.

Some frequently used words without a hyphen:

halfback	halftone
halfhearted	halftrack

Also: *halftime,* in keeping with widespread practice in sports copy.

Some frequently used combinations that are two words without a hyphen:

half brother	half size
half dollar	half sole (n.)
half note	half tide

Some frequently used combinations that include a hyphen:

half-baked	half-life
half-blood	half-moon
half-cocked	half-sole (v.)
half-hour	half-truth

I

Iberia Headquarters of this airline is in Madrid.

IBM Acceptable as first reference for *International Business Machines Corp.*

Headquarters is in Armonk, N.Y.

ICBM, ICBMs Acceptable on first reference for *intercontinental ballistic missile(s),* but the term should be defined in the body of a story.

Avoid the redundant *ICBM missiles.*

ice age Lowercase, because it denotes not a single period but any of a series of cold periods marked by glaciation alternating with periods of relative warmth.

Capitalize the proper nouns in the names of individual ice ages, such as the *Wisconsin ice age.*

The most recent series of ice ages happened during the *Pleistocene* epoch, which began about 1.6 million years ago. During that time, glaciers sometimes covered much of North America and northwestern Europe.

The present epoch, the *Holocene* or *Recent,* began about 10,000 years ago, when the continental glaciers had retreated to Antarctica and Greenland.

ice storm

Idaho Do not abbreviate in datelines or stories. Postal code: ID

J

Jacuzzi Trademark for a brand of whirlpool products. Generic terms are whirlpool bath or whirlpool spa.

jail Not interchangeable with *prison.*

Jane's All the World's Aircraft, Jane's Fighting Ships The reference sources for questions about aircraft and military ships not covered in this book.

The reference for nonmilitary ships is Lloyd's Register of Shipping.

Japan Airlines Corp. *JAL* is acceptable on second reference.

Headquarters is in Tokyo.

Japan Current A warm current flowing from the Philippine Sea east of Taiwan and northeast past Japan.

Jargon The special vocabulary and idioms of a particular class or occupational group. In general, avoid jargon. When it is appropriate in a special context, include an explanation of any words likely to be unfamiliar to most readers.

K

K Use *K* in references to modem transmission speeds, in keeping with standard usage: a *56K modem* (no space after numeral).

The abbreviation should not be used to mean 1,000 or $1,000.

Kabul The city in Afghanistan carries the name of the country in datelines.

kaffiyeh The men's headdress in Arab countries.

Kansas Abbreviate *Kan.* in datelines or stories. Postal code: *KS*

Kansas City Use *KANSAS CITY, Kan.,* or *KANSAS CITY, Mo.,* in datelines to avoid confusion between the two.

Kelvin scale A scale of temperature based on, but different from, the Celsius scale. It is used primarily in science to record very high and very low temperatures. The Kelvin scale starts at zero and indicates the total absence of heat (absolute zero).

Zero on the Kelvin scale is equal to minus 273.16 degrees Celsius and minus 459.67 degrees Fahrenheit.

The freezing point of water is 273.16 kelvins. The boiling point of water is 373.16 kelvins. (Note temperatures on the Kelvin scale are called *kelvins,* not *degrees*. The symbol, a capital K, stands alone with no degree symbol.)

To convert from Celsius to Kelvin, add 273.16 to the Celsius temperature.

L

Labor Day The first Monday in September.

Laborers' International Union of North America The shortened form *Laborers' union* is acceptable in all references.

Headquarters is in Washington.

Labrador The mainland portion of the Canadian province of Newfoundland and Labrador.

Use *Newfoundland* in datelines after the name of a community. Specify in the text that it is in Labrador.

Ladies' Home Journal

lady Do not use as a synonym for *woman. Lady* may be used when it is a courtesy title or when a specific reference to fine manners is appropriate without patronizing overtones.

lake Capitalize as part of a proper name: *Lake Erie, Canandaigua Lake, the Finger lakes.*

Lowercase in plural uses: *lakes Erie and Ontario; Canandaigua and Seneca lakes.*

M

Macau Stands alone in datelines. (Spelling is an exception to Webster's New World.)

Mace A trademark, shortened from *Chemical Mace,* for a brand of tear gas that is packaged in an aerosol canister and temporarily stuns its victims.

media law A briefing on media law appears in the current edition of the Associated Press Stylebook.

metric system For U.S. members, use metric terms only in situations where they are universally accepted forms of measurement (*16 mm film*) or where the metric distance is an important number in itself: *He vowed to walk 100 kilometers (62 miles) in a week.*

Normally, the equivalent should be in parentheses after the metric figure. A general statement, however, such as *A kilometer equals about five-eighths of a mile,* would be acceptable to avoid repeated use of parenthetical equivalents in a story that uses kilometers many times.

To avoid the need for long strings of figures, prefixes are added to the metric units to denote fractional elements or large multiples. The prefixes are: *pico-* (one-trillionth), *nano-* (one-billionth), *micro-* (one-millionth), *milli-* (one-thousandth), *centi-* (one-hundredth), *deci-* (one-tenth), *deka-* (10 units), *hecto-* (100 units), *kilo-* (1,000 units), *mega-* (1 million units), *giga-* (1 billion units), *tera-* (1 trillion units).

ABBREVIATIONS: The abbreviation *mm* for millimeter is acceptable in references to film widths (*8 mm film*) and weapons (*a 105 mm cannon*). (Note space between numeral and abbreviation.)

The principal abbreviations, for reference in the event they are used by a source, are: *g* (gram), *kg* (kilogram), *t* (metric ton), *m* (meter), *cm* (centimeter), *km* (kilometer), *mm* (millimeter), *L* (liter, capital *L* to avoid confusion with the figure *1*) and *mL* (milliliter).

midnight Do not put a *12* in front of it. It is part of the day that is ending, not the one that is beginning.

millions, billions Use figures with *million* or *billion* in all except casual uses: *I'd like to make a billion dollars.* But: *The nation has 1 million citizens. I need $7 billion.*

Do not go beyond two decimal places. *7.51 million people, $256 billion, 7,542,500 people, $2,565,750,000.* Decimals are preferred where practical: *1.5 million.* Not: *1 1/2 million.*

Do not mix *millions* and *billions* in the same figure: *2.6 billion.* Not: *2 billion 600 million.*

Do not drop the word *million* or *billion* in the first figure of a range: *He is worth from $2 million to $4 million.* Not: *$2 to 4 million,* unless you really mean $2.

Note that a hyphen is not used to join the figures and the word *million* or *billion,* even in this type of phrase: *The president submitted to a $300 billion budget.*

months Capitalize the names of months in all uses. When a month is used with a specific date, abbreviate only *Jan., Feb., Aug., Sept., Oct., Nov.* and *Dec.* Spell out when using alone, or with a year alone.

When a phrase lists only a month and a year, do not separate the year with commas. When a phrase refers to a month, day and year, set off the year with commas.

EXAMPLES: *January 1972 was a cold month. Jan. 2 was the coldest day of the month. His birthday is May 8. Feb 14, 1987, was the target date. She testified that it was Friday, Dec. 3, when the accident occurred.*

In tabular material, use these three-letter forms without a period: *Jan, Feb, Mar, Apr, May, Jun, Jul, Aug, Sep, Oct, Nov, Dec.*

MRI Magnetic resonance imaging, a noninvasive diagnostic procedure used to render images of the inside of an object. It is primarily used in medical imaging to demonstrate pathological or other physiological alterations of living tissues. *MRI* is acceptable on first reference and in all uses.

N

naive

names In general, use only last names on second reference.

When it is necessary to distinguish between two people who use the same last name, as in married couples or brothers and sisters, use the first and last name.

In stories involving juveniles, generally refer to them on second reference by surname if they are 16 or older and by first name if they are 15 or younger. Exceptions would be if they are involved in serious crimes or are athletes or entertainers.

nano- A prefix denoting one-billionth of a unit. Move the decimal point nine places to the left in converting to the basic unit: 2,999,888,777.5 nanoseconds equals 2.9998887775 seconds.

naphtha

noon Do not put a *12* in front of it.

numerals A numeral is a figure, letter, word or group of words expressing a number.

Roman numerals use the letters *I, V, X, L, C, D* and *M*. Use Roman numerals for wars and to show personal sequence for animals and people: *World War II, Native Dancer II, King George IV, Pope John XXIII.*

Arabic numerals use the figures *1, 2, 3, 4, 5, 6, 7, 8, 9* and *0.* Use Arabic forms unless Roman numerals are specifically required.

The figures *1, 2, 10, 101,* etc. and the corresponding words — *one, two, ten, one hundred one,* etc. — are called *cardinal numbers.* The term *ordinal number* applies to *1st, 2nd, 10th, 101st, first, second, tenth, one hundred first,* etc.

Follow these guidelines in using numerals:

SENTENCE START: Spell out a numeral at the beginning of a sentence. If necessary, recast the sentence. There is one exception — a numeral that identifies a calendar year.

Wrong: *993 freshmen entered the college last year.*

Right: *Last year 993 freshmen entered the college.*

Right: *1976 was a very good year.*

CASUAL USES: Spell out casual expressions:

A thousand times no! Thanks a million. He walked a quarter of a mile.

PROPER NAMES: Use words or numerals according to an organization's practice: *3M, Twentieth Century Fund, Big Ten.*

FIGURES OR WORDS?

For ordinals:

— Spell out *first* through *ninth* when they indicate sequence in time or location: *first base, the First Amendment, he was first in line.* Starting with *10th* use figures.

— Use *1st, 2nd, 3rd, 4th,* etc. when the sequence has been assigned in forming names. The principal examples are geographic, military and political designations such as *1st Ward, 7th Fleet,* and *1st Sgt.*

O

oasis, oases

Occupational Safety and Health Administration *OSHA* is acceptable on second reference.

occupational titles They are always lowercase.

occur, occurred, occurring Also: *occurrence.*

ocean The five, from the largest to the smallest: Pacific Ocean, Atlantic Ocean, Indian Ocean, Antarctic Ocean, Arctic Ocean.

Lowercase *ocean* standing alone or in plural uses: *the ocean, the Atlantic and Pacific oceans.*

P

pacemaker Formerly a trademark, now a generic term for a device that electronically helps a person's heart maintain a steady beat.

Pacific Standard Time (PST), Pacific Daylight Time (PDT)

page numbers Use figures and capitalize *page* when used with a figure. When a letter is appended to the figure, capitalize it but do not use a hyphen: *Page 1, Page 10, Page 20A.*

One exception: *It's a Page One story.*

palate, palette, pallet *Palate* is the roof of the mouth.

A *palette* is an artist's paint board.

A *pallet* is a bed.

Palestine Liberation Organization Not *Palestinian. PLO* is acceptable in all references.

pan- Prefix meaning "all" takes no hyphen when combined with a common noun:

panchromatic   pantheism

Most combinations with *pan-* are proper nouns, however, and both *pan-* and the proper name it is combined with are capitalized:

punctuation A guide to punctuation appears in the current edition of the Associated Press Stylebook.

Q

Q-and-A format   Use *Q-and-A* within the body of a story.

Qantas Airways   Headquarters of this airline is in Mascot, Australia.

QE2   Acceptable on second reference for the ocean liner Queen Elizabeth 2. (But use a roman numeral for the monarch: *Queen Elizabeth II)*

Q-tips   A trademark for a brand of cotton swabs.

quotation marks   (" ") The basic guidelines for open-quote marks (") and close-quote marks ("):

FOR DIRECT QUOTATIONS: To surround the exact words of a speaker or writer when reported in a story:
"I have no intention of staying," he replied.
"I do not object," he said, "to the tenor of the report."
Franklin said, "A penny saved is a penny earned."
A speculator said the practice is "too conservative for inflationary times."

RUNNING QUOTATIONS: If a full paragraph of quoted material is followed by a paragraph that continues the quotation, do not put close-quote marks at the end of the first paragraph. Do, however, put open-quote marks at the start of the second paragraph. Continue in this fashion for succeeding paragraphs, using close-quote marks only at the end of the quoted material.

If a paragraph does not start with quotation marks but ends with a quotation that is continued in the next paragraph, do not use close-quote marks at the end of the introductory paragraph if the quoted material constitutes a full sentence. Use close-quote marks, however, if the quoted material does not constitute a full sentence. For example:
He said, "I am shocked and horrified by the incident.
"I am so horrified, in fact, that I will ask for the death penalty."

But: *He said he was "shocked and horrified by the incident."*
"I am so horrified, in fact, that I will ask for the death penalty," he said.

DIALOGUE OR CONVERSATION: Each person's words, no matter how brief, are placed in a separate paragraph, with quotation marks at the beginning and end of each person's speech:
"Will you go?"
"Yes."
"When?"
"Thursday."

NOT IN Q-and-A: Quotation marks are not required in formats that identify questions and answers by *Q:* and *A:.*

NOT IN TEXTS: Quotation marks are not required in full texts, condensed texts or textual excerpts.

IRONY: Put quotation marks around a word or words used in an ironical sense: *The "debate" turned into a free-for-all.*

UNFAMILIAR TERMS: A word or words being introduced to readers may be placed in quotation marks on first reference:
Broadcast frequencies are measured in "kilohertz."
Do not put subsequent references to *kilohertz* in quotation marks.

AVOID UNNECESSARY FRAGMENTS: Do not use quotation marks to report a few ordinary words that the speaker or writer has used:
Wrong: *The senator said he would "go home to Michigan" if he lost the election.*
Right: *The senator said he would go home to Michigan if he lost the election.*

PARTIAL QUOTES: When a partial quote is used, do not put quotation marks around words that the speaker could not have used.

Suppose the individual said, *"I am horrified at your slovenly manners."*
Wrong: *She said she "was horrified at their slovenly manners."*
Right: *She said she was horrified at their "slovenly manners."*
Better when practical: Use the full quote.

QUOTES WITHIN QUOTES: Alternate between double quotation marks ("or") and single marks ('or'):
She said, "I quote from his letter, 'I agree with Kipling that "the female of the species is more deadly than the male," but the phenomenon is not an unchangeable law of nature,' a remark he did not explain."

Use three marks together if two quoted elements end at the same time: *She said, "He told me, 'I love you.'"*

(NOTE: Local style should ensure some differentiation between the single and double quotation marks, either with a "thin" space or by different typography, if not computer-programmed.)

PLACEMENT WITH OTHER PUNCTUATION: Follow these long-established printers' rules:
— The period and the comma always go within the quotation marks.
— The dash, the semicolon, the question mark and the exclamation point go within the quotation marks when they apply to the quoted matter only. They go outside when they apply to the whole sentence.

quotations in the news   Never alter quotations even to correct minor grammatical errors or word usage. Casual minor tongue slips may be removed using ellipses but even that should be done with extreme caution. If there is a question about a quote, either don't use it or ask the speaker to clarify.

If a person is unavailable for comment, detail attempts to reach that person. *(Smith was out of the country on business; Jones did not return phone messages left at the office.)*

Do not use substandard spellings such as *gonna* or *wanna* in attempts to convey regional dialects or informal pronunciations, except to help a desired touch or to convey an emphasis by the speaker.

Follow basic writing style and use abbreviations where appropriate, as in *No. 1, St., Gov., Sen.,* and *$3.*

FULL vs. PARTIAL QUOTES: In general, avoid fragmentary quotes. If a speaker's words are clear and concise, favor the full quote. If cumbersome language can be paraphrased fairly, use an indirect construction, reserving quotation marks for sensitive or controversial passages that must be identified specifically as coming from the speaker.

CONTEXT: Remember that you can misquote someone by giving a startling remark without its modifying passage or qualifiers. The manner of delivery sometimes is part of the context. Reporting a smile or deprecatory gesture may be as important as conveying the words themselves.

R

race Identification by race is pertinent:

—In biographical and announcement stories that involve a feat or appointment not routinely associated with members of a particular race.

—When it provides the reader with a substantial insight into conflicting emotions known or likely to be involved in a demonstration or similar event.

In some stories that involve a conflict, it is equally important to specify that an issue cuts across racial lines. If, for example, a demonstration by supporters of busing to achieve racial balance in schools includes a substantial number of whites, that fact should be noted.

Do not use racially derogatory terms unless they are part of a quotation that is essential to the story.

racket Not *racquet*, for the light bat used in tennis and badminton.

rack, wrack The noun *rack* applies to various types of framework; the verb *rack* means to arrange on a rack, to torture, trouble or torment: *He was placed on the rack. She racked her brain.*

The noun *wrack* means ruin or destruction, and generally is confined to the phrase *wrack and ruin* and *wracked with doubt* (or *pain*).

The verb *wrack* has substantially the same meaning as the verb *rack*, the latter being preferred.

radar A lowercase acronym for *radio detection and ranging*. Radar acceptable in all references.

radio Capitalize and use before a name to indicate an official or state-funded broadcast voice: *Radio Free Europe, Radio France International.*

Lowercase and place after the name when indicating only that the information was obtained from broadcasts in a city. *Mexico City radio,* for example, is the form used in referring to reports that are broadcast on various stations in the Mexican capital.

radio station Use lowercase: *radio station WHEC.*

S

Sabbath Capitalize in religious references.

saboteur

Sacagawea

sacraments Capitalize the proper names used for a sacramental rite that commemorates the life of Jesus Christ or signifies a belief in his presence: *the Lord's Supper, Holy Communion, Holy Eucharist.*

Lowercase the names of other sacraments: *baptism, confirmation, penance* (now often called the *sacrament of reconciliation*), *matrimony, holy orders,* and *the sacrament of anointing the sick* (formerly *extreme unction*).

sacrilegious

smartphone An advanced cellphone that allows for email, Web browsing and downloadable applications.

social media A list of social media guidelines appears in the current edition of the Associated Press Stylebook.

sports A list of sports guidelines and style issues appears in the current edition of the Associated Press Stylebook.

state names Follow these guidelines:

STANDING ALONE: Spell out the names of the 50 U.S. states when they stand alone in textual material. Any state name may be condensed, however, to fit typographical requirements for tabular material.

EIGHT NOT ABBREVIATED: The names of eight states are never abbreviated in datelines or text: *Alaska, Hawaii, Idaho, Iowa, Maine, Ohio, Texas* and *Utah.*

Memory Aid: Spell out the names of two states that are not part of the contiguous United States and of the continental states that are five letters or fewer.

ABBREVIATIONS REQUIRED: Use the state abbreviations listed at the end of this section:

— In conjunction with the name of a city, town, village or military base in most datelines.

— In conjunction with the name of a city, county, town, village or military base in text.

— In short-form listings of party affiliation: *D-Ala., R-Mont.*

Following are the state abbreviations (postal code abbreviations in parentheses):

Ala. (AL)	Neb. (NE)
Ariz. (AZ)	Nev. (NV)
Ark. (AR)	N.H. (NH)
Calif. (CA)	N.J. (NJ)
Colo. (CO)	N.M. (NM)
Conn. (CT)	N.Y. (NY)
Del. (DE)	N.C. (NC)

Fla. (FL)	N.D. (ND)
Ga. (GA)	Okla. (OK)
Ill. (IL)	Ore. (OR)
Ind. (IN)	Pa. (PA)
Kan. (KS)	R.I. (RI)
Ky. (KY)	S.C. (SC)
La. (LA)	S.D. (SD)
Md. (MD)	Tenn. (TN)
Mass. (MA)	Vt. (VT)
Mich. (MI)	Va. (VA)
Minn. (MN)	Wash. (WA)
Miss. (MS)	W.Va. (WV)
Mo. (MO)	Wis. (WI)
Mont. (MT)	Wyo. (WY)

These are the postal code abbreviations for the eight states that are never abbreviated in datelines or text: AK (Alaska), HI (Hawaii), ID (Idaho), IA (Iowa), ME (Maine), OH (Ohio), TX (Texas), UT (Utah). Also: DC (District of Columbia).

Use the two-letter Postal Service abbreviations only with full addresses, including ZIP code.

PUNCTUATION: Place one comma between the city and the state name, and another comma after the state name, unless ending a sentence or indicating a dateline: *He was traveling from Nashville, Tenn., to Austin, Texas, en route to his home in Albuquerque, N.M. She said Cook County, Ill., was Mayor Daley's stronghold.*

STATES IN HEADLINES: No periods for those abbreviated with two capital letters: NY, NJ, NH, NM, NC, SC, ND, SD and RI. Other states retain periods: Ga., Ky., Mont., Conn.

MISCELLANEOUS: Use *New York state* when necessary to distinguish the state from New York City.

Use *state of Washington* or *Washington state* when necessary to distinguish the state from the District of Columbia. *(Washington State* is the name of a university in the state of Washington.)

T

tablecloth

tablespoon, tablespoonfuls Equal to three teaspoons or one-half a fluid ounce.

The metric equivalent is approximately 15 milliliters.

television station The call letters alone are frequently adequate, but when this phrase is needed, use lowercase: *television station WTEV.*

time element Use the days of the week, not *today* or *tonight* in print copy.

Use Monday, Tuesday, etc., for days of the week within seven days before or after the current date.

Use the month and a figure where appropriate.

Avoid such redundancies as *last Tuesday* or *next Tuesday.* The past, present or future tense used for the verb usually provides adequate indication of which Tuesday is meant: *He said he finished the job Tuesday. She will return Tuesday.*

Avoid awkward placements of the time element, particularly those that suggest the day of the week is the object of a transitive verb: *The police jailed Tuesday.* Potential remedies include the use of the word *on,* rephrasing the sentence, or placing the time element in a different sentence.

times Use figures except for *noon* and *midnight.* Use a colon to separate hours from minutes: *11 a.m., 1 p.m., 3:30 p.m., 9-11 a.m., 9 a.m. to 5 p.m.*

Avoid such redundancies as *10 a.m. this morning, 10 p.m. tonight, 10 p.m. Monday,* etc., as required by the norms in time element.

The construction *4 o'clock* is acceptable, but time listings with *a.m.* or *p.m.* are preferred.

time zones Capitalize the full name of the time in force within a particular zone: *Eastern Standard Time, Eastern Daylight Time, Central Standard Time,* etc.

Lowercase all but the region in short forms: *the Eastern time zone, Eastern time, Mountain time,* etc.

Spell out *time zone* in references not accompanied by a clock reading: *Chicago is in the Central time zone.*

The abbreviations *EST, CDT,* etc., are acceptable on first reference for zones used within the continental United States, Canada and Mexico only if the abbreviation is linked with a clock reading: *noon EST, 9 a.m. PST.* (Do not set off the abbreviations with commas.)

Spell out all references to time zones not used within the contiguous United States: *When it is noon EDT, it is 1 p.m. Atlantic Standard Time and 8 a.m. Alaska Standard Time.*

One exception to the spelled-out form: *Greenwich Mean Time* may be abbreviated as *GMT* on second reference if used with a clock reading.

U

U-boat A German submarine. Anything referring to a submarine should be *submarine* unless directly referring to a German vessel of World War I or II vintage.

UFO, UFOs Acceptable in all references for *unidentified flying object(s).*

ukulele

Ulster Historically, one of the four Irish provinces, covering nine counties. Six of the counties became Northern Ireland, three became part of the Republic of Ireland. Avoid use as a synonym for *Northern Ireland.*

Ultimate Fighting A registered trademark. Use the generic term *mixed martial arts* for bouts featuring boxing, wrestling, taekwondo, judo and other disciplines. *Ultimate Fighting Championship* is acceptable for events sanctioned by that group.

V

vacuum

Valium A trademark for a brand of tranquilizer and muscle relaxant. It also may be called *diazepam*.

valley Capitalize as part of a full name: *the Mississippi Valley*.
Lowercase in plural uses: *the Missouri and Mississippi valleys*.

Vaseline A trademark for a brand of petroleum jelly.

Vatican City Stands alone in datelines.

v-chip

W

Wahhabi Follower of a strict Muslim sect that adheres closely to the Quran; it's most powerful in Saudi Arabia.

waiter (male), **waitress** (female)

waitlist (n.), **wait-list** (v.)

Wales Use *Wales* after the names of Welsh communities in datelines.

walk up (v.), **walk-up** (n. and adj.)

Wall Street When the reference is to the entire complex of financial institutions in the area rather than the actual street itself, *the Street* is an acceptable short form.

website A location on the *World Wide Web* that maintains one or more pages at a specific address. Also, *webcam*, *webcast* and *webmaster*. but as a short form and in terms with separate words, the *Web*, *Web page* and *Web feed*.

X

Xerox A trademark for a brand of photocopy machine. Never a verb. Use a generic term, such as photocopy.
Headquarters of *Xerox Corp.* is in Norwalk, Conn.

Xinhua News Agency The official news agency of the Chinese government is based in Beijing. It was founded in 1931 as the Red China News Agency and adopted its current name in 1937. *Xinhua* is acceptable on second reference.

XML For *extensible markup language,* used to sort, search and format information.

X-ray (n., v. and adj.) Use for both the photographic process and the radiation particles themselves.

Y

Yahoo A trademark for an online computer service. Headquarters of Yahoo Inc. is in Sunnyvale, Calif. Do not use the exclamation point in the formal corporate name.

yam Botanically, yams and sweet potatoes are not related, although several varieties of moist-fleshed sweet potatoes are popularly called yams in some parts of the United States.

yard Equal to 3 feet.
The metric equivalent is approximately 0.91 meter.
To convert to meters, multiply by 0.91 (5 yards x 0.91 = 4.55 meters).

year-end (adj.)

years Use figures, without commas: *1975*. When a phrase refers to a month, day and year, set off the year with a comma: *Feb. 14, 1987, is the target date*. Use an s without an apostrophe to indicate spans of decades or centuries: *the 1890s, the 1800s*.
Years are the lone exception to the general rule in numerals that a figure is not used to start a sentence: *1976 was a very good year*.

yellow journalism The use of cheaply sensational methods to attract or influence readers. The term comes from the "Yellow Kid," a comic strip in the New York World in 1895.

Z

zero, zeros

zigzag

Zionism The effort of the Jews to regain and retain their biblical homeland. It is based on the promise of God in the book of Genesis that Israel would forever belong to Abraham and his descendants as a nation.
The term is named for Mount Zion, the site of the ancient temple in Jerusalem. The Bible also frequently uses *Zion* in a general sense to denote the place where God is especially present with his people.

ZIP code Use all-caps *ZIP* for *Zoning Improvement Plan,* but always lowercase the word *code*.
Run the five digits together without a comma, and do not put a comma between the state name and ZIP code: *New York, NY 10020*.

zip line

Zurich The city in Switzerland stands alone in datelines.

Glossary

A

accuracy getting all the facts right and always seeking the truth.

active voice the subject performs the action expressed in the verb.

advertising paid medium concerned with sales; moving the audience to buy or do something.

advertising manager the person who heads up the advertising staff for a yearbook.

anchor the main news presenter, or reporter, to read broadcast news.

anchored regular features put in the same place so they are easily found each day.

anecdote a short personal story about an event or occurrence.

anonymous source a source who does not want to be named.

artists work with editors and reporters to produce illustrations, charts, graphs, maps or other materials that will help tell a story.

assets story elements.

Associated Press style style used by most news organizations for stories; usually referred to as AP style.

attribution giving the reader the name of your source.

B

backpack journalist a journalist who uses all the technical tools needed to produce the multiple elements of a story, such as a video camera and a laptop computer.

banner the long space across the top of the page.

beat topic or area of coverage such as sports or politics, but is even further defined and specific.

bio biographical sketch on a story subject.

biography an account of a person's life.

blog post blog entry.

body middle of the narrative story where the writer develops the story with details and quotes.

breaking news news that is happening now and that journalists must cover live and on deadline.

breakout box a black-outlined box that relates to, but is separate from, the story.

broadcast a radio or television program.

budget a document that sets out the expected expenses and income for the year.

business manager the person in charge of the money side of the yearbook.

C

caption also called cutline; copy adjoining the photo that relates to the photo.

celebrity a celebrated person; a person of note.

censorship the prevention, or attempted prevention, of printing or broadcasting materials that are considered by some to be objectionable.

central point the most important piece of information the writer wants to get across to the reader.

chart a graphic used to compare data such as amounts and percentages.

chronological order stories written in the order in which things happened.

chyron words superimposed on the lower third of the screen.

citizen journalism journalism in which the audience participates.

coaching guiding and training journalists to do their best work.

coaching editor an editor who helps reporters define stories, draft good questions for interviews and determine which sources are credible.

column a regularly appearing article that expresses the opinion of the writer; in sportswriting, a sports story that requires opinion and emotion.

computer-assisted reporting a name for the reporting that journalists do with data and documents that are stored electronically instead of on paper.

confidential source a person who provides information to reporters but who wants to remain anonymous, often because of fear of reprisals from authorities who may not want the information out.

conflict of interest a journalist has a personal interest in a topic that could influence his or her opinion; examples are writing about companies in which you own stock, an organization to which you belong or even the schools you or your children attend.

contact sheet photographic paper with the negatives printed on it at film size.

content editor an editor who works with reporters to produce content of all kinds — text, video and graphic.

content management system (CMS) a software program to manage all the information you produce.

content producers editors and reporters who continue to cover news of the day, as well as plan features and other stories for all their platforms.

convergence the merging of a news organization's operations; some combination of print, Web and broadcast; merging media with other platforms.

copy text of the story.

copy editors edit the text of a story, checking facts and correcting errors in spelling, grammar and word usage; they also write headlines for print and online stories and captions for photos.

copywriter the person who writes ad copy.

correspondents also called reporters, these journalists gather information for stories by researching, observing and interviewing, and they write most of the content.

credibility a reputation for being right; credible news organizations and their employees strive to be fair and independent, that is, free from the influence of government, businesses or individuals.

critic a reviewer who places a work in the context of the whole field.

crop taking out unnecessary elements in a photograph to improve the visual impact of the photo.

culture the set of attitudes that characterizes the group of journalists in a news organization.

cutline also called caption; the words under photos that explain who or what is pictured; generally written by editors from information supplied by photographers.

D

data information and statistics that bring perspective to a story.

deadline the date and time the story is due.

depth of field the amount of space that is in focus in your photograph.

descriptive lead lead that allows the writer to become a storyteller and hints at interesting things to come.

design also called layout; refers to the plan of how the different elements are presented on the page.

designers determine, with the top editors, where content will be placed on print pages or how it will be arranged on websites.

desks areas of designated specialties in a newsroom.

dialogue the back-and-forth conversation between subjects.

digest collection of stories.

digital journalism online journalism.

digital video camera a camera that captures images electronically.

direct address lead lead in which readers are told to do something.

direct quotation a reporter uses the exact words of the source.

diverse sources people who need to be interviewed to represent all sides of an issue on which a reporter is writing.

documents a paper trail, including tax records, licenses, death and birth certificates, and credit card and phone records.

dominance visual impact.

E

ears space on each side of the masthead at the top of each section, promoting what is inside the paper.

editorial voice of the newspaper.

editors assign and look over most of the content — stories, photos and video — that will be produced for a print, broadcast or online news report.

ellipses three dots that indicate something has been omitted from the copy.

enterprise news non-breaking news.

ethics the moral principles that govern the conduct of individuals and organizations.

executive editor top editor responsible for the entire news organization.

expenses all the things that cost money.

F

fabrication non-truthful writing, such as making up quotes and details, making a story more exciting or interesting or writing a whole story that didn't happen.

fact truths; information that can be proven.

feature story a story with all the journalistic elements of a news story but written with a beginning, middle and end like a short story.

First Amendment the First Amendment to the Constitution; provides the rights to free speech and a free press.

five W's and H questions all journalists ask to find the central point of a story: Who? What? When? Where? Why? and How?

focus style a style with four parts: the story lead, nut graph, body and kicker.

FOIA Freedom of Information Act; a law that says everyone should have access to federal public records.

found situation an event or scene a photojournalist comes across by accident that can make a good photograph.

freedom of information laws laws that protect the people's right to know what their government and government officials are doing, such as a law that says all records generated or meetings conducted by a public body are open to the public unless they are specifically exempted.

freelance journalists journalists who do not work for a particular news outlet and may cover stories for any news outlet that wants to hire them.

free writing an exercise many writers employ to move ideas out of their heads and onto a computer screen or piece of paper.

G

game story a story about an individual game; a news story about the contest and conflict between two teams.

general assignment reporters reporters who do not have a regular beat.

general in-depth reporting all in-depth stories that do not revolve around investigation of a particular issue.

Golden Age of Radio refers to the 1930s when Americans listened to their radios for music, drama, comedy, variety shows and news.

grid a framework or lines dividing a page into standardized columns.

H

hard news news about a serious or important topic with a sense of immediacy to it.

hierarchy refers to the order of things, with the most important at the top.

highlights important moments in the games and the final score.

hourglass style a combination of the inverted pyramid and narrative styles.

human interest story a feature story that is unusual, offbeat or just the result of keen observation.

I

impartial being objective and putting aside personal opinions when writing the news.

income the money to pay expenses.

independent sports bloggers writers who set up their own blogs on the Internet.

in-depth reporting reporting that gives critical analysis and careful consideration to all details and aspects of a subject.

indirect quotation a journalist rephrases the source's words for clarity.

influence to try to persuade a journalist to write favorably about certain people or businesses.

informational feature story a feature story that provides information.

informational graphics a visual display of information.

information center center of today's news operations; once called the newsroom.

insider a reporter who has access to the team and its managers.

integrity the quality of possessing an inner sense of knowing right from wrong and adhering to high moral principles or professional standards.

interview reporters talking to real people.

interviewing asking questions of knowledgeable people.

invasion of privacy an unwelcome intrusion into a person's solitude or personal affairs.

inverted pyramid a journalism style or news story format with the most important information at the top, in the first paragraph.

investigative reporting reporting that requires journalists to ask questions about the regular news stories and dig deeper to uncover what is hidden beneath the surface.

issue reporting in-depth reporting that looks at special issues of concern to society.

J

jargon language that pertains to a particular business or field; in sportswriting, words and clichés only sports fans use.

journalism the business of news-gathering and reporting.

journalists modern day storytellers who use all the technology available to them; journalists include reporters, editors, photographers, producers and camera crews.

K

kicker a feature such as good news or a human interest story to end the broadcast; conclusion of a story written in the focus style; ending of a story.

L

ladder a page-by-page plan of what will be included in the yearbook.

layout how the pages are presented.

lead the beginning of a story.

lead-in an anchor's introduction to a story.

libel making a false or damaging statement about somebody.

links avenues to other stories; the blue, underlined words in Web stories that take you to another story or informational site when you click on them.

Linotype a traditional way of setting newspaper type for printing; also called hot type.

locator map a map that helps the reader place the geographic area the reporter is writing or speaking about.

logo a company symbol.

M

managing editor an editor who is responsible for the day-to-day operation of the news organization.

mass media all the channels of communication that reach a large audience.

media kit provides elements beyond the press release and may also include still photography that could be used with a print or Web story, a video interview with a pertinent person or a video that shows the product.

muckraking the beginning of investigative journalism; journalists took on the role of promoting social responsibility by investigating corruption, especially in big business, social institutions and politics.

multimedia a Web story that is some combination of the written word, photographs, video clips, audio clips, graphics and an interactive element, such as a quiz or a poll.

multimedia journalists news and information gatherers who are comfortable working to produce all of the multimedia elements.

multiple media adding audio, video and graphic elements to print stories on the Web.

multiple platforms different ways of reporting and obtaining news, such as newspapers and news magazines, television, radio and the Internet.

N

narrate to tell a story in detail.

narrative a story that uses techniques of oral storytelling; a story told by a narrator.

narrative style a story written in chronological order, which uses dialogue, and has a beginning, middle and end.

navigate to be able to get around a page.

network a group of stations that broadcast regularly scheduled programs.

newscast a compilation of visual or audio broadcast stories.

news director the person responsible for all the news programming for a broadcast media outlet.

news magazine a format that allows for more in-depth coverage of traditional news and features.

news meeting a gathering of editors from each department where placement and deadlines of stories are discussed.

newspaper publication printed on large sheets of folded paper that contain information about current events, features on different topics and advertisements.

newsreaders anchors, disc jockeys and correspondents who deliver stories to listeners and viewers.

nut graph a paragraph that states the central point of a story written in the focus style.

O

objectivity the talent of remaining disinterested or impartial.

offensive language any words or remarks that offend, insult or threaten another person or group of people.

off the record information given by a source to a reporter that is not written down or recorded.

on background journalist may use the information a source is providing, but the information may not be attributed to the source.

online journalism journalism conducted on the Internet.

online publishing using the Web and its tools to get news and information to a targeted audience.

on the record information that can be attributed to a source by name.

op-ed newspaper page, often opposite the editorial page, devoted to editorial opinions.

open-ended question a question that encourages the subject to talk.

open-source or crowd-source reporting when the public helps news organizations report stories.

opinion point of view; your way of interpreting information; one side of an argument.

P

package the various elements of a newspaper, when put together; includes headlines, graphics, photographs, captions and stories.

pan moving the camera focus from one side to another in broadcast news.

partial quotation part of the source's actual words.

penny press newspapers that were named after the cost, one cent.

phoner interviews conducted over the phone.

photo editor the person in charge of the photography staff who also is a liaison with the news, feature, sports and any other departments necessary to producing news.

photo essay a series of photographs that tell a complete story.

photographers journalists who take still photographs of the people and events for the reporters' stories.

photojournalism visual reporting of facts and truths.

photojournalist a reporter with a camera.

photo request form a form yearbook staffers or editors fill out that details the who, what, when, where, why and how of the event or story.

pitching reporters and editors meet and share their ideas and expertise about a possible story.

plagiarism copying the work of others and passing it off as your own.

points of entry elements on a newspaper page through which readers enter, such as stories, photos and headlines.

posts updates added by a blogger to a blog.

precedent court cases that set what is legal for the future and what is not.

pre-reporting the process of determining whether a story is newsworthy.

press release a story written by a publicist to announce to the press something newsworthy, such as a restaurant opening.

preview story a story that does not focus on one game but takes a broader look at how a team may be expected to perform for a season.

primary headline the large, active, bold-face headline that states the story clearly and demands immediate attention.

primary source a person who gives the reporter the most thorough or best information because that person is the investigator, the witness or someone affected by the event.

print journalist a reporter who writes text for a print newspaper.

producer the person responsible for coordinating and organizing news coverage; an editor for a news website.

profile a feature story about an interesting person.

public figure a person whose achievements or notoriety put that person in the public spotlight.

publicist representative of businesses, colleges and universities, medical centers, individuals such as celebrities, governments and government agencies, and other types of organizations to manage their clients' relationship with the media.

public official a person who is paid with tax dollars, is elected, has control of government and has access to the media.

public relations often referred to simply as PR, it is the practice of presenting image and information.

Pulitzer Prize the top recognition journalists can receive from their peers.

Q

Q-and-A (question-and-answer) story written in the format of the reporter asking a question and the source answering that question.

question lead lead in which readers are asked a direct question.

quotation the exact words a source says during an interview that you use in a story, giving the source credit.

quotation lead lead that starts the story with something one of the subjects has said.

quotation marks the punctuation marks that go at the beginning and end of a source's words.

R

read-back reporters read portions of the story they are working on to their source to ensure accuracy.

real time while the event is taking place.

redundant information in copy that is repeated.

reporters also called correspondents, these journalists gather information for stories by researching, observing and interviewing, and they write most of the content.

review the view or opinion of the writer about entertainment and art or products and services.

reviewer person who writes reviews.

rhythm irregular alteration of the design elements.

S

sales pitch a presentation that briefly explains why your yearbook publication is a good place to advertise.

script a written broadcast story.

secondary headline the headline for a less important story.

secondary source a person who has information relevant to your story but is not a main official, eyewitness or directly affected by the event.

sections areas of coverage that go into a yearbook.

sequencing a variety of pictures that make a story move smoothly.

shield laws state laws that allow journalists to keep certain conversations confidential.

sidebar a secondary story that provides supplementary information about the main story.

Skype software program that allows real-time video chats.

slideshow a series of photographs that tell a story or add elements that will enhance a story.

slug the story name.

social media platforms online tools that people use to connect with one another using websites such as Facebook and Twitter.

soft news feature and human-interest stories; articles that are informational, educational, emotional or entertaining.

software tools computer programs that allow the user to write copy or design pages, among other uses.

sound bite a cut of an audio- or videotape that has the source's best quotes or quotes that end on a point the broadcaster wants to make.

sportswriting the reporting and writing of stories about the many different sports events and the people who play them.

still photograph a one-frame image taken on film or digitally.

storyboard a map or visual outline for a story and the elements you will use for each piece so you are clear about which aspects of the story will be covered by text, by video or by other media.

story budget a list of what stories need to be covered.

strategic plan a road map to achieving specific goals.

structure the way a story is organized.

subhead smaller headlines within the body of a story, used to make the story easy to read.

subjective writing expresses a point of view and is not concerned with being impartial.

summary lead the first paragraph of a news story.

sunshine laws also known as freedom of information laws; state laws that require open access for the media and a public representative to most government business and regulatory meetings; laws that protect the people's right to know what their government and government officials are doing.

surprise lead lead in which the writer supplies a twist.

T

tagline a motto or slogan for which the company is known.

team a group of journalists needed to cover a large event.

team leader a person who oversees the entire project for a team.

teleprompter device for displaying a script or prepared text so that the speaker or performer does not have to look down.

theme or concept the prism through which the yearbook staff may look at all the other coverage.

tip a phone call or email from a trusted source or an interested reader.

tipping point the point where something unique becomes mainstream.

touchstone the team leader who sets the standards by which the project is judged.

transition words that move the reader from one paragraph to the next; in broadcasting, the connecting words written for an anchor to say between stories.

transparency writing into the story where the information came from and allowing the public to decide for itself whether to believe the story.

trend a current style or what's in vogue, particularly when it comes to popular culture.

trend spotting reporters noticing the social trends in popular culture.

tweeted posted on a Twitter account.

U

umbrella lead a summary of multiple related stories in one lead.

unnamed source a person who asks that his or her name not be used, and, sometimes, that the information given reporters not be used.

V

videographers journalists who take videos of the people and events for the reporters' stories.

video journalism the art of telling the story with video.

visual journalism refers to the design of a newspaper.

voice style of writing.

W

weblog or blog a writer's personal opinions about a subject that is published on the Internet for public reading.

Web writing a combination (hybrid) of print and broadcast techniques.

Wikipedia an online open-sourced encyclopedia; not considered a reliable source.

wire services news agencies that send out syndicated news items to media by means of telephone wires or satellite.

Y

yellow journalism mid-1890s journalism that represented sensationalism, screaming headlines and cheap melodrama.

Index